The New Language of
Qualitative Method

The New Language
of Qualitative
Method

JABER F. GUBRIUM
JAMES A. HOLSTEIN

New York   Oxford
OXFORD UNIVERSITY PRESS
1997

OXFORD UNIVERSITY PRESS

Oxford   New York
Athens   Aukland   Bangkok   Bogotá   Bombay   Buenos Aires
Calcutta   Cape Town   Dar es Salaam   Delhi   Florence   Hong Kong
Istanbul   Karachi   Kuala Lumpur   Madras   Madrid   Melbourne
Mexico City   Nairobi   Paris   Singapore   Taipei   Tokyo   Toronto

and associated companies in

Berlin   Ibadan

Library of Congress Cataloging-in-Publication Data

Gubrium, Jaber F.
The new language of qualitative method / Jaber F. Gubrium, James
A. Holstein.
p.   cm.
Includes bibliographical references and index.
ISBN 0-19-509993-1. —ISBN 0-19-509994-X (pbk.)
1. Social sciences—Research—Methodology.   I. Holstein, James A.
II. Title.
H62.G82   1997   96-23816
300'.72—dc20

5 7 9 8 6

Printed in the United States of America
on acid-free paper

Contents

Preface

Method, for us, connotes a way of knowing. This means we take qualitative method to be more than a collection of research techniques and procedural guidelines. It's closer to what Thomas Kuhn (1962) describes as a paradigm—a distinctive way of orienting to the world. Of course this includes the practical *modus operandi* of empirical investigation, but, more importantly, it directs us to the broader sense in which method implicates perception, comprehension, and representation.

The new language of qualitative method is by no means our invention. Analytically self-conscious qualitative researchers have been crafting a variety of ways of discerning and describing social reality, a virtual medley of approaches to understanding the contemporary complexity and dynamics of lived experience. Each perspective has developed its characteristic assumptions, empirical sensitivities, and research strategies. We've come to think of the contrasting vocabularies out of which the new qualitative inquiry has emerged as idioms for apprehending and representing the real.

The new language of qualitative method is a response to the descriptive challenges posed by an unrelentingly multi-faceted empirical world. But it is also a recognition of the sharpening demand for theoretical sensitivity to the ways that experience is understood and represented by social researchers themselves. Descriptive richness has long been the stock-in-trade of qualitative inquiry. Still, enamored of the call to "thick description," qualitative researchers are sometimes overly captivated by their ability to "tell it like it is" without biasing preconceptions or theoretical prejudices. This seems naive. Every act of "seeing" or "saying" is unavoidably conditioned by cultural, institutional, and interactional contingencies. Our perceptual and representational frameworks are virtual theories of the possible. The new language of qualitative method reflects this, conflating theory and method. While it remains descriptively rich, it is also primed to engage the thorny epistemological questions that arise when researchers attempt to document the contours and workings of a constructed, yet substantial, world of everyday life.

This book is our attempt to articulate the new language, or at least enough of it so that readers can appreciate its composition, application, and utility. We intend this preface as a guide for how subsequent chapters should be read. Part I is expository. We've selected four familiar approaches to qualitative inquiry—influential research idioms—and devoted a chapter to describing each in exemplary detail. The chapters are not meant to be comprehensive. Rather, we try to give the flavor of each of the approaches, conveying the fundamental questions, concerns, and assumptions that practitioners bring to their craft.

Part I might be called an *idiomatic* history. Each chapter offers a discussion of family resemblances within each of the approaches. Let us be clear, however, that this is not a chronicle. We're not implying that one approach has supplanted another, or that the idioms we discuss represent an evolutionary ladder in the development of analytic self-consciousness. To the contrary, we view each of the idioms as central in its own right to the emergence of the new language.

Borrowing from the familiar, but also innovating to address the demands of empirical investigation in an increasingly postmodern world, this book also offers a trajectory for further renewal and the development of an idiom equally sensitive to the substantively meaningful and the artfully constructed nature of social reality. This renewed language combines the tried and true with more recently coined terminology, giving qualitative research a distinctive way of analytically addressing experience at the intersection of the modern and the postmodern.

Part II describes the renewal of the language in relation to recent encounters the various idioms have had with some difficult epistemological questions. Qualitative researchers of all persuasions have become increasingly self-conscious about their assumptions and research procedures. This has prompted many researchers to rethink traditional guidelines and analytic resources, seeking fresh ways of addressing and conveying the empirical. Newer forms of qualitative "method talk" are an inevitable result.

The second part of the book is more analytic than the first. It's also intended to be more instructional. In response to the emerging challenges confronting the research idioms, Chapter 6 begins by asking "Where does qualitative inquiry go from here?" Our answer points to the renewed language. After elaborating its theoretical and empirical motivations, we demonstrate the vocabulary *in use* by illustrating how various concepts and analytic terms can serve as resources for framing, examining, describing, and explaining the social world. As we proceed, we show in detail just how the researcher uses the terminology *in practice*. Our aim is to instruct readers about how the renewed language helps formulate a more inclusive, reflexive vision of social reality.

In contrast with most "methods" texts, we devote little attention to the nuts and bolts of research technique. Instead, we concentrate primarily on the relation between method and analysis, on the logic and theory of qualitative inquiry. Concrete research procedures are certainly important. But, since they attach directly to the theoretical scaffolding of the research enterprise, we want to establish that framework first, before engaging the practical questions of technique. Nevertheless, the procedural implications of our more analytic observations are implicit throughout the discussion.

Finally, while we draw many of the illustrations from our own work, this is as much a matter of convenience and familiarity as it is of design. The new language of qualitative method is now heard across a wide spectrum of qualitative studies, which should be apparent from the range of empirical research we cite. As we said at the start, we didn't devise the new language. It's a collective invention that we've found immensely useful. We hope this book makes its value apparent to others.

The idea of writing the book took hold a couple of years ago when we were doing a workshop on qualitative health research in Hershey, Pennsylvania. Using material from our own studies of nursing facilities, therapy agencies, mental health centers, and other people-processing settings, we intended to give our audience a taste of what could be done by bringing both naturalistic and ethnomethodological sensibilities to bear on health-related research concerns. Ambitiously, we titled our session, "The New Language of Qualitative Method."

Of course, that put us on the spot. This was a widely advertised international conference, and we were just the slightest bit apprehensive about who might show up to hear us talk about this *new* language. But the show went just fine, with no objections from the luminaries in the audience. Indeed, we even got a few interesting questions and comments from persons we suspected of being in the know.

As we left the lecture hall, however, John Heritage approached us. Anyone who knows ethnomethodology will tell you that John has written by far the most lucid and accessible commentary on Garfinkel and his legacy. A moment of truth was upon us. *Were we about to be exposed as charlatans touting the bastard child of naturalism and ethnomethodology for mass misconsumption?*

"I'm quite amazed at what I just heard," Heritage volunteered. "You were up there talking ethnomethodology, and you didn't seem to worry at all about mixing in naturalistic concerns. You got up there and got on with it beautifully. And everybody seemed to get what you were saying." *That was reassuring.*

Just then, David Silverman elbowed his way through the crowd now gathering for lunch. "So when's the book coming out?" David was apparently quite sincere. *What book?* "By all means, do it," teased Mel Pollner, who'd just materialized out of nowhere. "You might be able to resuscitate ethnomethodology's mundane intelligibility."

To that point, we'd never really envisioned a full blown writing project dealing with qualitative method. But with a little encouragement—and who better than Heritage, Silverman, and Pollner to give us a nudge—we began seriously to consider the claims we had been making about a newly emerging language of qualitative inquiry. We started to look more carefully and systematically at how qualitative researchers talked and wrote about their data, their findings, and their craft in general. It became clear that there was much to be said about the relationship between research and the idioms in which it is conducted.

We thought we knew quite a bit about that when we undertook this project. Little did we know how much we would learn. The tribe of qualitative researchers has been masterfully instructive; their work has taught us more than we can say. Throughout, we've relied on the research and counsel of a number of colleagues. John, David, and Mel did far more than just egg us on. Their work has inspired much of our own. Other friends and associates have directly and indirectly helped us formulate many of the questions and arguments we offer in this book: Bob Emerson, John Kitsuse, Doug Maynard, Gale Miller, Dorothy Smith, Joseph Schneider, Larry Wieder, and Pertti Alasuutari, just to name a few.

There's an even longer list of persons who are implicated in the project in one way or another, even if some would never admit to it. Sally Hutchinson, Doni Loseke, Joel Best, Hernan Vera, Carol Gardner, Jun Ayukawa, Norm Denzin, Mitch Allen, Steve Golant, Paul Rosenblatt, Jan Morse, Melvin Power, and Courtney Marlaire have helped us in ways they may not even recognize. Simply listing them can't adequately express our gratitude. And Dave Karp provided us with a thoroughly thoughtful review of the entire manuscript. We truly appreciate his efforts.

Finally, at the risk of sounding self-congratulatory (*Would anyone who knows us believe that was possible?*), we offer an endorsement for analytic collaboration. We've worked together for over a decade now, and we're quite pleased with what we've accomplished, if we must say so ourselves. But there's something more than mutual support and a division of labor that operates in our work. One of the themes of this book specifies a dialectic relationship between reality constructing activities and their substantive conditioning. It's quite possible that we would never have developed the theme had we not approached this project from slightly divergent—indeed, differently embodied—perspectives.

For example, both of us learned about ethnomethodology on our own. As most everyone knows, self taught ethnomethodologists can be a hazard to the community. Jay's appreciation for the constitutive side of interaction grew out of his early ethnographic studies of the multiple realities of caregiving. Initially, his forays into ethnomethodological analysis led editors to believe he had lost touch with the English language, but he got beyond that. At heart, however, he's still quite the naturalist, always concerned with the enduring and constraining meanings and regions of the social. Jim started out pretty innocuously at the University of Michigan, but something went awry, and he ended up writing what is believed to be the only *quantitative* ethnomethodological dissertation in existence. *Remember the dangers of self-education?* Fortunately, no one ever read it, so it's done little harm. A stint at UCLA allowed Mel Pollner and Bob Emerson to set him straight, and cultivated his appreciation for how artfully the social is constructed.

While we are now on the same analytic wavelength most of the time, we still retain our propensities and predilections. Jay can never ignore the conditioning influences of context and culture. Jim is intrigued by how adroitly we conjure structure and meaning out of the evanescent fabric of interaction. Occasionally, each of us goes off the deep end. But, after the accusations of "closet positivist" and "solipsistic navel gazer" have subsided, we both recognize that what's going on is the embodied replication of the cross-currents and tensions that we have come to see centered in reality construction. Our collaboration has reflexively related components, just like interpretive practice. Opposite sides of the same coin, as we are now wont to say, our personal preferences force us to confront the two sides of reality, the substantive and the artful, as an integral aspect of getting the work done. Maybe it could not have been otherwise, but we're fortunate that it worked out the way it did.

The New Language of
Qualitative Method

INTRODUCTION

CHAPTER 1

Method Talk

The strange idea that reality has an idiom in which it prefers to be described, that its very nature demands we talk about it without fuss . . . leads on to the even stranger idea that, if literalism is lost, so is fact.

Clifford Geertz, *Works and Lives: The Anthropologist as Author* (1988, p. 140)

The language of the social sciences shapes how researchers view the world. *Method talk* virtually leads them by the hand into the empirical realm. It is the working vocabulary of research procedure. One familiar idiom directs researchers to a real world of facts and figures. A second urges them to focus on how the real world is conceptualized or formed. Other research vocabularies stake out different empirical terrain.

If we accept the tenet that knowledge is humanly produced, it's not hard to conceive of sites of method talk as knowledge factories—places where the work of knowledge construction takes place. Extending the metaphor, colleges and universities stand out as production sites, since nearly all social researchers have professional ties to these institutions. A good way to hear method talk, then, might be to visit a production site, to drop in on a first-rate, if make-believe, department of sociology where research is the order of the day. We're certain to hear people discussing objectives and procedures, even "strange" ideas about reality.

Entering the department on the third floor of a weathered building near the center of campus, it's initially difficult to sort out exactly what's going on. There's not much to see, not a lot of action. But there's plenty of talk. Maybe it's important. Perhaps it's idle chatter. Let's listen.[1]

From offices and seminar rooms, in gatherings at mailboxes and computer terminals, we hear a distinctive vernacular, familiar, yet somehow arcane in its technical idiom. These sociologists are talking about our world, a reality we know in our commonsense fashion, yet the way they talk gives it an almost unrecognizable substance and force. "Structural variables and causal models." "Units of analysis and sampling frames." "Operationalization and measurement." "Cluster analysis and multidimensional scaling." "Stochastic processes, multicolinearity, and autocorrelation." The highly technical vocabulary of quantitative positivism rings down the corridors, virtually permeating the walls. It's just what we'd expect from folks committed to treating social facts as things, then measuring them, with the aim of describing and explaining their relationships.

Around the corner, down the hallway and off to the side, we hear different conversations. From one office comes the earnest exhortation to "go and find out what's really happening!" There's lots of talk about *meaning*, especially what things mean to the people being studied. This is decidedly not talk about predictive models. *Lived* experience is on stage here. Rich description is the name of the game. There's little mention of standardized measurement. Instead we hear the trials and tribulations of "entrée and engagement," "access and rapport." In contrast to descriptions of social facts and variable relations from an "objective" distance—held at arm's length, so to speak—we hear the admonition to get close to people, be involved. "You've got to get out there, into the nitty-gritty, real world. Get your hands dirty. See it up close, for yourself." This must be the qualitative contingent of the department.

A rather small group, this bunch, surrounded by the typical motley collection of skeptical graduate students and other souls who never mastered the nuances of linear regression. The group is easily identified by talk that seems more experientially poignant. If we listen closely, we can even detect distinct dialects, overlapping only slightly with the language of their quantitative cousins.

Here's someone saying that research has become "too damned behavioral, overly cognitive. We have to pay more attention to what really distinguishes human nature." We soon learn that this means paying attention to the truly subjective. "How do emotions *feel*?" "We can't be too scientific because human experience doesn't fit a completely rational model." "Deep down, we are more than cogs on social gears or actors in society's little dramas."

Next door, the discussion centers on human agency and the need to appreciate the richly layered skills, assumptions, and practices through which persons construct the very realities of their everyday lives. We hear that the researcher must always "be careful not to confuse the subjects' categories and concepts with her own analytic constructs." The point, the speaker reminds her listeners, is to see how members of social settings *accomplish* a sense of social order that they experience as real. And we hear words of caution: "Society members' constructions and categories are what we study, so we mustn't slip up by using members' categories as our own explanatory concepts. Remember, they are our topics, not our resources. And above all, *never argue with the members*!"

Across the hall, we hear a voice sounding unsettlingly like that of a literary critic. We haven't wandered into the English Department, have we? But as we listen, we're reassured that we are still in the right place. "Our own sociological work, qualitative work, is inscribed in realist terms that derive from our own authoritative voice." It seems like we're hearing that there's no possibility of unmediated, unfussy description, and that what we know is an artifact of our authority as researchers and writers. It's a matter of "displaced or projected desires." Nearby, we hear other, almost foreign, voices concerned with "image and simulacra," "decenteredness and polysemy," "electronic mediation," and "hyperreality." To what *are* we listening? What does this have to do with qualitative research? What's going on here?

VARIETIES OF METHOD TALK

At one level, everyone we've heard is talking sociology. But the diversity of lexicons strikes us as significant, the variety of messages crucial. We've overheard some not-so-idle chatter about research procedure and how that relates to empirical reality. The talk deals with how the researcher orients to and interprets facts. Broadly speaking, these are the concerns of any workplace. If we were seeking insight anywhere into how procedural knowledge relates to what is produced, we would certainly take this form of talk into account. Why not consider what method talk can tell us about social research and social reality?

That's what this book aims to accomplish. In its way, it is a sociology of knowledge. It's about what Clifford Geertz, in the opening epigram, refers to as "idioms" of reality. It considers the way the language of qualitative method relates to how researchers view and describe social life. We intentionally use the term *method* (rather than the plural, *methods*) to signal a primary interest in the knowledge-producing dimensions of the various research idioms comprising qualitative inquiry. We noted earlier that method implies a way of knowing as much as techniques for gathering information. In practice, it is, in Ludwig Wittgenstein's (1958) words, "a language game" or "way of life" in the sense that the manner in which one proceeds to do social research organizes the empirical contours of what is under investigation. Method connotes a manner of viewing and talking about reality as much as it specifies technique and procedure.

Qualitative research is a diverse enterprise (see Denzin and Lincoln 1994). Perhaps because it is typically counterposed with the contemporary monolith of quantitative sociology, qualitative method is often portrayed in broad strokes that blur differences. We believe it's important to recognize and appreciate these differences in order to evaluate their separate contributions as well as their overall direction. More importantly, we need to be more aware of the way the language of qualitative method shapes knowledge of social reality. This is impossible if we fail to distinguish working assumptions about the world, conceptualizations of everyday life, and, in particular, vocabularies of research procedure. Our strategy for understanding the diversity of qualitative research is to treat each variant as an enterprise that develops, and is conducted in, a language or idiom of its own. Accordingly, each idiom presents a distinctive reality, virtually constituting its empirical horizons. This chapter highlights just how revealing language is in this regard, setting the stage for the more detailed discussion that follows.

The sociology of work and occupations teaches us that a good way of understanding a profession or occupation is through everyday shoptalk, and we assume that the work of social researchers is no different (see Hughes 1971; Garfinkel 1986, 1995; Miller 1981). The language of quantitative, positivist sociology, for example, owes a profound debt to the natural sciences for both its empirical vision and its orientation to research procedure (Lepenies 1988; Filmer et al., 1973). It pervasively reflects the foundational presumption of an objective world of concrete components that can be represented in terms of "hard data." This world is obdurate and tangible enough in some cases, to put one's finger on, both metaphorically and literally. The research enterprise revolves around measurement and analysis, typically ordering numerically represented variables into explanatory models. The substantiality and coherence of the world so conveyed are impressive. But it is also an artifact of the procedural vocabulary itself. Method talk in the quantitative workplace conveys a deep commitment to systematically and rigorously representing a separate and distinct order of things without disturbing or distorting that order in the process. The talk provides communicative directives for just what the world might be; details are described and problems are solved against this linguistic backdrop.

The language of qualitative research is equally compelling, presenting its own distinctive reality-constituting endeavors, with different interests, goals, and strategies. Let us briefly describe four approaches whose procedural idioms have made their mark on contemporary qualitative research: naturalism, ethnomethodology, emotionalism, and postmodernism. While these are not the only, nor necessarily the "best," of qualitative approaches, viewed comparatively they help us demonstrate how differently method talk can convey the "facts" of the social world.[2]

Describing What Comes Naturally

Naturalism is the original and, arguably, the predominant language of qualitative research. The naturalistic impulse resonates at some level throughout the other idioms. Its goal is to understand social reality on its own terms "as it really is," to describe what comes naturally, so to speak. Taken in its simplest form, naturalism seeks rich descriptions of people and interaction as they exist and unfold in their native habitats. The people have ranged from prisoners and felons (Giallombardo 1966; Irwin 1970; Jones and Schmid 1997), the mentally ill or disturbed (Perrucci 1974; Estroff 1981), and the mentally handicapped (Edgerton 1967) to medical students (Becker et al., 1961; Haas and Shaffir 1987), surgeons (Bosk 1979), seminarians (Kleinman 1984), fantasy gamers (Fine 1983), the homeless (Snow and Anderson 1993), and the elderly (Hochschild 1973). Some of the distinct habitats have been nursing homes (Gubrium 1975; Diamond 1992), hospitals (Glaser and Strauss 1965, 1968), restaurants (Paules 1991), schools and playgrounds (Adler and Adler, 1991; Thorne 1993), households (Hochschild 1989; Rubin 1976), communities (Gans 1962; Suttles 1968), taverns (Spradley and Mann 1975), and street corners (Whyte 1943; Liebow 1967; Anderson 1976). The range of experiences and locales is breathtaking and the interpretations have been remarkably insightful.

Naturalistic method talk is replete with prescriptions and injunctions for capturing social reality on its home turf. Among the earliest and most colorful pleas came from Robert Park, one of the founders of the Chicago School of field research. Reacting to what he saw as "armchair sociology," Park insisted that social researchers become more involved in the real world (Bulmer 1984). Researchers had to get close to the sources of their data; data had to emanate directly from real life. Insisting that his students get "their hands dirty in real research," Park eschewed the research library and official statistics, preferring firsthand observation of city streets, dance halls, hotels, and the like. He virtually implored his students to find data in the natural settings that captured their interest:

> Go and sit in the lounges of the luxury hotels and on the doorsteps of the flophouses; sit on the Gold Coast settees and on the slum shakedowns; sit in Orchestra Hall and in the Star and Garter Burlesque. In short, gentlemen, go get the seat of your pants dirty in real research. (McKinney 1966, p. 71)

It was not enough for Park to simply exhort participant observation. He also insisted that "what sociologists most need to know is what goes on behind the faces of men" (1950, pp. vi–vii). Years later, Erving Goffman (1961) elaborated this appreciation for natively meaningful worlds:

> My immediate objective in doing fieldwork at St. Elizabeth's [psychiatric hospital] was to try to learn about the world of the hospital inmate, as this world is subjectively experienced by him. . . . It was then and still is my belief that any group of persons—prisoners, primitives, pilots, or patients—develop a life of their own that becomes meaningful, reasonable, and normal once you get close to it, and that a good way to learn about any of these worlds is to submit oneself in the company of the members to the daily round of petty contingencies to which they are subject. (Pp. ix–x)

From this language, we begin to see a working epistemology, a way of knowing that locates meaningful reality in the immediate settings of people's daily affairs. It is the settings' sheer naturalness that makes them authentic. Empirical inquiry must first of all respect the boundaries of real life, but at the same time penetrate them to reveal what is held in store. The added caution typically is to get close enough to people to recognize and describe the exquisite details of their social world, but without "going native."

Hearing How It's Done

If naturalism attempts to look inside the social worlds of real people as they experience those worlds, *ethnomethodology* and several related constructionist approaches want to look at, and listen to, the social activities through which everyday actors produce the recognizable features of those social worlds. Whereas the naturalistic researcher attends to what his or her informants say in order to understand what things mean to them, the ethnomethodologist listens to naturally occurring conversation in order to discover how a sense of social order is created through talk and interaction. At the heart of the research is a deep concern for the ordinary, everyday procedures and practices that society's members use to make their social experiences sensible, understandable, accountable, and orderly (Garfinkel 1967).

Rather than treating social facts or social structure as objectively natural parameters, ethnomethodologists approach structure and organization as achievements in their own right. They are interested in the interpretive activities that persons undertake, moment by moment, to construct, manage, and sustain the sense that their social worlds exist as factual and objectively "there." While its focus is more on the construction of social worlds than on experiential meaning, ethnomethodology still maintains a naturalistic orientation in the sense that it wants to describe in detail the everyday knowledge and interpretive procedures that are used to accomplish social reality (Heritage 1984b).

Given its concern with reality-constituting practices, ethnomethodological method talk must accommodate active, dynamic social process. Rather than focusing naturalistically on the more or less stable yet developing, experiential contours of everyday life, it examines how these contours are continuously "talked into being" in the first place (Heritage 1984b). The commonplace phenomena that interest the naturalist are temporarily set aside in order to examine the interactional processes through which those phenomena are constructed. This requires the ethnomethodological vocabulary to be one of actions more than things, of social practices more than social settings or social forces.

Ethnomethodology is especially attuned to communicative activity. From this perspective, conversation is the machinery of reality construction. Ethnomethodological method talk, then, is largely "talk about talk." Its mandate is for the researcher not only to watch, but also and especially to *listen*, in order to discern how reality is produced. Taking reality as an interactional activity (Mehan and Wood 1975) thus requires a vocabulary that can adequately convey what is learned when researchers "hear how reality is done."

As simple as this sounds, ethnomethodological method talk is often quite esoteric. Less patient or sympathetic observers might describe it as impenetrably complex. One must keep in mind, however, that ethnomethodology wants to make the taken-for-granted into its research problem. In a sense, it takes social structure—sociology's stock in trade—and turns it upside down. Structure is not viewed as a force compelling and constraining actors; instead it is taken to be a product of social action itself. Listen closely as the pioneer of ethnomethodology, Harold Garfinkel (1967), tells us how describing the "accomplishment" of the taken-for-granted is ethnomethodology's research mission:

> In doing sociology, lay and professional, every reference to the "real world" . . . is a reference to the organized public activities of everyday life. Thereby, in contrast to certain versions of Durkheim that teach that the objective reality of social facts is sociology's fundamental principle, the lesson is taken instead, and used as a study policy, that the objective reality of social facts *as* an ongoing accomplishment of the concerted activities of daily life, with the ordinary, artful ways of that accomplishment being known, used, and taken for granted, is, for members doing sociology, a fundamental phenomenon. Because, and in the ways it is practical sociology's fundamental phenomenon, it is the prevailing topic for ethnomethodological study. Ethnomethodological studies analyze everyday activities as members' methods for making those same activities visibly-rational-and-reportable-for-all-practical-purposes. (P. vii)

This extract is typical of what some might call Garfinkel's convoluted method talk, yet it also reveals the signal and unconventional aim of the ethnomethodological project. While the prose is uncommonly dense, it nonetheless provides the patient and careful reader with a sense of ethnomethodology's goal of analyzing and making visible the interactional practices that give taken-for-granted social facts their apparent reality.

Exploring Emotionality

As some qualitative researchers plunge headlong into the subjective, their method talk suggests that being "up close and on the scene" is not enough. For these researchers, subjectivity is truly understood only by delving "inside" experience, usually figuratively, but sometimes literally. Jack Douglas (1977), for example, argues that nearly all versions of sociology overrationalize lived experience, and, in qualitative research, he thinks this is most characteristic of ethnomethodology (see Douglas and Johnson 1977). For Douglas, "*brute being* is that core of feeling and perception that is our innermost selves, our being" (p. 3, emphasis in the original).

According to Douglas, this is hardly captured by the methodical analysis of talk and interaction that is limited to the transcripts of audiotapes. To comprehend the depths of social life and lived experience, the researcher must "understand the total man in his total natural environment" (p. 4). Significantly, this extends researchers' interest to *emotionality*. Partly echoing the voice of conventional naturalism, yet now distinctly romanticist, Douglas highlights an inner dimension of reality. Calling for "deep-deep probes into the human soul," he tells us (1985, p. 51) that access to the truths of experience is not gained by mere proximity. It requires open sharing and intimacy, affective sensitivity, even the surrender of "soul" necessary to developing true empathy and understanding. The goal is to capture, even *reenact*, the subject's experience and to describe that in full emotional color.

There is a conspicuous absence here of scientific sounding jargon. This emotionalist idiom is humanistic, even existential. While focusing on naturally occurring settings and interaction, method talk turns from what research subjects do and how they accomplish it, to what they feel. If Park's injunctions played up the need to get one's hands and pants dirty by observing on the scene, the talk of those investigating subjectivity calls for even more intimate contact. This typically is conveyed in the vocabulary of immersion and introspection:

> We do not stand outside experience. . . . We do not put society on a rack and try to torture the truth out of it. . . . We seek truth in the ways we find necessary in the natural social world. We create truth from within by finding what works, what enables us to understand, explain, piece together, and partially predict our social world. (Douglas 1977, p. 5)

The range of affective experiences studied by the emotionalists is broad and deep, from heart wrenching child custody hearings (Johnson 1975), emotionally draining abortion decisions (Ellis and Bochner 1992), and the experience of chronic pain (Kotarba 1977), to the seductions of crime (Katz 1988). Because the depths of experience are often considered to be outside the scope of traditional forms of documentation, these qualitative researchers have increasingly experimented with unconventional representational strategies (Richardson 1990). Some express emotional experience through poetry (Richardson 1992), while others turn to dramatic techniques (Ellis and Bochner 1992; Paget 1995) and introspective field notes (Ronai 1992).

For many, the final arbiter of authenticity is the subject. He or she alone knows what the experience under consideration is really like, especially how it feels. Use your own emotional experience, the researcher is told. Delve into personal biography and take the subject's point of view. Give voice to your own feelings (Ellis 1991b). This is not Park's exhortation to show up on reality's doorstep. It is a challenge to go inside, to the heart and soul of the matter.

Postmodernist Self-consciousness

Qualitative researchers have become more and more self-conscious, especially about the relation between method talk and the nature of social reality. There is a growing awareness that the relation is reflexive, that research procedure constructs reality as much as it produces descriptions of it. Listen as Joseph Schneider (1993) simulates a conversation about how sociologists use their analytic texts to bring themselves "into being" as descriptive authorities set apart from their subjects:

> We are the analysts; the experts; the scientists. Our project—our mandate—is to divide the world into them and us, and then to study them and explain why and how they do what they do. You've got to get that clear or you're in for serious personal problems. *They* don't analyze what they do—they don't think about it the way we do; they just do it. We analyze, sociologically, what they do and tell them (and each other) why they behave that way. That's our game (and "it is played").
> But what about us? What about what we do?
> You don't get it, do you? Our job is to analyze social *life*, not us.
> Oh. Yeah. (P. 103, emphasis in the original)

As qualitative research has become sensitive to the constructed nature of the social world—to the multiplicity of experiential realities that might be created, including the reality of method as a way of knowing—a crisis has developed concerning the relation between the researcher, representational practice, and those studied. The crisis provokes the question of how, if realities are accomplishments, those realities reported by researchers can be anything but accomplishments themselves. What is the basis for treating research reports as authoritative? How can they be authentic if they, too, are merely representations of experience, themselves grounded in particular places and perspectives?

Method talk becomes problematic in its own right as analysts begin to scrutinize the ways we "write culture" (Clifford and Marcus 1986) or write "against" it (Abu-Lughod 1991), read ethnography (Hammersley 1990; Atkinson 1992), or represent science and its findings (Lynch and Woolgar 1988). Sociological texts, and the practices and circumstances that produce them, become objects for analysis. We examine how qualitative researchers observe, listen, and write, asking, for example, how the exercise of "ethnographic imagination" or the ethnographer's craft constitutes ethnography. In the process, textual explication becomes a research method (Atkinson 1990).

The "crisis of representation" has inspired a host of attempts to "deconstruct" research to reveal its reality-constituting practices. This has produced its own brand of self-consciousness, embodied in *postmodernist* method talk designed to characterize a world whose "free-floating" signs and meanings are set loose from distinct social moorings. Some view this self-consciousness as self-indulgent (Best 1995), as it privileges the act of representation over the represented, sometimes completely upstaging reality. Nonetheless, the language of this so-called postmodern moment reveals an important formulation of what method can mean for the facts produced by researchers.

COMMON THREADS

This brief survey points out some key differences between idioms of qualitative inquiry. Before we are inundated by difference, however, we must remember that the approaches have a great deal in common regarding the research enterprise as a whole. These similarities become more apparent if we consider those concerns that have traditionally animated qualitative research. With common threads firmly established, we can then turn to a more extended discussion of differences in the following chapters of Part I. Part II will then attempt to show how the differences and the common threads might be woven into an analytic fabric that we call a renewed language of qualitative method.

Working Skepticism

Skepticism about what everyone ostensibly knows motivates much qualitative research. The skepticism derives from an uneasiness with the wisdom of received description. While this has been said to characterize the sociological imagination generally (see Mills 1959), it is the everyday calling card of qualitative researchers, who have traditionally tried to describe social life in ways that challenge popular understandings. The underlying presumption is that conventional appraisals, especially systematic quantitative assessments, fail to appreciate the nuances of the social world.

The skepticism prompts various strategies of inquiry, from "debunking" what is commonly thought to be true (that is, exposing the falsities of everyday understandings), to empathizing as completely as possible with those being studied and appreciating their articulations, feelings, and circumstances as they, themselves, do. At either extreme, there is the presupposition that what is conventionally known is somehow lacking. Indeed, as ethnomethodologists express it, the commonly known itself is subject to study for the way it is socially organized and taken for granted.

Commitment to Close Scrutiny

The orienting skepticism prompts qualitative researchers to scrutinize at close range, to place themselves in direct contact with, or in immediate proximity to, the lived world of those being studied. This is not done for the purpose of intervention or social reform, although such goals might indirectly motivate the research. Rather, researchers engage in close scrutiny in order to understand and document the organization of social life as it is practiced. The goal has been to look closely at social phenomena to see that which other kinds of inquiry may have missed.

Close scrutiny may involve a variety of techniques, from trying to document the naturally occurring details of talk and interaction to attempts to reenact subjects' feelings. While methods of close scrutiny vary, the goals are basically the same: to see the unseen in its own right, to represent the unknown in living color. Qualitative researchers are typically committed to viewing the details of experience, deferring if not eschewing the broad strokes of generalization in favor of describing particulars. Sweeping claims about the influence of social forces that often characterize sociological research are likely to be softened, qualified, set aside, or replaced by more painstaking accounts of the complex minutia of everyday life. But the detail is not trivial; qualitative researchers characteristically maintain that only close scrutiny can give voice to the eloquence of the commonplace.

Search for the "Qualities" of Social Life

Concern for detail allows qualitative research to pay special attention to the "qualities" of experience, aspects of life that quantitative approaches typically gloss over.

Indeed, this may be a defining distinction between the two. Rather than simply enumerating categories of social structure or interaction, qualitative researchers seek to understand and describe the categories as problematic in their own right. What quantitative researchers take for granted, their qualitative kindred study for meaningful substance, working boundaries, and everyday usage. For qualitative researchers, categories of social life are not so much given as they are subject to careful and systematic scrutiny in themselves.

Those seeking predictive or explanatory models of social behavior often decry qualitative studies as "merely descriptive," but qualitative researchers have staunchly resisted the pejorative connotation. Instead, they insist that we must have a good, clear picture of the qualities of the world before we can attempt to explain it, let alone predict or modify it. Thus, description justifies itself, as researchers aim to apprehend and comprehend the diversity, intricacy, subtlety, and complications that compose the social.

Focus on Process

Qualitative research also is distinguished by a commitment to studying social life in process, as it unfolds. Researchers extend their analyses of the qualities of the social to the ways its processes both enter into, and reflexively constitute, everyday life. Because the various idioms share an understanding of the social world as fluid and elastic, they direct their attention to the working definitions and procedures by which that world is given meaning. Seeing people as active agents of their affairs, qualitative inquiry has traditionally focused on how purposeful actors participate in, construct, deeply experience, or imagine their lives.

The various approaches may differ on just what role process plays, however. For some, it is a configuration of meaningful responses to the circumstances and contingencies of an obdurate, yet manageable reality. For others, social process constitutes the very circumstances, contingencies, and meanings of everyday life. Yet, while it differs from one idiom to the next, there is an enduring appreciation for the working subject who actively injects life into, and shapes, her or his world.

Appreciation for Subjectivity

For better or worse, qualitative inquiry has long been associated with subjectivity. One misinformed criticism alleges that qualitative research is little more than a set of subjective impressions, unsubstantiated by rigorous research procedure or "hard" data. This ignores the subject and the subjective as integral features of social life, and neglects the fact that the researcher is a subject in his or her own right, present in the same world as those studied. As we will see in Chapter 5, some qualitative researchers have taken this to heart and it has led to a crisis of representation. At the same time, both the focus on subjectivity and the crisis have enhanced the appreciation for subjectivity. This is now tied to the key question of how to represent matters that cannot be literally described by an objective observer.

Qualitative researchers have long insisted that they are not lax, imprecise, or unsystematic, and have now assembled a massive technical literature attesting to this (see Denzin and Lincoln 1994). Still, they can never completely distance themselves from subjectivity, inasmuch as subjectivity, broadly speaking, is their domain. Reluctance to standardize data collection and unwillingness to sacrifice depth for generality are matters of analytic necessity, not technical inadequacies. A world comprised of meanings, interpretations, feelings, talk, and interaction must be scrutinized on its own terms. Qualitative inquiry has always maintained this commitment, now more than ever.

Striving for rigor, qualitative research also honors perspective. For some researchers, this means documenting versions of subjectivity, such as describing how something looks or feels from various subjects' viewpoints. Indeed, portraying the world from alternate vantage points has been a goal of qualitative research from the earliest ventures of the Chicago School, all the way to the imperatives of contemporary, poststructuralist feminists (Reinharz 1992; Harding 1987; Smith 1987). As different as qualitative researchers' descriptions might (indeed, must) be, the common thread here is the recognition that subjectivity is perspectival. While some qualitative researchers are not so much interested in subjects' inner experiences as they are in the possibility of subjectivity and subjects' mundane belief in the perspectival nature of experience and personal knowledge (see Pollner 1987), the topic of subjectivity nonetheless is paramount.

Tolerance for Complexity

Finally, qualitative researchers maintain an abiding interest in interactional complexity. While this is sometimes mistaken for analytic fuzziness or a reluctance to generalize, it more accurately reflects the researchers' orientation to the working intricacies of human agency and circumstance. A skeptical orientation to the commonplace, a commitment to the close scrutiny of social action, the recognition of variety and detail, the focus on process, and the appreciation of subjectivity, all, in one form or another, suggest that everyday life is not straightforwardly describable. This could hardly be captured by the operational designation of variables, social forces, and the like. A subsequent tolerance for complexity militates against the impulse to gloss over troublesome uncertainties, anomalies, irregularities, and inconsistencies in the interest of comprehensive, totalizing explanation. As a matter of principle, qualitative inquiry accommodates and pursues the problematic finding or the unanticipated occurrence. The research in many ways mirrors, and is mirrored by, its findings, offering the world as fine-grained, variegated, and to some extent, always resistant to comprehensive explanation.

The common threads combine to underscore the complexity of meaning. Writing of the methodological position of symbolic interactionism, but speaking in terms congenial to most qualitative approaches, Herbert Blumer (1969) articulated the following principle:

The meanings that things have for human beings are central in their own right. To ignore the meaning of the things toward which people act is seen as falsifying the behavior under study. To bypass the meaning in favor of factors alleged to produce the behavior is seen as a grievous neglect of the role of meaning in the formation of behavior. (P. 3)

The methodological implications are clear, as Blumer once again notes:

We can and, I think, must look upon human group life as chiefly a vast interpretive process in which people singly and collectively guide themselves by defining objects, events, and situations which they encounter.... Any scheme designed to analyze human group life in its general character has to fit this process of interpretation ... interpretation is a formative or creative process in its own right. It constructs meanings which, as I have said, are not predetermined. (Pp. 132–35)

The pursuit of meaning plunges qualitative inquiry into the complexities of social context. On the one hand, context is interactive. People develop and use meanings with respect to themselves and others. Because interaction resists analysis in terms of fixed variables (Blumer 1969), qualitative research has taken responsibility for its "thick description" (Geertz 1973). The constitutive theoretical linkage to method is undeniable: if everyday life is construed as ongoingly social, it can be analyzed only by way of flexible, empathetic, qualitative technique. On the other hand, context implies circumscribed configurations of understanding, or culture. Here, we take culture in its broadest sense, as complexes of shared usages that distinguish a community, a setting, or a situation. These are webs of significance, more or less fixed, that variably suffuse and surround everyday life, yet also offer members resources for further interpretation (Geertz 1973). Taken together, interaction and culture both specify and generate meaning, the study of which is necessarily complex.

LEADING QUESTIONS

The common threads lead qualitative inquiry to an array of research questions. Typically at the forefront are the *what* questions. The commanding focus of much qualitative research is on questions such as *what* is happening, *what* are people doing, and *what* does it mean to them? The questions address the content of meaning, as articulated through social interaction and as mediated by culture. The resulting research mandate is to describe reality in terms of what it naturally is.

At the same time, a sensitivity to the ways people participate in the construction of their lives and social worlds has led qualitative inquiry towards equally compelling *how* questions. While not ignoring *what* concerns, those pursuing *how* questions typically emphasize the production of meaning. Research orients to the everyday practices through which the meaningful realities of everyday life are constituted and sustained. The guiding question is *how* are the realities of everyday life accomplished?[3]

The method talk associated with these *what* and *how* questions is telling. It all but specifies the objects and events that qualitative researchers choose to study and analyze. To answer *what* questions, one must focus on people and settings, looking for the meanings that exist in, emerge from, and are consequential for, those settings. Researchers seeking answers to constitutive *how* questions temporarily set meaning aside as they identify meaning-making practices.

Among qualitative researchers who have engaged the postmodern debate, the sensitivity to *how* has increased to the point that the question no longer applies to the empirical world, but turns on method talk as a form of rhetoric. Here, ways of asking and answering questions such as how the world of everyday life operates, are themselves subject to study, notably in relation to the research texts that tacitly direct the reader to distinct empirical worlds. The *how* question here is radically epistemological, concerned with how we can possibly know anything (any thing) at all.

There are, of course, other questions, most notably those dealing with *why* things are as they are, *why* people act in particular ways, and the like. Such questions, while not uncommon in qualitative research, are typically deferred until the *what* and *how* questions are dealt with. Still, qualitative researchers can engage *why* questions (Katz 1994; Silverman 1993a), and we take this up in Chapter 9.

In the chapters of Part I, we examine in greater detail the four idioms we have introduced, discussing their assumptions about the fundamental parameters of the social world and the research procedures used to make that world visible. We will demonstrate the ways in which the ostensibly neutral medium of language is enduringly and unavoidably implicated in the decisions qualitative researchers make about how to study social life. As we proceed, we will describe the empirical implications that stem from conceiving of—talking about—the social world in the respective research vernaculars. In the course of the discussion, we will hear traces of the new language of qualitative method.

We proceed by means of exemplification. Rather than surveying the full range of studies animated by the alternate forms of method talk, we concentrate on leading exemplars of each approach. For instance, while myriad studies deal with the native *whats* of social life, three exemplary ethnographies provide a basis for examining naturalistic method talk. The advantage of this approach is a more nuanced consideration of the talk as a set of procedural and empirical language games.

In Part II, we respond to the increasing empirical nihilism that postmodernism brings to qualitative inquiry, offering prospects for a more positive approach built on a newly emerging analytic vocabulary. This approach is deeply indebted to those we discuss in Part I, but its method talk departs from exclusive attention to either *what* or *how* questions. Instead, we propose a "renewed" language that focuses qualitative inquiry on both the interpretive processes of a constructed social world and the substantive meanings, contexts, and conditions that shape its inhabitants' actions.

That we write in terms of a renewed language of qualitative method means we think that a new language has been developing for some time, one increasingly conscious of its empirical claims. From qualitative researchers' first naturalistic forays into the field, *what* questions have been paramount. Ethnomethodologists offered an important turn by self-consciously radicalizing the *how* question, transforming method talk from talk about the meaningful contours of the world of everyday life and the way it operates into talk about *how* that world is constituted by its members. Emotionalists have warned against the over-rationalization of *whats* and *hows* of everyday experience, especially the *whats* and *hows* of the emotional. Their self-consciousness orients to feelings, both their subjects' and their own. Finally, the postmodernist sensibilities that now suffuse certain quarters of qualitative inquiry have made procedural self-consciousness a central concern, sometimes to the detriment of empirical analysis itself.

While this emerging self-consciousness has sensitized qualitative researchers to many important procedural issues, we believe that it too often infringes upon the key concerns of qualitative inquiry. Sometimes it unravels the common threads that have traditionally animated and united qualitative research. Other times it unnecessarily undermines the separate contributions of the various research idioms. Some manifestations of the self-consciousness seem to be turning qualitative research more and more into a self-representing enterprise. Even while reflexive consciousness is an important ingredient of science—alerting us to the part that we, as researchers who ourselves are located in the world, play in what we study and describe—it has become a preoccupation that too often supplants empirical inquiry.

The new language of qualitative method is increasingly concerned with representational issues. In a form of social research that closely scrutinizes reality and representation it could hardly be otherwise. But these concerns now risk overwhelming systematic inquiry itself. It is time not only to take stock of the method talk that has led to our present state, but also to reappropriate the common threads for continued empirical analysis and to present the possibility of method talk that is sensitive to both the real in everyday life and the representational practices of participants. This doesn't mean we long for a nostalgic return to the days and ways of more simplistic analysis. To the contrary, we want to refurbish and reinvigorate some valuable traditions in order to better address the increasingly complex existential contours of contemporary social life.

PART I

Idioms of Qualitative Inquiry

CHAPTER 2

Naturalism

Naturalism is a cornerstone of qualitative sociology.[1] This approach presumes that reality exists in textured and dynamic detail in the "natural" environment of the social world. The meaningful features of everyday life consist of participants' orientations to, and actions within, this world as they purposefully manage their realities. The naturalistic researcher strives to richly and accurately describe these realities without unduly disrupting—thus distorting—these worlds in the process (see Adler and Adler 1994; Denzin 1989b). From the start, researchers have described all sorts of everyday settings, formal and informal, revealing the distinct ways of life of their participants. As Goffman (1961) noted, the aim has been to carefully document these ways of life on their own terms by participating in them and discreetly observing people, events, and interaction.[2]

Ethnographic research on neighborhoods and communities is perhaps the oldest tradition of qualitative sociological inquiry. Sometimes called "urban ethnography," this research conceives of places as "natural areas" in the sense that social conditions native to the locales combine to give them a particular shape and flavor. One of the earliest and best studies is William Foote Whyte's (1943) now-classic book about a neighborhood Whyte calls Cornerville. It is a richly textured account of the social structure of an Italian-American slum in the late 1930s that systematically focuses on indigenous patterns of meaning and social interaction. Whyte is the consummate participant observer, whose naturalistically being on the scene and carefully documenting what goes on is evident on almost every page (see Geertz 1988).

We begin this chapter by examining the naturalistic method talk in Whyte's landmark study *Street Corner Society* and move on to two other exemplary urban ethnographies, Elliot Liebow's (1967) *Tally's Corner*, and Elijah Anderson's (1976) *A Place on the Corner*. As we shall see, each author orients to the natural world in terms of a three-part vocabulary. They view their respective settings as *geographic* fields of experience, and each researcher seeks to "be there" in time and space. Each aims to document the real-life drama of "participants' worlds," in order to convey participants' "own story." From our perspective, it is of more than passing interest that the word "corner" appears in the titles of all three studies. We will see that the street corner is both the common empirical mooring of the studies and the narrative foundation of the authors' claims to naturalistic authenticity.

"BEING THERE"

Where is "there" for these naturalists? What anchors their search for the facts?

Cornerville

In *Street Corner Society*, "there" is an Italian-American neighborhood located in what Whyte calls "Eastern City." He names the neighborhood "Cornerville" because so much of its social life is conducted on street corners. From the book's appendix, where Whyte describes how the study was done, we surmise that Eastern City is Boston. Harvard University has awarded Whyte a three-year research fellowship and now, with considerable effort, he enters into Cornerville life and finds it an appealing and intriguing location to study. Whyte notes that Cornerville presents the researcher with a different set of local challenges than does the Cambridge campus. "Being there" requires more than simply finding a location on a map. The unknowns of the area make it difficult to be "on location" as an outsider, much less as a sociologist. This is evident in the first paragraph of Whyte's Introduction:

In the heart of "Eastern City" there is a slum district known as Cornerville, which is inhabited almost exclusively by Italian immigrants and their children. To the rest of the city it is a mysterious, dangerous, and depressing area. Cornerville is only a few minutes' walk from fashionable High Street, but the High Street inhabitant who takes that walk passes from the familiar to the unknown. (P. xv)

Here, and throughout subsequent descriptions, "there" takes on elements of the exotic, conveyed by way of contrasts that Whyte draws between Cornerville and settings that are likely to be more comfortable and familiar to most readers (cf. Said 1978; Torgovnick 1990). Pointing out that Cornerville is not High Street is more than an informational gesture; it is a rhetorical maneuver that begins to establish Cornerville's special character and uniqueness. The timing of the Cornerville study—during World War II—introduces another element of concern. What is this community of recent *Italian* immigrants really like? Are they really American? Whyte writes that much of the general public feared that the "Italian slum dweller might be more devoted to fascism and Italy than to democracy and the United States," which would put "Cornerville at odds with the rest of the community." Then he adds that "respectable people have access to a limited body of information about Cornerville," explaining that much of what is known about the area is limited to what a sightseer might observe—bad housing conditions, narrow and neglected streets—or what available statistics tell, such as the lack of bathing facilities and a high juvenile delinquency rate. Whyte portrays the mystery of Cornerville in the form of a faceless mass, the implication being that, for outsiders, "there" is an unknown place, undifferentiated and strange.

Whyte goes on to conclude that the popular image of districts like Cornerville is not true to life. Not denying that Cornerville is a poor, crime-ridden slum, he nonetheless contends that there is something missing from this view:

There is one thing wrong with this picture: no human beings are in it. Those who are concerned with Cornerville seek through a general survey to answer questions that require the most intimate knowledge of local life. The only way to gain such knowledge is to live in Cornerville and participate in the activities of its people. One who does that finds that the district reveals itself to him in an entirely different light. The buildings, streets, and alleys that formerly represented dilapidation and physical congestion recede to form a familiar background for the actors upon the Cornerville scene. (Pp. xv–xvi)

Tally's Corner

Fast-forward twenty years or so to the early 1960s and we find Elliot Liebow participating in the streetcorner life of his African-American informant Tally Jackson. This time, "there" is an African-American neighborhood located in the inner city of Washington, D.C. Liebow has set out to study the "lower-class Negro man [who is] neglected from a research point of view simply because he is more difficult to reach than women, youths and children" (Liebow 1967, p. 7). Again, geography anchors method talk. Tally's corner is a distinct place, inhabited by real people, whose equally real lives are a mystery to social researchers.

Liebow points out that research on lower-class life is cursory, offering a thin body of facts in the form of social statistics based on surveys:

There is, for example, a growing uneasiness about the validity of much of the data already gathered, especially data gathered by interview and questionnaire. Appeals for data in depth go hand in hand with a widespread suspicion that lower-class persons are less tractable to interview and questionnaire techniques than are persons in the middle and upper strata. (P. 9)

Thus, the mystery of places like Tally's corner is both public and scientific. Such places not only are a public quandary, but also present a "thereness" not readily revealed by standard survey research techniques. If geography introduces us to the subject matter, it also clearly poses a challenge to one's research procedure.

Liebow accepts the challenge and sets out to give his readers the lay of the land, so to speak. Not only is Tally's corner part of an African-American, inner city neighborhood, but it is also a setting for the "life of ordinary people," which Liebow seeks to document "on their grounds and on their terms" (p. 10). "Their grounds" are again presented by way of familiar contrasts, this time against well-known Washington landmarks. Referring to what he calls the "New Deal Carry-out shop," a take-out restaurant and convenience store that is the social hub of Tally's corner, Liebow tells us that the unknown can be found in close proximity to the familiar, indeed in its geographic shadow:

The New Deal Carry-out shop is on a corner in downtown Washington, D.C. It would be within walking distance of the White House, the Smithsonian Institution, and other major public buildings of the nation's capital, if anyone cared to walk there, but no one ever does. (P. 17)

As Liebow proceeds through the area, he reveals more of the setting to his reader: "Across the street from the Carry-out is a liquor store. The other two corners of the intersection are occupied by a dry cleaning and shoe repair store and a wholesale plumbing supplies showroom and warehouse" (pp. 17–18). Moving on, he describes dwellings and other businesses. There are the old, red-brick buildings, some con-

verted to rooming and tenement houses, standing alongside liquor stores, pawnbro-
kers, poolrooms, beauty parlors, barber shops, and launderettes. Here and there, one
finds a storefront church, corner grocery, or funeral parlor.

For Liebow, "being there" is initially more scenic than it is for Whyte. Liebow
throws the geographic contours of the setting into high relief from the start. Virtually
escorting us down the street, his aim is to move us bodily to the site in order to take
in the sights and sounds pedestrians do. Stopping to look around, Liebow describes
the daily rhythms of corner life. Focusing on the Carry-out shop, where the action
is, Liebow writes:

The Carry-out shop is open seven days a week. Two shifts of two waitresses spend most
of their time pouring coffee, opening bottles of soda, and fixing hamburgers, french fries, hot
dogs, "half-smokes," and "submarines" for men, women, and children. The food is taken out
or eaten standing up because there is no place to sit down. But in the 10' × 12' customer
area, there is wall space and other leaning facilities which lend themselves nicely to the Carry-
out's business and social functions. (P. 21)

Small as it is, and as poor as the participants may be, the setting teems with life.
Liebow implies that one has to be there in order to fully appreciate this. We immediately get a tantalizing glimpse of the forthcoming social drama as Liebow describes some of the business conducted on the shop's premises:

On top of the cigarette machine or on the jukebox, for example, Bumdoodle, the Carry-
out's numbers man in residence, conducts his business dealings with the white numbers backer
who comes by daily to settle accounts with him and with other numbers men from the neighborhood. (P. 21)

The continuing implication is that only close, on-site observation can reveal the
setting's natural aura. This sort of intimate observation opens to view the many "odd
jobs" and ways of making a living that are available in circumstances with few
proper sources of income (see Miller 1978, 1981). The broader implication will be
that circumstances, when intimately understood, reveal complex courses of action
and indigenously reasonable ways of life, as "deviant" as they might otherwise seem
to outsiders.

As if this glimpse were not enough, Liebow makes a final effort to give the reader
a genuine feel for the place before introducing the cast of characters and beginning
the drama. After taking us to the inner-city street corner, walking us down the streets
and giving us the lay of the land, Liebow tells us that the final, and crucial, step in
being there is to "hang out." This means one must actually participate in the setting
that animates its inhabitants. "Being there" becomes a literal "assault [on] the five
senses":

For those who hang out there, the Carry-out offers a wide array of sounds, sights, smells,
tastes, and tactile experiences which titillate and sometimes assault the five senses. The air
is warmed by the smells from the coffee urns and grill and thickened with fat from the deep-
fry basket. The jukebox offers up a wide variety of frenetic and lazy rhythms. The pinball
machine is a standing challenge to one's manipulative skill ... colorful signs exhort customers to drink Royal Crown Cola and eat Bond Bread. (Pp. 21–22)

Another Place on the Corner: Jelly's Bar and Liquor Store

Ten years later, in the mid 1970s, Elijah Anderson (1976) takes us to yet another place on the corner, this time in a poor, African-American neighborhood on the south side of Chicago. "Being there" is once again a geographic orientation, focusing on a corner establishment that Anderson calls Jelly's bar and liquor store. The outsider who passes by observes the usual buzz and seeming confusion. Neighborhood people, mostly men, mill about. Some are drunk, some sober. A few appear to be furtively skulking about. Street noises and voices sound chaotic, with the occasional surprise of loud shouting or argument. As Anderson writes:

> Periodically, the humdrum routine is punctuated with some excitement. An elderly black woman bursts out of Jelly's, clutching her jug of wine and her pocketbook as she hurries along minding her own business. The group on the sidewalk comes to life as one of the men grabs at her purse and yells, "Gimme some o' what you got there, woman!" "I'll geh ya' this fist upside yo' head!" she responds, shaking her fist and confidently moving on about her business. (P. 2)

But the apparent pandemonium at Jelly's is only superficial. Once more, a set of contrasts introduces the reader to an underlying order that only close scrutiny reveals. Anderson tells the reader that what the casual observer may view as chaotic, the insider knows is socially regulated and meaningful. The implication is that this world, like others, operates by certain rules. If one is to understand it, one must enter and view it on its own terms. Being there is not only a practical challenge to inhabitants, but a methodological one for researchers. Anderson offers the following lesson:

> After being around Jelly's neighborhood for a while and getting to know its people, the outside observer can begin to see that there is order in this social world. For example, the wineheads turn out to be harmless, for they generally do the things people expect them to do: they drink on the street, beg passersby for change, and sometimes stumble up and down the street cursing at others. One also begins to understand that what looks like a fight to the death usually doesn't come near a fatal end. Often such a "fight" turns out to be a full-dress game in which only "best friends" or "cousins" can participate—but at times even they can't play this game without its ending in a real fight. After a while one gets to know that old black woman leaving Jelly's with the "taste" as Mis' Lu, "a nice ol' lady who been 'round here fo' years," and "studs 'round dese here streets'll cut yo' throat 'bout messin' with her. She hope raise half the cats 'round here." Secure in her knowledge of how she is regarded, she walks the streets unafraid, "back-talking" to anyone "messin' " with her. (Pp. 2–3)

Anderson asks two questions: What does it take to "be somebody" in this world, and how is it that, in a world offering comparatively little of material value by which to claim status, deference, and respect, one can still amount to something? He goes on to argue that what it takes to "be somebody" is continuing interpersonal work, which not only reaps the advantages and disadvantages of a system of respect, but serves to actively construct that system in the process. What appears from a distance to be fruitless mutual insults and baseless boasting, is, on closer observation, the construction of status and respect, or their opposite, as the case might be. The status system needs continual demonstration and renewal because it has little material warrant of its own.

Jelly's is the heart of the system in microcosm, and Anderson takes us inside to reveal its workings in detail. What is natural on this particular street corner is vividly played out indoors. Anderson's working skepticism and commitment to close scrutiny now reveal the interactional complexities of the contrasting inner social worlds of the barroom and the liquor store:

Jelly's bar and liquor store has two front entrances, one leading to the barroom and the other to the liquor store. Each room has its own distinctive social character. The barroom is a public place . . . It invites almost anyone to come in and promises he will not be bothered as long as he minds his own business. In this sense it is a neutral social area. Yet people who gather on this side of Jelly's tend to be cautiously reserved when approaching others, mainly because on this side they just don't know one another. In contrast, the liquor store [which is separated from the barroom by an open doorway allowing regulars to pass from one side to the other] is more of a place for peers to hang out and outwardly appears to have a more easygoing, spontaneous ambiance. (P. 4)

As an African American himself, Anderson has relatively easy access to the barroom, where regular customers mingle with visitors. The liquor store is another matter, almost another world for Anderson. This is a more exclusive world. The goings on here, Anderson guesses, are more likely to reveal the organization of status and respect among the regulars. This regular clientele and their interactions in the liquor store intrigue Anderson, challenging him to become an insider. The liquor store—this place within a place—ultimately represents "being there." Like Cornerville and the New Deal Carry-out shop, Jelly's is bursting with life, but only for an "insider" who is actually "there" and willing to pay really close attention.

Spanning nearly four decades of qualitative research, these exemplary ethnographies introduce us to natural worlds concretely placed in time and space. The research settings resemble those that field biologists call natural habitats. Words like *corner*, *place*, *neighborhood*, *turf*, *hangout*, *grounds*, *scene*, and *setting* disclose a geographic orientation to the field and present the physical constraints on direct observation. These worlds genuinely come into view only when the observer gets close to them. This gives rise to procedural expressions of the need to be "on the scene," to "become an insider," and to "hang out." As we shall see later, this method talk will encounter serious challenges from qualitative approaches that detach experiential reality and social order from geographic location, transforming them into interpretive constructs (see Gubrium and Holstein 1987).

"THEIR WORLDS"

Natural habitats are full of life, which leads to another strand of the naturalist's working vocabulary. Being at the scene of the action is a necessary, but not a sufficient, condition for authentically capturing the real-life drama of participants' worlds. Not only must the naturalist see things up close, but he or she must get into the action. Being "there" is an ideal vantage point, but to really understand participants' lives, the researcher must get inside "their worlds."

Becoming Part of the Action

Each of our exemplary naturalists carefully describes how he became part of the action. For Whyte, it is not enough to walk through Cornerville and spend time there, day after day. He quickly recognizes that territorial presence merely transplants the stranger from an outer to an inner landscape; it does not provide automatic access to everyday experience. That requires the sort of diligent fieldwork that Whyte's book makes apparent. The eighty-page appendix, entitled "On the Evolution of Street Corner Society," devotes less than one page to "Finding Cornerville" and 68 pages to how Whyte became part of the community. Similarly, Liebow is accosted by the smells, sights, and sounds of the New Deal Carry-out shop, but that alone does not open its social world to view. Anderson is a mere bystander at Jelly's until he meets Herman, his key informant. Only then does he begin to feel like a part of that world. Note, for example, the implicit desire to be an insider that is evident in Anderson's description of the liquor store area he initially views only from the adjacent barroom:

In that [liquor store] room people were engaged in spontaneous fun—laughing, yelling, playing with one another, and being generally at ease. To me that room seemed very exciting, but it was clear that I would have been out of place there for it seemed to be only for peer-group members. I sensed that there I would have been reminded of my outsider status again and again. While in the barroom, among the visitors and a few of the peer-group members who gravitated over now and then, I felt *in place*. Looking into the liquor-store room, I saw Herman. Catching his attention, I beckoned to him, and he came over to me in the barroom. We shook hands and greeted each other, then held a friendly conversation over a couple of beers. But soon he returned to the liquor-store area, where more of his buddies seemed to be. That Herman had buddies, and so many of them, was one of the important distinctions between him and many of the visitors I had previously met at Jelly's. (P. 14)

"Inner" realms, such as the liquor store, virtually *belong* to their participants. They are not merely locales for living, but represent social domains within which insiders establish who they really are and what their actions are authentically about. As Anderson explains, referring to "special hangouts for the urban poor":

Here they can sense themselves to be among equals, with an equal chance to be somebody, even to be occasional winners in the competition for social esteem. This is their place. They set social standards. And when they feel those standards are threatened, they can defend them. (P. 1)

It is as if Anderson, as well as the other authors, had to convincingly ingratiate himself to the participants in order to gain access to their worlds and secrets. Each world, while "there," also seems to distance itself from outsiders, concealing its natural realm and requiring exceptional effort to get inside.

For the authors, the process of getting inside, while still being sociologists, centers on the key informant, who gets star billing in the social dramas that eventually will be produced. Whyte's key informant is Doc, the central figure in the "Norton gang." Doc is both socially and sociologically savvy. When Whyte presents his research project to Doc, Doc seems to know immediately what needs to be done to integrate Whyte into his world and sets about vigorously, but tactfully, doing so.

With Doc's help, Whyte becomes part of the action and begins to encounter the complex details of Doc's world. Doc virtually trains Whyte—his "friend"—to see the inchoate shape of gang social organization. Ultimately, Whyte comes to view Doc as a collaborator in the research as much as its central subject:

> As I began hanging about Cornerville, I found that I needed an explanation for myself and for my study. As long as I was with Doc and vouched for by him, no one asked me who I was or what I was doing. . . . My relationship with Doc changed rapidly in this early Cornerville period. At first he was simply a key informant—and also my sponsor. As we spent more time together, I ceased to treat him as a passive informant. I discussed with him quite frankly what I was trying to do, what problems were puzzling me, and so on. Much of our time was spent in this discussion of ideas and observations, so that Doc became, in a very real sense, a collaborator in the research. . . . Actually, without any training he was such a perceptive observer that it only needed a little stimulus to help him to make explicit much of the dynamics of the social organization of Cornerville. Some of the interpretations I have made are his more than mine, although it is now impossible to disentangle them. (Pp. 300–301)

Liebow's key informant is Tally Jackson. Tally, too, is socially and sociologically perceptive. He knows his way around the neighborhood and commands considerable respect there; he understands its social secrets. Liebow describes the need to "belong" in the same way that Whyte does, conveying the achievement as being "up tight" with Tally:

> By the end of the second day I had met nine men, learned the names of several more, and spent many hours in close public association with several men, at least two of whom were well known. And perhaps most important of all, in my own mind I had partly sloughed off that feeling of being a stranger and achieved that minimum sense of "belonging" which alone permits an ease of manner and mind so essential in building personal relationships. (Pp. 241–42)
>
> By the middle of March, Tally and I were close friends ("up tight") and I was to let him know if I wanted or needed "anything, anytime." By April, the number of men whom I had come to know fairly well and their acceptance of me had reached the point at which I was free to go to the rooms of apartments where they lived or hung out, at almost any time, needing neither excuse nor an explanation for doing so. Like other friends, I was there to pass the time, to hang around, to find out "what's happening." (P. 246)

For Anderson, insidership comes with the friendship of Herman, his key informant. Anderson links belonging to trust. He knows that he has arrived in "their world" when he begins to sense an openness between Herman and himself. As trust develops, he feels he belongs in the inner reaches of the world he wants to study, especially in the presence of the liquor store regulars. Hinting at an increased self-consciousness more in tune with ethnomethodology, Anderson points out that his own and others' belonging in "their world" is socially constructed in the open give-and-take of native participants. He, together with the natives, establishes an insider's membership through the banter of casual conversation. Anderson describes his social entrée this way:

> My openness encouraged Herman to be open with me. As a result, there was now some basis for trust in our relationship. In telling me more about himself, Herman said he was a

janitor but quickly added, "I'm a man among men," implying that, contrary to what some might expect of a janitor, he held himself in high esteem. . . . It was encounters like this that made me conscious that who I was and how I fit into the cognitive picture of Jelly's did preoccupy some of its more persistent members. (Pp. 13–14)

[After Anderson had joined Herman and some of his friends inside the liquor store:] The men of the group continued to check us out. Herman was treating me as a friend, as an insider, as though my status in the group were somehow already assured. Certainly Herman would not invite just anyone to a party at work. Other group members wouldn't have expected this and in fact would have been surprised if he had asked one of them. After this demonstration by Herman, I could feel the others in the group warm up to me; they looked at me more directly and seemed to laugh more easily. (P. 16)

For me the evening had been remarkable. It was the first time I had been introduced to anyone well connected within the social setting of Jelly's; the first time I had actually been sponsored by someone with an important social stake there. And no less significant, it was my first social venture on the liquor-store side of Jelly's—a real achievement. I had become involved with peer-group members, people for whom others at Jelly's really mattered. The whole experience marked the real beginning of my entrée: It was the time from which I began to gain a feeling of place at Jelly's. Moreover, it pointed up to me the importance of this setting as one in which social selves were cast, debated, negotiated, and then defended—in a word, socially constructed. (P. 17)

Signs of belonging are highlighted in all three texts, with the authors' sense of the field apparent in their method talk. The signs are a combination of territorial and social presence. Geographically passing through their world signals what a corner bystander, a bar visitor, or a carry-out stopover would encounter—being close to nature, so to speak. As method talk would have it, this amounts to being "on the scene." But frequenting private rooms, the premises of gambling, or an informant's private parties is to become an actual part of the natural environment, in this case, to have "made the scene." Making the scene is indexed by events like being told about another's personal life or about illicit activities and relationships. Each author searches for such signs in his developing fieldwork and knows he has arrived when they become evident.

The Cast of Characters

"Their worlds" are full of dramatic detail, evincing both ordinary and extraordinary scenes and a full range of motives and emotions. Having arrived and made the scene, each author presents the cast of characters who are its principal actors. Foremost, of course, is the key informant. He serves a dual purpose, being both natively informed and informative, as well as providing sponsorship for the research. Doc, Tally, and Herman loom in importance as spokespersons and get star billing in their respective ethnographies. Indeed, as noted earlier, Whyte even acknowledges Doc's analytic partnership. The authors devote many pages to their key informants, and while they take others' stories into account, they clearly consider the key informant to be the consummate insider, the one who best "tells it like it is."

Other informants become minor characters. Having introduced Doc, Whyte presents the Norton gang, which, at various stages, includes Nutsy, Danny, Joe Dodge, Frank Bonelli, Carl, and Tommy. A rival Cornerville group, the "college boys," are presented next and include Chick Morelli and some of his Italian Community Club members. Later in the book, Whyte introduces still others—racketeers and politicians—who also figure in Cornerville life. Similarly, having given star billing to Tally Jackson, Liebow describes other players in the daily drama of the New Deal Carry-out shop's environs: Sea Cat, Richard, and Leroy. Liebow then lists sixteen additional minor actors according to their ages and usual employment. Anderson's cast of characters is a bit smaller and is presented through the interpersonal linkages of a developing plot centered on his key informant, Herman.

"THEIR OWN STORIES"

Having taken us "there" and introduced the cast of characters, the naturalist is ready to tell "their stories," that is, the stories of subjects' worlds. While the stories will focus on the key informants and other actors in the informants' lives, the crucial point, as far as storytelling is concerned, is that the stories told will be the *subjects' own* stories, not the naturalist's. The naturalist merely serves as the observant and sensitive vehicle by which others' experiences are conveyed. The tale of these experiences is reproduced in its essential detail by the skillful ethnographer.[3]

Here again, method talk is illuminating. For Whyte, the ethnography is a story within a story. After introducing Doc and the Norton gang, Whyte tells us that the drama about to unfold is, by and large, the story of Doc's life: "The story of the evolution of the Nortons can best be told as Doc's story" (p. 3). It's clear that what will be conveyed as the general story of street corner society will be told from Doc's perspective, as represented by Whyte. Indeed, for all practical purposes, the Nortons are Doc. Doc is a *key* informant not only because he has the insight and broad knowledge with which to accurately and fully convey the world under consideration, but also because that world is duplicated in its essential social details in the story of Doc's own life.

Liebow describes "their stories" as tales told on subjects' "own terms." He not only wants to portray the social world he finds on Tally's corner from its participants' standpoint, but also wants to use their own language in telling it. He uses street talk to convey the "sounds, sights, smells, tastes, and tactile experiences" of the locale. At one point, Liebow writes, "The present study is an attempt to meet the need for recording and interpreting lower-class life of ordinary people, on *their* grounds and on *their* terms" (p. 10, our emphasis). As he states in his conclusion:

> This study has been primarily concerned with the inside world of the streetcorner Negro man, the world of daily, face-to-face relationships with wives, children, friends, lovers, kinsmen and neighbors. An attempt was made to see the man as he sees himself, to compare what he says with what he does. (P. 208)

However, as later, more self-conscious, ethnographic critics might point out, none of these ethnographies is fully aware of its perspectival character. Whyte's book, for example, is decidedly not written from the standpoint of Nutsy, Joe Dodge, Frank Bonelli, or other Nortons. It reflects even less the experience of more peripheral members of Chick Morelli's Italian Community Club. Rather, the story is a composite, told through Doc's life. This story, critics might conclude, could never have been told in this way had Whyte not assumed the authoritative stance he did. The singular narrative is possible only by way of the omniscient language of natural-ism.[4] The same criticism, of course, would apply to Liebow and Anderson. What story would Sea Cat, himself an avid storyteller, relate about Tally or about the daily goings-on at the New Deal Carry-out shop? What story would the wives and girl-friends of Jelly's regulars tell about the culture of respect in the place on the cor-ner? Would these stories challenge Doc's, Tally's, and Herman's as valid portray-als of their world?

The problematic narrative status of "their stories" notwithstanding, our natural-istic researchers get "ready to roll," as it were. The scene has been set, casts have been introduced, and the action is about to begin. Liebow's opening scene is espe-cially compelling, drawing the reader into a scenario he will eventually question in ironic sociological terms, contrasting what the action falsely appears to convey with the "real" story:

> A pickup truck drives slowly down the street. The truck stops as it comes abreast of a man sitting on a cast-iron porch and the white driver calls, asking if the man wants a day's work. The man shakes his head and the truck moves on up the block, stopping again whenever idling men come within calling distance of the driver. At the Carry-out corner, five men de-bate the question briefly and shake their heads no to the truck. The truck turns the corner and repeats the same performance up the next street. In the distance, one can see one man, then another, climb into the back of the truck and sit down. In starts and stops, the truck finally disappears. (P. 29)

Liebow then asks:

> What is it we have witnessed here? A labor scavenger rebuffed by his would-be prey? Lazy irresponsible men turning down an honest day's pay for an honest day's work? Or a more complex phenomenon marking the intersection of economic forces, social values and individual states of mind and body? (Pp. 29–30)

Having led us "there" and asked his leading questions, Liebow is about to tell "their story" in order to show us how to appreciate what it means to be a participant in this real-life drama.

Time and again, the authors remind us that, above all, "their story" should be told on their own terms, in the characters' own voices. This mandate to be as true to life as possible translates directly into a method of communication with the reader that strives to convey the natural. We are offered personal stories, native testaments, and conversations in the words of the natives, all of which disclose authenticity.

The Personal Story

The personal story is used to recount extended actions. It is a way of letting infor-mants tell what happened in considerable detail and in their own fashion, without spoiling the coherence of the larger story of which the personal stories are a part. In the ethnographies, personal stories do not contend with each other for the right to be considered the whole story. Rather, as discordant as the stories seem to be at times, the authors work them together to present a well-integrated text. For exam-ple, while Doc's story of Cornerville life might in certain respects seem to contradict Chick's story, Whyte treats the differences as parts of *the* Cornerville story, conveyed in relation to the complex social fabric he is trying to describe.

Over thirty years later, Anderson relies just as much on the personal story, but he is becoming more attuned to how the story both conveys and constitutes his informants' realities. While never losing track of his naturalistic project, Anderson lets Herman tell us about his world in his own words, but also shows us how Herman uses the emerging story of his growing friendship with Anderson to construct respect for himself (Herman) within that world. This hints at a reflexive sensitivity that is uncharacteristic of traditional naturalists, but later becomes a major ethnomethodological and postmodernist concern.

For instance, when Anderson meets Herman and strikes up a friendly relationship, Herman learns that Anderson is a graduate student working on his doctorate at the University of Chicago. Anderson, in a phrase, "is somebody," which immediately impresses Herman. He soon asks Anderson to "share his turf" by inviting him to a Christmas party where Herman works. Herman expects this to confirm that he (Herman) "is somebody" in his own right because, as he tells it, he associates, indeed is "going for cousins" with, someone who is clearly "somebody" (Anderson). Anderson does not describe in discursive detail *how* Herman's storytelling constructs status, but, rather, focuses on *what* the resulting story preparation and storytelling accomplish in "their world."

In one example, Anderson tell us that, in a world where material conditions of life precariously align with status, claims to be "somebody" are quickly challenged or "shot down" by those ostensibly in the know. Anderson goes on to explain how Herman anticipates such contingencies in preplanning his stories:

> These notions, grounded in Herman's experience on the streets around Jelly's, are the background to his careful preparation of our "story" for the people at the Christmas party. At the party, Herman introduced me as his cousin who "goes to the University of Chicago, gettin' his Ph.D." He even told one black secretary that I was the cousin he had long been telling her about. Herman was the only janitor at the party; the others present were professionals and office workers. He and I were the only representatives from any setting at all like Jelly's. Yet with Herman's direction we moved easily among these people. With each introduction he beamed with pride over his " 'cousin,' who's gettin' his Ph.D." (P. 19)

Anderson's story thus becomes a narrative about Herman's storybuilding and story telling.

Despite his clear sensitivity to the constructed nature of Herman's reality, Anderson's working naturalism holds forth in his account; he uses the language of reality construction mainly to inform us of *what* members of Jelly's world work at constructing, not *how* this is done in methodic detail. The vocabulary of social construction is not so much method talk for Anderson as it is an adumbration of what such a vocabulary would show if it were applied to the analysis of life on the corner. It merely alludes to the possibility of analyzing the social constitution of Herman's status in relation to his story.

Native Testaments

"Their stories" are supplemented by native testaments to events otherwise described by the authors. Verbal snippets are sprinkled throughout each of the books, subjects' voices confirming what the larger ethnographic account is about. For example, describing what he calls an indigenous "theory of manly flaws" that the inhabitants of Tally's corner use to explain (away) sexual infidelity, Liebow first notes:

> In each instance, the man is always careful to attribute his inadequacies as a husband to his inability to slough off one or another attribute of manliness, such as independence of spirit, a like for whiskey, or an appetite for a variety of women. They trace their failures as husbands directly to their weaknesses as men, to their manly flaws. . . . One of the most widespread and strongly supported views the men have of themselves and others is that men are, *by nature,* not monogamous; that no man can be satisfied with only one woman at a time. (Pp. 118, 120, our emphasis)

Liebow then offers the following quotation from Sea Cat in support of the theory, which receives unanimous approval from the men on the corner:

> Men are just dogs! We shouldn't call ourselves human, we're just dogs, dogs, dogs! They call me a dog, 'cause that's what I am, but so is everybody else—hopping around from woman to woman, just like a dog. (Pp. 120–21)

As naturalists, Whyte, Liebow, and Anderson do not systematically examine such testaments for how they are used in talk and interaction to produce and warrant what is indigenously taken to be real and true. In the preceding example, the naturalist would be less interested in how gender differences are narratively constructed than he or she might be in how naturally occurring differences were reported. A concern with the production of gender in social interaction would relate to a contrasting analytic language, one less interested in representing the natural world of everyday life for men and women than in documenting *how* members methodically use accounts like the theory of manly flaws to produce a semblance of order and reality centered on gender differences (see Kessler and McKenna 1978; Holstein 1987). In the next chapter, we will show how ethnomethodology takes up this concern, making the natural a topic for research in its own right.

Conversation

Naturalists boldly illustrate the social contours of their subjects' lives with samples of real conversation. For example, in describing the social organization of Chick Morelli's Italian Community Club, Whyte underscores the interpersonal forces that shape leadership and decision making. What Doc, Chick's rival, tells us in various stories is elaborated on in extracts from Cornerville talk and interaction. At one point, Whyte highlights the competition between Cornerville leaders as it bears on the Club's viability by presenting an extract from a conversation between Chick and Doc after a club meeting. The exchange centers on the enforcement of a club rule requiring dismissal if a member misses three meetings in a row:

> CHICK: Where were you tonight?
> DOC: I had important business.
> CHICK: That's what you always say . . . . You better come to the club meetings or you'll get thrown out.

Doc: I'll skip two meetings and come to the third. And you won't be able to
        do anything about it.
Chick: That's what you think.
Doc: All right. If you don't believe me, put a little side bet on it, and we'll
        see what happens. You can't put me out without changing the consti-
        tution, and if you try to do it, you won't have a leg to stand on.
Chick: You'll see.
Doc: Want to bet on it?
Chick: No. . . . . But you better come to meetings. (P. 71)

Later, Whyte describes, but does not reproduce, a street corner conversation to again elaborate on the social relations between the Nortons and the Italian Community Club. A diagram shows various stages in the flow of the conversation between members of the groups and their intermediaries (p. 95). Whyte explains that, while members of each group join the corner gathering, there is no general conversation. Members of each group readily talk with co-members, but only talk to members of the other group through intermediaries. This conversational organization prevails throughout the gathering and illustrates the interactional by-product of group differences.

In a similar fashion, Liebow elaborates his description of the social rules governing the relations between what he calls "lovers and exploiters." Having described the operation of the theory of manly flaws, Liebow explains that it can manifest itself in considerable male bravado, which is accentuated in the presence of women. An exchange between Wesley, Richard, and Richard's 22-year-old half-sister Thelma, who is visiting from New York, provides an illustration:

Wesley: From now [on], if a girl ain't got money and a car, I'm not talking to
         her.
Thelma: But you don't find very many of those girls.
Wesley: My buddy next door, he's got one. She's got a '58 Mercury and I hear
         she's got a whole lot of money.
Thelma: How old is she?
Wesley: I don't know how old she is but she sure parks that Mercury in front
         of that door.
Richard: She could be sixty if she give me some of that money, let me drive
         that new car.
Wesley: [Agreeing vigorously] What'cha talking about, man!
Thelma: But won't you be embarrassed—to be seen with an older woman?
Wesley: No. I was dumb one time. This lady, she was about forty-five. She
         got her own home. She got a white Cadillac, '60. She got a restaurant
         and she tried her best to talk to me. She told my landlady, told my
         landlady to get me to call and I wouldn't. But now let her come around!
         I'll tell the landlady, "Anytime she come around, call Wesley." I was
         crazy then. And all that money! Ooh, I could play a long time! I could
         cool it. All that money and riding around in a big Cadillac. I'd ride
         the other women around. (Pp. 140–41)

Anderson makes a point about the continuing construction of status by describing the ritual insults that mark differences in social standing on the corner. Outside of friendship, such insults would be considered verbally abusive and offensive. Anderson uses the following extract from a corner exchange between Herman and Bucky, who are best friends, to show otherwise:

"Hey, motherfucker," Herman greeted [Bucky] in a loud voice, then went on to tell him, "I'm gettin' ready to go get me some o' Edna's [Bucky's wife] good pussy."

Bucky, with no apparent sense of outrage or embarrassment, calmly said, "I just left Butterroll in yo' bed, and she told me she'd have my supper ready afterwhile."

Herman then grabbed Bucky affectionately and said, "Aw, you dirty motherfucker, you."

The two men stood there laughing and talking for a while, as the others, now apparently satisfied, turned and looked away. (P. 193)

Naturalists provide conversational displays like these to illustrate the functioning of social organization, not to analyze *how* talk and interaction build up social organization, utterance by utterance. For the naturalist, social organization is "there," an essential part of its members' world, even while its qualities often go unrecognized and its complexities are commonly ignored by the public at large. In contrast, as we will show in the following chapter, ethnomethodologists view conversation as part of the machinery for *constructing* social organization. The principal question for them is not *what* the social organization under consideration is, but *how* it is constituted in speech and interaction. Conversation analysts, in particular, examine in systematic detail what members *do with words*, rather than just use subjects' words to show what members are thinking and doing. Regarding conversation as their topic, they refuse to treat it as epiphenomenal, as merely a source of illustration for other concepts and constructs the analyst has uncovered (Zimmerman and Pollner 1970).

A TRADITION OF GUIDELINES

Naturalists have developed a variegated tradition of guidelines for research. In contrast to the method talk of ethnomethodologists, emotionalists, and others, advisory method talk has become an enterprise in its own right. Much of it is atheoretical, which reflects in part the methodological presumption that "their story" is, indeed, located in "their world" and that the primary function of naturalistic study is to represent it as accurately and colorfully as possible.

Now in its third edition, John and Lyn Lofland's (1995) popular text, *Analyzing Social Settings*, is exemplary in this regard. From the start, the Loflands emphasize a commitment to naturalistically rigorous, close scrutiny:

We have a fondness for the term *naturalism* or *naturalistic research*. This term has a tradition (e.g., Matza 1969, Blumer 1969, Denzin 1971) and possesses transdisciplinary neutrality. Further, it suggests an appropriate linkage to *naturalist* as that word is used in field biology. From the realms of philosophical discourse, it has acquired the connotation of minimizing the presuppositions with which one approaches the empirical world—a laudable resonance indeed. Moreover, as a literary genre, *naturalism* involves a close and searching description of the mundane details of everyday life, a meaning we seek to foster in the social science context. (Pp. 6–7, emphasis in the original)

Various chapters are meant to take the researcher to the action: "Evaluating Data Sites," "Getting In," and "Getting Along." Chapter 6, "Thinking Topics," directs the reader to worlds of meaning, which link what is observed to what participants themselves make of it.

At the same time, in a curious turn of phrase for a naturalist text, the Loflands refer to naturalism as a "literary genre." This could raise serious representational questions by casting "being there," "their world," and "their story" as a *rhetoric* for a separate and distinct reality, rather than as terms of reference for reality itself. However, reading on in the text, we learn that the Loflands intend this merely to suggest a close inspection of the details of "their worlds," not a radical deconstruction of naturalism itself. In a sense, the Loflands tacitly preview, but do not develop, a self-conscious challenge to naturalism. As we will show in Chapter 5, this challenge emerges full-blown in the postmodernist portrayal of naturalistic ethnography as tacitly a *theory* of "being there" that turns "their worlds" and "their own stories" into artifacts created by the naturalistic story itself.

Minimizing Presuppositions

The directive to "minimize presuppositions" in order to witness subjects' worlds on their own terms is key to naturalistic inquiry. Repeatedly, methods books caution researchers to let "members' meanings" come through and not to substitute sociological or popular interpretations. The operating principle is to allow people to tell their own stories, with theory taking a back seat, at least initially.

Naturalistic method talk even extends to mundane research activities like taking field notes. As Robert Emerson, Rachel Fretz, and Linda Shaw explain in *Writing Ethnographic Fieldnotes* (1995):

We see ethnography as committed to uncovering and depicting indigenous meanings. The object of participation is ultimately to get close to those studied as a way of understanding what their experiences and activities *mean to them*.

Ethnographers should attempt to write fieldnotes in ways that capture and preserve indigenous meanings. To do so, they must learn to recognize and limit reliance upon preconceptions about members' lives and activities. They must become responsive to what others are concerned about, in their own terms. (P. 12, emphasis in the original)

Sharing this reluctance to impose meaning or a priori theoretical frameworks, Barney Glaser and Anselm Strauss (1967) see the process of qualitative inquiry as an opportunity to discover theory:

Our book is directed toward improving social scientists' capacities for generating theory that *will* be relevant to their research. . . . We need to develop canons more suited to the discovery of theory. . . . We argue in our book for grounding theory in social research itself— for generating it from the data. (Pp. vii–viii, emphasis in the original)

However, as the extract from the Loflands' book intimates as it draws our attention to the "genre" of naturalism, researchers are becoming progressively more uneasy with this guideline. While the directive to minimize presuppositions still holds in most methods books, naturalistic researchers are increasingly loath to claim that their orientation to members' worlds is completely atheoretical. This is reflected in contemporary naturalists' growing sensitivity to the constitutive relation between method talk and social reality. Anderson's overture to the "construction" of status at Jelly's, for example, is an incipient critique. Emerson, Fretz, and Shaw's (1995) naturalistically oriented book on writing field notes also cautions against an atheoretical view:

Members' meanings, however, are not pristine objects that are simply "discovered." Rather, these meanings are interpretive constructions assembled and conveyed by the ethnographer. This process certainly begins with asking questions and paying attention to what is relevant to people in some indigenous group. But the key to the process lies in sensitively representing in written texts what local people consider meaningful and then in making their concerns accessible to readers who are unfamiliar with their social world. (P. 108)

Regarding the writing of field notes in particular, the authors caution:

While fieldnotes are about others, their concerns and doings gleaned through empathetic immersion, they necessarily reflect and convey the ethnographer's understanding of those concerns and doings. Thus, fieldnotes are written accounts that filter members' experiences and concerns through the person and perspective of the ethnographer. (Pp. 12–13)

Being with the People

Guidelines about actually becoming a participant in "their world" are also prominent in naturalistic methods books. For example, the lead heading of Robert Bogdan and Steven Taylor's *Introduction to Qualitative Research Methods* (1975) announces the central directive of the naturalistic stance: "Go to the people." Calling their approach "phenomenological," but using the term in the same way we have used "naturalistic," Bogdan and Taylor explain what it means to deal "with how the world is experienced."

The phenomenologist . . . seeks understanding through such qualitative methods as participant observation, open-ended interviewing, and personal documents. These methods yield descriptive data which enable the phenomenologist to see the world as subjects see it. This book is first and foremost about qualitative methodologies: how to collect data in the form of people's own words, utterances, gestures, and behavior. (P. 2)

Regarding observation in particular, Bogdan and Taylor add that observers:

immerse themselves in the lives of the people and the situations they wish to understand. They speak with them, joke with them, empathize with them, and share their concerns and experiences. Prolonged contact in the setting allows them to view the dynamics of conflict and change and thus see organizations, relationships, and group and individual definitions in the process. (P. 5)

The chapters immediately following this imperative advise researchers about how to get to "the people." Their prescriptions have the characteristic geographic tone, dominated by the vocabulary of barriers and location. Before the fieldwork proper can begin, there is "pre-fieldwork," which amounts to "choosing a field site," dealing with gatekeepers, and establishing rapport. Geographic and social factors, we are told, pose ongoing challenges to the researcher.

The organization of William Shaffir and Robert Stebbins's (1991) collection of essays on fieldwork experience expands on these geographically oriented lessons. Shaffir and Stebbins not only indicate that "getting in" to a field site poses a distinct procedural barrier, but "learning the ropes" and "maintaining relations" are equally significant hurdles. The various essays show that geography and native meanings not only offer obstacles at the start, but persist even after the researcher has departed the field. Shaffir and Stebbins's message is insistent: from start to finish, and afterward, naturalistic inquiry centers enduringly on the procedural contingencies of "being there," becoming part of "their world," and getting "their stories."

Yet, "being there" as part of "their worlds" poses a distinct problem of its own, putting the naturalist at risk of becoming too much a part of what he or she is ostensibly studying. Method talk here typically warns against "going native," as Shaffir and Stebbins (1991) explain in the following extract. Note, however, that they treat this problem as a matter of sustaining an objective orientation, not as a representational dilemma:

In learning the ropes, a basic problem revolves around the delicate balance required between involvement, or the attempts to acquire an insider's perspective, and the possibility of "going native" (Miller 1952), or the danger that excessive involvement may thwart the ability to conduct dispassionate research. The rather extensive literature concerning this topic indicates that field research is characterized by a combination of engrossment and distance (Gordon 1987, Karp and Kendall 1982, Robbins, Anthony and Curtis 1973, Thorne 1979), both of which are necessary to gain an appreciation of the actor's perspective. The dynamics of this balance, however, are not determined by research alone but are shaped by the demands and expectations of the researched (Pollner and Emerson 1988). (P. 85)

Faithful Representation

Whether the specific research procedure is participant observation, in-depth interviewing, or a combination, the ultimate aim is to represent subjects' worlds in writing as faithfully as possible. Naturalistic guidelines for writing at all stages of research point to the goal of producing a kind of "realist tale" (Van Maanen 1988). Emerson, Fretz, and Shaw (1995), for example, present writing field notes as an activity to be done immediately. Stressing the danger of losing the immediate reality and native details of the social world, they caution the reader to write field notes soon after one has left the research site:

Over time, people forget and simplify experience; notes composed several days after observation tend to be summarized and stripped of rich, nuanced detail. Hence we strongly encourage researchers to sit down and write full fieldnotes as soon as possible after the day's (or night's) research is done.

Writing fieldnotes *immediately* after leaving the setting produces fresher, more detailed recollections that harness the ethnographer's involvement with and excitement about the day's events. Indeed, writing notes immediately on leaving the field offers a way of releasing the weight of what the researcher has just experienced. . . . In contrast, those who put off writing fieldnotes report that with the passage of time the immediacy of lived experience fades and writing fieldnotes becomes a burdensome, even dreaded experience. (Pp. 40–41, emphasis in the original)

The Loflands and others also recommend writing up field notes as soon as possible, lest the researcher lose the details of "small gestures, facial expressions, bodily movements—those important ephemera that we so easily forget" (Lofland and Lofland 1995, p. 92). Given the vicissitudes of memory and the demands on the researcher's time, the promptness guideline is good advice, of course. But there also is something analytically significant about this, underscoring our theme concerning the relationship between method talk and social reality. The authors express the goal of minimizing the time between observation and writing because they desire to capture lived experience "there" in living color, as they aim to be true to "their worlds." It is not just validity that is at stake here. It is also a matter of living up to the naturalist creed of "being there," in "their worlds," and accurately telling "their stories." Because it is assumed that "there" is a richly textured, yet separate and distinct, social location, the reasonable thing to do is to promptly, completely, and carefully record it, lest the details be forgotten or confused. This position and the resulting procedural guideline are precisely what more analytically self-conscious naturalists, such as ethnomethodologists, and more radically skeptical critics of the natural, such as emotionalists and postmodernists, increasingly question, and to which we turn in the following chapters.

CHAPTER 3

Ethnomethodology

If traditional naturalists believe that meaningful social worlds can be discovered by "being there," some qualitative researchers argue that there is no "there" until it has been constructed. For them, method talk and social reality come by way of a different idiom. Since the 1960s, a family of qualitative approaches has been arguing that what passes for everyday reality is in one way or another produced by those engaging it. This family is not close-knit, however, and some have chosen to dispute kinship claims (see, for example, Lynch 1993, Lynch and Bogen 1994; Zimmerman and Wieder 1970). Still, at some level, the premise that reality is accomplished rather than merely experienced unites social phenomenology (Schutz 1967, 1970), ethnomethodology (Garfinkel 1967), social constructionism (Berger and Luckmann 1966; Spector and Kitsuse 1987; Holstein and Miller 1993; Miller and Holstein 1993), and some versions of symbolic interactionism (Blumer 1969) and labeling theory (Kitsuse 1962; Pollner 1974; Holstein 1993), providing sufficient justification for considering them together. This chapter will concentrate on ethnomethodology because it has been the most systematically self-conscious and explicit about its sense of the empirical status of the social world and how it might be studied.

As we stated earlier, naturalism strives to report the rich and variegated texture of everyday social worlds. Ethnomethodology and its constructionist kin also hold the "natural" in high regard, but their appreciation is of a different order. Whereas naturalists want to be there, inside the worlds of their subjects, ethnomethodologists aim to describe the natural as a matter *in the making*. Like the naturalists, they want to get close to the action, but they don't want to overdo it. Borrowing from Wittgenstein, ethnomethodologist Melvin Pollner (1987) goes so far as to suggest that getting too close to the natural is apt to blind us to some of its most interesting and intriguing qualities:

The aspects of things that are most important for us are hidden because of their simplicity and familiarity. (One is unable to notice something—because it is always before one's eyes.) The real foundations of his inquiry do not strike a man at all. Unless *that* fact has at some time struck him. And this means: we fail to be struck by what, once seen, is most striking and most powerful. (Wittgenstein 1958, p. 50; cited in Pollner 1987, p. ix, emphasis in the original)

While this sort of method talk conflicts with naturalistic guidelines, there is still a strong commitment to close scrutiny, but, this time, of the *production* of social reality.

Ethnomethodology, according to Pollner (1987), holds the natural in particular awe, not so much for its richness or authenticity, but for the masterful handicraft that goes into its construction:

One of ethnomethodology's contributions to the understanding of social life is its capacity to produce a deep wonder about what is often regarded as obvious, given or natural. Whether it be the interpretation of documents, the utterance of "uh-huh" or the flow of everyday interaction, ethnomethodology has provided a way of questioning which begins to reveal the richly layered skills, assumptions and practices through which the most commonplace (and not so commonplace) activities and experiences are constructed. (P. ix)

This "attitude of wonder"—ethnomethodology's working skepticism—encourages a heightened self-consciousness about the conduct of social research as well as a set of revealing questions about just what the product of social scientific inquiry turns out to be. Where naturalistic inquiry tries to capture experience "up close," ethnomethodology "steps back" in order to gain purchase on just how everyday realities are experienced and conveyed as such. Where naturalism looks upon the social world as an experiential object, ethnomethodology encourages a more radical stance vis-à-vis that world. As Pollner (1987, p. 7) puts it:

The phenomenon *par excellence* is not the world *per se* but worlding, the work whereby a world *per se* and the attendant concerns which derive from a world *per se*—truth and error, to mention two—are constructed and sustained.

"Worlding," not the world, is the object of ethnomethodological inquiry, shifting the focus from the substance of reality to reality construction *practices*.

THE ROOTS OF ETHNOMETHODOLOGY

Alfred Schutz is often singled out as the precursor to ethnomethodology and sociological constructionism, but ethnomethodology, in particular, is more than an elaboration of Schutz's work. Still, there are clear theoretical and methodological connections. Most importantly, Schutz (1967, 1970) introduced phenomenology to sociology, pointing out the constitutive nature of consciousness and interaction. He argued that the social sciences should focus on the ways that the life world—the experiential world every person takes for granted—is produced and experienced by members.

While most naturalistic approaches are interested in members' subjective experiences, it is the emphasis on *production* that distinguishes ethnomethodology and its kin. These approaches depart radically from the naturalistic view that the social world is "out there," separate and distinct from acts of perception or interpretation, available to be observed and described if the researcher has adequate access, proximity, and technology. As we shall see, ethnomethodology confers much greater agency and responsibility upon society's members by attributing the very existence of an apparently real world to their interactional and interpretive skills.[1] People are seen as possessing the practical linguistic and interactional competencies through which the observable, accountable, orderly features of everyday life are produced. Accordingly, ethnomethodology's topic becomes members' practical procedures for creating, sustaining, and managing a sense of objective reality.

This gives a radically empirical turn to Schutz's program, uniting a "phenomenological sensibility" (Maynard and Clayman 1991) with an abiding concern for interactional process. While some versions of constructionism are more cognitively oriented (see Berger and Luckmann 1966; Cicourel 1974), ethnomethodology's emphasis is decidedly social, holding that members accomplish the world of "social facts" through visibly public, interactional, interpretive work. Its empirical initiatives pointedly accentuate talk-in-interaction.

In part, Garfinkel's program was a response to the dominant sociological paradigm of the day, most elaborately articulated by Garfinkel's mentor Talcott Parsons (Heritage 1984b). In Parsons's theory of action (1937), institutionalized systems of norms, rules, and values were internalized by individuals, making social order possible. Garfinkel (1967) rejected this approach, which portrayed social actors as "judgmental dopes" responding to external social forces and motivated by inner moral directives and imperatives. As an alternative, he offered a model of social order grounded in contingent, embodied, ongoing interpretive work. To use a telling term of method talk, Garfinkel was more interested in how members *do* social order, than in how they are animated by it.

BRACKETING SOCIAL REALITIES

To make visible the practices through which taken-for-granted realities are accomplished, ethnomethodologists temporarily suspend all commonsense assumptions about those realities, employing a procedure resembling phenomenological "bracketing" (Schutz 1970). One's everyday orientation to the real is set aside in order to focus on the ways in which members themselves interpretively produce the recognizable, intelligible forms they treat as real. Schutz (1970) provides a compelling rationale:

> In our everyday life . . . we accept as unquestionable the world of facts which surrounds us as existent out there. To be sure, we might throw doubt upon any *datum* of that world out there, we might even distrust as many of our experiences of this world as we wish; the naive belief in the existence of *some* outer world, this "general thesis of the natural standpoint," will imperturbably subsist. But by a radical effort of our mind we can alter this attitude, not by transforming our naive belief in the outer world into a disbelief, not by replacing our conviction in its existence by the contrary, but by suspending belief. We just make up our minds to refrain from any judgment concerning spatiotemporal existence, or in technical language, we set the existence of the world "out of action," we "bracket" our belief in it. (P. 58, emphasis in the original)

Contrary to a common misconception, bracketing the life world does not mean that the analyst challenges the existence of reality. Schutz is explicit about this. Bracketing is not an ontologically radical attack on the substantiality of experience.

Rather, it is a strategic move to suspend everyday assumptions in order to view the processes by which the apparent concreteness of lived experience is assembled. As John Heritage (1984b) explains, "The investigator *suspends* his or her belief in . . . the objective existence of the objects of perception in order to examine *how* they are experienced as objectively existent" (P. 41, emphasis in the original). Bracketing thus allows the researcher to "objectify" social practices, making them into research objects, which go unnoticed when one assumes the attitude of everyday life.

Don Zimmerman and Melvin Pollner (1970, p. 98) point out that this "reduces the features of everyday social settings to a family of practices and their properties." Where naturalistic inquiry describes the "normal, natural facts of life" that are taken to be essentially independent of the subject's perceptual or descriptive acts, a bracketed scene can be examined ethnomethodologically for the "particular, contingent accomplishments of the production and recognition work" conducted by participants (p. 94). Bracketing allows the researcher to ask different kinds of questions about social reality, questions oriented to "*how* the structures of everyday activities are ordinarily and routinely produced and maintained" (Garfinkel 1967, p. 38, our emphasis).

This reorientation from *what* to *how* questions points ethnomethodology down an empirical path quite distinct from that traveled by more naturalistic investigators. According to Zimmerman and Pollner (1970), it is a major methodological and conceptual departure:

> Instead of an ethnography that inventories a setting's distinctive, substantive features, the research vehicle envisioned [in ethnomethodology] is a *methodography* . . . that searches for the practices through which those substantive features are made observable. (P. 95, emphasis in the original)

The focus shifts from the scenic features of everyday life onto the ways through which the world comes to be experienced as real, concrete, factual, and "out there." An interest in members' *methods* of constituting their worlds supersedes the naturalistic project of describing members' worlds as they know them.

Heuristic Distance

A distinctive analytic vocabulary, including terms like "bracketing," "suspending," and "setting aside," underscores ethnomethodology's need to distance itself from its subjects' life world. But this is a *heuristic* distancing since close scrutiny is still required to bring practice into focus. Proximity to the action is still essential, but one mustn't be engrossed by the natural standpoint. As the goal shifts from describing reality to describing reality-constituting procedures, the researcher separates himself or herself from the commonsense assumptions that underpin everyday beliefs about the factual character of the life world. This spawns interest in what Pollner (1987) calls "mundane reason," and that becomes the focus of ethnomethodological inquiry.

Pollner warns of the problems the researcher encounters when attempting to describe the reality-creating practices that produce the same world in which the researcher experiences his or her own everyday life. Writing metaphorically, he likens this to the problem confronted by the tribal anthropologist who tries to study his or her own tribe. Rhetorically, Pollner asks:

Insofar as mundane reason comprises an activity of the "tribe," to what extent does mundane reason infiltrate the discourse of those who would be students of tribal life? What consequences for sociology flow from naive participation in the mundane idiom? To what extent, if any, can sociology transcend mundaneity? (P. xi)

Answering, Pollner offers ethnomethodology's classic methodological admonition:

Beware of confounding the *topic* of one's studies with the *resources* for studying them (Cicourel 1964; Garfinkel 1967). In subtle ways, the warning goes, sociologists have naively taken for granted the self-same skills, practices and suppositions as members of the society. The confounding has the consequence . . . of rendering sociology a folk discipline: sociology becomes naively ensnared in the very practices it ought to be describing. The methodological warning turns into a substantive recommendation: the ethnomethodologist is to search out these hidden resources and describe the ways in which they are used by members in the construction of "rational," intelligible or "accountable" action and discourse. (Pp. xi–xii, our emphasis)

This distinction between topic and resource is fundamental to ethnomethodological inquiry. It is achieved only by setting the researcher apart from the life world so that the ongoing achievement of the phenomena of that world can be treated as topics (Zimmerman and Pollner 1970). For example, Whyte (1943) found it interesting that, when members of the Norton gang went bowling, Doc won more than his share of the games, even though it was apparent to Whyte that Doc was not the best bowler. Whyte's naturalistic analysis uses the pattern of Cornerville roles and statuses to explain differences in gang members' bowling scores, suggesting that lower status members allowed Doc to win out of deference to his position in the group. In this explanation, Whyte employs "status" and "role" as analytic *resources*. In contrast, ethnomethodologists would turn these resources into topics in their own right. They would formulate a different sort of research question: *How* do members of Cornerville society construct a sense of their relationships as organized in terms of roles and statuses? *How* is that sense of social order used by members to explain bowling performances that follow status lines? Ethnomethodologists do not draw upon commonsense accounts from everyday life to explicate what is going on. Members' explanations are not imported, elaborated on, or systematized in order to employ them as explanatory devices. Instead, they are treated as *indigenous* understandings to be studied as topics, not used as resources.

Where naturalistic inquiry attempts to get close to its subjects in order to capitalize upon their familiarity with the topic of study, ethnomethodology strives for a kind of closeness that both appreciates the fine-grained details of social life and promotes the "strangeness of the familiar world" (Zimmerman and Pollner 1970, p. 98). This strangeness is made possible, in part, by problematizing the myriad taken-for-granted activities through which social order is constituted. The naturalist tends to overlook these activities, considering them uninteresting compared to the accounts and descriptions that comprise these practices. From an ethnomethodological viewpoint, however, it is only when the familiar becomes "strange" that it is available for description.

Adopting the member's perspective can be naturalistically valuable, but ethnomethodologically costly. Borrowing from the familiar—relying upon or co-opting indigenous explanations—places the investigator on the same analytic plane as those being studied, an uncomfortable position for an ethnomethodologist. As Zimmerman and Pollner (1970) suggest, naturalistic ethnographies often incorporate informants' reports

> about otherwise unobservable or difficult to observe aspects of "inside life" of various social settings. When ethnographers assemble *their* descriptions of settings, by reference to informants' formulations, the members' descriptions and the ethnographer's description have identical status in relation to the events reported on. The member's formulation, like that of the ethnographer, is a possible reconstruction of the setting, that is, a version of the setting's reigning norms and resident attitudes, and it is often the case that the ethnographer must rely on the member's formulation as the definitive characterization of the setting. (Pp. 90–91, emphasis in the original)

In doing so, the researcher and the informant form a kind of "reality reporting" team that offers insiders' insights.[2] Informants provide the voices of authority, while researchers facilitate descriptions, mediate between conflicting stories, scrutinize and filter out unreliable statements, and generally work to assure quality control over the insiders' reports (see Becker 1958). And of course the researcher is ultimately responsible for organizing the stories and pointing out the generalizations that they support. Recall how Whyte's analytic collaboration with Doc follows this prescription.

From an ethnomethodological point of view, however, one loses the ability to analyze the commonsense world and its culture if one uses analytic tools and insights that are themselves part of the world or culture being studied. That is the gist of confounding topic with resource. As Zimmerman and Pollner (1970) note, sociology's (especially naturalism's) reliance upon members' formulations prevents it from becoming anything more than an integral component of the very world it seeks to describe, leaving sociology as "an eminently *folk discipline* deprived of any prospect or hope of making fundamental structures of folk activity a phenomenon" (p. 82, emphasis in the original).

Indifference

Separating topic from resource produces a particular kind of detached attitude that Garfinkel and Harvey Sacks (1970) call "ethnomethodological indifference." As Garfinkel and Sacks explain, "Ethnomethodological studies . . . describe members' accounts of formal structures wherever and by whomever they are done, while abstaining from all judgments of their adequacy, value, importance, necessity, practicality, success, or consequentiality" (p. 345).

While the attitude of indifference precludes a priori judgments regarding the correctness or appropriateness of persons' practical reasoning, it does not mean that the researcher loses interest in mundane phenomena, or disregards them because they are insubstantial or inwardly subjective. To the contrary, it means that one adopts a perspective outside of, apart from, the social objects of inquiry, so as to dispassionately examine in detail the practical activities that constitute the objects. Analytic indifference allows the ethnomethodologist to respect and topicalize members' constitutive practices, to discern and describe how they produce and manage the objects of their lives without judging their actions against some transcendent standard of what the life world is "really" like. Focused on practice, it is the study of subjectivity par excellence, notably, how it is that subjects derive a sense of their relation to objects, events, and beliefs taken to be separate and distinct from themselves. In this context, there is no basis for invidiously comparing commonsense practices with idealized standards, no warrant for pointing out errors in members' interpretations. As Garfinkel (1967) clearly indicates:

> Ethnomethodological studies are not directed to formulating or arguing correctives. They are useless when they are done as ironies. . . . They do not formulate a remedy for practical actions, as if it were being found about practical actions that they are better or worse than they are usually cracked up to be. (P. vii)

This precludes all commitments to privileged versions of social structure, focusing instead on how members accomplish, manage, and reproduce a *sense* of social structure, and themselves confer privilege on select versions. Research centers on the properties of practical reasoning and the constitutive work that produce the unchallenged appearance of a stable reality, while resisting judgment of the "correctness" of members' activities. Contrary to conventional sociology's tendency to ironicize or criticize members' commonsense formulations in comparison with sociological findings—a rampant practice in sociology textbooks—ethnomethodologists resist "arguing with the members," as their method talk would have it.

This appreciation of mundane reasoning and indigenous claims places ethnomethodology in a somewhat paradoxical relationship with respect to what members say about their own lives, especially when compared with what naturalism makes of those same reports. For the naturalist, the objective is to obtain the most authentic accounts, from the member's point of view. A mark of success might be found in the member's validation of the researcher's report. In principle, if an informant reads a naturalistic account, and says, "That's what it's really like," the naturalist would be satisfied.[3]

But an ethnomethodologist's report is likely to puzzle its subjects. Viewing the "seen but unnoticed" aspects of everyday life may unsettle members' assumptions about the life world, radically undermining the foundations of mundane reason, to put it in Pollner's terms. As appreciative of members' methods as ethnomethodology might be, reducing the substance and order of members' worlds to a congeries of practices cannot fail but produce an ironic "debunking" of sorts, revealing what is typically thought to exist separately from members to be members' virtual productions.[4]

ETHNOMETHODOLOGICAL DESCRIPTION

Ethnomethodology approaches the production of social order from a distinct theoretical perspective. The topics are virtually unlimited, ranging from the constituting practices of commonplace, informal settings, to science labs, bureaucracies, courts, and schools.[5] The objective is to describe how order—say, the recognizable structures of observable behavior, systems of motivation, or causal ties between motivations and patterns of behavior—is made visible through members' descriptions and accounts (Zimmerman and Wieder 1970). An immense tolerance for complexity is apparent as ethnomethodologists methodically describe members' own descriptive practices.

Whereas conventional sociology, including naturalism, might focus on rules, norms, and statuses as explanations for patterned behavior, ethnomethodology makes them topical, but in a distinctly different way. The notion that behavior is rule-governed or motivated by shared values and expectations is "bracketed" in order to observe how members themselves describe and explain by referring to rules, values, motives, and the like. From this analytic stance, the appearance of behavior as being the consequence of a rule is treated as merely, but importantly, "just that": the appearance of an event as an instance of compliance or noncompliance with a rule. Ethnomethodology focuses on how members, by invoking rules and elaborating their application to specific cases, describe and constitute their activities as rational, coherent, precedented, and orderly (Zimmerman 1970).

D. Lawrence Wieder's *Language and Social Reality* (1988 [1974]) is a study of the informal rules governing conduct in a halfway house for convicted narcotics offenders. It provides a now-classic example of what an ethnomethodologist might study and how analysis proceeds. The book is especially instructive because Wieder intentionally contrasts naturalistic and ethnomethodological approaches. Part One presents a traditional ethnography of the halfway house; Part Two examines how the "social facts" recounted in the ethnography were themselves produced by halfway house members and the ethnographer himself. In the process, Wieder explores several important ethnomethodological topics and themes.

The Convict Code as an Explanation of Behavior

Wieder began his study as Garfinkel's graduate student, seeking a research position on a project dealing with some sort of "deviance." At the time, the State Department of Corrections was running a halfway house designed to help ease inmates' transition from prison to community. Wieder reports that state officials and staff variously conceived of the halfway house as a "decompression chamber" that would gradually prepare the ex-prisoner for the pressures of normal life by providing a "homelike" environment or a "bridge to the community," with staff members running interference, helping residents to find work, keep jobs, solve problems, and generally establish themselves in viable independent living arrangements (pp. 46–52).

The Department of Corrections was concerned that the halfway house was not functioning as planned. Indeed, officials felt that participation at the halfway house did not seem to improve a parolee-addict's chances of abstaining from drug use, and department administrators were anxious to study the structure of the organization and the lives of residents in order to discern why the organization did not have the intended effect (pp. 132–33). Wieder took the job and set out to conduct participant observation at the halfway house as naturalistically as he could. To this end, he avoided the professional corrections literature so that he would not be predisposed to observe patterns of conduct reported in other studies. He arranged for his introductions to the halfway house staff and residents to be as informal as possible, and took an office far from where the staff had their offices and conducted most of their work. Wanting to experience the halfway house as it "really" was, Wieder attempted to

> avoid identification as a staff member, to observe what I could of the organization by being around it in as many places as I could, and to become friends with residents so as to spend time with them in order to see what it was that they were doing and saying. To assist in doing this, I wore casual clothes . . . while the staff wore coat and tie, and intended not to locate myself next to staff while in the presence of the residents. (P. 133)

Wieder's attempt at "being there" led him to seek out the residents on their own "turf," often taking informants out for a beer at bars where they would feel more comfortable away from the surveillance of staff members. The aim was to secure naturally occurring data about life at the halfway house, to get the residents' "own stories."

Part One of the book reports patterns of resident deviance and rule violation that seemingly doom the halfway house to failure in terms of its stated goals. Over the eighteen-month period of his observations, Wieder was able to describe behavior that consistently undermined the efforts and objectives of the halfway house staff. In staff terms, the behaviors were serious departures from the official aims of the program, behaviors that were causing the program to fail.

Wieder identified six main categories of routinized deviance that worked at cross-purposes with program goals (pp. 76–112). Residents were continuously *distancing* themselves from staff members, using particular body movements and positioning and speaking Spanish (many residents were Latino, while most staff were Anglo). The result was an obvious physical and social segregation of residents and staff members. This was compounded by open displays of *disinterest* and *disrespect*. Residents made it obvious that they were not interested in the program, were unconcerned with what staff had to say, "couldn't care less" about rehabilitation, and felt the program was "not for them." The residents refused to enthusiastically participate in house programs, conceding only *passive compliance* to what staff tried to enforce. Residents would, however, make continuous *requests* and *demands* on staff members. Staff generally saw this as evidence of an inappropriate "dependence," and were constantly vigilant about giving in to the requests and being exploited. Residents also were routinely *dishonest* or *unreliable* in their dealings with staff, and constantly *violated* the routines, requirements, and regulations of the halfway house. This included missing meetings, being late for curfew, failing to look for jobs, ignoring house work assignments, stealing equipment and money from the house and its residents, and using and selling illicit drugs on the premises.

Wieder initially explained this "deviance" in terms of residents' adherence to an indigenous normative order—a set of rules, roles, and prescriptions generally known as the "convict code." The code, he suggests, acts like a set of subcultural counter-directives, compelling residents to defy the objectives of the staff and to violate house rules. Wieder's report shows that residents observed and followed the code in a variety of ways that led directly to rule violations, refusal to cooperate, and open defiance of requests to participate in house programs. It would, he writes, "explain the patterns of deviance I observed there. The code provides the motivations to engage in those patterns, to positively sanction those patterns, and to not interfere with those patterns even if a resident were to find it in his own interest to do so" (p. 120). In the words of resident informants, "regular guys" abide by the code; "kiss asses," "snitches," and "snivelers" do not (p. 114).

While residents generally could not recite all of the maxims, or articulate them in precisely the same fashion, the specifics of the code took the following form (paraphrased from pp. 115–20):

1. *Above all else, do not snitch.* Do not inform on other residents. Never suggest that any resident has done something illegal or illegitimate.

2. *Do not cop out.* Do not admit that you have done anything illegal or illegitimate. Never "turn yourself in" for rules violations. Copping out is a form of "defecting" to the other side, agreeing with the standards of the staff.

3. *Do not take advantage of other residents.* This is primarily a directive not to steal from other residents. But if someone has something stolen, it is his responsibility to do something about it himself. Fellow residents cannot intervene and staff should never be involved.

4. *Share what you have.* Residents are expected to be relatively generous towards other residents with regard to money, clothing, and alcohol. Even drugs should be offered to close friends and sold to others if there is a surplus.

5. *Help other residents.* This refers to helping fellow residents avoid detection and punishment for house violations. Helping might involve assisting in deviant activities or refusing to support staff efforts to detect deviance.

6. *Do not mess with other residents' interests.* A resident should not disapprove of others' deviant activities or keep others from enjoying their activities. In no way should a resident endanger others by attracting attention to their activities. This includes "bringing the heat" by attracting unnecessary attention to oneself.

7. *Do not trust staff; staff is heat.* Under no circumstances should a staff member be trusted with any information that might be used against residents.

8. *Show your loyalty to residents.* Staff members are to be treated as "the enemy." Residents are never to side with staff against a fellow resident. Any act of solidarity with staff should be interpreted as a defection. Residents should not "kiss ass," do favors for staff, be friendly toward staff, or accept the legitimacy of any of the staff's rules. Conversely, one must always demonstrate solidarity with residents and support their interests.

Treating the code as rules of conduct that residents follow and enforce upon each other, Wieder provides a traditional sociological explanation for the deviance at the halfway house: actions in accord with the code are positively received by the residents; violations are negatively sanctioned. In general, normative expectations promote allegiance to the code, and the code encourages violations of house rules, undermining all that the official order stands for.

Telling the Code: Instructions for Interpretation

Readers might conclude from this that the code promotes motivations and sanctions that lead to deviance. Indeed, this sort of explanation permeates the criminological and deviance literatures (see Clemmer 1940; Sykes 1958). The studies comprising this literature are typically based on insiders' accounts of "their worlds" told, in part, in their own words. However, as convincing as the explanation sounds, Wieder remains dissatisfied. While acknowledging the importance of classic studies of "the code" (like Clemmer's and Sykes's), he turns an ethnomethodological eye (and ear) in Part Two of his book to their findings and his own halfway house material. Starting with the observation that these studies are all derived from inmate accounts, Wieder attempts a new framing. Whereas, naturalistically, he initially treated the accounts as informed reports from residents about their lives and activities, he now begins to consider what would emerge if the reports themselves were treated as reality-producing activities:

> Inasmuch as these data are inmate-produced accounts, like most of the data of sociology, they are visible phenomena in the way they occur as interactional events between an investigator and his subjects. . . . the convict code could be examined as something like a language event that inmates or residents, staff, and researchers employ to "interpret" conduct. . . . the code, in fact, was encountered by me . . . in the very setting that it was being used to "tell about." That is, the activity of "telling the code" was informing the investigator about actions in the same setting in which the act of "telling the code" was itself a part and was included in the actions being described." . . . the activity of "telling the code" in a behavioral environment accomplished (or created or sustained) a particular kind of social reality for those who witnessed the "scene." (Pp. 130–31)

For Wieder, the fact that researchers regularly incorporated informants' analyses into their own explanations signaled a confusion of topic with resource, a failure to distinguish between members' and researchers' accounts: "this explanatory use of the code parallels its uses by staff members and residents in the very settings in which the code is detected" (p. 126). In other words, telling the code was a way of doing "folk sociology," initially done by residents, then subsequently adopted as "professional sociology" by researchers. The folk and professional sociologies (accounts) were indistinguishable.

The ethnomethodological alternative is to analyze the telling of the code as constitutive activity. This leads Wieder to approach the code as a set of "embedded instructions" for seeing the formal structures of resident conduct. He frames "telling the code" as a set of actions that have immediate consequences within the circumstances of the telling. The code is an indigenous interpretive schema for seeing and describing halfway house events and behavior. It requires constant application and articulation with concrete events and actions in order to make the actions and events meaningful, accountable, and orderly. In effect, the code is *used* to constitute what is deviant and what is not; it does not simply lead members to be deviant. This simultaneously makes the code visible (hearable) as an explanation for what takes place.

Wieder's initial encounters with residents are significant in this regard. Early on, Wieder persuades a resident named Sanchez to talk about things that residents should or should not be doing. During the conversation, Sanchez explicitly cites "the code":

> I [Wieder] asked him . . . were there things that they should and should not do. He [Sanchez] said that "guys" should not snitch (inform on each other) or steal from one another. I asked

him if there were anything else, and he replied that, yes, there was more to *the code* than that. (P. 134, emphasis in the original)

This was Wieder's first encounter with the code, and he began to recognize its importance as a source of indigenous explanation. In other words, members themselves seemed to be accounting for their actions by referring to the code. Struck by the actual articulation of these rules of conduct, Wieder initially wondered if residents were so familiar with social research that they had come to naturally describe their lives in such "theoretical" terms. But encountering the code was usually not so straightforward or formalized. Indeed, as Wieder later remarked, he was often unaware that he was hearing rules of conduct being specified until he recognized that "the very matters being talked about in the conversation . . . made the course of that conversation understandable as rule-governed" (p. 135).

Residents were often "evasive" in conversations with Wieder, so they rarely described the code for him in detail. Instead, he discovered the code being expressed in the very acts of evasiveness that seemingly hindered his research:

In various ways, residents offered me moral characterizations which made reference to the code. Some of these references were included in their complaints about the program. On a number of occasions, residents complained to me about the group therapy they experienced at the narcotics treatment center and under the old halfway house program. They said that such programs were based on "snitching, sniveling, and copping out." They explained that to engage fully in group therapy meant that you had to talk about what other guys were doing and to talk about your own private life, which was certain to include deviant episodes. They told me that trying to get another man to talk about his life was just like snitching, because you were getting him to cop out on himself. They spoke of guys who like to "score points" with staff, and said that was the principal motivation for guys' talking about themselves. In their terms, a "good grouper" was likely to be a "kiss-ass."

Through bits and pieces of moral characterization like those above, the code could be assembled. . . . I began to see that the difficulty I was experiencing [residents' reluctance to talk to Wieder] was produced by the same phenomenon that I was trying to investigate. I came to see that my experience of not being able to join conversations over the dinner table, although conversations were going on all around me, was being produced by the code that I was trying to explicate. (Pp. 137–38)

It became clear to Wieder that residents were doing much more than merely reporting on the features of their lives when they "told the code." They were trying to accomplish things in the telling, "doing things with words" to create the very social structures they were otherwise apparently just describing. They were, in practice, actively marking the border between deviance and nondeviance through talk and interaction. In the process, they let Wieder know where he stood in relation to their activities: "resident recitations of the code . . . were done in such a way that the residents were not simply describing a set of rules to me, but were also simultaneously sanctioning my conduct by such a recitation" (p. 138).

Wieder realized that the code was not a separate and distinct normative structure, available to the researcher for explaining why residents acted as they did. Rather, it was variably conjured up by the residents themselves, who used it to account for matters in need of explanation. Applicable to any form of conduct, the code was a living embodiment of social control, serving as a shared accountability structure for residents' actions. Wieder illustrates this with excerpts from a conversation he had with a resident named Arnaldo. Arnaldo and Wieder had been talking in the resident dormitory and as they carried out some chores at the request of the halfway house manager. They then headed off to a local tavern for a beer:

> We continued our talk about "regulars," "snitching," and "kiss asses," and about getting stopped by the police because one lives at halfway house.... Though our conversation had been long and friendly, when I started to ask about the clientele of the bar and the fact that I had heard that there were lots of guys "holding" (possessing drugs) there, Arnaldo said, "I don't know, but you'd be the last one I'd tell if I did." ... I did not know what to say and did not press the matter ... by asking him why I would be the last one he would tell. "The reason" seemed immediately obvious ... for him to have told me would have bordered on snitching. (P. 139)

Wieder thus takes a new slant on what he was being told, and he begins to analyze talk as consequential activity in its own right, as embodying and enlivening social structure *in use*. In the process, he documents how a normative order is locally constituted and reproduced:

> It was through ordinary interactions in the setting in which the "business" of the setting was being accomplished that the code was empirically manifested as a part or feature of the setting as well as being about it. In their occasioned talk, residents provided descriptions and explanations of their conduct. They identified (largely by naming) their actions as instances of patterned, more or less uniform conduct that would be done by any resident. They pointed to the ways that these patterns of action were produced by the constraint of normative requirement. (P. 145)

It follows that, when the code was not in use, neither were its particular normative order and resulting social categories. In talk and interaction, the everyday reality and social effects of deviance were not constant artifacts of an ever-present set of norms. Rather, the normative order (in this case, the convict code) was an indigenous resource for invoking normative accounts for whatever residents did or did not do in the halfway house. In other words, applicable social categories and their normative order were phenomenally present, in practice, only upon the occasions of their use. Ethnomethodologists argue that this "useable" resource is precisely what traditional sociological accounts depend on to explain deviance and other forms of action. They treat the resource as if it were enduringly applicable—24 hours a day, so to speak—to all conduct in a social setting.

A naturalistic analysis, for example, might be content with the discovery and description of the code, treating it in the same fashion as the residents did—as an explanation for behavior. The ethnomethodological approach, in contrast, resists the wholesale adoption of indigenous analysis, preferring to make members' descriptions and commonsense reasoning topics in their own right. The objective is to move beyond the resident's own explanation (the telling of the code) in order to analyze what is accomplished by the resident's use of the code as an explanation of behavior. The focus of the analysis thus shifts from *what* is said, to *how* it is said and what is socially realized in the process. This marks a clear difference in emphasis between naturalism and ethnomethodology. Where naturalism capitalizes on, even adopts, members' analytic insights, ethnomethodology brackets members' claims about the causes of behavior, suspending belief in whether or not the claims are true in order to examine what is accomplished by making the claims (see Holstein and Jones 1992).

Wieder goes on to show how an analysis of this sort proceeds, highlighting and detailing the way references to the code can be treated as reality-producing "work," as a consequential move in the field of action, which it also defines. Note how Wieder's analytic focus in the following extract is trained on what speakers are doing with their talk. In the ethnomethodological idiom, research subjects do not merely inform the researcher of their social world (as the naturalist might contend). They also communicatively constitute the gamut of structures of those social worlds. In practice, invoking "you know I won't snitch" at that very moment constructs a whole context of relationships and understandings for what is going on:

> Let us examine the range of "work" that a single utterance can accomplish. When talking with residents, staff and I often had a relatively friendly line of conversation terminated by a resident saying, "You know I won't snitch." Hearing such an utterance functioned to re-crystallize the immediate interaction as the present center of one's experiential world. "You know I won't snitch" multiformulated the immediate environment, its surrounding social structures, and the connections between this interaction and the surrounding social structures. It (a) told what had just happened—e.g., "You just asked me to snitch." It (b) formulated what the resident was doing in saying that phrase—e.g., "I am not saying that this is my answer to your question. My answer is not to answer." It (c) formulated the resident's motives for saying what he was saying and doing what he was doing—e.g., "I'm not answering in order to avoid snitching." Since snitching was morally inappropriate for residents, the utterance, therefore, formulated the sensible and proper ground of the refusal to answer the question. It (d) formulated (in the fashion of pointing to) the immediate relationship between listener (staff or myself) and teller (resident) by re-locating the conversation in the context of the persisting role relationships between the parties—e.g., "For *you* to ask *me* that, would be asking me to snitch." This, saying "You know I won't snitch," operated as a renunciation or a reminder of the relationships involved and the appropriate relations between members of those categories. . . . It (e) was *one more* formulation of the features of the persisting relationship between hearer and teller—e.g., "You are an agent [or state researcher] and I am a resident-parolee. Some things you might ask me involve informing on my fellow residents. Residents do not inform on their fellows. We call that snitching." . . . the features of that trans-situational role relationship were originally and continuously formulated through such utterances as, "You know I won't snitch." (Pp. 168–69, emphasis in the original)

Wieder's conclusions in Part Two of his book are quite different from those in Part One. Naturalistically, the code initially was portrayed as a moral structure that shapes and constrains behavior. Ethnomethodologically, it is something else, as Wieder explains:

> [The code] did not simply describe, analyze and explain the environment, but was as well a way in which residents (and staff, when they "told the code") guided conduct through effective persuasion. The code operated as a device for stopping or changing the topic of conversation. It was a device for legitimately declining a suggestion or order [whatever that suggestion or order might be, whether apparently deviant or not]. It was a device for urging or

defeating a proposed course of action. It was a device for accounting for why one should feel or act in the way that one did as an expectable, understandable, reasonable, and above all else acceptable way of acting or feeling. It was, therefore, a way of managing a course of conversation in such a way as to present the teller (or his colleague) as a reasonable, moral, and competent fellow. The code, then, is much more a *method* of moral persuasion and justification than it is a substantive account of an organized way of life. It is a way, or set of ways, of causing activities to be seen as morally, repetitively, and constrainedly organized. (P. 175, emphasis in the original)

THE TALK OF *HOW*

The key to ethnomethodological analysis is obvious in its method talk. In contrast to naturalism, the ethnomethodological field is not bound to specific geographic locations. Nor does it require "getting inside" social worlds in order to describe them. Instead, the field can be found wherever reality-constituting interaction takes place (see Gubrium and Holstein 1987, 1990; Turner 1989). As we will discuss in greater detail later, talk about the reality of, say, a household's domestic life, conducted in a family counseling agency, is as much an empirically constituting field as talk and interaction in the household itself. The language of ethnomethodology is designed to describe members' methods of reality construction, not to discern what is subjectively meaningful within that reality.

The differences between ethnomethodology and naturalism become more apparent as we compare key terms of their respective idioms. Naturalistic inquiry typically raises questions about what is going on from the members' perspective, where it takes place, and, perhaps, why it is happening. Put most simply, the vocabulary highlights *what* and, to some extent, *why* questions. Ethnomethodological method talk, on the other hand, is dominated by a vocabulary focused on *how* realities are constituted. It is method talk about members' talk. Note how obvious this becomes as Wieder explains his ethnomethodological approach to analyzing life in the halfway house:

How the resultant experiential environment was thereby constituted through the concerted efforts of those who "told the code" and those who heard it will be a principal topic of the ethnomethodological analysis. In that analysis, we will also see *how* the behavior of parolee residents is recognizable and reportable by lay and professional sociologists (myself and the staff) as deviant behavior that is produced by rule, *how* that deviant behavior has the observable, reportable properties of formal structures and social facts . . . , and *how* the residents' deviant rules have the observable, reportable properties of formal structures and social facts. The "how" of these questions pertains to how the residents, in their interactions with staff and researcher, made it happen that their behavior was observable and reportable as deviantly rule-governed conduct having the status of formal structure and social fact, i.e., what Garfinkel and Sacks (1970) formulate as "accountable phenomena as practical accomplishments." (Pp. 44–45, emphasis in the original)

The focus on the *hows* of social life reflects the fundamental ethnomethodological tenet that one cannot distinguish what is going on in social interaction from how it is accomplished:

What the parties talked about could not be distinguished from *how* the parties were speaking. An explanation of what the parties were talking about would then consist entirely of describing how the parties had been speaking . . . the recognized sense of what a person said consists only and entirely in recognizing the method of his speaking, of *seeking how he spoke.* (Garfinkel 1967, pp. 28–29, emphasis in the original)

Garfinkel (1967) makes the literal meaning of ethnomethodology clear: "the activities whereby members produce and manage settings of organized everyday affairs are identical with members' procedures for making those settings 'accountable' " (p. 1). *Ethno-method-ology* refers to the logic of people's everyday methods for rendering the circumstances of everyday life recognizable. The focus is on

the objective reality of social facts *as* an ongoing accomplishment of the concerted activities of daily life, with the ordinary, artful ways of that accomplishment being by members known, used, and taken for granted. . . . Ethnomethodological studies analyze everyday activities as members' methods for making those same activities visibly-rational-and-reportable-for-all-practical-purposes. (P. vii, emphasis in the original)

The ethnomethodological mandate is to study the "ethno-methods" of reality construction rather than "reality" per se.

The Importance of Talk

With *how* questions at the forefront, Wieder emphasizes that ethnomethodology requires its own brand of close scrutiny:

To show *how* "telling the code" was productive of a social world of real events and to show *how* talk could be heard as "telling the code," however, requires a closer look at experience than ethnographic reportage as ordinarily practiced can provide." (P. 183, emphasis in the original)

This "closer look" amounts to an analytic focus on talk and interaction that contrasts with the earnest attention that naturalism also grants them. Traditionally (and naturalistically), qualitative researchers have treated members' talk as expressing an underlying, shared, cognitive order, but have not explicated the ways in which talk itself is an essential feature of the settings that it describes. Talk is typically seen as descriptive, not constitutive. Members are treated as reporters on experience, not the authors of that experience.

Ethnomethodology treats talk as social action. Wieder, for example, viewed residents' tellings of the code as "mini-ethnographies" that members themselves used to explain their circumstances and experiences. He analyzed these stories as "language events" that reflexively constituted the very circumstances in which the events took place. For Wieder, the code constructed the very situations where he encountered it as a description: "(T)he activity of telling the code . . . accomplished (or created and sustained) a particular kind of social reality for those who witnessed the scene" (p. 131).

In conventional social science analysis, as in everyday life, the meaning of a word is taken to be what it references, relates to, or stands for in the real world, following a correspondence theory of meaning (Heritage 1984b). In this framework, the essential task of language is to convey information, to describe reality. But when viewed as components of a system of linguistic construction, words become the constitutive building blocks of reality. The analytic schemes of conventional sociology and ethnomethodology assign quite different roles to talk, according to Wieder:

> Traditionally sociology has been concerned with talk only as a source of data for analysis. What is said as such, how it is said, and the interactional and other contexts for what is said is [sic] generally disregarded in favor of exclusively examining *what was meant* by some utterance or collection of utterances as that meaning is relevant to some sociological theory or frame of reference. . . . the remarks that an ethnographer receives to his questions (or simply overhears) are of interest in the ways that they can be understood as substantive reports *about* such matters as norms, values, customs, and the like. The meanings of a societal member's talk, as understood in terms of the social scientist's theory or frame of reference, is [sic] often analytically related by him to the meaning of some other remark. In this way talk is both of overwhelming interest to social science and of little concern. (P. 129, emphasis in the original)

Rather than analyzing members' descriptions as more or less accurate reports, the ethnomethodologist treats them as events within, and constitutive of, the setting. Talk in interaction becomes the object of inquiry, the very field itself, with the ethnomethodologist viewing members' descriptions as both "done from within the world" and as "part and parcel of that world" (Zimmerman 1988, p. 23). This implicates two essential properties of social interaction that are revealed by ethnomethodological analysis. First, the meanings of words and objects are *indexical,* that is, they depend on context. It is only through their situated use in talk and interaction that words become concretely meaningful. Second, the circumstances that provide context for meaning are themselves *reflexively* generated through talk and interaction, from within the circumstances themselves. Recall, for example, how invoking "I won't snitch" immediately created a context of roles and relationships pertinent to what was said. This is the sense in which talk is both *in* and *about* the settings to which it orients. Words give shape and meaning to settings, while simultaneously deriving their meaning from these very same settings. Wieder distinguishes the indexicality and reflexivity of talk and circumstance by contrasting the telling of the code with a travelogue narrative:

> While one *could* propose an analysis of the code as. . . . something like a narrative which is offered by the tour guide of a museum or the narration for a travelogue film, to do so would be misleading. . . . In the travelogue story of a voyage, one encounters the story shown on the screen and the identifications, explanations, and descriptions of the narrative heard over a loud speaker as discrete occurrences—narrative and picture. One hears the narrative as an outside commentary on the events depicted visually. . . . The narrative begins with the beginning of the film and "completes itself" by the end. Whoever speaks on the sound track is doing narration. Typically, explanations are juxtaposed to the scenic occurrences they explain. Finally, one listens to the narration and sees the film passively as a depicted scene for one's enjoyment or edification, not as an object that one must necessarily actively encounter and immediately deal with. (P. 165, emphasis in the original)

Telling the code is different because the code is not encountered "outside" the scene it purports to describe. Instead, it is told within that very scene as a continuous, connected part of the scene, constructing the scene as both talk and scene unfold. In this way, it is reflexively constitutive of the scene. Opposite sides of the same coin, indexicality and reflexivity are integral features of the halfway house's social reality.

Conversation Analysis

Given ethnomethodologists' penchant for differentiating topic and resource, the recognition that talk is both in and about the situations it describes provides a puzzle and a challenge. How can the researcher conduct his or her studies of linguistic phenomena without relying upon aspects of those very phenomena? For Sacks (1963), the solution is straightforward. Language ought not be part of an analytic apparatus until it has been thoroughly described. This provides the impetus for topicalizing the conversational machinery of interaction.

In collaboration with Emanuel Schegloff and Gail Jefferson, Sacks offered the fundamentals for an ethnomethodologically inspired program of conversation analysis (CA) (see Sacks 1992; Sacks, Schegloff, and Jefferson 1974). According to Douglas Maynard and Steven Clayman (1991, p. 396), CA has emerged as "perhaps the most visible and influential form of ethnomethodological research."[6] Committed to viewing talk as constitutive activity, Sacks and his colleagues began to develop an elaborate and detailed system for transcribing audiotaped conversations. The general strategy was to take note of how speakers achieved some recognizable interactional effect. The studies were motivated by questions such as: Was this outcome accomplished methodically? Can we describe it as the product of a method of conduct such that we can find other instances of that method? Do other enactments of the method yield the same outcome or the same recognizable effect? (Whalen 1992).

The initial ties between CA and ethnomethodology were close. Taking up themes found in Wieder's ethnographic study, conversation analysts sought to carefully and systematically examine the machinery of conversation in order to recover the structures that undergirded interaction, yet which were seldom noticed or acknowledged. Sacks points out that it was critical to frame talk as an object for analysis and to attend to previously unsuspected details as critical resources for understanding what was getting done in and by the talk (Schegloff 1992). Jack Whalen (1992) underscores the importance of attending to these microstructures when he writes, "It was in the details of the talk that we could discover just *how* what was getting done in the activity was accomplished, systematically and procedurally, then and there, by the co-participants themselves" (p. 304).

To accomplish detailed descriptions of talk-in-interaction, Sacks developed an "apparatus" that would provide a way of analyzing how conversational participants orient and respond to one another in an orderly, recognizable fashion. Following Sacks, conversation analysts have been assembling a large corpus of observed patterned regularities, describing what speakers are doing in their talk. The aim is to document the systematic practices used to achieve social order.

Observing ethnomethodological principles, both the production of conduct and its interpretation are seen as the accountable products of a common set of methods or procedures (Heritage 1984b). It is through these procedures that the intelligibility of the social world is made evident. As Schegloff and Sacks (1973) argue regarding the patterned conversations they inspected:

Insofar as the [conversational] materials we worked with exhibited orderliness, they did so not only to us . . . but for the co-participants who produced them. If the materials were . . . orderly, they were so because they had been methodically produced by the members of society for one another. (P. 290)

Heritage (1984b) summarizes the fundamentals of conversation analysis in three premises. First, interaction is structurally organized, and this may be observed in the regularities of ordinary conversation. All aspects of interaction can be found to exhibit organized patterns of stable, identifiable structural features. They stand independent of the psychological or other characteristics of particular speakers, representing ubiquitous features of talk-in-interaction itself to which participants orient. Second, all interaction is contextually oriented, in that talk is both productive of, and reflects, the circumstances of its production. Third, these two properties characterize all interaction, so that no order of detail can be dismissed as disorderly, accidental, or irrelevant to the ongoing interaction.

Strategically, CA seeks to exploit these premises, asking how particular conversational outcomes happen (or do not happen). The goal is to document indigenous methods of conversational conduct that will yield outcomes in other situations that will be recognized as similar by both participants and analysts. The approach eschews a priori dismissal of any feature of conversation as trivial, as "merely" a way of talking (Schegloff 1992, p. xxx).

This appreciation of complex detail and commitment to close scrutiny reminds us that CA is not entirely different from other qualitative approaches. Indeed, Schegloff (1992) argues that CA has

mixed a kind of naturalism (in its insistence on noticing and crediting the potential seriousness of particulars of the natural occurrences of conduct) with the ethnomethodological concern for the Member's methods for the production of the mundane world and commonsense understandings of it. [It asks] how the recognizably detailed ordinary world of activities gets produced, and produced recognizably. (P. xxx)

Of course this brand of naturalism is more self-conscious than the traditional version, reflecting a trend that we shall re-encounter as we discuss other idioms of qualitative inquiry.

CHAPTER 4

Emotionalism

The depths of experience pose a major challenge to qualitative method. For decades, many qualitative researchers have been pointedly concerned about the neglect of "inner" realms, arguing that theory and methodology do not adequately take account of deep emotions or what some call "brute being." Traditional naturalism, they contend, is too superficial; it simply falls short of reaching important dimensions of what is actually experienced. Ethnomethodology, on the other hand, seriously shortchanges the heart and soul of everyday life by conceptualizing the social world in terms of constitutive processes, neglecting interaction's affective dimensions (Johnson 1977). Excessive attention to constitutive *hows* virtually obliterates the panoply of lived experience. Critics note that ethnomethodologists, who assiduously claim that nature is as much socially produced as it is "just there," have led sociology further and further away from the animatedness of life and the sheer scenic presence of being, in particular the feelings that enduringly suffuse action (Douglas 1977, pp. 62–63).[1] In general, those concerned with emotions suggest that a "cognitive bias" in sociology has led researchers to neglect the affective, visceral, and subjective dimensions of experience (see Ellis and Flaherty 1992).

The challenge to seriously engage emotionality has gone by various names. In the 1970s, Douglas and his associates called it "existential sociology" (Douglas and Johnson 1977). While the terminology is admittedly rooted in philosophical existentialism, its practitioners claim that the approach is also directly informed by their own experience and their disenchantment with both classical and phenomenological (that is, what we are calling ethnomethodological) sociology. Douglas (1977) explains:

All of us who have contributed . . . to existential sociology began our sociological work within the confines of classical sociology. We early found that tradition inadequate to deal with the problems and truths we encountered in our everyday lives and in our research into a broad spectrum of American society. . . . [After turning to phenomenology], we came increasingly to see the limitations of [phenomenological ideas] and then discovered that the existential philosophers had followed a similar line of development in moving beyond Husserl's phenomenology. All our work remains fundamentally grounded in our own experience . . . . (P. 11)

The inward thrust is shared by another group of qualitative researchers who Carolyn Ellis and Michael Flaherty (1992) call "students of emotionality." This group is equally concerned with the passions of inner experience, but its analytic heritage is more an outgrowth of the naturalistically oriented symbolic interactionist tradition (see Denzin 1984, 1985, 1989a; Kleinman and Copp 1993) and less a reaction to ethnomethodology.[2] Other qualitative approaches to the sociology of emotions (see Hochschild 1979, 1983; Scheff 1990; Scheff and Retzinger 1991) relate to different traditions, so that there is no single designation that presently includes all the variants. Consequently, we have advisedly chosen to refer to existential sociology and the entire range of qualitative studies of emotion and emotionality as "emotionalism."

We find this generic designation useful because it provides us with the vocabulary to compare this research idiom with those of naturalism, ethnomethodology, and postmodernism. We chose the term "emotionalism" for theoretical as well as practical reasons; it alludes both to the topic of "studies of emotionality" and to many of its practitioners' commitment to convey, even embody, the very personal depths and passions of lived experience within their texts. Since it is almost axiomatic that studies of emotionality be conveyed *with emotion* (Ellis 1991a, 1991b), we believe that the terms "emotionalism" and "emotionalist" faithfully connote what practitioners are trying to do, and be, in offering their work. That emotionalists might be emotional themselves in their presentations is a theoretically motivated aspect of their program, one that is every bit as thoughtful and methodical as other qualitative approaches. The goal is for researchers and their readers to virtually *feel* experiential truths, "to become more fully immersed—morally, aesthetically, emotionally, and intellectually" (Bochner and Ellis 1996, p. 4).

The emotionalist program emphasizes the depths of experience. While this often implies the need for intimacy with research subjects, it also calls for researchers to reflect upon their own lives. Indeed, as Douglas, Ellis, and others suggest, researchers' own experiences can, and should, serve as rich sources of "data." This admonition reflects the theme that, ultimately, each of us naturally and fundamentally owns the real stuff of experience, the "brute being" of our existence (see Douglas 1977). As far as research is concerned, it directs us to the personally intimate, for both research subjects and those who study them. From the start, emotionalist sociologies have included researchers themselves as subjects. Introspection, in which researchers examine both their own and others' private thoughts and feelings, becomes a method of choice (Ellis 1991b). Variations of the procedure continue to be a hallmark of the approach.

From the mid-1980s into the 1990s, the focus on emotionality and inner experience continued to be a criticism of traditional and constitutive sociologies, but centered more mundanely on the body as the leading site of experience.[3] For example, Norman Denzin (1984, 1985) urges us to focus our attention on the body as known and considered, not just on emotion in the body. According to Denzin, emotion is "self-feeling," which is linked with the passions, related thoughts, and sentiments about these thoughts and feelings. Ellis and Flaherty's collection of essays, *Investigating Subjectivity* (1992), gets directly to the point, offering glimpses, even performances, of how the body mediates experience. This can literally become "emotional sociology" (Ellis and Bochner 1992, p. 80), an attempt on the written page or on the stage to get the reader or the audience to "feel the passion" of the circumstance under consideration.

Whether as existential or emotional sociology, these are the received sensibilities and methods of romanticism. The goal is to get behind the increasingly rationalized analytic languages for investigating everyday life; researchers are counseled to move beyond traditional naturalism and ethnomethodology, to break free of the prison house of language. The aim is to really get "inside," to the hidden "wellsprings" of the natural, a field of experience that ethnomethodologists and others exclusively concerned with the *hows* of social life tend to neglect. Emotionalist method talk virtually takes naturalism to heart.

THE TONE OF EMOTIONALIST METHOD TALK

The working vocabulary of emotionalism establishes its empirical horizons. Just as the naturalistic language of "being there" in "their worlds" constituted a geographic field and related methodology, the emotionalist idiom bespeaks the passions of existence as the field of study.

Passionate Engrossment

Consider the tone of emotionalist method talk in comparison with the naturalists and ethnomethodologists. Of course, Whyte (1943), Liebow (1967), and Anderson (1976) do offer absorbing texts. For example, as Liebow takes us to Tally's corner, we feel the buzz and apparent chaos of the environs. We literally sense the sounds and smells of rooms, streets, and neighborhoods. In striking contrast, the tone of ethnomethodologists' method talk is much more guarded. Their field does not so much display an absorbing panorama of subjective or interpersonal experience as it trains a dispassionate eye and ear on the potentially-absorbing-in-the-making. For ethnomethodologists, the natural is not yet "there," as it were. Perennially bracketed, the objects or events of experience (including, one would think, emotional experience itself) are necessarily coolly scrutinized for the details of how they are constituted.[4]

As in naturalistic texts, the emotionalists' tone of writing and its substantive concerns resonate with the sights and sounds of its subject matter. The difference, however, is that, while the naturalist accompanies the reader to, say, the charms or dangers of a neighborhood tavern, the emotionalist directs us straightaway to the feelings surrounding the actions, characteristically in florid terms. Of course Whyte, Liebow, Anderson, and other naturalists do describe what participants feel in various circumstances, just as they convey their own trepidation as participant observers, but their writing style is otherwise concertedly neutral. At most, naturalists provide the reader with brief glimpses of what might be called the human side of "their story." The emotionalists, in contrast, plunge directly into the subjective fray, at times becoming passionately engrossed.

Douglas (1977), for example, describes a fellow researcher who inadvertently becomes involved in a life threatening assault, what Douglas calls a "near murder." As Douglas discusses the events that led up to the assault, he turns the reader's attention directly to the emotional contours of the action, including the researcher's feelings. Just before he writes about the scene and events that presumably prompted the assault, Douglas explains:

We [he and his research associates] have also experienced and observed many situations in which built-up hatred and anger became so intense that people went berserk, threatening their own lives and the lives of others. One social researcher inadvertently became involved in a near murder that resulted from a slow buildup of resentments, hatreds, and many other feelings that erupted in an instant, appearing almost totally to flood out conscious thought and were followed by deep feelings of guilt and remorse. (P. 36)

Douglas then presents the interactions and events that climax in an argument between Bob and his wife Chris, next-door neighbors of the researcher in question. The account is poignantly detailed, as we see in the following excerpt, which is told from the researcher's point of view:

We [the researcher and his wife] settled down to watch some television movie. About midnight we heard screams from next door. At first we thought Bob and Chris were playing around, but as the shouts and screams got louder we realized they were having a serious fight. Though we didn't say anything, we were clearly in agreement that we didn't want to get involved. But it kept up. Finally my wife said, "Fuck it. I'm going over." I didn't like it at all, but I followed her. The screams were terrible. We kept pounding at the door. Suddenly it flew open. Chris ran by us. Bob then picked up my wife and me in turn and threw each of us across the patio against the wall. . . . [After some time], Bob seemed suddenly quiet [and] I went into the house with him to discuss what had happened. (My only serious injury was a badly cut knee.) He told me they had gone to bed and had started making love. Bob then asked Chris if she still cared for [a] boy friend. She said yes. He blew up and, after shouts and screams, tried to strangle her. . . . I stayed close to Bob for the next few weeks because I was afraid he might commit suicide. He decided once again to forgive Chris. He said only, "You've got to sink to the bottom of your soul and existence to understand what is really important to you." She returned. (P. 37)

In this excerpt, and in the fuller account from which it is taken, feelings are communicated, interactions unfold, and a complex series of activities develops in the process—the empirical grist of both naturalism and ethnomethodology. But the tone of the text makes it evident that the field of feelings is the most captivating, as we can see in Douglas's language as he interprets the scenario:

It seemed clear in this case that the slow buildup of resentment and anger was closely related to the deep threat Chris's sexual activities posed for Bob's existential self, his primal feeling of masculinity. His reaction of rage came in precisely the situation where this threat was total. Behind most feelings of deep hatred and rage is a threat to the core of the individual's being, his existential self. If the threat is manageable but persistent, the individual's hatred may be hidden for years, yet smolder behind his fronts of affability, even friendship, and lead him to attack his enemy secretly. If the threat is great, but manageable, he may be thrown into furious attack, a towering rage. If he cannot win in such a total war, he may sink into deep anxiety and lasting depression. . . . If an individual is carried to the ultimate extreme of deep, primal emotion, all symbolic thought may be swept away. (Pp. 37–38)

Feelings about Feelings

The emotionalists' working vocabulary characteristically refers to the feelings of both subjects and researchers. This further contrasts emotionalism with other idioms. Naturalists commonly relegate detailed accounts of the researcher's feelings to appendices. The emotionalists, who figure that researchers' feelings constitute empirical material as much as empirical material naturally speaks for itself, weave their own feelings into their analysis. From the start in the 1970s, through more recent experiments in textual representation, emotionalists' own responses to the people and situations under study have been treated as valid data. As Ellis (1991b, p. 29) states in discussing introspection as a source of interpretive materials, "Sociologists . . . can generate interpretive materials about the lived experience of emotions by studying their own self-dialogue in process. Who knows better the right questions to ask than a social scientist who has lived through the experience?" Ellis (1991a) also advises that emotionalists should try to convey the experience emotionally.

We noted earlier that, for the emotionalists, method talk necessarily bespeaks the "real" passion of existence. It would be a mistake to consider this working vocabulary and its related tone as gratuitous "wallowing" in feelings. Like other researchers, the emotionalists' vocabulary forms a well-defined analytic program whose methodology designates a particular field of inquiry, in their case the field of emotional experience. Given the resulting empirical horizons, the emotionalists necessarily aim to document feelings by way of their own emotionality.

A FIELD OF EMOTION

Method talk both locates and structures the field for research. References to the actual experience "behind" or "underlying" appearances signal the emotionalists' working skepticism. The word "mysterious" especially locates a domain of experience separate and distinct from the discursive processes that in Chapter 3 served to construct the sum and substance of everyday life. Even while the mysterious is admittedly part of the natural, it is a part that no amount of reasoning or talk can fathom. If mere words, explanations, or accounts begin to describe the mysterious, in the final analysis this "rational" veneer only hints at more basic qualities.

Ellis and Flaherty (1992) call upon John Keats, the English romantic poet, to describe the common aim of the idiom. The goal is

> to capture and evoke the complex, paradoxical, and mysterious qualities of subjectivity. Instead of subordinating lived experience to the "tyranny of reason" or the "consolation of order" (Jackson 1989, p. 16), they follow Keats (1958, p. 193) in their attempt to cultivate the apprehension of "being in uncertainties, /Mysteries, doubts, without any irritable reaching after fact and reason." (P. 5)

Douglas (1977, p. 10) contrasts this sense of the field with the overly rationalized view of social life that he sees in other sociologies. He argues that the "unexpressed, even unexpressable" netherworld of experience is consciously ignored by those who focus exclusively on the spoken *hows* of everyday life, especially the "symbol mongers" (p. 28), who limit themselves to the rationally accountable. Specifically targeting ethnomethodology, Douglas writes:

> This is seen in the very definition of ethnomethodology: the study of "accounts" in everyday social life (Garfinkel 1967). More specifically, this study of accounts focused on the ways in which the members of society show their actions to each other to be "rationally accountable." A huge realm of commonsense considerations was immediately shorn away by the definition of the term. . . . At the ultimate extreme, as found in the writings of Harvey Sacks and his co-workers [see Sacks 1992], this form of linguistic ethnomethodology [conversation analysis] imposed the further constraint that only those accounts that could be tape-recorded or videotaped could be studied. . . . As a result, the enterprise became a narrow one, with little or nothing to say, by self-imposed definition, about the experiences that concern human beings the most in their everyday lives. Love, hate, anxiety, agony, order, disorder, deceit, lies, truth—all were supposedly irrelevant to the study of man and should, by definition, be ignored [except] indirectly in terms of what linguistic statements suggested about them. (Pp. 10–11)

Other terms of reference further constitute the emotionalist field. While lived experience admittedly is multi-layered—shared, meaningful, rational, irrational, complex, and mysterious—its depths are occupied by the passions. Reason, as represented, say, by the spoken word, does not necessarily convey "real" reason, the feelings at the root of, "behind," or hidden by what is said about one's actions. Reason is the mere surface of more basic motives, expressed desires, and "darker" intents. In his inimitably passionate style, Douglas (1977) describes the place of feelings in this regard, noting nonetheless that feelings without thought are blind and that thought guides feelings:

> We live for feelings. Feelings lie behind, are the foundation of and the goal of, all thought. Feelings pervade thought, are fused with thought, inspire thought, and at the extreme, destroy thought. But feeling without thought is blind. Thought (reason, rationality) is the guide of feelings. . . . To present the whole picture we must begin with the beginning, the foundation and the end of all else: feeling. We begin with what Merleau-Ponty called "brute being." But we must also see how necessary and valuable reason is to all human life, how reason guides feeling to expression, gratification, fulfillment, and growth. We must then see that reason can do this only by becoming fused with feeling, that it is inevitably pervaded by feeling, and that reason in its most exalted form—Absolute Truth—is commonly a naked and perverted form of man's darkest, most dangerous passions. (Pp. 14–16)

Emotionalists do not ignore reason, but they rail against what they perceive as an exclusivity evident in various domains of sociology. Ethnomethodology's focus on accounts and survey research's analysis of proffered opinions and causal explanations are prominent targets. It is clear in the emotionalist vernacular that they think of feelings as "fused" with, not separate from, reasoning. While feelings constitute the "depths" of lived experience, it is through the various surfaces of experience—talk, conversation, gesture, posture—that the depths are conveyed.[5] The exception, which is evident in the extracts from Douglas's description of the assault, ostensibly shows "blind" feelings without thought.

Several related metaphors are a regular part of emotionalists' method talk, revealing their view of the ultimate core of experience and the field of inquiry. The metaphor of the "pressure cooker," for example, portrays constrained feelings left undisclosed, the idea being that the "wellsprings" of experience need regular release, presumably through some form of communication. Kept in confinement, emotions are virtually under pressure, ready to explode into blind rage, perhaps, or other raw feelings. The "tornado" metaphor is used similarly to describe what uncontrolled feelings can do if they burst forth out of control. Explicitly recognizing this metaphor, Ellis (1991b) describes how the symbol of the tornado conveys the lived experience of managing depression that she and an interview "co-respondent" mutually disclose:

A co-respondent discussing control and depression said: "Sometimes life is overwhelming. I feel like I'm holding on in a tornado. And, the tornado threatens to pull off my arm if I don't let go. I get scared, let go, and go into depression." I replied, "When I'm in danger of losing control, it appears as a tornado to me, too. But, I quickly try to get control of some arena in my life, something to hang on to, so that the tornado won't engulf me." Both strategies, although different, protected us from the tornado, the symbol for being overwhelmed. (P. 41)

Other emotionalist metaphors are not so explosive, yet still convey the deep affect of lived experience. David Karp (1996), for example, provides a rich description of the experience of depression and, in the process, shows how metaphors can serve to convey what simple words cannot. Karp explains that "like literary prose writers whose art depends on translating ineffable emotions into written words" (p. 28), many of the people he interviewed used metaphors equating depression with experiences such as descending into a bottomless pit and being in a dark tunnel. By borrowing from a special language to address what it feels like to live with depression, interviewees provided accounts of what was deeply felt, but otherwise would remain silent.

While seeking to reveal the depths of feelings, emotionalists attempt to avoid the segmentation of experience into distinct domains of thought and feeling. Separating the cognitive from the emotional, they argue, is a pervasive problem in conventional sociological analysis. They contend, to the contrary, that lived experience is a complex, multifaceted whole. To divide it into discrete parts and then reformulate analytic wholes from the segments is to violate the characteristically interwoven quality of experience. Ellis and Flaherty (1992) make the point directly, in relation to sociological treatments of the body and emotions:

Emotional processes are treated [in conventional sociological approaches] as separate from other kinds of subjectivity, such as thinking and somatic experiences. With few exceptions (Glassner 1988; Jacobus, Keller, and Shuttleworth 1990; Kemper 1990; Sanders 1989), sociological writing has ignored the body. Moreover, many who do consider the body tend to sever it from subjective experience (Denzin 1985). Sociologists have paid more attention to cognitive process, but this represents vestiges of the rational-actor model. The cognitive bias in sociology has put those who study emotion in a defensive position, in which many act as if they must choose between emotion and cognition. As a result, emotional and cognitive orientations are viewed as competing perspectives, instead of "blurred together in the person's stream of experience" (Denzin 1989a, p. 121; James 1950[1890], pp. 185–87). (P. 3)

The emotionalists, however, appear to be responsible themselves for some of the segmentation. To presume that a domain of experience, variously termed the emotional depths or "brute being," is foundational to speech and reasoning automatically separates the emotional and the rational. As we will show at the end of the chapter, emotionalists often distinguish mere words from actors' passions. Their dramatic presentational techniques contrast the rational and the emotional, thus highlighting, not eliminating, segmentation.

Denzin (1985) seems to be aware of the segmentation problem when he writes that emotion as a field of experience is located in the *relation* of the subject to the self and the body; emotion is not just in the body or in the self. Denzin structures his field by locating the meaning-making process in close proximity to where the person and others are situated in time and space as embodied beings. Indeed, Denzin is the consummate anti-segmentalist when he emphasizes that "emotion is self-feeling." Because emotionality draws the subject into relations with others, there are also "emotional associates," including those who interpret the individual's emotional experience, which by implication applies to researchers themselves and their informing representational cultures. This provides a highly articulated and unsegmented domain for the study of emotional experience, incorporating both the body and the self, on the one side, and extending into the cultural contexts of emotional experience, on the other. In this field, both words and feelings matter; they are not separated into exclusively cognitive or emotional domains. This field constitutes the subjective whole that is lived experience.

Focusing on a deep field of lived experience has clear procedural implications: if access to the field is by and large public, its public veneers must be peeled off or worked through, in order to render the depths visible. This means that, as much as possible, research procedures must close the gap between subjectivity and its public data. Ellis and Flaherty (1992) state the common aim of the contributors to their book in this way: "While realizing that writing about experience always is removed from actual 'raw' experience, the overriding concern of these writers is shrinking the distance between the experiencing subjects and their accounts of lived experience" (p. 4). Among other things, the effort to shrink distances has led to innovative research techniques, including creative interviewing (Douglas 1985), emotional fieldwork (Johnson 1975), introspection or auto-ethnography (Ellis 1991b), experimentation with dramatic performance (Ellis and Bochner 1992), and the use of narrative forms other than prose as legitimate methods of research.

CREATIVE INTERVIEWING

The word "creative" in the title of Douglas's *Creative Interviewing* (1985) refers as much to the interviewer as to the respondent. According to Douglas, creative interviewing derives from the difficulties he encountered attempting to probe respondents' "deep experience." Douglas reports that in his many empirical studies, he repeatedly discovered how shallow the standard recommendations for conducting research interviews were. Canons of rational neutrality, customary in survey research, for example, failed to capture what Douglas refers to as his respondents' "emotional wellsprings." This view of the subject calls for a methodology of deep disclosure.

The Vessel of Feelings

Douglas's image of the subject is decidedly romanticist. Douglas imagines his subject, like the image implicit in survey research, to be a repository of answers, but in his case, the subject is a well-guarded vessel of feelings, not simply a collection of attitudes and opinions (see Holstein and Gubrium 1995a). Emotionalists like Douglas cannot address heartfelt, cloistered feelings in any simplistic, straightforward way, no matter how sensitive or empathetic they might be. Emotional life, after all, runs deep and with passion, and it is not readily or fully disclosed through superficial interview exchanges. Douglas's respondent authentically communicates from within only in response to an interviewer who knows that mere words cannot convey what experience ultimately is all about.

Tapping into this inner field of feelings, unexpressed or unexpressable, of hidden desires, and submerged or repressed passions, places a considerable methodological burden on the interviewer. Since emotional experience is often buried, mysterious, and inarticulate, questions and answers can miss what the respondent actually feels "deep down." According to Douglas, superficial standardized interviewing can actually do more harm than good in getting the respondent to disclose emotionality. Because emotional experience is often considered to be embarrassing, respondents might actually offer surface opinions in order to throw the interviewer offtrack.

Douglas aims deeper, trying to "get to know" the real subject behind the respondent. Creative interviewing is his procedure for moving past the words and sentences exchanged in the interview process. To achieve this, the interviewer must establish a climate for mutual disclosure, which, of course, implicates the researcher's own emotional experience. According to Douglas, the interview should be an occasion that displays the interviewer's willingness to share his or her feelings and deepest thoughts. This is done to assure respondents that they can, in turn, share their thoughts and feelings. Douglas suggests that this is thoroughly suppressed by the cultivated neutrality of the standardized survey interview. In contrast, Douglas writes that "creative interviewing . . . involves the use of many strategies and tactics of interaction, largely based on an understanding of friendly feelings and intimacy, to optimize *cooperative, mutual disclosure and a creative search for mutual understanding*" (1985, p. 25, emphasis in the original).

Orienting Principles

Douglas offers abundant practical advice for creative interviewing. One rule of thumb is to figure that, as he puts it, "genius in creative interviewing involves 99 percent perspiration" (p. 27); getting the respondent to deeply disclose requires much more work than obtaining mere opinions. Douglas (1985) enthusiastically advises:

If your one overriding motive in life is to be a creative designer of papier-mâché dolls, or an organic gardener, then do so; do not become a creative interviewer. The great creative interviewers, those discoverers of the uncharted truths about human life and the soul, find the exploration of human beings very exciting in itself and a source of joy in accomplishing something very difficult. Excitement and the feeling of accomplishment are some of the most powerful emotions that govern our lives, so it is little wonder that they can drive mere mortals on to become the creative handmaidens of Goddesses. (P. 28)

The creative interviewer must take the time and make the effort to know the subject as more than a respondent, committing himself or herself to being part of the respondent's life and forming relationships with the respondent that move beyond interview roles. According to Douglas, this is necessary because deep disclosure is ostensibly unlikely to occur between strangers or mere acquaintances. While the standard interview might offer glimpses of emotional experience, respondents are not likely to present the passionate and often contradictory elements of their feelings or their typically hidden desires.

There can be no formal procedural guidelines for creative interviewing, only orienting principles. The interviewer must be prepared to creatively surmount the hurdles of mutual disclosure in relation to each respondent. Unfortunately, the respondent's experience is unavailable until trust and openness are established and cultivated. This process requires patience and imagination. The trick is to approach the relationship with the respondent as one might a friend or a neighbor. As the interviewer's interpersonal style and commitment are accepted, the process bears emotional fruit.

Douglas describes the fine creative interviewers he has known, and it is evident that they have become deeply involved in their respondents' lives. In some instances, they have risked harm to themselves in the process. Note how, in the following extract, Douglas (1985) traces interview effectiveness to creative interviewers' own emotional lives:

Each individual's motivation to undertake these voyages of human discovery bubbles up from somewhat different subterranean sources. A great voyager ["into human discovery"] like John Johnson, infamous for being too friendly and caring for his own material good, is driven by those caring and adoring feelings, those yearnings for intimacy and togetherness, to launch grandiose voyages into very troubled waters indeed, such as the boiling turbulence of family violence. Ann Bedard, a neophyte creative interviewer who has done some wondrously revealing life studies with me, is driven by these same friendly caring and adoring feelings, but adds to those an endearing, wide-eyed sense of wonderment at the mysteries unveiled before her. (P. 29)

Douglas goes on to admonish the researcher to "know thyself and play to thy strengths." This calls for continual self-analysis, which is necessary, lest the creative interviewer's own defense mechanisms work against mutual disclosure and understanding. For example, the creative interviewer who unknowingly harbors deep conflicts about his sexuality can hardly provide the openness a respondent needs to disclose his or her own sexual desires. Similarly, the creative interviewer who is unaware of her latent animosities toward her parents, can't readily establish grounds for asking others to disclose their own sentiments about intergenerational responsibility. In other words, the creative interviewer needs to ask whether or not the subject matter of interviews has been addressed in his or her own life:

No one should be an explorer of human beings unless he can face painful self-discoveries, unless he has already undertaken a great deal of self-exploration and exploration by others, especially by probing close friends who have *shared* the joy and anguish of the endless search for mutual understanding. Even more important, an interviewer should not try to discover truths about those areas where he has major emotional problems until these have been thoroughly explored and resolved. (Pp. 39–40, emphasis in the original)

The creative interviewer must be strongly committed to mutual disclosure. This can take considerable ingenuity, as each case is different. But, here again, there are proven rules of thumb. One is to actively listen to the respondent. The creative interviewer needs to convey expressions and exhibit gestures that show he or she is genuinely interested in what the respondent has to say, especially its emotional underpinnings. Another rule of thumb is for the interviewer to forthrightly reveal his or her sentiments in the interview process, not just ask questions and seek responses. A third rule involves the expression of caring. Open displays of personal concern and offers of emotional support are helpful. Douglas states the underlying principle: "In general, the more of a listener the interviewer is, the more sensitive, the more openly intimate, the more sincerely interested in and warmly caring about the other person, the more he can temporarily surrender to the experience and soul of the other person, the more successful he will be as a creative interviewer" (pp. 57–58).

The admonitions to "know thyself" and be willing to disclose one's self place a heavy burden on the creative interviewer's own emotions. Creative interviewing becomes almost a way of life for the researcher, consuming his or her very being, as Douglas might put it. It means virtually dedicating one's emotional self to the feeling respondent. As Douglas (1985) explains: "The creative interviewer is a handmaiden of knowledge and wisdom who must become a supplicant to those who have both" (p. 55). The reward is interpersonal understanding. Aiming for "soul communion," each party to creative interviewing not only discovers, but makes, meaning. The process, then, is always partially productive of new selves for both the interviewer and the respondent. If properly done, it reaps harvests of self-discovery, for the subject and the interviewer.

THE EMOTIONAL FIELDWORKER

While creative interviewing contains elements of participant observation, it is not ethnography. One of Douglas's associates, John Johnson (the "great voyager" to whom Douglas referred earlier) has written an engaging account of ethnography that orients to and reconstructs the emotional experience of the fieldworker. As Johnson poignantly explains, the personal investments and hazards of fieldwork can be as emotionally harrowing as creative interviewing is personally taxing.

Fusions of Thinking and Feeling

Johnson's *Doing Field Research* (1975) is an important contribution to the study of emotionality. Johnson notes that traditional naturalistic methods books frame accounts of fieldwork almost exclusively in terms of the "steps" that make for successful ethnography: gaining entry, establishing rapport, building trust, and managing oneself in the field. Having gained entry, for example, one ostensibly takes up the challenges of rapport and, having solved that problem, one moves on to building trust, and so forth. Traditional representations of fieldwork portray it as a kind of observational plan, each of whose elements can be completed and evaluated in turn. A research proposal, for instance, might describe *the* process by which one will obtain consent for studying a particular field site, how participants will be informed of the risks involved, and what the observational process will entail.

This model is far too simplistic, according to Johnson, because it lacks any sense that field experience can be diversely interpreted by various participants and at different times. In Johnson's words, ethnographic representation also leaves out fieldwork's integral "fusions of thinking and feeling," the documentation of which would show that ethnography is anything but a series of resolvable problems. He argues that ethnographic representation is often too cognitive and does not take account of the emotional contours and diversity of a setting.

Johnson refers to conclusions that Kurt Wolff (1964) reached after reviewing the anthropological and sociological literatures and comparing ethnographic representation with his own extended fieldwork experience in a small Mexican village. Commenting on the literature, Wolff writes:

> The relevance of what is observed is transformed into theoretical relevance, and the relevance of the observer into theoretical interest. Even the field worker's confusion has a purely theoretical meaning; when he writes, "I did not clearly see any reason why I should inquire into one matter rather than another," there is no affective or interactive component in his meaning: interaction and affect are limited for him to interaction with and affect for cognitive problems, although they are more purely limited and more passionate, more unconditional within these limits than anywhere else in a community study that I know of. (P. 256)

According to Johnson, Wolff's reflections provide a rare example of how the emotional aspects of research can be considered for how they inform and organize what is observed and interpreted.

Johnson similarly reflects on his own field research, which took place in five offices of two large metropolitan welfare departments. A major portion of the fieldwork was undertaken at the agency he calls the "Metro office." Johnson spent ten months participating in the everyday routines of work at Metro and it was there that much of the "fusions" of thinking and feeling developed.

Johnson had intended to write a more-or-less conventional ethnography, documenting the social organization of welfare work in the agencies, especially how social work was conducted in child welfare services. He had not intended to write a book about field research methods. The actual experience of the fieldwork, however, made Johnson acutely sensitive to what he might be representing in an ethnography. In his opinion, the related methodological literature did not convey what field research was actually like.

Asking what the field and fieldwork would resemble if its lived experience were opened to view, Johnson relates the fusions of thinking and feeling that he experienced as a participant observer. *Doing Field Research* shows how each ostensible step in the fieldwork process is not isolated, but is instead suffused with the prospective or retrospective relevance of other steps. Each step is affected by the developing interpersonal contingencies of daily occurrences in the setting. Entry, for example, is not just a starting hurdle, but is an integral, ongoing feature of social relations in the field. Johnson illustrates how, even after episodes of participant observation in which he comfortably felt "in" the field—in "their world," as a naturalist would put it—he learned that being "in" was surrounded by the real-life con-

tingencies of being "in" only in relation to particular (perhaps originally unspecified) matters, such as particular personalities, ongoing social service developments
in the metropolitan area, and Johnson's own unfolding confidence in the research
process. Being "in," in other words, was not so much experienced as a stage of fieldwork as it was an enduring problematic of social interaction in the field. Nor, as
Johnson soon discovered, could trust be thought of as a problem to be dealt with at
a particular point in the research process or as some absolute characteristic of field
relations. While the methodological literature suggested that a leading goal was to
develop trusting relations early in the research process, Johnson found that the changing circumstances of fieldwork required recasting trust as a problem of "accom-
modative morality." Trust was best conceived in terms of the situational and political dimensions of ongoing field relations.

Visceral Reactions

As Wolff reminds us, an emotional, not just a cognitive, fieldworker initiates, conducts, and completes participant observation. Johnson describes how this can have
concrete visceral results, again not much in evidence in traditional ethnographies.
For example, while rational self-presentation may be the received wisdom for the
fieldworker, participant observation can induce considerable anxiety. Johnson (1975)
describes his own early days in the welfare offices and the anxieties that prompted
him to engage in "demented [fieldnote] recording rituals" to prove that he was doing a good job:

> In my field research in the welfare offices, I experienced all these feelings [private fears,
> apprehensions, feelings of ignorance, confusion, incompetence, and incomprehension] at the
> beginning, and some periodically thereafter, and mine were complicated by distinct physical
> manifestations of various kinds. When I returned to my apartment at the end of the very first
> day of fieldwork at the Lakeside office, several of the blood vessels in my nose broke. Blood
> spewed forth at a frightening rate onto the floor and the carpet. I was taken to the emergency
> room of a local hospital by one of the social workers I had met that day. The doctor said the
> event was "inexplicable." Upon coming home again, I recorded field notes for *seven hours*.
> In retrospect, that also appears to be a reflection of my feelings of anxiety, apprehension,
> worries about doing a good job, and the like. (Pp. 151–52, emphasis in the original)

Such visceral reactions and other fusions of thinking and feeling do not stop after one has gained entry to a field setting, established rapport, and ostensibly achieved
trust. The following excerpt from Johnson's field notes, written after two months
of participant observation at Metro, illustrates his reactions to a conversation with
Buzz, a social worker:

> I began by asking him what had happened recently with the kids at the Young foster home,
> where we were last week. Buzz began his account by saying, "Oh wow, J.J., you wouldn't
> believe how bad I blew it," and then he proceeded to describe the details of what he called
> his own ignorance, unprofessional conduct, erroneous judgments, sentimental and sloppy
> thinking, bad social casework, and so on. Now I'll admit that I don't know all there is to
> know about social workers or social casework, but I sure as hell know enough about it to
> know that all the examples he cited from his case wouldn't be similarly defined by *any* other
> social worker, that there isn't a social worker in the world who would see that as unprofes-

sional conduct, or anything else. . . . It's fairly obvious he was giving me some kind of short-con this afternoon, although I'll be damned if I have any idea why. The thing really got to me. After taking leave of the situation, I walked out of the office and over to the parking lot whereupon I proceeded to break into a cold sweat, felt weakknee'd and nauseous. (Pp. 153–54, emphasis in the original)

One of the inherent hazards of studying emotionality is that researchers, for good theoretical reasons, consider it necessary to become emotionally involved with subjects. Douglas insists on this in creative interviewing and, later, it is also explicit in Ellis and her associates' writings. Because emotionalists need to put their emotions on the line, as it were, not just apply their thinking skills as researchers, they risk the emotional consequences of their field relations. It is important to emphasize that, while these emotional experiences might vary among individual researchers, or even be selected for by those who commit themselves to studying emotionality, the idiom itself makes a commitment to this method. Emotionalism *should* take its practitioners' hearts away; anything less would be methodologically remiss.

Emotional Field Notes

The analytic necessity of emotionally experiencing, as much as cognitively considering, the field extends to the most mundane activities. Take the matter of writing ethnographic field notes, which we discussed in Chapter 2 in the comparatively "cool" context of naturalistic method talk. The imperative there was to write field notes as soon as possible after one departs from the field, the reason being that events should be recorded when they are freshest in the researcher's mind. Evidently, any delay makes the researcher vulnerable to the vicissitudes of recall and the confounding effect of the competing details of subsequent field experiences, among other sources of contamination.

But, as we can infer from Johnson's field experience, waiting may also detach the researcher from events that have been very emotional. The passage of time affects the field-note-writing process by allowing the researcher time to "cool down." Johnson points to both the advantages and disadvantages of this. For example, one custody hearing in juvenile court so upset Johnson that he was ready to give up his work as "the cool, objective, calculatingly rational social scientist." After the hearing, he cried most of the evening. He reports that "field notes were not recorded in the heat of the moment, then, but the following day; this was one of the few times I didn't record notes on the day of the observation" (p. 159). Rather than allowing the resulting fusion of thinking and feeling in the field to affect field-note writing, Johnson chose to wait, becoming a party to the "transformation of interactive and affective elements into *cognitive* problems," and losing something "real" in the process. Johnson was not completely willing to accept the methodological consequences of his operating idiom, which required the merger of thinking and feeling:

It is wiser to conceive the tensions between thinking and feeling as necessary and inevitable ones. They are necessary and inevitable ones, that is, as long as one retains a moral commitment to the observations. To observe sociologically means that one deliberately cedes experiencing the things in themselves to the members of the setting; observation entails seeing phenomena as "exhibits" of the things in themselves. If one elects to do observation sociologically, there is and can be no other way. (Pp. 159–60)

Ultimately, according to Johnson, the decision regarding the writing of field notes reverts to scientistic justification. Strictly speaking, following the existential sociologists' own conception of the field as fused thought and emotion, Johnson actually had good theoretical grounds for writing field notes in the passion of the moment rather than later. To borrow an existentialist phrase, the later, cooler, cognitive field notes became a form of "bad faith," even while they were presumably sociologically more acceptable. As we shall see in the next section, two decades later, emotionalists are not as convinced of this "necessary and inevitable" tension between thinking and feeling. Rather, they self-consciously take on board the constitutive relation between reality and method, directly incorporating their own fusions of thinking and feeling into research texts.

REENACTING EMOTIONALITY

In their "agenda for the interpretation of lived experience," Ellis and Flaherty (1992) maintain that sociology must not be hampered by traditional methods of representation. Qualitative researchers especially need to engage in representational practices and create texts appropriate to the full range of lived experience, integrating cognitive, emotional, and somatic dimensions. This moves the enterprise beyond fusions of thinking and feeling in the field, to the infusion of thinking and feeling throughout the descriptive project. While the existential sociologists of the 1970s, like their later compatriots, built their field of inquiry on inner lived experience, they kept (cool) representational practices separate and distinct from (often hot and passionate) field activities. The new emotionalists, in contrast, draw from postmodernist sensibilities to create texts that themselves "capture and evoke the complex, paradoxical, and mysterious qualities of subjectivity" (Ellis and Flaherty 1992, p. 5).

Performing Experience

If naturalist and existentialist texts take us "there" to "their world," the more contemporary emotionalists explicitly construct their field as part of the process of representation. The aim is a poetics of experience, not just the construction of a window on the world or into inner realms. To illustrate, Ellis and Bochner (1992) have written a play to convey the emotional experience of pregnancy and abortion for a woman, Alice (who is Ellis), and her male partner, Ted (who is Bochner). As the authors state:

> The text was written with the express purpose of being performed so that nuances of feeling, expression, and interpretation could be interpreted more clearly. . . . An audience that witnesses a performance of this text thus is subjected to much more than words: they see facial expressions, movements, and gestures; they hear the tones, intonations, and inflections of the actors' voices; and they can feel the passion of the performers. (P. 80)

Note that there is little distinction between the field and its representational venue, nor is there a separation between subjects and researchers. The play is a kind of auto-ethnography, whose data are drawn from "systematic introspection" (Ellis

1991b). In this postmodern context, emotionalists attempt to reenact, not just represent, lived experience.

Ellis and Bochner report that during the time the dramatized events took place, they were too absorbed in what was happening to write about them. Two months afterward, they began the process of transforming events into a "dialogic mode of narration that attempted to capture the processual and emotional details of what happened." The result is a written text intended to be performed in five scenes: "The Pregnancy Test and the Test of Pregnancy," "Making the [abortion] Decision," "Dealing with the Decision," "The Preabortion Procedure," and "The Abortion." The performance is emotionally charged. Alice, 39 years old and committed to her career, has never before been pregnant. She is attracted to the idea of having a baby, but weighs that against her professional aspirations. Ted is engrossed in the notion of becoming a father, but after a failed marriage does not want to spoil a relationship that he values highly. The performance conveys and highlights the deep and nuanced emotions that might be lost in a more conventional, academic text.

Staging Devices

Still, the emotional and visceral dimensions of the experience are not as directly conveyed in the performance as the authors suggest. Indeed, they employ two important textual devices that are also staging directions to render visible and audible what otherwise would be hidden from view: the actors' positioning on stage and the use of quotation marks in the script of the play. When either Alice or Ted faces the audience as the other turns away, the authors write as if the audience is hearing and seeing Ted and Alice's separate inner ruminations and feelings. As such, the audience is dramaturgically brought "inside" their private thoughts and emotions. When Alice and Ted face each other and there are quotations marks in the script around what they say to one another, the speech and action that the authors are presenting to the audience are meant to be available to any bystander. This is the public side of the situation and is narratively thin. As the script shows, what we know of the couple's lived experience by way of their private inner conversations without quotation marks is textually much richer, deeper, more evocative, even more mysterious—virtually the entire gamut of emotional experience—than what the actors convey when they openly speak to one another in quotation marks.

Compare, for example, how Alice and Ted, in Scene 3, describe their separate inner experiences. At one point, Ted has turned away, and Alice faces the audience:

ALICE: For the hundredth time, I think through the pros and cons of abortion. Abortion gets rid of the problem. I don't have to make major life decisions, everything continues on the same trajectory, my relationship with Ted is not artificially accelerated, I don't have to be pregnant for nine months. My work won't suffer. How would I meet all the obligations I've taken on? On the other hand, I have to go through the physical and emotional pain of abortion and cope with having killed a living being. It feels so wrong, selfish. Why is this happening? Was it meant to be? I'm 39. Is this my last chance to have a baby? Perhaps I would find meaning being a mother that I could not know any other way. Ironically, I think of another advantage of having a baby—I wouldn't have to be department chair. Who would ask a pregnant woman/new mother to be department chair? . . . Sometimes I fantasize that I am going to have a baby, not an abortion. Then I like the feeling of the pressure on my abdomen. I shake my head so that I don't get carried away with this thought. Then I grieve for the child that I will give up. (Pp. 86–87)

Following a pause, there is a brief, comparatively thin conversation between Ted and Alice, who now face each other and speak textually in quotation marks:

TED: "You don't have to do this."
ALICE: "What?"
TED: "Have this abortion. I'm with you all the way. I'll do whatever you want." (P. 87)

Then, Alice turns away as Ted faces the audience, and we are presented a medley of reported conversation (in quotation marks) and inner thoughts and feelings (without quotation marks):

TED: "Alice is pregnant," I say to Diane, one of only two people I talk to about the pregnancy. I do not want to share my conflicts, be judged, questioned, or challenged. Nor do I want to be pitied or sympathized, but I feel obligated to tell Diane because she knows something is wrong. "I feel foolish about how careless we were. We're not teenagers, although we acted like we were." Then I am distracted by the crying infant and two other young children scooting around the table near us as we finish our lunch. (P. 87)

Are we to conclude from this "reenactment" that emotionalists have finally found a means of directly representing subjectivity? Do performances, poetry, and other innovative texts do a better job than other representational practices of communicating fusions of thought and feeling? Typically, these creative representational forms are more emotionally evocative and descriptively captivating than conventional academic texts. Indeed, the mere use of such unconventional forms is a kind of cultural signal, virtually instructing consumers to listen and view the materials more deeply, to see and hear emotionality and scenic presence in the format itself (see Gubrium 1988b). Culturally cued, and invoking more of our senses, these reenactments appear to take us closer to, even inside, the richness of lived experience and emotion.

Still, as Schneider (1991) implies in a discussion of "performance science" (see McCall and Becker 1990), dramatic performance and other innovative forms are themselves "re-presentations" that rely upon their own formats and devices to convey the realities in question. As Schneider (1991, p. 303) asks, "We can't get away from format, can we?" Stories conveyed by means of performances, poetry, and other nontraditional texts are themselves discursively formulated. That leaves them just as "contrived" as any other textual practice. Moreover, as Richard Hilbert (1990, p. 134) questions, "Why is this method [dramatic performance] superior to even more 'direct access' to actors through documentary films or videotapes?" This, of course, raises even further questions relating to both authenticity on the one hand,

and analysis, on the other. We are still left to ponder how to faithfully convey experience. And if the answer lies in getting at, and making available, the unadulterated "data" of actual lived experience, then we have to ask about the role played by the researcher/writer, if he or she is left with any role at all (see Hilbert 1990).

The adequate representation of emotions clearly remains a problem for qualitative researchers. Many emotionalists seem convinced that traditional modes of representation, especially academic texts, have impeded our understanding of feelings. Novelist Umberto Eco (1994), however, suggests a further complication. Agreeing that the portrayal of emotions is indeed challenging, Eco poses an even thornier dilemma:

> It is difficult to reconstruct the actions and feelings of a character surely afire with true love, for you never know whether he is expressing what he feels or what the rules of amorous discourse prescribe in his case—but then, for that matter, what do we know of the difference between passion felt and passion expressed, and who can say which has precedence? (Pp. 5–6)

Questions abound. How do we distinguish between emotions felt and emotions expressed? Do we have any evidence of emotion other than its expression? Can researchers give us access to "real" emotion simply by re-presenting or reenacting subjects' *expressions* of those emotions? Do emotions exist apart from culturally available modes of expression, beyond the rules of discourse to which Eco refers? These questions go right to the heart of the relationship between nature and its signs. They lead us uneasily toward the looming analytic self-consciousness of postmodernism and the crisis of representation that the postmodern debate poses for qualitative inquiry.

CHAPTER 5

Postmodernism

Postmodernism has caused quite a stir in the social sciences. Pauline Rosenau (1992) goes so far as to say that it "haunts" them. Frequently misunderstood, reviled, or faddishly embraced (Best and Kellner 1991), postmodernism offers an idiom for characterizing lived experience that challenges, if not subverts, each of the research idioms that we've discussed in the preceding chapters. Of course, postmodernism speaks in diverse voices, so we must be cautious in making blanket assertions about what it is or is not, what it does or does not do. In its more extreme, *skeptical* incarnations, for example, postmodernism questions the very foundations and core of the social sciences, radically dismissing them. Its more moderate, *affirmative* formulations set up camp outside of modern paradigms in order to deconstruct them. They encourage reexamination of social scientific goals, assumptions, logic, and methods and promote innovation in how studies might be done and presented (Rosenau 1992).

Paradoxically, the lack of unity within postmodernism reflects one of its most widely shared tenets: the possibility of certainty must be regarded skeptically, if not rejected outright. This reverberates through the social sciences as a challenge to comprehensive or veridical descriptions of the social world. Postmodernism doubts the possibility of *any* totalizing or exhaustive theories or explanations. Its objective, writes Rosenau, is to

support a refocussing on what has been taken for granted, what has been neglected, regions of resistance, the forgotten, the irrational, the insignificant, the repressed, the borderline, the classical, the sacred, the traditional, the eccentric, the sublimated, the subjugated, the rejected, the nonessential, the marginal, the peripheral, the excluded, the tenuous, the silenced, the accidental, the dispersed, the disqualified, the deferred, the disjointed.... Postmodernists, defining everything as a text, seek to "locate" meaning rather than to "discover" it.... They offer "readings" not " observations," "interpretations" not "findings." ... They never test because testing requires "evidence," a meaningless concept within a postmodern frame of reference.... They look to the unique rather than to the general, to intertextual relations rather than causality, and to the unrepeatable rather than the re-occurring, the habitual, or the routine. Within a post-modern perspective social science becomes a more subjective and humble enterprise as truth gives way to tentativeness. Confidence in emotion replaces efforts at impartial observation. Relativism is preferred to objectivity, fragmentation to totalization. (P. 8)

Clearly, with the postmodern turn, social reality comes on extraordinarily hard times. The substantiality of social forms is constantly assaulted. Even the central constructs of sociology—the self as a central presence in experience, for example—may dissolve in the onslaught.[1] While there are certain affinities between some of the postmodernist impulses that Rosenau chronicles and the qualitative research approaches we discussed in preceding chapters, some versions of postmodernism deny the very possibility of qualitative inquiry.

Indeed, the challenge comes in crisis proportions, taking qualitative inquiry away from, and beyond, empirically grounded *what* and *how* questions. The crisis is about representation itself, with radical postmodernism completely displacing reality with representation.[2] In this context, the *how* question shifts from the substance, process, and indigenous constitution of social life, to the representational devices used by society and the sociologist to convey the image of objective (or subjective) reality. Postmodernist inquiry tends to veer away from how members of society interact to produce their lives and experience, turning more toward the representational practices used by those claiming the authority to offer "true" representations. If the postmodern challenge abides any concern with *what* questions, it is less with the substance of experiential reality than it is with what images are produced and how they are used to signify the real.

EXPRESSIONS OF POSTMODERNISM

Postmodernism is expressed in a variety of ways, across many disciplines. The version we discuss here as the postmodernist idiom is gleaned largely from the influential work of Jean-François Lyotard and Jean Baudrillard.[3] In Lyotard's (1984) expression of the postmodern, master narratives evaporate, as do master vocabularies. The signal terms of classical social theory—self, community, class, society, attitude, sentiment, and reason—no longer apply in the same way. Master narratives once called "theories," which centered on the relation of the terms to their respective empirical realities, are now viewed as "stories," grand tales told about social life and linked with the perspectives and interests of their storytellers. This deprivileges their status as master narratives, or even theory. If the terms are used at all in postmodernism, they are necessarily written in quotation marks, alerting us to postmodernism's nihilistic tendencies.

Incredulous Method Talk

How has the language of inquiry changed in this new idiom? The Introduction to Lyotard's *The Postmodern Condition* (1984) describes postmodernity as a condition of knowledge in highly developed societies that prevents us from simply speaking, writing, or referring to objects and events the way we did before the late nineteenth century (p. xxiii). Literalism has been completely lost. We can infer that before this, words in principle referred to things separate from the words themselves. Of course, words could incorrectly represent things and, in that sense, transmute knowledge. The "thingness" of things, however, was not so much at issue in description as was their accurate representation. One could, for example, misrepresent situations or incorrectly interpret them, but the discrepancies between representation and reality were taken as a matter categorically distinct from the reality of the situations in their own right.

Lyotard regards the hallmark of postmodernism to be the "breaking up" of the grand narratives, or theories, of the disciplines (pp. 15 and 31–41). "Simplifying to the extreme," he writes "I define *postmodern* as incredulity toward metanarratives" (p. xxiv). With respect to social and behavioral research, we take him to mean that method talk can no longer be accepted as principally about a scientific relationship with the entities being studied. Instead, method talk is essentially about itself, a point of view that, to a degree, informs a theme of this book. One might argue, for instance, that naturalism's analytic vocabulary not only shapes its empirical horizons, but at the same time representationally constitutes the object of its descriptions. In other words, a discipline has tacit ontological (or foundational *what*) rules about how to proceed in "doing" or fabricating the reality under consideration. This is postmodern because such disciplinary rules are viewed as creating what the rules are about, making disciplinary realities into empirical language games (cf. Wittgenstein 1958). As we will see later in the chapter, the resulting crisis turns qualitative inquiry into the study of representational practice, leaving it conceptually and methodologically skeptical about the possibility of empirical footing.

According to Lyotard (p. 15), lived experience and the postmodern self do not amount to much; he grants them little substantiality. Still, for postmodernists, the self and experience remain objects of discussion and debate. Two ironies result. First, postmodernists want to erase essential presence because there is no warrant for it outside its empirical language game, yet they tell us what that lack of presence is like. This, of course, requires presence or at least some semblance of empirical substantiality to communicate what absence resembles. There needs to be something modern, something principally distinct from representation, about the postmodern for the postmodern to be about anything other than an instantaneous swirl into itself or no-thing.

It is also ironic that, as irascibly reluctant as postmodernists are to be categorized as pre- or post- anything, they do bring intellectual (re)sources to their writing. While they resist the notion of "source," modern theoretical differences, from structuralism to hermeneutics, pervade their descriptions of the postmodern condition as informing narratives. For example, what "postmodernist" Denzin (1988, 1991, 1992, 1993) conveys about self and experience reflects his deep involvement in the symbolic interactionist tradition (see, for instance, Lindesmith, Strauss, and Denzin 1988). A related naturalism evidently grounds Denzin's evaluation of the reality of cinema images in postmodern or "cinematic" society (Denzin 1991). This contrasts with Baudrillard's (1983a, 1983b, 1988b) postmodern vision, whose point of departure was critical theory (see Baudrillard 1981).

Hyperreality

Because there is no substantial *what* to liken to anything in a radically reflexive postmodern mode, nor a distinct empirical *how* to attribute either to the operation or social constitution of the *what,* it is useful to think of these ironies in relation to imagined, empirical sites. Metaphorical fields can be used to address questions of "what it's like" and "how it works" when there is no field in sight. Baudrillard, for example, locates the postmodern condition in what he terms "hyperreality." He describes the postmodern condition in parallel to electronic, not print, media. The print media are linear, "wordy," and relatively slow. They chronicle experience in terms of before, now, and later. A grand theme of the modern thus undergirds the written media: time is ordered sequentially and divided into periods; space is allocated within time so that we peruse one event, another, and then another, akin to the empirical impulse animating naturalism.[4]

According to Baudrillard, the electronic media, especially television, change this. Through television, we are taken instantaneously to distant and disparate places. Space in terms of distance doesn't seem to matter. In seconds, contrasting images are juxtaposed, jarring a modern sensibility built on things that are separate and distinct from one another. An advertisement for cotton fabric, sung in nostalgic, melancholy tones, fades into the fantastic glitz and dizzying pastiche of the violent spectacle of professional football, which soon flashes into ads for the coolness and masculinity of light beer and fast cars. This peaks during the Super Bowl and its all-encompassing hype, where the represented and the representational become so intertwined that time, space, and substance—distinguishable order—virtually warp and collapse.[5] And if that is not enough, the viewer can increase the speed of disorder by "channel surfing" via remote control.

Reality, or modern time and space, are "cranked up" to the point where the objects and order normally associated with the real no longer apply. As simulation supplants the actual, substantiality becomes a matter of images. Presence is thrown to the wind in a literally mindless project. Subjects with footing in the world disappear, and significances are so flattened that representation ceases to have any particular reference to things. Reality becomes a playful field of signs, signs of other signs and other signs of signs. The hyperreal offers the Gulf War to the American public in the shape of a media simulation or video game—sheer events with no center (Baudrillard 1991a, 1991b). As Douglas Kellner (1992, p. 147) puts it, in this mode, television is a site of "pure noise," "a black hole where all meaning and messages are absorbed into the whirlpool and kaleidoscope of radical semiurgy, of the incessant dissemination of images and information to the point of total saturation."

The stuff of sociology—distinct social objects—hardly matters in hyperreality. The self, in particular, is nowhere and everywhere at the same time, totally abstracted and rapidly flitting about in myriad versions without reference to source or defining circumstance. For example, we hear self's authentic, yet fleeting, secrets in gaudily romanticized form on talk shows, as the troubled, tormented, and morally triumphant speak of their inner sorrows, deepest fears, and hidden desires. What had once been ostensibly profoundly personal becomes unending grist for public display. Social objects are fully visible, commodified for mass consumption.

The hyperreal obviates all attention to the natural, which becomes just one more set of images whose erstwhile metanarrative merely harkens to a *rhetoric* for time, being, and authenticity. From a postmodernist perspective, Cornerville, the New Deal Carry-out shop, and Jelly's are less actual places methodologically urging us on to "be there" in order to know "their worlds" and convey "their stories," than they are rhetorical anchors for images of a particular moral space. The depths of experience, which are claimed by emotionalists to ultimately shape the natural, become romanticized representations of the (genuinely) real. Whereas the ethnomethodologists, who study the use of indigenous methods for systematically managing and constituting the natural, merely set aside (that is, bracket) the natural or real for research purposes, postmodernists might bracket the entire possibility of "reality" itself, totally, ontologically eclipsing the natural or real. What remains is the hyperreal—not reality, not nature, not subjects with agency, not feelings, not members' methods, but a world of images and pure representation.

Hyperreality, of course, has its detractors (see Poster 1988; Best and Kellner 1991; Lash and Friedman 1992; Seidman and Wagner 1992). Mike Featherstone (1988, p. 200), for example, cautions that, while Baudrillard describes hyperreality as a representational site epitomized by television, he offers few clues to how the hyperreal relates to practice: "For all the alleged pluralism and sensitivity to the Other talked about by some theorists, one finds little discussion of the actual experience and practice of watching television by different groups in different settings." Referring to the penchant for siting postmodern experience in channel hopping and multiphrenic imaging, Featherstone also notes that "evidence of the extent of such practices, and how they are integrated into, or influence, the day-to-day encounters between embodied persons is markedly lacking."

In his introduction to *Selected Writings* from Baudrillard, Mark Poster (1988) offers some additional criticisms, even while he later appreciates Baudrillard's contributions to our understanding of the impact of electronic media on society. He elides an appreciation of Baudrillard's need to write as he does in the constitutive context of his postmodernism.

[Baudrillard's] writing style is hyperbolic and declarative, often lacking sustained, systematic analysis when it is appropriate; he totalizes his insights, refusing to qualify or delimit his claims. He writes about particular experiences, television images, as if nothing else in society mattered, extrapolating a bleak view of the world from that limited base. (P. 7)

Sociological Manifestations

The more radical version of the postmodernist idiom is enamored with a nihilistic vision of a world of ungrounded representation. However, as Rosenau suggests, there is a more affirmative variant of the idiom that emphasizes innovative and deconstructive forays into new fields of inquiry, including the social sciences themselves. There is even a developing sociology of postmodernism (see Lash 1990). Sociologists adopting (and adapting) the postmodernist impulse have generally come to terms with "reality" in such a way as to permit the examination of the social "content" of lives and experiences. But this notion of content, suggests Rosenau (1992, p. 111), is " 'soft,' provisional, and emotional," a far cry from the vision of content held by positivist sociology. While stressing the complex interrelations between "texts," or phenomena, postmodernist sociologists allow for the possibility of relational patterning. And explanation is not anathema, as it might be for skeptical postmodernists. Indeed, some affirmatives introduce forms of teleological interpretation, while others reassert the role of unconscious processes in human conduct. Some more sociological versions of postmodernism even remind us of their critical ancestors, risking theoretical inconsistency in order to resist radical relativism and offer an authoritative voice of their own (Rosenau 1992).

While lagging considerably behind their anthropologist kin (see Clifford and Marcus 1986; Marcus 1994; Marcus and Fischer 1986), qualitative sociologists have fashioned significant empirical projects that retain sociological orientations and objectives within more-or-less postmodernist frameworks.[6] Their approaches differ considerably from one another, offering a wide spectrum of adaptations of postmodernist sensibilities to qualitative research, staking out different positions in relation to the landmark convictions of postmodernism. The following sections illustrate some of these efforts at postmodernist qualitative inquiry.

STUDYING CINEMATIC SOCIETY

Affirmative postmodernists have reservations about doing away with "reality" altogether. According to some, the radical denial of all substantiality and the dissolution of master categories undermines our ability to comprehend the postmodern condition. For example, some argue that a blindness to class, race, and gender, combined with nihilistic tendencies, is having a deleterious impact on qualitative inquiry (Denzin 1991). In his book *Images of Postmodern Society* (1991), Denzin offers an alternative that draws upon the postmodern idiom without abandoning modernist concerns. He suggests that the idea of the field, so dear to qualitative researchers, can no longer be viewed as geographically, emotionally, or even discursively anchored. In postmodern society, the field needs to be viewed as residing within the prevalent social images that mediate lived experience. As never before, images loom large and are ubiquitous across the social landscape. It is a telling characteristic of postmodern society that images take a seat within, if not constitutively in front of, the theater of life they represent. As Baudrillard (1981) argues, contemporary reality has become a political economy of signs, if not a landscape of hyperreality. Denzin (1991) puts it succinctly in stating the basic thesis he examines:

> This society, Baudrillard argues, only knows itself through the reflections that flow from the camera's eye. But this knowledge, Baudrillard contends, is unreflexive. "The cinema and TV are America's reality!" (Baudrillard 1988a, p. 104; 1988b). I examine the basic thesis (taken from Baudrillard) that members of the contemporary world are voyeurs adrift in a sea of symbols. They know and see themselves through cinema and television. If this is so, then an essential part of the contemporary postmodern American scene can be found in the images and meanings that flow from cinema and TV. (Pp. vii–viii)

From this point of departure, Denzin sets out on a program of empirical inquiry into the nuances of "cinematic society."

Cinematic Ethnography

What Denzin calls the "cinematization" of society makes it necessary to rethink the idea of the field in qualitative method. While in the modern era subjects, things, actions, events, and their environs could be viewed as located in clock time and in physical or social space (or interpretively constituted in relation to these parameters), in the postmodern era[7] the field is confounded by a sea of images. For Denzin (1991), postmodern social relations, even economic formations, become reflections in sometimes dazzling displays in the electronic media:

Postmodernism is more than a series of economic formations. The postmodern society . . . is a cinematic, dramaturgical production. Film and television have transformed American, and perhaps all other, societies touched by the camera, into video, visual cultures. Representations of the real have become stand-ins for actual, lived experience. Three implications follow from the cinematization of contemporary life.

First, reality is a staged, social production. Secondly, the real is now judged against its staged, cinematic-video counterpart (Baudrillard 1983b, p. 152). Third, the metaphor of the dramaturgical society (Lyman 1990, p. 221), or "life as theater" (Brissett and Edgley, 1990, p. 2; Goffman, 1959, pp. 254–55) has now become interactional reality. The theatrical aspects of the dramaturgical metaphor have not "only creeped into everyday life" (Goffman 1959, p. 254), they have taken it over. Art not only mirrors life, it structures and reproduces it. The postmodern society is a dramaturgical society. (Pp. ix–x)

Denzin borrows from Goffman, cautiously making the point that, while Goffman likened contemporary life to the theater and described its interactional order in dramaturgical terms, postmodern society *is* theatrical, not merely informed by a theatrical metaphor. This is an important distinction, both empirically and methodologically. Empirically, the postmodern condition cannot be marked by a vocabulary of nature, where time, space, and activity are concretely designated; it resists description in naturalistic, ethnomethodological, or emotionalist terms. This has significant procedural consequences, requiring what Denzin calls a "cinematic-ethnographic interpretive sociology" (p. 157):

The postmodern terrain is defined almost exclusively in visual terms, including the display, the icon, the representations of the real seen through the camera's eye, captured on videotape, and given in the moving picture (see Ulmer 1989, p. ix–x). In these traces of the visible and the invisible, the figures of postmodern man, woman, and child emerge, as if out of a misty fog. The search for the meaning of the postmodern moment is a study in looking. *It can be no other way.* This is a visual, cinematic age. The collage and the mixed-media–tele/audio text are the iconic markers of this moment (Hebdige 1988, pp. 13–14; Ulmer 1983, 1989). (Pp. viii–ix, our emphasis)

In other words, Denzin claims that there are significant empirical grounds for a cinematic-ethnographic interpretive sociology. "It can be no other way," he argues, precisely because the condition of postmodern society is visual and cinematic. His method talk does not present yet another procedural option for documenting contemporary life. Rather, he suggests that the old analytic vocabularies no longer apply because social reality has changed into the hyperreal. The postmodern moment demands a new idiom of inquiry, which, in this case, requires sociological observation of, "notetaking" about, and the ethnographic documentation, of images of the real. To continue to search, say, for the natural and "their story" by "being there" in order to present "their world" would be tantamount to searching for the real in a room of mirrors.

Against this background, Denzin presents his project, pointing to the theoretical urgency of experimenting with new modes of representation:

Classical sociological ways of representing and writing about society require radical transformation. If sociology and the other human disciplines are to remain in touch with the worlds of lived experience in the late twentieth century, then new ways of inscribing and reading the social must be found. Throughout, my analysis works back and forth between two kinds of texts: social theory . . . and cinematic representations of life in contemporary America. I take six late 1980s award-winning films, *Blue Velvet, Wall Street, Crimes and Misdemeanors, When Harry Met Sally, sex, lies and videotape,* and *Do the Right Thing,* as readings of life in contemporary America, finding postmodern contradictions in these texts that mirror the everyday in this society and its popular culture. (P. ix)

In his descriptions of the postmodern scene, we begin to see Denzin assert his commitment to modernism, even as he attends to postmodern culture. He writes, for example, that the same postmodern condition that permits endless images of the real to represent society provides countless options for assigning meaning to lived experience. This implies that lived experience remains to be mediated. Contrary to Baudrillard's (1983b) claim, Denzin would argue that TV (and cinema) are not the world, but "merely" the centrally significant and ubiquitous means of articulating it in contemporary life (the textual mirrors of the everyday in the extract above). This leaves Denzin with a not-quite-postmodernist footing for evaluating and resisting prevalent media images, especially those he calls "astral" or Hollywood star-quality glosses of the lived realities of class, race, and gender. Denzin summarizes:

I offer, then, a critical ethnographic reading of this world and its meanings, as given in the ["two kinds of" (p. xi)] texts listed earlier, [which] means that I am neither a custodian of nor a defender of postmodern culture, and the theories generated about it. I seek instead to write a postmodernist theory of cultural resistance, which acknowledges and explores my place in the creation of this culture and its meanings. I seek not a theory of cultural indifference (Connor 1989, p. 181), but a theory of resistance (Fields 1988). Such a theory examines how the basic existential experiences with self, other, gender, race, nationality, family, love, intimacy, violence, death, and freedom are produced and given mythical meaning in everyday life. (P. xi)[8]

No apologist for postmodern culture, Denzin backs away from the postmodernist rejection of theorizing and authoritative representation in order to preserve a space for qualitative inquiry and description of the postmodern landscape. He clearly remains committed to examining the "essential" foundations of social life and experience in terms that are sociologically traditional.

The Field of Film

Turning to the films, Denzin asks his leading question: "How are the crucial cultural identities grounded in class, gender, and race defined in the postmodern moment?" He goes on to trace postmodern themes in each film, teasing out their specific emphases, and comparing the themes and emphases for how imaged or realistic they are. The films are a postmodern field within which Denzin sets about doing a kind of modernist fieldwork. His cinematic ethnography is highly evaluative, grounded as it is in the "real," notably, in the ostensibly lived realities of race, gender, and class.

In *Blue Velvet,* the postmodern accent is on gazing and voyeurism. According to Denzin, the film "celebrates the voyeur as postmodernism's penultimate, iconic figure," "elevating the look and the gaze to new voyeuristic levels." *Wall Street,* in contrast, presents a "purely imaginary ideological site, which has no concrete referent in the real world." Denzin (1991) comments about the Wall Street of the bullish mid-1980s, echoing Baudrillard's analysis of the postmodern political economy of signs:

> In this political economy only signs, representation, and simulations of the real circulate. . . . Money attached to nothing but imaginary numbers attached to made-up accounts, built on the transactions and imagined doings of imaginary companies. Careers built on who can best manipulate this imaginary political economy of signs. (P. 91)

Denzin suggests that Woody Allen's film *Crimes and Misdemeanors* "celebrate[s] the voyeur as a cultural figure who, in his (and her) looking, becomes a tourist of the contemporary scene" (p. 105). Looking and the visual are cinematically evanescent, crisscrossing the film's moralistic plot. A "lightness of being" (see Kundera 1984), characteristic of the tourist's orientation to his or her environs, suffuses a cinematic field in which crime becomes a misdemeanor requiring only a small punishment.

Images of the postmodern sexual order emerge in *When Harry Met Sally,* and in *sex, lies, and videotape.* Here the voyeur and the gaze are taken to new heights, yet Denzin still considers them in terms of (modernist) falsification. Sexuality, notably orgasm and masturbation, are mediated by representations of themselves, indulged in and consummated through claims, testaments, and videotaped images. The sexually real is less significant than are signs of the real. The fake and "faking it" supplant the authentic. As Denzin explains, referencing Baudrillard:

> Underneath this system of romantic love and its renewal of the traditional meanings of family and marriage lurks the hyperreal, the lie, the simulation, the faked orgasm, and the sexual truths about male and female sexuality. . . . The new sexual order is based on lies. It is a marriage of convenience. It reflects not what is real, or truthfully felt, but what is pretended, what is thought to be appropriate, not what is. Baudrillard's hyperreal has become the real; the lie has become the truth. . . . This is what *sex, lies, and videotape* and *When Harry Met Sally . . .* are all about: the fraudulent foundations of the postmodern sexual order. (P. 122)

Finally, Denzin turns to Spike Lee's 1989 film, *Do the Right Thing,* referring to it as "an ethnography of the lived experiences of ordinary, everyday black and white, Italian, Korean, Puerto Rican, and Spanish-American men, women, and children in Brooklyn" (p. 126). That it is called an ethnography reminds us of Denzin's postmodern field site: media images. This film, in Denzin's judgment, comes the closest to representing the real, and it is thus a critical benchmark for postmodern reality. According to Denzin, it presents this reality better than any of the other films because, while it gazes at the real, it is self-reflective, and offers viewers choices. But, characteristically, it offers no clear solutions:

> *Do the Right Thing* provides an apt contrast to the films thus far considered. It takes its problems seriously, critiques its own solutions, and offers no easy answers to the conditions that it sees. It forces the viewer (black and white) to confront hard, moral choices concerning the racial order in America today. . . .
> In asking us to do the right thing, Spike Lee asks that we reconsider the meanings we have thus far brought, unthinkingly, to the ordinary signifiers that we wear on our backs.

In opening our eyes in this way Lee has created a way to see past semiotics to a political economy of signs that does more than set the postmodern world adrift in a sea of unattached signifiers without meaning. Race is the unraveled sign of the contemporary age. (Pp. 126, 135)

Ultimately, Denzin's critical footing, which is apparent in this extract, promotes what resembles an innovative version of postcolonialist ethnography (Bhabha 1992; Fahim 1982) applied to the postmodern filmic field. The project teeters on the brink of modernism, returning us to an "unraveled" reality of contemporary life. Denzin's analytic idiom is as much an updated and emended naturalism as it is an affirmative postmodernism.

PSYCHOANALYTIC READING

In contrast to Denzin's cinematic field, the field in Patricia Clough's book, *The End(s) of Ethnography* (1992), is the corpus of texts written about doing ethnographic research.[9] Her vehicle is a psychoanalytically informed, critical reading of the method talk in Herbert Blumer's, Howard Becker's, and Erving Goffman's writings about qualitative inquiry. These works, she suggests, recall the realist sentiments of the modern novel, cinema, television, and computerized simulation. We concentrate here on her deconstruction of Blumer's methodological essays, since they reflect the realism of qualitative method most directly, and because Clough's particular reading of, and commentary on, Blumer's writing are especially direct and sustained.

Clough orients her project to several representational issues. From the start, she is concerned with how ethnographic authority mediates the reality of experience. Her analysis focuses on the invisible forces that work to constitute both the natural and naturalistic methodology:

With few exceptions, sociologists seemed yet unable to make much sense of the so-called crisis of representation and the deconstruction of the subject, both of which follow in the wake of poststructural accounts of discourse and representation.
    While the 1983 publication of James Clifford's essay on ethnographic realism did lead to a more general criticism of anthropological discourse, sociologists, even those receptive to discursive and textual criticisms, seemed unable to extend the criticism of ethnographic writing to a more general criticism of sociological discourse. . . . if the ethnographic tradition is to be the focus of a poststructural criticism of sociology or empirical social scientific discourse generally, then the way ethnography has functioned in the construction of the authority of empirical social scientific discourse, sociology in particular, must be made more visible. (P. xi)

Clough's very next sentence points out the acutely self-conscious *how* question that arises from these representational concerns: "The aim of this book is a critical reading of the ethnographic tradition in sociology that explores the way [*how*] ethnographic writing functions in the construction of the authority of sociological discourse" (pp. xi–xii).

A Field of Desire

Clough's critical footing is psychoanalytic feminism. From her perspective, the invisible force that works to constitute the distinct reality of the empirical world is *desire*. While, on the surface, traditional sociological research and writing (ethnography in particular) aim for the objective documentation of the empirical world, the aim is simultaneously an unconscious expression of the desire for a separate empirical world to document. A distinct empirical world is part and parcel of desire, not separate from it. Clough suggests that unconsciously, through their methods of inquiry, naturalistic qualitative researchers unconsciously desire the very world they purport to represent.

As long as this remains unconscious, Clough argues, those things held to be separate and distinct endure as components of an obdurate reality that has the capacity to resist and "talk back," as Blumer (1969, p. 22) writes. When we become conscious of this, however, it poses a crisis of representation. Naturalists of all ilks can no longer merely carefully, empathetically, and systematically inspect and document the world of everyday life, because the very acts of doing so—penetrating, examining, probing, and presenting—derive what is unwittingly desired. The *how* of this unconscious process is the centerpiece of Clough's project.

For Clough, realism and desire are cultural forces that work themselves out in object relations, especially in the objectifying method talk about that which is considered natural. The reality of the natural is necessarily constituted by denying the reality of desire. Conversely, the reality of desire necessarily requires making visible, that is, deconstructing, the constitutive contours of related method talk. Commenting on the interrelatedness of ethnographic authority and narrative form, Clough describes what is lacking in recent criticisms of authority, suggesting the need for a psychoanalytically sensitive approach:

> While these criticisms [Brown 1987; Clifford 1988; Smith 1989] pointed to the interrelatedness of ethnographic authority and narrative form, they did not further explicate the relationship in narrative of desire and authority. What was not made clear is *how* the desire that narrative puts into play is nonetheless disavowed so that the unity of the subject and the completeness of knowledge might appear as factual representations of empirical reality rather than the imaginary constructs they are not criticized to be. It was not shown *how* narrative desire is itself narratively disavowed. I want to propose that it is the realist narrative that informs ethnography that produces the narrative effects of a disavowed desire. It is a realist narrativity that makes narrative appear as if nearly dead, dead to desire. (P. 3, our emphasis)

Clough then turns to realist narratives, aiming to make visible how naturalistic method talk renders invisible the production of reality. She writes that "the subject is constructed in unconscious desire" (p. 3), as if to say that the narrative realities of Tally's corner, ethnomethods, and brute being are unconscious denials of the desires of their respective authors. She goes on to invoke the significance of psychoanalysis by highlighting the oedipal traces of desire. For Clough, ethnographic authority, and the distinct social worlds ethnographers authoritatively describe, unconsciously stem from (masculine) narratives of separation and identity.

Deconstructing Naturalism

The significance of psychoanalysis established, Clough proceeds to deconstruct Blumer's methodological writings. She argues that what operates oedipally to generate the separateness of male identity is reproduced in the unconscious separation of naturalistic objects from their authoritative (literally authored) sources. The unconscious separation of the author from a distinctly identified world of objects and activity reflexively distinguishes the author's identity. This reality-sustaining phallic function is everywhere, especially in Blumer's procedural vocabulary, reflecting what Clough calls the "cinematic realism" of his informing idiom. Needless to say, this would apply to the naturalists we described in Chapter 2, as well as to the objectifying practices of ethnomethodology and emotionalism. The phallic tone, Clough suggests, is characteristic of Blumer's treatise on doing "penetrating" participant observation:

> If for the researcher the purpose of participant observation is to test his own images deliberately, then the narration of the observer's struggles must demonstrate his moving from what Blumer describes as "the position of the outsider" in order to get "in close touch with the action and experiences of the people who are involved" [Blumer 1969] (p. 35). Thus the narration of the observer's struggle comes to be thematized in terms of getting in and getting out of close touch with the observed. (P. 41)

Referring to the following extract from Blumer's writing, Clough continues, arguing that Blumer's method talk preserves a separate and real (or masculine) field:

> The metaphor that I like is that of lifting the veils that obscure or hide what is going on. The task of scientific study is to lift the veils that cover the area of group life that one proposes to study. . . . The veils are lifted by getting close to the area and by digging deep into it through careful study. . . . This is not a simple matter of just approaching a given area and looking at it. It is a tough job requiring a high order of careful and honest probing. . . . It is not a "soft" study (Blumer 1969, p. 40). (P. 41)

Blumer's terminology—"lifting the veils," "cover the area," "getting close," "digging deep," "looking at," "honest probing"—serves to authoritatively deny the distinct reality it unconsciously constructs.

Clough concludes that Blumer's methodology for systematic and careful observation is highly eroticized. Participant observation, she argues, is centered in the oedipal tension between connectedness and separation. The methodology sustains itself by denying what it simultaneously desires, that is, a highly proximate world to penetrate and probe. In the final analysis, Clough explains:

> The narration of participant observation thus turns from the researcher's own struggle with his own images to focus on his struggle against the resistance that the empirical world seemingly offers. . . . What is first understood as the researcher's struggle with his imaging is displaced on to the spectacle itself. Now it is the spectacle that is difficult, that is resistant to penetration. The spectacle now threatens with castration, so that what comes to motivate participant observation is the desire to get as close as possible to what is observed without getting lost in it, without becoming completely absorbed in what is to be made visible. . . . Thus,

in its narration, participant observation becomes eroticized with the anxiety and excitement of the sexual scenarios of vision. (P. 41)

Clough's postmodernism leads her to challenge the underpinnings of accepted realities by looking deeply inward into the unconscious for their foundations rather than outward, into the "real" world. From her perspective, a representational dilemma emerges with the realization that it is the "feminine threat of castration and (re)absorption"—tantamount to going epistemologically native—that sustains the distinct authority of the real for ethnography, as much as the real "obdurately" fends for itself. The threat of connectedness challenges Blumer and other naturalists as participant observers. In effect, the tradition of ethnography neglects the feminine (the connection of authority with description and writing) in order to preserve the masculine (the separate and distinct subject matter of the field).

CONFRONTING THE CRISIS OF REPRESENTATION

The "crisis of representation" to which Clough and others refer is gaining momentum as postmodernist sensibilities infiltrate the social sciences. It emanates from postmodernists' deep skepticism about reality. For Baudrillard, reality yields to the hyperreal. Lyotard (1984) offers a different slant, contending that the aim of postmodernist commentary and description "is not to supply reality, but to invent allusions to the conceivable which cannot be presented" (p. 81). Still others argue that reality is neither the object nor the cause of scientific description but is instead its consequence (Latour and Woolgar 1979). The most radical postmodernists even doubt the need for a *conception* of reality (Rosenau 1992).

This view clearly imperils the social sciences. If there are "no independently identifiable, real-world referents to which the language of social description is cemented" (Gergen 1986, p. 143), scientific description, like any other account of reality, amounts only and entirely to representation. In the absence of an independent reality, all representation refers to other representations; it can never be authentic (Baudrillard 1981). In postmodernism, with reality reduced to linguistic convention (Eagleton 1983), representation is relative and arbitrary—linguistically reflective rather than reality related. Signs "no longer represent anything and no longer have their equivalent in reality" (Baudrillard 1983b, p. 19).

Consequently, there is no substantial basis for distinguishing true from false in the postmodernist scheme of things. And there is no content to experience apart from the rhetoric of representation. Rhetoric creates the world that it is supposed to be merely representing; representation produces the truths it supposedly reflects (Ryan 1988). At the same time, however, the modern commonsense belief in an objective world helps conceal the constitutive power of representation. For postmodernists, modern representation promotes deception, desecration, and domination:

It signals distortion; it assumes unconscious rules governing relationships. It concretizes, finalizes, and excludes complexity. . . . representation is fraudulent, perverse, artificial, mechanical, deceptive, incomplete, misleading, insufficient, wholly inadequate for the post-modern age. (Rosenau 1992, pp. 94–95)

If everything is representational rhetoric, where does that leave qualitative inquiry and its authoritative texts? Many qualitative researchers are troubled, some even paralyzed, by questions regarding just what their own texts represent. In postmodernism, the *how* question for qualitative inquiry must focus on the researcher's method talk as it relates to the production of social reality. Advanced systematically, this has resulted in what might be called the "ethnography of argument" (Woolgar and Pawluch 1985). It has even turned qualitative inquiry toward the "ethnography of ethnography" (Van Maanen 1995a)—re-presentations of others' representations (Marcus 1994).

Of course, the postmodern impulse has not captivated everyone; indeed, it remains on the margins of qualitative sociology and in the dungeons of positivist analysis. Many are not convinced of the constitutive hegemony of representation. For the most part, qualitative researchers remain committed to objectivist description in one way or another. According to Dmitri Shalin (1993), undue concern with the crisis of representation risks the loss of reality altogether. It portends the transformation of social experience into a postmodern field of nothing but texts, with the likelihood of that field turning into yet another field of texts, where the real is less grounded in lived experience than embedded in the written page.

Developing a Reflexive Sensitivity

This dire appraisal is not universal, however. George Marcus (1994), for example, points out that studying a field of representations is not necessarily a diversion from fieldwork, but rather an exploration of consummate social facts that might help us better understand the assumptions and practices underpinning what comes to pass for knowledge. Generally agreeing, others, like Schneider (1991), are sensitive to the call for reflexively examining the representational practices of the social sciences, but remain concerned about the consequences for empirical description. Geertz (1988) has observed the effects of these concerns on ethnographic writing, but has made it a point not to succumb to the anxieties.

Commenting on the "nervous present," Geertz contrasts the "scene-setting, task-describing, self-presenting opening pages" of two epistemologically distinct ethnographies. One, Raymond Firth's book *We, the Tikopia*, published in 1936, is written with classic authorial presence. The other, Loring Danforth's book *The Death Rituals of Rural Greece*, which appeared in 1982, is decidedly more self-conscious. Compare the first paragraph of Firth's opening chapter, "In Primitive Polynesia," with the start of Danforth's introduction, called "Self and Other." The difference in tone is remarkable:

We, the Tikopia

In the cool of the early morning, just before sunrise, the bow of the *Southern Cross* headed towards the eastern horizon, on which a tiny dark blue outline was faintly visible. Slowly it grew into a rugged mountain mass, standing up sheer from the ocean; then as we approached within a few miles it revealed around its base a narrow ring of low, flat land, thick with vegetation. The sullen grey day with its lowering clouds strengthened my grim impression of a solitary peak, wild and stormy, upthrust in the waste of waters. (Quoted in Geertz 1988, p. 11)

The Death Rituals of Rural Greece

Anthropology inevitably involves an encounter with the Other. All too often, however, the ethnographic distance that separates the reader of anthropological texts and the anthropologist himself from the Other is rigidly maintained and at times even artificially exaggerated. In many cases this distancing leads to an exclusive focus on the Other as primitive, bizarre, and erotic. The gap between a familiar "we" and an exotic "they" is a major obstacle to a meaningful understanding of the Other, an obstacle that can only be overcome through some form of participation in the world of the Other. (Quoted in Geertz 1988, p. 14)

The authorial presence of Firth's writing recalls the naturalism of *Street Corner Society, Tally's Corner,* and *A Place on the Corner.* Firth literally takes us "there" aboard the *Southern Cross.* As the ship nears the beach, we come face-to-face with the native environs and inhabitants. Echoing Whyte, Liebow, and Anderson, Firth is about to open "their world" to view and tell "their story." Secure in his mission and only musing about the complexities of what he is about to encounter, Firth asks, "I wondered how such turbulent human material could ever be induced to submit to scientific study" (quoted in Geertz 1988, p. 12). In contrast, Danforth echoes the representational questions that, for him, now overshadow anthropology. His concern over how to write the Other lurks at the very heart of the possibility of doing ethnography and writing the real.

Undaunted, Geertz argues that the issue of "being there," as he puts it, is perhaps not so new. It has been a rhetorical problem of ethnography from the start, but we have never been as self-conscious about it. He compares the rhetorical styles of "being there" of four quite different anthropologists—Claude Levi-Strauss, Edward Evans-Pritchard, Bronislaw Malinowski, and Ruth Benedict—who hail from distinct generations. The crisis of representation that now radicalizes the *how* question, it would seem, has been an enduring hurdle of transforming the ethnographer's actual presence in the field into authorial presence.

Geertz recognizes that this barrier, while not necessarily insurmountable, makes us more critically aware of the constitutive relation between method talk and social reality. As Geertz explains, "The advantage of shifting at least part of our attention from the fascinations of field work which have held us so long in thrall, to those of writing is not only that this difficulty will become more clearly understood, but also that we shall learn to read with a more percipient eye" (p. 24).

A Growing Appreciation for Rhetoric

Van Maanen, a sociological ethnographer, is equally optimistic. Succinctly stated, the back cover of his book, *Tales of the Field* (1988) reads:

Once upon a time ethnographers returning from the field simply sat down, shuffled their note cards, and wrote up their descriptions of the exotic and quaint customs they had observed. Today scholars in all disciplines are realizing that *how* their research is presented is at least as important as *what* is presented. Questions of voice, style and audience—the classic issues of rhetoric—have come to the forefront in academic circles. (Emphasis in original)

Van Maanen argues that a growing recognition of the place of rhetoric in representation of all kinds, including ethnography, unshackles traditional forms of writing, providing a basis for experimentation in representing worlds of experience and thus reflexively preserving common threads with other qualitative research idioms. For example, it doesn't trivialize naturalistic accounts of street corner life if we know that naturalists convince us of reality as much by *how* they present their stories as by *what* they convey. Rather, it tells us that "being there" in "their world" in order to convey "their story" is one among many compelling means of writing culture.

Van Maanen focuses on authorial presence in his own writing, distinguishing two primary narrative styles whose tales vary in how the author insinuates himself or herself into the text. The "realist tale" is cool, self-assured, and objective. "Their story" is center stage. When the realist author chooses to take account of the personal trials and tribulations of the ethnographer in the field, details are relegated to a methodological appendix. Consider our classic naturalist texts in this regard. If Whyte is present at all in the text proper, it is mostly as a bystander, only occasionally as an active participant in the action. The overall sense of the ethnography is that the reality of corner life is derived from a separate and distinct locale, not from the author's attempts at documentation. Liebow and Anderson give us the same sense.

In contrast, what Van Maanen calls the "confessional tale" is suffused with concern over how the author has figured in the telling of "their story." While not necessarily empirically nihilistic, it is nonetheless a self-absorbed account that communicates as much about how the ethnographer contends with his informants and manages his presence in the field as it presents a picture of "their world." Douglas's (1985) account of creative interviewing, for example, shows confessional self-absorption reaching agonizing heights.

Geertz and Van Maanen provide few details about how ethnographic writing might account for the author's construction of his or her subjects and their lives. Paul Atkinson (1990), however, takes us full tilt into rhetorical territory. Atkinson situates his analysis in two ways. First, he points to qualitative researchers' growing awareness of the constitutive relation between the language of analysis and social reality: "Sociologists have become increasingly sensitive to the cultural significance of spoken and written accounts, texts, and the nature of 'discourse' in the production and reproduction of social forms" (p. 6). While theoretical perspectives have varied, he argues, the reflexivity of texts increasingly preoccupies researchers. They now pay systematic attention to the way texts of all kinds, from media images to methodological writing and ethnographies, construct the realities they otherwise presume to represent.

Second, like Denzin, Geertz, and Van Maanen, Atkinson (1992) denies that representational matters necessarily cripple social science. He argues instead that all description is rhetorical, including all forms of scientific description:

The position I adopt . . . will recognize that our methods of reading and writing in ethnography are thoroughly conventional and contrived; it will endorse the view that our social-scientific texts draw on the same conventions as other literary forms, including fictional types; but it will find no reason for anxiety on that score. Many of the cherished parallels and contrasts with "science" are totally misleading. First, the texts of the natural sciences are as rhetorical as any other. . . . Secondly, the recognition that all human inquiry and reportage are essentially the same is not a recipe for nihilism or a loss of scholarly standards. (P. 3)

Atkinson maintains that this provides greater critical consciousness, an awareness of the diverse and complex relation that languages of analysis have with what they are meant to represent. Situated as social science is between literature and natural science (Lepenies 1988), its representational practices necessarily straddle the constructive impulses of literature and the objectifying tendencies of natural science. To take notice of this, Atkinson argues, is to enrich the interpretation of the experiences and worlds social scientists aim to understand.

Atkinson (1990) turns to ethnographic texts as a field within which to document rhetorical practices. To illustrate "textual constructions of reality," Atkinson asks us to consider the distancing devices used by ethnographers to separate their own writing from what they write about. The devices are not unique to ethnography, but apply to objectifying accounts of various kinds. As far as ethnography is concerned, the devices deflect the reader from attending to the possibility that ethnographic writing itself "writes" culture, as the title of Clifford and Marcus's (1986) edited volume on the poetics and politics of ethnography suggests.

One distancing device is the use of exemplary extracts from informants' comments or conversations. While much ethnographic writing is a multifaceted description of events and interactions observed in the field, such as accounts of gang member interactions in Cornerville, the ethnographer regularly supplements and rhetorically confirms his or her descriptions with exemplary extracts. In a manner likened to Ricca Edmondson's (1984) characterization of "rhetorical induction," the extracts literally set off and, in effect, separate the ethnographer's commentary from concrete instances of the lived (actual) data that the ethnographer's commentary, and the ethnography as a whole, are taken to be about. Atkinson (1990) explains that "the text [thereby] persuades in so far as the reader concurs or acquiesces in the dialogue between the exemplar and the commentary, and draws on the exemplar so as to find the commentary adequately plausible" (p. 83).

Atkinson describes a related device that capitalizes on a distinction Emile Benveniste (1970) makes in differentiating *histoire* and *discours*. *Histoire* refers to the story that a text deals with, that is, the actions and events that are commented upon in the text. In the case of qualitative research, the story (*histoire*) ostensibly is what field notes and in-depth interviews are about. On the other hand, *discours*, or narration, presupposes a narrator and refers to the narrator's or author's commentary on the story.

While postmodern sensibilities question this distinction, the distinction nonetheless can be a persuasive rhetorical device. Atkinson points out that shifts between *histoire* and *discours* in ethnographic writing are commonly marked by changes in tense. What is referred to as the "ethnographic present" often marks *discours,* while *histoire*, or the story, is told in the past tense. Atkinson uses a passage from *Tally's Corner* to illustrate, which we quote in part. Note the change in tense in the second sentence of the second paragraph extracted below. This serves to persuade the reader that the subjects and their accounts are something separate and distinct from the author's ethnography, providing an analytic distance that underscores the researcher's authority:

The men had their reasons. Some had separated from their wives and children and did not know their children were hospitalized. Others knew but couldn't or wouldn't make it. Richard had intended going but if something came up, he would probably go tomorrow, and anyway, he never did like being in a hospital, not even to visit someone else.

But whether the fathers were living with their children or not, the result was the same: there were no men visiting the children in Ward E. This absence of the father is one of the chief characteristics of the father-child relationship. The father-child relationship, however, is not the same for all streetcorner fathers, nor does a given relationship necessarily remain constant over time. (Liebow 1967, pp. 72–73, quoted in Atkinson 1990, p. 98)

Atkinson goes on to discuss and illustrate several other rhetorical devices, such as the use of "characterization." For instance, "memorable characters" such as Whyte's Doc and Liebow's Tally Jackson anchor the reader's attention to a story in a way that a flatter characterization would not. Such devices persuade by textually highlighting "their world," keeping it open to view and distinct from what writing otherwise does to separate it from itself.

POSTMODERNISTIC REPRESENTATION

The notion that representation is more rhetorical than reportorial can lead us to both nihilism and guarded optimism. Skeptical postmodernists, for example, suggest that because "truth" is necessarily relativized, if not impossible, then social scientific reports should enjoy no special privilege over any other set of accounts (see Schneider 1991). Atkinson (1990), on the other hand, is more positive. Claiming that social science relies upon the same authorizing devices that support other discourses, he argues that social scientists, especially qualitative researchers, should not be so self-conscious or modest in relation to representational issues that they abandon their work of describing lived experience and social worlds. He doesn't ignore the crisis of representation, but he believes that it shouldn't inhibit social scientific inquiry.

Others have been more radical in addressing representational dilemmas. One response comes in the form of unconventional modes of representation that acknowledge postmodernist concerns while still trying to sustain the conventional goal of empirically based description. Steve Woolgar (1988, 1989a, 1989b), Schneider (1991), and others, for example, have experimented with textual forms in which multiple voices both present and "interrogate" the emerging narrative. These experiments suggest that by reflexively examining representational practices at the same time that we rely upon them, we might better understand how authoritative texts are constituted. In the process, we might see how textual authority is rendered "transparent"—its sources made invisible—by practices that are typically cast as "objective" or "neutral" tools for analysis or reporting.

Other encouraging responses to the postmodernist critique involve even more radical textual forms—"messy texts" as Marcus (1994) calls them (also see Krieger 1979, 1983; Richardson 1990, 1991; Richardson and Lockridge 1991; Paget 1995). Laurel Richardson (1992), for example, self-consciously uses poetry as a means of representing lived experience. In one particularly interesting project, she writes a poem to convey the life story of one of her interview respondents, an unwed mother named Louisa May. Richardson keeps the crisis of representation at bay by making use of, not despairing over, the epistemological reflexivity that a postmodernist per- spective entails.

Richardson is concerned that a simple transcript of Louisa May's story might not faithfully represent its lived qualities, particularly its "core" tone. She also worries about how the sociological reader relates to the story being told. According to Richardson, a sociologist who reads the transcript of the life story is likely to view it as "data," searching for "background variables" to explain what Louisa May says and does. Such a reading would, inadvertently perhaps, stereotypically construct a sociological subject in the transcripts, taking away from Louisa May's own version of her life.

As a result, and after careful preparation, Richardson presents Louisa May's story by reconfiguring the transcript into a poem. Richardson explains her motivation:

> I transcribed the tape [of Louisa May's interview] into 36 pages of text and then fashioned that text into a three-page poem, using only her words, her tone, and her diction. . . . For so- ciological readers, the poem may seem to omit "data" that they want to know. But this is Louisa May's narrative, not the sociologist's. She does not choose, for example, to talk about her educational level or her employment. The questions the poem raises for readers about Louisa May thus reflect their own particular subtexts, not universal texts. If they wonder, for example, how Louisa May supports herself, are they tapping into stereotypes about "unwed mothers"? If they feel they cannot understand her unless they know about her schooling, are they telling us something about their own relationship to education, its meaning in their own lives? More generally, have the concepts of sociology been so reified that even interpretivists [among whom Richardson would presumably be counted] cannot believe they "know" about a person's life without refracting it through a sociologically prescribed lens? (Pp. 126–27)

Ultimately, Richardson argues that poetry provides a basis for reading and hearing Louisa May's story that other forms might preclude because the literary form is de- cidedly interpretive and relatively open to understandings grounded in the subject's perspective, not the sociologist's.

Richardson wants to be faithful to, or at the very least, be more open to diverse interpretations of Louisa May's life. Regarding the transcript of Louisa May's in- terview, the initial question for Richardson was, should the transcription be turned into substantive sociology? Richardson (1992) describes how she resolved the dilemma, leading her to use poetry as a means of conveying that which she figured sociological writing could not capture (also see Gubrium 1988b):

> About this time, a part of me that I had suppressed for more than eight years demanded attention: the part that writes poetry. Writing poetry is emotionally preoccupying; it opens up unexpected, shadow places in my self. As a kind of time-saving/snaring-two-birds-with- one-net strategy, I decided to fashion material from an unmarried mother interview [Louisa May] into a poem. That, I thought, would get me started . . . acknowledge my need for po- etry/play, and maybe—just maybe—provide a new strategy for resolving those horrid post- modernist writing dilemmas. (P. 131)

Richardson goes on to discuss the personal consequences of this decision. As she notes, while the task of presenting Louisa May's story is daunting, it provides an opportunity to respond to both the veridical challenges of positivism and the "hor- rid" representational hurdles of postmodernism:

Louisa May brings me to different sites and allows me to see familiar sites in new ways. Disillusionment is one of the outcomes. When, for example, a symbolic interactionist conventioneer asks me to "prove" Louisa May exists by showing him the transcript of my interview (as if transcripts were real), or when my feminist postmodernist reading group wants to know about the "validity" of the poem, I experience deeply the hold of positivism on even those I consider my allies, my intellectual companions. In the chasm, I experience isolation, alienation, and freedom, exhilaration. I want to record what they are saying; I want to do fieldwork on them. Science them. My romanticized vision of a postmodernist sociology shaken, I seek alternative sites for sharing sociology. Louisa May's life takes me to poetry bars, literature conventions, women's studies classes, social work spaces, and policy making settings. (Pp. 135–36)

Richardson's writing certainly has elements of Van Maanen's (1988) "confessional tale;" her account is self-revelatory and, for that reason, can be viewed as a kind of "personal sociology" that "understandably" leads to a professional career of related work (Higgins and Johnson 1988). Her responses also place her among those (as described in Chapter 4) who self-consciously attempt to plumb the emotional depths of experience. But, significantly, Richardson is pointing to something more, bearing directly on the crisis of representation. Her own writing experience is not just a personal field of concern, informing the overall effort but kept scrupulously separate from it in the final analysis. Rather, Richardson actually blends her own writing desires and experience with her respondent's narrative, to produce what she believes to be a new, more open mode of representation. Further, she believes that a merely accurate transcript would literally misrepresent experience sociologically. Richardson necessarily must write differently, poetically. Her project demands a presentation that would less determinantly lead us to read Louisa May's story.

Here again, method talk is telling. Every statement of "fact" about Louisa May's story is written in relation both to Richardson's own developing self-understanding and to her understanding of the "Other," who in this case is Louisa May. Richardson affirmatively resolves the crisis of representation by simultaneously, now necessarily, writing herself along with the Other. Poetry, she argues, permits this, as it quintessentially implicates its subjects, author, and the reader. Good, conventional sociological writing, in this context, unfortunately can only be about its subject matter. Richardson concludes:

Representing the sociological as poetry is one way of decentering the unreflexive "self" to create a position for experiencing the self as a sociological knower/constructor—not just talking about it, but doing it. In writing the Other, we can re(write) the Self. That is the moral of this story. (P. 136)

PART II

Renewing the Language

CHAPTER 6

Analytic Choices

Reflecting on the idioms of qualitative inquiry—naturalism, ethnomethodology, emotionalism, and postmodernism—we can see how each is fashioned to address its own sorts of questions, specify different objects of inquiry, and define contrasting fields of study. Sometimes, the approaches take exception to one another. Postmodernism can be the most aggressive and purposeful in this regard, virtually defying, even denying, the others, and staking out a radically different analytic space in relation to empirical "reality." While postmodernism does suggest intriguing new fields for exploration, and entices us with the charms of narrative invention, it is also shadowed by the specter of an empirical nihilism that threatens to undermine, if not eradicate, the other idioms. Indeed, skeptical postmodernism challenges even the possibility of empirical research as we have come to know it.

Preferring a more affirmative stance, we are loath to accept this as the ultimate or inevitable upshot of postmodernism and the crisis of representation. We believe that postmodernism contributes most significantly to qualitative inquiry by spurring researchers to critically examine their methodological assumptions and choices with an eye to expanding their own epistemological and empirical horizons. This, of course, is one of the principal objectives of this book, but we don't want to let the postmodernist critique run amuck, overwhelming an appreciation of its alternatives. Instead, we have positioned ourselves to more clearly see and hear the epistemological challenges of the various idioms at work. With the benefit of hindsight we now take up these challenges by considering the analytic choices entailed in answering the question: Where does qualitative inquiry go from here?

WHERE DO WE GO FROM HERE?

Let's reconsider the epigram that introduced Chapter 1. Perhaps reality doesn't have a *single* idiom in which it prefers to be described as much as it offers *choices* among idioms for rendering its description. Taking this to be the case, we see a substantial challenge for qualitative inquiry in how to deal with the myriad options that researchers confront as they define their projects and select their methods. The choices virtually guide how reality will speak to its observers.

With naturalistic, ethnomethodological, emotionalist, and postmodern idioms at their disposal, qualitative researchers make reality-shaping choices at every turn. Yet, too often they fail to consider the ramifications of these choices. Each approach—the use of each analytic vocabulary—offers both incentives and risks. Postmodernism, especially, points out how deeply research strategies are implicated in the production of findings, leaving significant epistemological questions to emerge in the process: What, if anything, is left for qualitative inquiry? How can qualitative method respond to the crisis of representation? And, if it survives the myriad challenges, how might it deal with the postmodern condition? Analytic choices and methodological solutions issue from the range of possible answers to each question.

In its skeptical form, postmodernism disturbs traditional qualitative researchers. Of course, for some, the crisis of representation is overblown, nothing to fret about as long as one sustains a pervasively realist orientation. As we saw in Chapter 5, others acknowledge the crisis, but try to maintain their focus on a reality that is something more than rampant, unfettered representation. For them, an empirical world remains to be described, but it needs to be re-apprehended in new form. At the same time, they seem to admit that the researcher's representational machinery might need to be tuned up, if not retooled. In their respective fashions, each of the analysts we discussed in Chapter 5 affirms a postmodern possibility for qualitative inquiry.

Richardson (1990), for example, tells us that the self-consciousness deriving from postmodernism unshackles the procedures we use to represent that world, encouraging, even celebrating, representational diversity and innovation. She believes we can avert representational crises and self-indulgent wallowing in epistemological doubt by adopting new textual forms of expression and taking advantage of qualitative method's open empirical horizons. Atkinson (1990, 1992) chooses a different path in reassuring us that qualitative inquiry need not relinquish the possibility of empirical description. He tells us to cultivate a reflexive awareness and be open to alternative ways of writing and reading texts, but not to abandon qualitative research just because it relies on rhetorical presentation. He specifically warns us not to "flock towards alternative literary modes" (1990, p. 180) in an unprincipled rush towards postmodern "cleverness and pretension."[1]

This, of course, alludes to the popular conviction that postmodernism is merely an intellectual fad. Many would add that it is also counterproductive, leaving systematic inquiry with no ground to stand on. Marcus (1994, p. 573) comments, for example, that qualitative social scientists have tended to skirt the postmodernist debate for fear of yielding to what they see as postmodernism's "excessive skepticism" and "paralyzing relativism"—out of apprehension about crossing the limits beyond which "anything goes." Others resist on the grounds that unfettered reflexivity misplaces the social sciences' attention, diverting it away from subjects and subject matter and onto the researcher. This sentiment is amusingly, yet aptly, projected in an apocryphal tale attributed to anthropologist Marshall Sahlins. Quoted by Judith Stacey (1990, p. 232), Sahlins recounts an exchange between a postmodernist field-worker and his native Fijian informant: "But as the Fijian said to the New Ethnographer, 'That's enough talking about you; let's talk about me.'"

Joel Best (1995) is far from amused by postmodernism; he vehemently denounces it. Striking a contrast with Robert Park's naturalist admonition to get out into the streets to see what's going on in the world, Best writes:

Today, the postmodernist slogan might be: "out of the streets, into the armchairs." After all, if the analyst inevitably shapes the analysis, the reasoning goes, we should focus our attention, not on the subject of analysis, but on the analytic act. The focus shifts from social life to the analyst's self, a shift which is self-centered, self-congratulatory, and self-indulgent. Anything—but especially anything personal—is grist for the postmodernist mill—sexual memories, reactions to movies or fast-food restaurants, recollections of life's disappointments. All musings are equally worthy. All styles are equally legitimate. . . . When we adopt the postmodernist fad, we surrender our ability to do what we have always done best [naturalistically oriented qualitative research], in return for some new jargon. It's a bad trade. . . . No doubt we can always call our assumptions into question, we can always seek to improve on what we do. But there is a difference between doubt as constructive criticism and doubt for the sake of academic gamesmanship. [Qualitative researchers] ought to stop playing games, and get on with their work. (Pp. 128–30)

Clearly, Best is caricaturing postmodernism, and pointedly needling postmodernists. Still, his diatribe reflects a common discomfort, if not disillusionment, with the reflexive demands that postmodernist sensibilities place on qualitative inquiry. More importantly, like Sahlins, Best highlights the displacement of the analyst's focus, which postmodernists transfer from the "real" world onto signs, images, representations, and textual practices. To be sure, many of the "old guard" still care about what the empirical world is like and what their informants have to say.

In many respects, we are part of that "old guard." In writing this book, we retain some quite "modernist" commitments to empirical description. At the same time, however, we are intrigued by many of the postmodernist questions and excited by the prospect of describing the postmodern condition. Postmodernism opens up new fields (e.g., Denzin's cinematic field or Clough's field of desire) and offers fresh ways of expressing findings in unorthodox modalities arguably more faithful to their phenomena. And reflexive sensitivity and an awareness of the roles occupied by authority and authorship in the production of knowledge invite us to examine our own claims as well as the claims of those we study.

But, while we appreciate Atkinson's reassurance of the ubiquity of scientific rhetoric, and admire the courage of those venturing into unconventional fields and inventive forms of representation, we find something compelling in both Sahlins's subtly chiding anecdote and Best's two-fisted indictment. Not only are we reluctant to fully embrace the unbridled relativism and "self"-ish orientation of skeptical postmodernism, but we don't want to give up on reality, so to speak. While we do not reject postmodernism out of hand, we do share Best's commitment to documenting the social world, to the possibility of empirically based description of everyday life. For us, this is the enduring stuff of qualitative inquiry. In the wake of postmodernism, the challenge lies in cultivating these objectives in light of new epistemological questions and analytic sensibilities.

But the postmodernist crisis of representation is not the only hurdle. In the preceding chapters, we have presented what might be read as an idiomatic history of the development of qualitative method. One might infer a progressive trajectory of epistemological concerns extending from naturalism towards postmodernism. As we noted at the start, this is *not* our intention. Qualitative inquiry has become increasingly self-conscious with the development of ethnomethodology, emotionalism, and postmodernism, but that does not necessarily imply that each of the idioms that we

reviewed has somehow successively eclipsed, obviated, or rendered the others ob-
solete or surpassed them in terms of analytic sensitivity or sophistication. Instead,
we are now aware that each idiom offers its own groundings, assumptions, topics,
and analytic machinery that comprise distinct descriptive projects. Each asks and
answers its own kinds of questions. Increased self-consciousness makes researchers
more inclined to examine their presuppositions and the foundations of their analyses, but self-consciousness alone is not the mark of a useful analytic paradigm. If
we resist applying some sort of implicit hierarchy or developmental model to the
various research idioms, we can approach them in terms of the choices they offer
concerning how we might view the world. These are choices about the very possibilities of what the world might look like when apprehended by way of a distinctive analytic stance and vocabulary.

It is clear that the various qualitative research idioms create analytic tensions in
relation to one another. Following their own commitment to diversity, qualitative
researchers should embrace and exploit—but not necessarily try to eliminate—these
tensions. For example, rather than merely asking what results if one postmod-
ernistically deconstructs naturalism's practices of realistic description, one could
also ask what the postmodern world might look like, approached more naturalistically.[2] Alternatively, instead of simply declaring ethnomethodology to be insensi-
tive to the emotional side of experience, one might explore the situated accomplishment of emotional inner life (as we did at the end of Chapter 4).

Each of the qualitative idioms raises important questions and pursues cogent answers in its own terms, on its own grounds. Each idiom sustains its distinctive issues and questions, and transforms, or fails to recognize, the fundamental questions
of the other approaches. Each is likely to "unravel" when held up to the assumptions of the others. Nevertheless, this is not an argument for giving up on qualitative inquiry as much as it is a complication that in many ways mirrors the cultural
representations of social life.

Qualitative researchers have always tolerated complexity. The dilemmas and tensions deriving from increasingly divergent research idioms test this traditional resolve. An affirmative approach to these tensions provides new opportunities to understand how the empirical world is implicated in these tensions, how it provokes
the development of alternate approaches, and how reality inevitably remains elu-
sive within the separate boundaries of a discipline, perspective, or idiom. There is
far too much of value in each of these traditions, even as they antagonize one another, to merely abandon them to the radical bugaboos of postmodernism, or to insist upon idiomatic purity. Instead, we might reinvigorate qualitative inquiry by taking notice and making use of the sources of analytic tension among the idioms, and
between the idioms and the empirical world.

In part, the tensions emerge because each approach is especially well-suited to
examine and portray particular senses of everyday reality. This translates into distinctive and contrasting analytic sensitivities. The idioms are not tools for uncovering various aspects of reality; they are not the machinery of methodological trian-
gulation (see Denzin 1989b). Rather, they are culturally recognizable approaches
for distinctively constituting realities and rendering them visible. As such, each approach can flirt with its own epistemological and empirical hazards. But the situation is not inevitably daunting. Collisions between idioms need not be destructive;

cultural self-consciousness is not necessarily immobilizing. Internal strain can signal the opportunity for transformation and revitalization. The friction releases energy, which can be as invigorating as it is destructive. Considered affirmatively, the various tensions and the sites of idiomatic collision may constitute "growth plates" (Pollner 1993) for the sociological imagination as well as for the continued development of qualitative inquiry. Let us consider how these diverse tensions, risks, and sensitivities are implicated in the further development of qualitative inquiry.

AT THE LIVED BORDER OF REALITY AND REPRESENTATION

Wolf Lepenies (1988) maintains that sociology grew out of the dilemmas of depicting industrial society in the nineteenth century. It emerged to occupy an analytic space between positivist scientific description and literary representation. Born between science and literature, sociology continues to draw its inspiration, but also derives its lament, from this peculiar placement. The discipline's "human interests" are quite paradoxical at times, as sociology alternately strives for explanation and control, on the one hand, and for meaning and empathy, on the other. At times, it is both a source of social enlightenment and a critic of social order (cf. Habermas 1971). Located as it is, sociology is enduringly confronted with epistemological crosscurrents, continuously raising issues of representational practice, both its own and that indigenous to the world it seeks to represent.

Qualitative inquiry is especially sensitive to representational matters because of its unique position at the *lived border* of reality and representation. By "lived," we mean the actual locations within the lifeworld where those things, events, and circumstances that people experience are meaningfully described and conveyed, to one's self as well as to others. Being at this lived border, qualitative inquiry assumes a distinctive vantage point from which to observe how actors "in the world" both participate in and re-present experience.

For us to conceptualize a border between reality and representation implies an empirical distinction between the two. It presupposes the possibility of an analytic footing existing in some space apart from either one, which allows for sightings of, and at, the border. It is our position that a world of *possible* things—that is, objects, events, experience, and the like—exists prior to its mediation by signs and signs of signs. But this world requires representation for it to take the shapes in which we recognize it, for example as obdurate or as invariable. It is at the lived border of reality and representation that meaning is attached to raw materials to make the "things" of experience. Interpretation makes reality come alive for us; interpretive work at the border constitutes social reality, producing what we apprehend and treat as meaningfully real. Each of the qualitative research idioms we have discussed focuses on this border activity, but each also distinguishes the border in its own fashion, locating meaning differently in relation to where it situates itself.

The special sensitivities of the various approaches are heightened because qualitative inquiry demands analytic proximity to the lived border. In one way or another, qualitative researchers characteristically locate their work—even their work lives—there. The competing goals of explanation and control versus meaning and understanding are not just distant epistemological options or expressions of contrasting sociological interests, but also are immediate practical concerns. The ethnographer who aims for scientific explanation, for example, may personally encounter fluid and complex situations and meanings that will challenge his ability to offer detached and "objective" accounts. The in-depth interviewer may organize her research around particular hypotheses, but her respondents' narratives can offer understandings or "hypotheses" of their own that do not accord well with the interviewer's preliminary conjectures or the interview schedule's format or content. In that regard, we might say that the lived world of experience doesn't hold to a strict schedule.

As we saw in Part I, there are differences among qualitative researchers in just how this engagement transpires at the lived border of reality and representation. At one extreme, some emotionalists feel obliged to become directly involved in their subjects' lives as a way of establishing grounds for mutual and deep disclosure. For others, conveying experience means reenacting it. Less deeply personal, the naturalists and ethnomethodologists, respectively, attempt to "be there" in order to represent "their worlds" or try to document the naturally occurring ways that members constitute their realities in practice. In short, the approaches offer different takes on "border work."

The willingness of qualitative researchers to engage lived experience reflects their special sensitivities to representational matters precisely because qualitative research is a kind of lived border activity itself. Borders separate, but they may be more or less elastic, permeable, and visible. One's vantage point in relation to that border shapes what one might observe; being close to a border reduces the clarity of what, from a distance, seems distinct.[3] At a distance, objects, events, sentiments, and actions appear to be more solidly self-evident. Engaging lived experience at the border of reality and representation virtually incites issues relating to meaning, subjectivity, practice, and complexity.

Naturalism's Special Sensitivity

Consider the special sensitivity revealed in *Street Corner Society*. Representation is clearly an issue on the very first pages of the Introduction. While, earlier, we highlighted the message of these pages in procedural terms, there is also a lurking concern with how to convey Cornerville life. Should it be represented in terms of what it is "to the rest of the city," as a "mysterious, dangerous, and depressing area"? Will it be described as a "problem area"? Should its inhabitants be depicted as "undifferentiated members of 'the masses' " whose lives have no rules and whose world is bereft of order? Should the meanings and categories in the rest of the city be used to represent native Cornerville and the experience of its inhabitants?

Whyte's naturalistic aim is clear. He plans to stand at the lived border of Cornerville reality, observing and listening to the way its inhabitants represent that reality. He relies upon both his senses and the reportorial skill of his informants, letting these indigenous ethnographers show and tell him what life is like in their world. His decision to let their interpretations represent the reality of Cornerville suggests that what lies on their side of the lived border can be adequately conveyed if subjects are allowed to describe Cornerville life *on its own terms*. Consequently, Whyte's methods are not especially sensitive to the border per se. They acknowledge its existence but seek mostly to get beyond it to where reality is found. Whyte believes that his informants can figuratively cross the border, bringing with them reports that describe accurately and authentically what is on the other side. As a naturalist, he is especially attuned to the represented reality of the insider. While the accuracy of the insider's reports is never taken for granted, the *possibility* of authentic representation is not in question.

Ethnomethodology's Special Sensitivity

Ethnomethodology approaches the lived border differently. For example, Wieder's initial attempt to study "the" convict code brings him up against an ever-changing social entity-in-the-making. His brand of close ethnomethodological scrutiny of constitutive processes leads him to focus on *how* members of the halfway house community use the code to represent what they take to be the real life structures surrounding them. Ethnomethodology's special sensitivity allows Wieder to examine how the practical reality of the code is produced through members' interactions at the border between the experientially real and indigenous explanations of that reality. As Wieder participates in house activities, observing and documenting the ways the code is applied, he eschews his subjects' explanations as analytic resources, making them into his research topic. In a sense, he is looking at *members'* border activity, focusing on their representational methods. His aim is to demonstrate how, for members, each use of the code produces a practical sense that those events and actions to which the code applies are a separate and distinct reality, and an equally convincing sense that the code itself is real, taking the form of a set of rules governing conduct. His research questions relate to the interpretive work his subjects are doing. Treating residents' explanations as rhetorical accounts rather than informative reports, he asks: How is the code used *by residents* to explain conduct?

This means that Wieder must consider the issue of where the code stands in relation to the "reality" it ostensibly explains. How should *he* represent both the reality of the code and the reality of the everyday lives that the code serves to represent, to which the code ostensibly applies? At the lived intersection of the activities of everyday life and subjects' representations of those activities, the reality–representation border is blurred. The reality to which the code reportedly (by subjects) applies is not distinctly on one side and the code on the other. If anything, Wieder shows us that the code itself is a border-in-the-making.

The special sensitivity here lies in Wieder's ethnomethodological interest in the relation between language and reality, an interest ethnomethodology shares with postmodernism. Wieder's observations of rule use in the halfway house tell him that the code is a part of members' social reality in the house. The code constitutes (by way of rhetorical representation) the very circumstances that members contend it merely regulates. In a sense, the code stands on "reality's" side of the lived border from the members' point of view, but on the representational side from the ethnomethodological vantage point. (And, we might add, the ethnomethodologist's description of the code stands as one more idiomatic representation of the border in its own right.)

Emotionalism's Special Sensitivity

Emotionalism's special sensitivity also derives from a lived border engagement. From its perspective, reality is hidden from plain view. The lived border between reality and representation is characteristically strewn with cognitive hurdles. Because the reality of the passions is deep and mysterious, researchers exploring for the "core" facts of life must get beyond mere linguistic representations, wending their way, often wrenchingly, through a thicket of superficial signs and symbols. They must penetrate the border more deeply than even the naturalists might attempt, trying to existentially apprehend the real before representations have a chance to merely catalog it.

Plain words, the emotionalists figure, cannot convey, and may even conceal, what is inside experience. Even when the emotionalists tap into the deep wellsprings of reality, transporting their findings back across the representational border is as daunting a task for them as it is for their subjects. The analyst's own words and descriptions transform and transfigure—rationalize—what they have discovered on reality's side of the border. Reality, from this perspective, is often too "deep" or impassioned to be just reported, either by those who actually experience it or by analysts who attempt to systematically describe subjects' experiences.

For emotionalists, the lived border poses a communicative stumbling block, a translational dilemma. Words are hardly up to the task of conveying the "actual." Subjects cannot articulate what they feel or deeply know without help and empathy from the researcher. Even then, subjects' words may not adequately disclose what dwells within. Researchers cannot conventionally impart what they discover because academic textualization, according to emotionalists, strips experience of its life, passion, and vigor. For the emotionalist, the task is to find modes of communication that can truly, richly represent that which the researcher needs to convey. As if getting beyond the lived border were not enough, transporting the mysterious character of what is ultimately discovered poses this additional predicament. It's no wonder that the emotionalists, more than other qualitative researchers, have been attracted to, and encouraged by, postmodernism's openness to representational experimentation.

From the emotionalists' point of view, social researchers have traditionally employed a very sterile set of technical resources for conveying lived experience. What makes border activity problematic for emotionalists are the experientially limiting transmutations that inevitably occur when lived realities must be conveyed by linguistic, not lived, representation. As a result, emotionalists have turned to dramatic performance and poetry, among other innovative representational forms, in order to reenact or otherwise communicate the incommunicable. In doing so, they attempt to take their respective audiences and readers to areas of lived experience where plain words and mere prose fear to tread.

Postmodernism's Special Sensitivity

For skeptical postmodernism, as reality's "thingness" evaporates into myriad fleeting sensations, spinning into a free play of images, the putative border between reality and representation is overrun by signs. With no "there" to be studied and described, a field of representations is all that's left. Postmodernism's special sensitivity therefore focuses intensely on representational practice, typically on the practices of researchers themselves. Guidelines for inquiry are both problematized and problematic; for some the mere idea of conventional empirical method is anathema. For them, inquiry is guided only by the antirule of skeptical rigor; method-ologically, it is possible that "anything goes," as we noted earlier (see Rosenau 1992).

Less radical versions of postmodernism rely on research procedures resembling post-positivist or anti-positivist methods (see Denzin 1989b). These approaches look to feelings, personal experience, empathy, emotion, intuition, subjective judgment, imagination, creativity, and play for insight into the postmodern condition. At the most affirmative end of the continuum, postmodernism begins to resemble the more "realist" emotionalist idiom we have discussed, resurrecting and existentially af-firming the lived border of reality and representation. Skeptical postmodernists, on the other hand, staunchly deny the distinction and, with it, the possibility of formal method for knowing anything, including the deeply emotional (Rosenau 1992).

Inspired by literary studies, deconstructive analysis (see Derrida 1974; Norris 1982) may come the closest to being a systematized enactment of postmodernism, even a postmodernist method. It typically involves demystifying a text by pulling it apart to reveal its internal groundings and contradictions. Postmodernist decon-struction is concerned as much with what a text suppresses or silences as it is with what it makes explicit; it searches for what a text excludes, conceals, or marginal-izes. The goal is not to reveal "error," however, for this would admit to "truth" (Rosenau 1992). Instead, it aims to transform or redefine a text, undoing, reversing, displacing, and resituating the categories that constitute the text in the first place. Deconstruction seeks the tensions in texts, but does not try to resolve them. And ul-timately, the deconstructive text is itself subject to deconstruction (de Man 1986).

Deconstruction in particular, and postmodernism more generally, attempt to show how the lived border between reality and representation is an artifact of represen-tational practice, that the border ineluctably represents itself. Postmodernism's spe-cial sensitivity to representation places it close to sites of "border construction," and, in this respect, it resembles ethnomethodology. But the postmodernist sensitivity in-cludes the deconstruction of the lived border as a textual project, laying it open to inspection as an authoritative, or author's, construction. (This book and its inform-ing metaphors would be no exception.) Where ethnomethodology temporarily sus-pends belief in the real in order to focus on indigenous representational practices, postmodernism's skepticism can be more pervasive and lasting. It is especially cap-tivated by representation writ large, which is both its strength and its affliction.

ENDURING RISKS

Qualitative inquiry's engagement at the lived border of reality and representation yields diverse insights into the *whats* and *hows* of everyday life. But allowing the border to be radically deconstructed—dissolved completely—jeopardizes the sig-nificant empirical accomplishments of qualitative research and threatens to unravel its common threads. In the wake of postmodernism, the eclipse of the real by the representational is the enduring risk of qualitative inquiry's lived border engage-ment. With postmodern consciousness, the culturally prompted special sensitivities of the respective qualitative research idioms can be their own undoing.

The Risk for Naturalism

For naturalism, the risk is the decomposition of that which is culturally received as substantial. Naturalists like Whyte, Liebow, and Anderson, for example, observe and describe others' lives from "up close," but they still look across a divide between the empirical and the representational. Because they view the border as a mere *technical* hurdle that can be overcome through methodological skill and rigor, they lose sight of the border as a region where reality is constituted within representation. For them, reality has its own turf, and the naturalist's job is to accurately re-present what goes on there. This is feasible for them because representation, in principle, is considered to be a neutral process of recounting that which really is. Informants provide reality reports; they don't literally make things up (unless, or course, they are lying). Researchers then systematically and accurately convey those reports to wider audiences. Ultimately, the naturalist is interested in *what* informants say, in *what* subjects lives are like, and not in *how* those lives might be talked (represented) into being.

In naturalism, the real ascends to its rightful place of prominence; representation is merely its minion. Taken to its extreme, this consigns naturalistic inquiry to the status of something like systematic journalism; the researcher is charged with eliciting and organizing indigenous characterizations of the realities in question (see Becker 1958). The naturalist assumes no special *analytic* vantage point, but instead tries to get inside "their world" to take the member's perspective on reality's side of a lived border that is all but ignored. Representation, both members' and researchers,' is merely reportorial.

When Anderson tentatively introduces the constructionist idiom to his descriptions, we can see how the lived border becomes more salient, more perceptible. As he cautiously gazes across what begins to look like a divide between his subjects' reality and their constructions of it, he jeopardizes the security of his naturalistically apprehended reality, opening the possibility that all is not as solid as one might have believed. As immersed as he is in the life world of Jelly's patrons, Anderson nonetheless senses that this world is phenomenally one of their own making, not so much a "thing" given and containing subjects' conduct, as it is an artifact of their actions. His immersion sustains the insight, as well as the world under consideration. However, casting the insight in radical postmodern terms stands to "de-solidify" the world Anderson otherwise so forthrightly studies, giving cause to ask not only how the appearance of solidity is constructed at the lived border, but how naturalism is implicated in the process.

The Risk for Ethnomethodology

Ethnomethodologists turn the appearance of solidity into a full-blown project. Wieder, as we saw, finds that the code is less a stable set of directives for conduct than it is a variable way of using rules of conduct to account for interaction in the halfway house. If there is anything (any "thing") natural about this, it is the taken-for-grantedness of members' orientations and responses to the code. Members use and respond to the code in the natural attitude, in terms of the working assumption that the code is categorically distinct from the things and actions to which it is applied (Schutz 1970). The reality/representation border that members take for granted makes it altogether reasonable for them to account for their conduct in terms of the code's regulating function. Like other kinds of "common sense," their reasoning in relation to the code is practical, recognizing a distinction between the code on the one hand and the code's ordinary applications on the other. The ethnomethodologist, however, sees the conflation of the two, with reality and its representations being reflexively related.

Ethnomethodology risks reality's melting into representation as it focuses on the *hows* of reality construction at the expense of the *whats* of lived experience. Procedurally bracketing the *whats* of the code, Wieder documents how the code is used in the halfway house, providing us with a view of the code's role in socially organizing everyday life. Members' representational practices displace the separate realities they represent. The risk for ethnomethodological analysis is that in radical postmodern consciousness, procedural bracketing is catapulted into a full-fledged epistemological doubt. Unless ethnomethodologists keep a guarded eye on the real—as separate, distinct, and as analytically significant as the real's representational machinery—they stand to technically support the dissolution of the lived border by default. Because the *whats* of a particular code, say, as opposed to other codes, are technically undistinguished, the sociological message can become more about members' methods than about a concrete code (this particular code) as an object of experience. This serves to obscure the distinct, meaningful consequences that specific applications of methods have for members' lives.

Viewed in this way, Wieder's analysis becomes morally empty and might as well have been a study of *any* kind of rule use, in the halfway house or anyplace else. Consider, for example, what might have happened if Wieder focused exclusively on *how* concerns and swapped settings with Anderson in order to conduct an ethnomethodological study of the culture of respect and the code of honor that distinguishes Jelly's social environs. As an ethnomethodolgist, Wieder would have been intent on describing the indigenous accounting practices that he encountered. His attention would turn to the culture of respect as a set of interrelated accounts that socially organized life on the street corner. The analysis would likely parallel the description of the use of the convict code. But, apart from introductory remarks and the obligatory scene-setting passages, what would distinguish a description of the use of the culture of respect from a discussion of the use of the convict code?

With *usage* center stage, content is ushered to the wings. By focusing on the *hows* of indigenous accounting and explanation at the border of reality and representation, ethnomethodologists risk losing track of the *whats* that anchor matters of local concern, even as they describe the "seen but unnoticed" realm of constitutive practice. As the substantively meaningful aspects of local culture are shunted aside in order to concentrate on constitutive interactional activity, the content of lived experience becomes almost incidental. Setting substantive differences aside risks turning lived experience into a homogeneous world of members' representational practices, shorn of meaning and emotional content.

The Risk for Emotionalism

Quite to the contrary, emotionalists approach lived border engagements with a keen desire to explore the depths of lived experience. Standing at the border of words

and passions, at the frontier of what is difficult, if not impossible, to conventionally communicate, they are especially sensitive to the cognitive absorption of af-
fectivity. Emotionalists are vigilant that they not lose the impassioned and poignant
to the cool, phlegmatic domain of plain words. Their own absorption in the inner
passions, however, risks the objectification of emotion nearly to the point of reification. By peering so intently into subjects' interior lives and inner realms, emotionalists can blind themselves to the ways that subjects shape these spheres by way
of their own interpretive actions. If ethnomethodology loses touch with scenic presence as it tracks reality's constitutive process, emotionalism slights interpretive
agency and linguistic construction as it searches for affective foundations.

Nevertheless, and paradoxically, language and cognitive categories appear to
be necessary to depict a world that emotionalism casts as beyond words. As
Johnson (1975) reminded us when he decided not to write field notes while in the
throes of an emotionally charged moment, it is important to "retain a moral commitment to the observations." As he explained, "To observe sociologically means
that one *deliberately cedes* experiencing the things in themselves to the members
of the setting; observation entails seeing phenomena as 'exhibits' of the things in
themselves" (p. 159). Exhibits call for words and representation; they are not realities in their own right. The result is that emotionalists sustain the lived border
of reality and representation for sociological reasons—that is, reasons of fact gathering and factual representation—even as they resist the linguistic distortion of
pure experience.

As humanistically appealing as this is, the emotionalists' special sensitivity to the
often unspoken (or unspeakable) richness of reality flirts with the daunting epistemological challenge of re-presenting that which can only be directly experienced.
Noting that the passions are highly resistant to description, emotionalists charge toward ineffability. Yet they insist on the representational quest. Ellis and Bochner
(1992), for example, cannot just carefully document and describe an abortion decision; this would erase the emotional experience it was for both of them. They choose
instead to reenact the experience in performance because, that way, the viewer
"comes away with a sense of what it must have been like to live through what happened" (p. 80), as we noted earlier. Nevertheless, the performance, in script and
dramatization, uses words to keep the message alive, to duplicate what the authors
felt. As they strive to avert the risk of simply feeling and not communicating experience, the unacknowledged complicity of language unavoidably transmutes what
they authentically felt.

Epistemological risks abound when emotionalists toy with postmodernism.
Because plain prose—the communicative resources of scientific description—
cannot do the trick, postmodern emotionalists look for alternate means of conveying authenticity. Since the essentially emotional is bereft of categorical contours, any and all forms of representation become valid. In the postmodern version, only the fantastic productions and subsequent displacements of one form of
representation after another do empirical justice to the mysteries of lived experience. Lest nothing at all be said about the ineffable, innovative representation becomes the method of choice. The consequent danger, however, is that representational free play inundates whatever independent reality is claimed for the
wellsprings of experience.

The Risk for Postmodernism

Turning qualitative inquiry into the ethnography of representation takes us directly into postmodern territory. Denzin (1991), for example, argues that, in postmodern context, the field becomes a sea of images. Representation is paramount. A cinematic society blurs the difference between lived experience as depicted on the movie screen and on television and that which is located in the concrete niches of everyday life. This invites the obliteration of borders altogether, risking the total collapse of reality into representation. Denzin rebuilds the boundary by arguing that even cinematic society is set against the harsh realities of daily living, but he is, at most, involved in a stopgap maneuver in the face of postmodernism's persistent assault on the lived border.

Atkinson (1990) offers a defense of his own against the fears of rampant representation, persuading us that, while qualitative method has a special sensitivity to representational matters, it is no different from other forms of scientific description in its representational practices. Qualitative researchers, he argues, can rest assured that their border work is not uniquely threatening. Seeming to say that everyone does it, Atkinson advises us not to worry and to just get on with whatever we were doing, while of course remaining alert to the rhetorical nature of our work and being open to representational innovation. He persuades by transforming the ostensible crisis of representation into a situation which, in the broader scheme of things, is a rather ordinary, routine epistemological dilemma that really cannot be laid to rest.

But qualitative inquiry is *not* just like any other descriptive enterprise. Its special sensitivity is different enough from the sensitivities of other scientific activity to make Atkinson's argument a rather small comfort in the face of the postmodernist onslaught. Engaged as qualitative method must be at the lived border of reality and representation, it is not afforded the epistemological safety of distance that sustains variable-type quantitative analysis, for example. Nor does it possess sociology's customary technical armament that preserves the distinction between empirical reality and its mere depictions. Indeed, qualitative inquiry has traditionally and assiduously eschewed such distancing operations. Nothing of the sort protects it from the emerging challenges at the lived border.

Postmodernism in the guise of qualitative inquiry is very risky business. Rhetorical ubiquity notwithstanding, at the lived border, reality is always on the verge of collapsing into representation, taking with it the substantively distinct parameters of experience whose "qualities" are qualitative method's unique subject matter. Trying to capture that which is not there, or to describe the inexpressible, using mere rhetoric that begs its own deconstruction, is hazardous indeed. Qualitative inquiry is surely in peril as it gambles with empirical nihilism.

WHAT ARE THE OPTIONS?

Can this gamble pay off? Has the increasing self-consciousness been worth the risks? Bringing qualitative method self-consciously to bear on the lived border of the real and the representational results in several analytic tensions. For naturalism, there is the tension between the "out-thereness" of natural social order and the self-conscious turn toward constitutive and rhetorical practice. For ethnomethodology, there is tension between the bracketed reality of interactional construction, on one hand, and the technical complicity with the moral emptiness of radically reflexive inquiry, on the other. For emotionalism, the thrust toward postmodernism suggests the possibility of never coming to descriptive grips with the essential, yet unexpressable, essence of brute being. And, for postmodernism itself, the tension centers between empirically affirmative deconstruction and complete skepticism regarding the possibility of empirical description. Short of eliminating the lived border, in effect elevating either reality or representation while dismissing the other, it seems that the tensions will remain a fact of analytic life.

How can we profit from any of the tensions that arise within or between the various qualitative idioms and their border engagements? With so much at stake, can we exploit the tensions while preserving, perhaps even enriching, the unique contribution of qualitative inquiry?

There are no easy answers, only informed choices. We believe that accepting empirical complexity and analytic tension is crucial to sustaining qualitative method's special engagement with lived experience. Our choices cannot eliminate the complexity or the tensions, but they can specify how we will deal with them, and what opportunities we will sacrifice or reject. While self-consciousness can become a preoccupation, it also helps uncover the various options available as qualitative researchers designate their objects of inquiry and stake out their positions in relation to empirical reality.

Methodological self-consciousness itself gives us choices. Without it, qualitative inquiry cannot move beyond the most traditional of naturalistic approaches. Failing to recognize that representation is implicated in social reality and is not merely outside of it, qualitative researchers have no choice but to search out native, naturalistic truths, capture them on their own terms, then naively re-present them as accurately as possible. The aim of an old-fashioned naturalism is to provide an ostensibly neutral conduit for knowledge, nothing more nor less.

As researchers increasingly appreciate reality's representational constitution, however, they become progressively more concerned with questions about how reality is constructed. Analytic choices multiply, providing us with new challenges: What is it that is constructed? Who does the constructing? Under what circumstances? Using which resources? Self-consciousness ultimately leads us to consider how we, as analysts, are implicated through our own representational practices.

But does that mean that researchers must inevitably end up on skeptical postmodernism's doorstep, reflexively inquiring about their own constitutive complicity while reality slips out the backdoor? We hope not. Indeed, our optimism derives from the analytic choices that remain available to us. As qualitative researchers, we have a host of alternatives regarding who, or what, we choose to study as a constitutive source of "reality." Shall we turn inward with radically reflexive inquiry? Should we interrogate our own practices, engage in the ethnography of argument, do ethnographies of our own ethnographies? This is certainly a viable option. Indeed, it may be especially important that we look into the production of social scientific knowledge because social scientists are granted a privileged place with regard to telling others what is going on in the social world. Because we speak and write a discourse of scientific "truth" and there are substantial institutional arrangements that lend credence to what we say, self-consciousness obligates us to reflexively deconstruct our own "truths" and consider the power that resides in producing and owning knowledge (see Foucault 1980).

Logical questions remain to be answered, however, regarding both analytic vantage point and product. In order to deconstruct method, one must have some independent analytic footing from which to operate. The establishment of this footing and the analysis it supports relies upon practices that are subject to further description, and so on, *ad infinitum*. But it is not merely the possibility of infinite regress that is daunting. The most radically reflexive forms of inquiry position themselves outside of the processes and practices that create the ontological space for the very possibility of conventional inquiry (Pollner 1987). Such ventures, in their examinations of the discursive bases of mundane reality, virtually undo their own findings. The substantive meanings of their accounts are canceled out by their claims that all accounts are essentially arbitrary—lacking in particular truths. Having no ground to stand on, no substance to convey, and no means of communicating the authentic, the radical postmodernist project deconstructs itself (as does a radically reflexive ethnomethodology). Tension and choice thus undo the enterprise.

While some might assume that this leaves qualitative inquiry with nowhere to go, Pollner (1991) suggests that radical reflexivity can be empirically useful in that it stimulates the sluggish imagination at the "metalevel." It disturbs, even disrupts, the complacency of ordinary inquiry by moving outside the fundamental premises and practices of Western epistemology to "make problematic the universality of the conceptions of mind, individuality, reality, and representation that ground the social sciences" (p. 376). Pollner argues that to "settle down" to produce conventional representations of reality means one has to be involved in the very discourses and practices that sustain mundane belief in that reality, practices that are themselves invisible to those engaging in them. The *careful* pursuit of radical reflexivity attempts to avoid this trap. While it may not be able to extend past the "outer rim of conventional discourse," according to Pollner, it hints of what lurks beyond:

> By inducing equivocalities that threaten to paralyze or subvert ordinary analytic discourse, radical reflexivity interrupts its normal operation, unsettles any version of reality, and makes visible the work of settling. . . . Radical reflexivity within the human sciences reconnoiters the regions beyond and beneath the settled territories. It returns to the [conventional analytic] community with new phenomena and contingencies whose origins, implications, and organization are elaborated in the settled ontological space. (Pp. 376–77)

Of course, Pollner also notes that radical reflexivity is likely to demand an "abnormal discourse" (Rorty 1979) to both provoke and convey its phenomena. Abandoning conventional discourse as an analytic resource virtually decimates anything reminiscent of scientific inquiry and description. The very possibility of conventional inquiry is constituted within the ontological space carved out by conventional discursive idioms. Reflexively undermining them, we cannot possibly know what might emerge to replace them. Not only is this another bit of risky business, it's also empirically costly. As Pollner puts it, radical reflexivity may hint of deep insight into the foundations of the mundane, but "the price is mundanely intelligible description" (1987, p. 150).

That is a cost that qualitative inquiry cannot bear. Nor can it afford to focus exclusively on itself. Postmodernist sentiments notwithstanding, we still have the option of examining phenomena other than analytic method or academic text. Qualitative inquiry by no means denigrates constitutive processes by looking beyond the analyst and his or her text to investigate other reality constructors and their projects. Indeed, there is something narcissistic, even presumptuous, about an exclusive concern for reflexively examining scientific arguments, even if such examination leads to their deconstruction.

As postmodernism dissolves reality into representation, it can all but eliminate "the other." It de-emphasizes the subject as an object of analysis, as a thinking, active, agentic presence. Whereas denying the subject (and the author, for that matter) may be possible in literary studies, it threatens the very possibility of the social sciences, stripping them of their most prized phenomena (Rosenau 1992). It also flirts with solipsism. Taken to its extreme, a preoccupation with representational practices leaves one with no-thing and no one to study, save one's own constitutive practices, which ultimately is also inconceivable. But this is a *choice* that the analyst makes in accepting the fundamentals of the postmodernist argument. Self-consciousness offers analytic options, not inevitability. The outcome is inevitable *only* after the choice has been made, and subsequent choices can always alter the analytic trajectory, forestalling what can be a plunge into nihilism.[4]

This does not imply a rush to re-embrace an unreflective naturalism, however. Ethnomethodology and affirmative postmodernism provide ample analytic leverage on "reality-in-the-making," allowing us to move beyond naive descriptions of the "naturally" given without leaving reality completely behind. If we grant the existence of *any* reality outside of representation, our analytic choices often boil down to deciding whether to highlight reality or representation, and which to consign to the background, if only temporarily. With reality and representation both on the conceptual scene, each deserves its moment in the empirical spotlight. Qualitative inquiry should be sufficiently versatile and adaptable to accommodate them both.

Unrepentant positivism's arrogance, of course, is that it insists on the preeminence of "objective" reality while denigrating as mere interference or contamination any representational or interpretive static that intervenes between the obdurate world and its scientific descriptions. In contrast, radical postmodernism's conceit is to "write off" reality by single-mindedly insisting that representation be given its due. Somewhere in between, we should be able to locate options for reclaiming reality without discounting representation, for acknowledging that reality is not merely given, but constructed. While we are compelled to investigate rhetorical production, we can't afford to ignore the substantive aspects of what is received and what is produced in the end.

CHOOSING AN ANALYTIC VOCABULARY

Researchers exercise options, embrace epistemologies, designate empirical fields, and formulate orienting questions by virtue of the analytic vocabularies they employ. In our view, qualitative inquiry must take a middle ground that sustains a sharp focus on lived realities. It should appreciate reality's interactional constitution while reining in postmodernism's unbridled concern with representational practice. It must capitalize on an increasing self-consciousness while simultaneously resuscitating the "other" who is fading into the shadows of reflexivity. And it must be sensitive to the interactionally emergent, yet substantively recognizable, quality of everyday realities. For qualitative inquiry to accomplish all this, it must choose its research idiom judiciously. It must renew the language of qualitative method.

An analytic vocabulary composed of terms like "setting," "naturally occurring," "status," and "social structure" takes us to places where the action is, to scenes like Cornerville, the New Deal Carry-out shop, and Jelly's bar and liquor store. Once there, the vocabulary brings native participants into view. We see them in terms of roles, rules, performances, authority, leadership, obligation, responsibility, achievement, and failure. Naturalistic method talk makes it possible to discern pattern in relationships. What is "there" is seen and reported as the "facts" of life as they naturally occur. The *whats* of the setting are paramount, as the constitutive *hows* are mainly taken for granted.

A different analytic vocabulary, composed of terms like "talk-in-interaction," "situated accomplishment," and "social construction" takes us elsewhere. The way members of a setting interactionally convey a sense of their roles and social structure commands the analytic stage. The vocabulary reveals pattern in the process by which roles and performances are communicatively constituted. What is "there" is not viewed as simply evident upon close inspection; instead, it is treated as constructed through social interaction. Status and authority, for example, enter into and recede from view as members take up and drop the topics as matters of practical concern. Having set aside the *whats* of social reality, method talk orients us to how reality is produced and sustained through everyday representation, bringing social *process* to the foreground.

Uniting these vocabularies provides an idiom that conflates reality and representation. It fashions a renewed language, blending naturalistic and constitutive traditions to capture the constructed yet familiar character of social life. But this renewed method talk must also allow us to interpretively appreciate the depths of emotional experience without analytically succumbing to the ineffability of affect, on the one hand, or the representational free play of postmodernism on the other. It must keep the constructed *whats* of "their world" in focus without totalizing the constitutive *hows*. The task is to preserve the substantive realities of lived experience without sacrificing the important gains that have been made in understanding their representational practices.[5]

This means we must accept a necessary tension between focusing on the *hows* of lived experience, on one side, and independently specifying the integral *whats* and related *whys*, on the other. The challenge is to balance the analytic attention paid to each of these countervailing concerns. Accepting the tension modifies ethnomethodology's special sensitivity by having it view reality *in relation to*, not simply in terms of, ethno-methods. Procedurally, this combines traditional naturalistic concerns for subjective and situated meaning with ethnomethodology's emphasis on constitutive interaction. And, as we will show in the following chapters, it also leaves a space for a kind of postmodern concern for representation, authority, difference, and diversity.

When we say that qualitative inquiry should claim a middle ground in order to manage the tensions between reality and representation, we are not suggesting a retreat from the difficult issues emerging from the postmodern crisis of representation. We are certainly not advocating a conservative retrenchment to the tried-and-true of qualitative method. To the contrary, we view the analytic middle ground at the lived border as a site for a radical recombination of analytic orientations, concerns, and vocabularies that can turn emerging tensions into productive energy and empirical insight.

ANALYZING INTERPRETIVE PRACTICE

Accepting analytic tension does not resolve it. The challenge to qualitative inquiry is to develop a renewed language that deals productively with diverse idioms, not dismiss them, to describe life's empirical complexities without getting lost in them or losing them to postmodern nihilism. From our perspective, the initial step is to focus on what is most distinctive and most definitive of social life: *interpretive practice*.

The Work of Everyday Life

Reality construction is practical activity. It involves a craftlike process of articulating meaning with experience to give one's circumstances and actions the appearance of substantiality, an appearance that conducting the routine business of everyday life demands (Gubrium 1988a). We use the term "interpretive practice" to convey both the artful and substantive aspects of this process; it refers to the constellation of procedures, conditions, and resources through which reality is apprehended, understood, organized, and represented in the course of everyday life (Holstein 1993; Holstein and Gubrium 1994b).

Interpretive practice is the work of everyday life. Like method talk itself, it links the concrete and the representational. People conduct their lives in diverse social circumstances, encountering reality in myriad forms. Cultural conventions and institutional settings specify possible complexes of meanings and definitions which serve as interpretive resources, promoting some interpretations, impinging upon others, eschewing still others. While this configuration of *whats* does not determine the course of talk and interaction, it makes it understandable in its related terms. For example, the institutional surroundings, say, of a therapy agency or a counseling center, provide relatively specific definitional frameworks and vocabularies for deciding the nature of personal and interpersonal troubles (Gubrium 1992; Miller and Silverman 1995). But these frameworks do not strictly govern interpretations; rather, they provide participants with familiar and accountable ways of representing conditions and concerns. In effect, the potentially real is sorted for what will be taken to be the actual, using the resources at hand. Local interpersonal engagements serve as the interactional scaffolding and definitional venues for this interpretive work, both configuring the *hows* and implicating the *whats* of interpretation. As W. I. Thomas's (1967) famous dictum would have it, definitional resources not only frame the lived sense of the realities at hand, but also mediate the course of interaction.[6]

In everyday experience, the representational is the other side of the real. Interpretive practice gives us the *real-in-the-making*. In counseling settings, for example, while there are empirically specifiable, institutional frameworks for defining the meaning and relevance of case material, the frameworks must be articulated with each case's particulars. The real-in-the-making relies upon representational methods, what ethnomethodologists call "practical reasoning" (Garfinkel 1967). But these *hows* of reality construction are enduringly linked with *what* is under construction, because interpretive practice unfolds within practical definitional circumstances. So, while interpretive practice is actively constitutive, if it were conceived exclusively in interactionally artful terms, it would seem to be out of place and time, without the interpretive building blocks that reality construction demands.

Studying interpretive practice thus takes qualitative method right to the border of a working dialectic of the real and the representational, of the macro and the micro, of objects and subjects. This serves to prevent positivistic excess by tying the real, in practice, to symbolic work. At the same time, this resists nihilism because it locates representation in the lived context of empirical circumstances. In analyzing interpretive practice, we do not aim to derive *the* real—"their world" or "their story" as such. Nor do we exclusively seek to discern the methodical or rhetorical contours of the real, or to co-opt innovative representation of the "really" real or the wellsprings of true emotion. Rather, our goal is to make visible how practitioners of everyday life constitute, reproduce, redesign, or specify locally, what the institutional and cultural contexts of their actions make available to them.

Classic Foundations

Our objectives resonate with several classic sociological concerns (cf. Hilbert 1992). Recognition of the importance of method talk, for example, invites the connection between our vocabulary of interpretive practice and the terminology Karl Marx applied over 150 years ago. Using the term "social praxis," he underscored the practical side of social, political, and economic action. While Marx did not envision the analytic project we propose, he nonetheless adumbrated the position that reality construction is far from abstract, cognitive, arbitrary, or merely linguistic. Indeed, he viewed the meanings of social life as bound to the social relationships of particular concrete circumstances (Bottomore 1956).

Similar to Marx's notion of praxis, interpretive practice involves two reflexive components, one constitutively active, one meaningfully substantive. One is situated, dynamic, and interactional; the other is more encompassing, more enduring. Practical, artful interpretation stands as the active side of practice; substantive resources and constraints as the other. Social interaction is possible only as the two reflexively intertwine in the social machinery that dialectically constructs meaning to meet the demands of the circumstances at hand.

Emile Durkheim offers a way of conceiving of the substantive side of this version of practice. While the positivist underpinnings of contemporary sociology are often traced to Durkheim's (1964) call for the scientific study of social facts, aspects of his work also provide a basis for relating meaning to the objects and actions of everyday life (Pfohl 1992; Silverman 1985). For example, in *The Elementary Forms of the Religious Life* (1961), Durkheim argues that "experience is not sufficient unto itself, but presupposes certain conditions which are exterior and prior to it," but he goes on to ask "how it is that these conditions are realized at the moment and in the manner that is desirable?" (p. 27). His answer suggests that Durkheim was far more sensitive to the interpretive—and interpreted—side of social reality than is typically acknowledged: "the categories of human thought are never fixed in any one definite form; they are made, unmade, and remade incessantly; they change with places and times" (p. 28).

The term Durkheim (1961) uses to address the relation between social reality and human agency is *collective representation*. Significantly, the term is both noun and verb. Social objects, he argued, are "things" that come to us by way of categories that order and arrange our perceptions. In their application, these categories represent, both in source and substance, what we otherwise collectively engage. Collective representation is something we do together that realizes social life. The *whats* of social reality are reflexively related to *how* reality is represented. Durkheim is clear about the social contours of the process:

> Society is a reality *sui generis*; it has its own peculiar characteristics. . . . The representations which express it have a wholly different content from purely individual ones. . . . Collective representations are the result of immense cooperation, which stretches out not only into space but into time as well; to make them, a multitude of minds have associated, united and combined their ideas and sentiments; . . . There are two beings in (man): an individual being which has its foundation in the organism and the circle of whose activities is therefore strictly limited, and a social being which represents the highest reality in the intellectual and moral order that we can know by observation—I mean society. This duality of our nature has as its consequence in the practical order, the irreducibility of a moral idea to a utilitarian motive, and in the order of thought, the irreducibility of reason to individual experience. In so far as he belongs to society, the individual transcends himself, both when he thinks and when he acts. (P. 28–29)

Socially formulated categories, including social forms such as religion, family, class, and community, are thus used to meaningfully represent members' lives. As Mary Douglas (1986, p. 96) puts it, Durkheim considered collective representations to be "publicly standardized ideas (that) constitute social order." As such, they can be substantively appropriated to interpretive practice in a manner similar to Schutz's (1970) "schemes of interpretation." These socially acquired frameworks for organizing and making sense of everyday life mediate individual experience and interpersonal relations. They reflect and perpetuate culturally promoted understandings of, and orientations to, the life world. As foreign to one another as they sometimes seem, Schutz and Durkheim both point us to a dialectic of social interpretation.

While Durkheim paid little attention to the interactive processes through which representation and representations develop, he provides a basis for orienting to meaning as a collective social accomplishment. Decades later, the work of Michel Foucault suggests a connection between the collectively representational and the interactional, arguing that interpretive structures are embodied in discourse. Interested in the relation between knowledge, language, and action, Foucault explicitly focuses on the role discourse plays in constituting, configuring, and conveying knowledge. He contends that the way we understand and represent experience derives from, and is constrained by, sociohistorically anchored discourse structures (Wuthnow et al.,

1984). But these structures are not mere linguistic templates for expressing knowledge. Foucault argues that discourses are more than systems of signs or signifying elements that refer to the content or meanings of objects and actions. They are not "a mere intersection of things and words: an obscure web of things, and a manifest, visible, coloured chain of words" (1972, p. 48). Instead, discourses are "*practices* that systematically form the objects of which they speak. Of course, discourses are composed of signs; but what they do is more than use these signs to designate things" (p. 49, our emphasis).

Foucault thus points directly to discourse, both its structures and articulations, as the essence of reality construction. The notion of practice provides the vehicle for linking substantive meaning to experience. For Foucault, "discourse is not a slender surface of contact, or confrontation, between reality and a language, the intrication of a lexicon and an experience" (p. 48). It is much more like a complex and dynamic *border engagement* at the lived intersection of reality and representation.

Throughout his work, Foucault is skeptical of individual agency, tending to reject the active subject (Best and Kellner 1991). Moving away from the interactional dynamics of reality construction, he engages in the archaeology and genealogy of knowledge. Still, his recognition of discourse-as-practice hints at the importance of understanding the more interactional side of language-in-use. Indeed, in an interview conducted shortly before his death, Foucault makes overtures in this direction, at least partially resurrecting the active subject, going so far as to suggest that an interpretive dialectic exists between the active and creative agent and a constraining social field (Best and Kellner 1991). While this points toward the process of connecting substantive meaning to objects and experience, it doesn't imply an incipient de-emphasis of the constitutive and constraining power of discourse:

> If now I am interested . . . in the way in which the subject constitutes himself in an active fashion, by the practices of the self, these practices are nevertheless not something that the individual invents by himself. They are patterns that he finds in his culture and which are proposed, suggested and imposed on him by his culture, his society and his social group. (Foucault 1988, p. 11)

It is ultimately left to ethnomethodology to round out a renewed language of qualitative method by providing a vocabulary for appreciating the *interactional* constitution of reality. Where other classic sociological approaches emphasize a terminology of interpretive structures and resources, ethnomethodology is an idiom of constructive process. But, as we have noted, Garfinkel, Pollner, Wieder, and others have urged qualitative inquiry to describe members' methods as the bedrock of meaningful interaction. For them the question of *how* reality is accomplished overshadows concerns with *what* things might mean, or *why* this is so. Indeed, in ethnomethodological method talk, questions of *what* and *why* might completely be subsumed by *how* concerns, as Garfinkel (1967) insists:

> What the parties talked about could not be distinguished from how the parties were speaking. An explanation of what the parties were talking about would then consist entirely of describing how the parties had been speaking . . . the recognized sense of what a person said consists only and entirely in recognizing the method of his speaking, of *seeing how he spoke*. (Pp. 28–29, emphasis in the original)

Our own notion of interpretive practice is more balanced in this regard; we want to address both *how* and *what* concerns. Conceiving of the production of meaningful reality as similar to other practical "construction projects," we seek an analytic idiom that recognizes that a sense of meaningful order is assembled from constituent parts and resources as well as through constitutive work. As Hugh Mehan argues, "the social world is not made up anew on each occasion of interaction" (1991, p. 73). Reality is built out of something (some thing). Therefore, we read Garfinkel's statement more symmetrically. That is, if *what* is talked about can't be separated from *how* the talk is conducted, the *whats* and *hows* of meaningful interaction are equally important to understanding whatever has interactionally transpired.[7] A renewed research idiom should speak to each of these classic concerns.

Analytic Bracketing

Given that both constitutive activity and substantive resources are necessary to produce everyday reality, and given their unavoidable reflexivity, we need an analytic procedure that dialectically acknowledges, accommodates, and explicates both sides of the process, while remaining sensitive to the ways in which the two sides are inseparable. Moreover, given the reflexivity of constructive activity and contextual resources, it would be futile and pointless to try to establish the primacy of one over the other. Because interpretive practice is two-sided, there is an inescapable analytic tension within it. To the extent that the researcher focuses on one side of practice, the other must be ignored, and vice versa. The trick is to accept and balance the tension derived from the competing sides (and their reflexive relationship), assembling descriptions that intelligibly convey a practical sense of the phenomenon under study.

This is no mean feat, for reflexivity all but defies linear description. M. C. Escher's well-known illustration of "Drawing Hands" (reprinted in Mehan and Wood, 1975, among other places), for example, can capture such a process in a single glance, yet one cannot adequately describe the picture without foregrounding some feature of the drawing in order to convey what the rest of it is about. Reflexivity thus poses a serious challenge to any analytic strategy and vocabulary, one daunting enough for some to respond that the enterprise itself is tautological. Others, such as Pollner (1987, 1991), suggest that the pursuit of reflexivity as a topic is tantalizing and provocative, but, as we noted earlier, he also reminds us of its cost: the sacrifice of mundane intelligibility.

We are unwilling to pay that price in the all-out pursuit of the intrigues of reflexivity itself, but we are challenged to find a way of managing our empirical descriptions so as to convey the reflexive dynamics of meaningful interaction. So, while we must decline the opportunity to engage reflexivity on its own terms, we do want to fashion a not-quite-so-postmodern approach that retains both classic sociological concerns and a version of sociology's empirical grounding.

As a point of departure, we return to the phenomenologically inspired practice of bracketing. Our use of bracketing differs somewhat from the ethnomethodological version discussed in Chapter 3, however. In that approach, bracketing is an a priori procedural strategy, designed to permit the asking of a particular kind of *how* question about social reality. It refers to the temporary suspension of belief in the substantive realities of everyday life in order to examine constitutive activity. Bracketing in this sense is an operation conducted prior to actual analysis, a procedural move that provides an opportunity to describe processes of social construction while holding in abeyance things produced and things used in their production. It is not, as some might incorrectly assume, an ontological challenge that fundamentally questions the empirical status of everyday life (Silverman and Gubrium 1994). It does not suggest that there is no substance to reality, or that nothing is real. Rather, it is a means of temporarily suspending belief in the substantial (the *whats*) in order to better view the processes (the *hows*) by which substantiality is produced.

Yet, in order to convey what is going on in a bracketed setting, the researcher unavoidably must reference meanings and circumstances external to the bracketed scene. We take note of this not as a critique, but as a recognition of the reflexive quality of interpretive practice. Given this inevitability, coupled with our framing of interpretive practice as both a *what* and a *how* phenomenon, we offer an adaptation of bracketing that is less static, more capable of accommodating and reflecting social complexities and the key tensions of reality production. Rather than bracket the phenomenon as a prelude to analysis, we work with what we call *analytic bracketing*, which operates along with analysis. This procedure amounts to alternately bracketing the *whats*, then the *hows*, in order to assemble a more complete picture of practice. The objective is to move back and forth between constitutive activity and substantive resources, alternately describing each, making informative references to the other in the process. Either the activity or the substantive context becomes the provisional phenomenon, while interest in the other component is temporarily deferred but not forgotten. The constant interplay between the analysis of the two components mirrors the interplay between artfulness and substantive resources that characterizes interpretive practice.

Because the process of accomplishing reality, and the objects and events that are ultimately constructed, are mutually constitutive, one cannot argue that analysis must begin or end with one or the other. Neither constitutive activity nor substantive resources predetermines the other. As with asking "Which came first, the chicken or the egg?," a definitive answer is impossible. If we set aside the need for an indisputable resolution, we can arbitrarily designate an analytic point of entry and proceed with our descriptions—so long as we keep it firmly in mind that we must continue to move back and forth between the components that comprise interpretive practice. Analysis itself constantly shifts focus, from artfulness to resources and back again.

The two forms of bracketing have different technical implications. Discursively oriented ethnomethodology, for example, relies upon a priori bracketing, which, in turn, leads to the use of a variety of conversation analytic techniques. Real-time interactional practice is the crucial object of study, and conversation analysis becomes (for some) the apparatus of choice for capturing it (see Sacks, Schegloff, and Jefferson 1974; Psathas 1995). But if research is guided by analytic bracketing, it directs us to a different set of procedural choices. Technically, we are encouraged to use both discourse analytic techniques and methods of "constitutive ethnography" (Mehan 1979), the "ethnography of practice" (Gubrium 1988a), or other circumstantially sensitive constructionist approaches (see Holstein 1993; Miller 1994).

Analytic bracketing reaffirms the ethnomethodological claim that we must focus on language use, and appreciates the necessity of studying how reality is methodically accomplished, through talk and interaction, from the bottom up, so to speak.[8] But it also requires that analysis be constantly attuned to interpretive resources and conditions. This position is not altogether foreign to ethnomethodology, for Garfinkel (1967) asserted from the start that all meaning is indexical. Even Sacks (1974), a pioneer of conversation analysis, acknowledged early on that culture provides the material conditions and resources for interpreting experience.[9]

But here, once again, we encounter tension. While our analysis is informed by awareness of substantive conditions, we must be careful not to appropriate these conditions naively into our analyses. We share ethnomethodology's desire to distinguish between members' analytic resources and our own. Therefore, as we focus on the substantive resources used in interpretive practice, we attempt to understand and describe them *as they relate to members' activities.* Our interest lies in how members apprehend, employ, and are constrained by interpretive resources and conditions; we want to document ethnographically how members' interpretive activities are conditioned by what they experience as the circumstantial realities of their lives. In doing so, we must appreciate and describe how members respond to, and represent, their circumstances, but, at the same time, guard vigilantly against appropriating their explanations as our own. Put differently, we must describe members' interpretive circumstances and cultures, but not reify those cultures and circumstances in the process.

As we turn to circumstance and interpretive resources, we must be careful not to engage in a selective relativism in the sense that we privilege particular aspects of experience, treating them as exogenous resources that stand outside of interpretive practice. This is a problem that has afflicted other attempts at constitutive analysis. Steve Woolgar and Dorothy Pawluch (1985) have suggested that many constructionists are, in fact, selective "objectivists" who render problematic the truth status of certain matters that they single out for analysis, while treating other matters as unproblematic, as unquestionably "real." In doing so, the analyst places a boundary between assumptions that are understood to be problematic and those that are not. The analyst then uses the unexamined "truths" as resources for analyzing and critiquing the construction process. Woolgar and Pawluch call this strategy "ontological gerrymandering."

Our strategy of analytic bracketing bears a superficial resemblance to this, but it is hardly the same. First, analytic bracketing is always *substantively temporary* and never dissolves the constitutive role of representation. It merely suspends attention to selected phenomena, for the time being, in order to concentrate on other phenomena. Analytic bracketing allows us to set aside the "constructedness" of contextual features in order to describe their apparent contours and substance. But we never abandon the position that the circumstantial phenomena under consideration are themselves constructed and subject to further constitutive analysis (including analysis of how the analyst comes to identify and represent them). When constitutive practice is bracketed, it does not mean that the substantive conditions under consideration should be treated as unproblematic or immutable. Their meaning and organization are only provisionally highlighted. A shift in brackets brings constitutive practice back into focus, with analytic attention trained on the processes by which meaning or substantiality are themselves constructed.

Second, analytic bracketing is *enduringly empirical* in that it does not take substantive conditions for granted, as given truths of the settings under consideration. The resources and circumstances that condition interpretive practice must be discerned and described through systematic observation. Sometimes circumstantial contingencies will comprise contextual features as they are known and experienced by members. The analytic task then tilts toward the phenomenological, reporting subjective experience. At other times, analysis may focus on conditions that are "seen but unnoticed" by members, but which are available through ethnographic observation. Members, for example, may naively employ cultural resources in conversation and interaction—institutional discourse structures or professional gazes, to single out two Foucauldian terms of reference—and be largely unaware of the limitations and possibilities that these pose. They may use other substantive and interactional resources without acknowledgment. The fact that these contingencies and resources are "unnoticed," however, does not diminish their role in the interpretive process. The analytic task is to observationally identify occasions of their use or nonuse, then discern pattern, context, and content as they are, or are not, brought to bear in practice.[10]

Finally, analytic bracketing *does not privilege conditions or artfulness.* Being the two sides of interpretive practice, conditions and artfulness are reflexively intertwined so that the reification of one in service to the analysis of the other is virtually impossible. While a simultaneous focus on the artful *and* the substantial is a practical impossibility, analytic bracketing allows us to appreciate their respective contributions to interpretation while respecting their reflexive relationship.

This sensitivity to both sides of interpretive practice expands ethnomethodological horizons by reemphasizing naturalistic concerns for the configurations of meaning in relation to which reality construction takes place. While it remains important to understand how meaningful social order is built up, it is also imperative to engage the overarching issues of what meanings are available for construction, how circumstances condition the construction process, and the manner in which the animatedness and sheer scenic presence of the process brings all of this to life.

This interplay is the heart of interpretive practice, but it assuredly complicates analysis. The constant moving back and forth—the shifting between constitutive activity, culture, circumstance, and scenic presence—yields a less-than-tidy picture. But qualitative researchers have come to accept that as the nature of everyday life. It isn't tidy; its production is fraught with nearer and more distant contextual complications. To reveal the interpretive capabilities people possess, we need to give them full credit for the massive challenge they undertake at each engagement with the world of experience. As we mentioned at the start, an enduring strength of qualitative inquiry is its willingness, indeed its eagerness, to skeptically confront, digest, and attempt to document the intricacies and complications of the social. The analytic tension that exists between constitutive activity and substantive resources is the price we pay for attempting to capture this in practice.

A renewed language of qualitative method centered on interpretive practice appreciates the analytic tension at the lived border of reality and representation. The vocabulary accepts the epistemological risk of border engagement by conceptualizing agents of lived experience as practitioners of everyday life. These are agents who both draw on the real and represent it, in the course of defining and responding to their worlds. Practitioners of everyday life conduct their business making use of what is available—what their immediate and broader circumstances provide them—to construct the meanings that inform and guide their actions. These are agents who not only methodically produce their worlds in talk and interaction, but also do so within discernible circumstances. These worlds, in turn, are variably linked to cultural and institutional formations. While practice is ineluctably local, it is selectively fed by and selectively draws from what is immediately and more broadly available. As Marx (1956) would have it, people actively construct their worlds, but not completely on, or in, their own terms.

CHAPTER 7

The "Artful" Side of Interpretive Practice

In outlining his program for ethnomethodology, Garfinkel (1967) uses the term "artful" to convey how adroitly, spontaneously, resourcefully, and creatively people accomplish social order. The term refers to the myriad processes and procedures that everyday actors engage as they produce, moment-by-moment, the realities they inhabit. Most importantly, interacting persons artfully construct reality by doing things with words, talking reality into being, so to speak.

This chapter illustrates a vocabulary for understanding the artful side of interpretation, offering a perspective for examining *how* members articulate meaning and order with experience. "Articulation" is an apt term for this since it connotes both expression in a verbal form and a joining together—an act of connection and construction. Recalling that we don't intend to privilege either the artful or the substantive side of practice, we begin by looking at method talk that describes what some have called the interactional machinery of reality construction: ordinary conversation (see Maynard 1988; Sacks, Schegloff, and Jefferson 1974). Let's consider some terminology that proves useful for studying this active side of interpretive practice.

CONVERSATIONAL STRUCTURE AND INTERACTIONAL COMPETENCIES

Conversation analysis offers one idiom for examining *how* speakers in face-to-face interaction constitute the realities of concern to them. It provides a vocabulary for recognizing and analyzing a basic interactional competency underpinning social life, the fundamental exchange procedures and expectations speakers rely upon when they engage in intelligible conversation (Heritage 1984a). Put simply, CA furnishes us with an analytic apparatus for talking about talk.

This approach starts from the position that both the production and interpretation of conduct are responsive to a common set of conversational methods or procedures (Heritage 1984b). Social order is "methodically produced by the members of society for one another" (Schegloff and Sacks 1973, p. 290); hence the means of production are visible (hearable) and available for analysis. The work of Sacks,

Schegloff, and Jefferson launched a project that has identified diverse properties of speech exchanges, revealing the vast "seen but unnoticed" structures and contingencies of competent conversation. While we cannot do justice here to the wide-ranging, interlocking, and cumulative body of empirical descriptions inspired by CA, we offer a brief summary of some of the findings, to illustrate what is revealed by closely examining the structure and dynamics of everyday talk. Let us sketch out some observations of what unfolds in the simple act of trading conversational turns back and forth, as a way of demonstrating how CA helps to "unpack" what is interactionally going on.

Conversational Organization

The central finding and tenet of CA is that ordinary conversation is a highly coordinated, organized form of activity requiring keen attention and conspicuous competence. Most fundamentally, talk proceeds in an orderly fashion, one person speaking at a time, in sequences of exchanges:

> Turns at talk do not simply happen to occur one after another but rather "belong together" as a socio-organizational unit and where there is thus a methodic relationship between the various turns or parts. . . . a set of mutual obligations is established by the structural relations between these sequence parts, with each action projecting some "next." (Whalen 1992, p. 306)

An obvious example of this sequential organization is the question-answer pair, in which the asking of a question "demands" an answer or some accountable substitute. Changes between speakers occur at recognizable speakership transition points, preserving single person speakership, with orderly mechanisms for designating who will speak next.

A more detailed look at this simple but basic phenomenon allows us to discern what is going on in what are generally taken to be unimportant conversational actions. The organization of single-speaker turns, for example, is not socially trivial. Speakers take their turns at talk, with one party speaking at a time. A conversation may involve several speakers, however, so transitions from one speaker to the next must be achieved in an orderly fashion or conversational chaos ensues. The trick is to transfer speakership from one person to a single next speaker, without having speakers overlap one another's talk, and without an extended pause or gap between adjacent turns. As Sacks, Schegloff, and Jefferson (1974) note, coordinated, single-speaker turns are achieved with remarkable regularity, regardless of substantive variations in the conversation, such as participants' identities, topic of conversation, setting, and the objective of the conversation. This is also the case when the task is complicated by the participation of multiple potential speakers.

Sacks, Schegloff, and Jefferson (1974) have outlined the "context-free" but "context-sensitive" means through which this regularity is achieved and managed. One mechanism identified is the practice of the current speaker's allocating the next turn by selecting the next speaker by virtue of the design of his or her turn and its completion. Alternatively, another party may select himself or herself to speak at the completion of a turn if the current speaker's utterance does not allocate the next turn. There are "rules" or normative expectancies for this process. First, a current speaker may construct his or her turn so as to select the next speaker by a variety of direct and indirect techniques (e.g., explicitly asking a designated person for a response). The person so designated then has the right and obligation to speak next. If the current speaker does not allocate the next turn, at the first possible speaker transition point—a place in the conversation at which the possible completion of the original turn might be detected—another person may select himself or herself to speak. Finally, if the first speaker fails to designate the next speaker, and if no one self-selects at the first transition relevance point, the current speaker may (but does not have to) continue, until one of the above transfer mechanisms results in a change in speakers, thus sustaining the interaction.

These "rules" coordinate turn taking, organizing the transition from one speaker to another, and minimizing gaps and overlaps (Sacks, Schegloff, and Jefferson 1974). Whether someone has been selected to speak next, or the next speaker selects himself or herself, speakership transfer is determined turn-by-turn. That is, speaker selection is *locally managed* within the series of exchanges. The obligation to listen to the conversation, to monitor the possibilities it may hold for the next turn, is thus built into the conversation, since any participant may be selected to participate at any time. The production of some current conversational action proposes a local, here-and-now definition of the situation to which subsequent talk will orient. One turn projects a relevant next activity or response that must be fashioned to meet the demands of the immediate occasion. Thus, each utterance is "sequentially implicative" (Schegloff and Sacks 1973).

Schegloff and Sacks observed some more generic features of conversational sequences centered around what they called the "adjacency pair" structure. Summarized by Heritage (1984b), an adjacency pair is (1) a sequence of two utterances that are (2) adjacent, (3) produced by different speakers, (4) ordered as a first part and a second part, and (5) typed, so that a first part calls for a second part (or range of second parts). Schegloff and Sacks offer a simple rule of adjacency pair operation: "Given the recognizable production of a first pair part, on its first possible completion, its speaker should stop and a next speaker should start and produce a second pair part from the pair type the first pair part is recognizably a member of" (p. 206) These sequences are normatively invariant:

> The adjacency pair structure is a *normative* framework for actions which is *accountably* implemented . . . the first speaker's production of a first pair part proposes that a second speaker should relevantly produce a second pair part which is accountably "due" immediately upon completion of the first." (Heritage 1984b, p. 247, emphasis in the original)

Even when the second pair part is not forthcoming, this format requires the second speaker to show that he or she is oriented to the normative framework, regardless of its substance, and that the action taken is accountable in some other fashion. When turn-taking errors or adjacency pair violations occur, participants invoke "repair mechanisms." For example, when more than one speaker talks at a time, one of them may stop before a normally anticipated completion point, recognizing the basic "rule" of one speaker at a time. Or if speakership transfer fails to occur at an appropriate place, the speaker may repair the sequence by speaking again, respecting the ongoing sequence-in-progress. Or, in still other instances, if repairs by someone other than the current speaker are in order, the next speaker waits until the next possible completion point before speaking again. Thus, the turn-taking system is respected, even when violations and repairs occur.

In a sense, turn taking and repair are embedded in one another (Silverman 1993a). The turn-taking system lends itself to, and incorporates, devices for repairing its troubles, while simultaneously providing the basic mechanism for repairing other troubles in conversation. As Sacks, Schegloff, and Jefferson (1974, p. 723) put it, the turn-taking system and the organization of repair are "made for each other."

To understand what is happening in the course of ongoing talk, then, one must view conversation as *sequences of action*. According to CA, these sequences, and the exchange of turns within sequences, rather than individual utterances or sentences, are the most consequential conversational components, the units most responsible for the production of interactional order. Because the turn-taking sequence also compels potential participants to pay attention to the ongoing conversation, and to be prepared to display an understanding of what is going on, it virtually binds them into a joint, collaborative enterprise. This is the scaffolding of social interaction, action that, through the sheer sequential mechanics of exchange, takes account of others. The basic pattern provides a framework of accountability to which any competent conversational practitioner must orient.

CA, of course, has moved far beyond the description of regularities in turn taking, laying out an impressive array of basic mechanisms attendant on the organization of ordinary conversation. The list of conversational mechanisms that have been considered includes conversational openings and closings, and the myriad activities in between.[1] Built on this foundation, an equally impressive body of studies of "institutional talk" is emerging (see Drew and Heritage 1992). This work examines similarities and modifications of the routine properties of talk that are present in formal organizational settings (e.g., medical clinics, courtrooms, classrooms). All told, a massive literature is now available to help us understand the regularities of conversational practice. This literature provides an extensive vocabulary for understanding talk-in-interaction as artful *social action*. The language of CA virtually transforms conversation from a vehicle for *conveying* reality into a machinery for *producing* it.

Caveat: Don't Forget Other Contexts

If conversational competence is on the artful side of interpretive practice, we must still bear in mind that interpretive resources and conditions are its reflexively related siblings. These provide contexts other than conversation's sequential organization that bear upon reality construction. Their description requires an analytic vocabulary of its own.

The empirical horizons of the term "context" are especially important to our formulation of interpretive practice. Conversation analysts tend to limit their interest in context to what is immediately and discursively apparent *within* conversational exchanges. The parameters of the contextual are defined by what is ongoingly available, or being built up, in conversation. Ethnographers, in contrast, traditionally view context as more scenically and culturally inclusive, extending to matters not readily evident in conversational exchanges per se (e.g., performance rituals, institutional missions, and broad cultural understandings). Our view of interpretive practice is that, while it is suffused with talk and interaction, it is only partially driven by sequential imperatives. It also unfolds within interpretive circumstances that provide resources and constraints that may remain unspoken but nonetheless insinuate themselves into the social constitution of reality. Consequently, we take neither artfulness nor resources and conditions to supersede the other; one is always dependent upon the other. The caveat for this chapter on the artful, then, is: Don't forget the substantive contexts of what is going on!

Let us underscore this point by examining the meaning of interactional "competence." It may by now seem self-evident that such competence is prerequisite for orderly interaction. But is that, by itself, an unchallengeable analytic claim? And is such competence locally identifiable in speech exchanges, a quality that is objectively ascertainable apart from broader social contexts?

Consider the following illustrations that call into question just what it takes to achieve interactional competence and incompetence. In an observational study of involuntary mental hospitalization hearings (Holstein 1988a, 1993), one of the authors repeatedly observed sequences of testimony delivered by candidate mental patients that representatives of the district attorney's office (DAs) and the presiding judges described as evidence of severe and debilitating mental problems.[2] "Crazy talk," as they sometimes called it, is speech that they believe clearly displays the candidate patient's interactional incompetence. In an extract from one hearing presented below—in which a judge (J1), a district attorney (DA2), a public defender (PD2), a psychiatrist (Dr12), and the candidate patient (LS) participate—the DA asks the candidate patient, Lisa Sellers, a series of questions about the routine circumstances of her life. After initiating fourteen question-answer pairs (one immediately following the other) regarding the patient's intended residence and who she planned to live with, the DA enters into the following exchange. The sequence culminates in what is later described as Ms. Sellers's hearably delusional references to a "rocketship":

1. DA2: How do you like summer out here, Lisa?
2.   LS: It's OK.
3. DA2: How long have you lived here?
4.   LS: Since I moved from Houston
5.   ((Silence)) [Note: If unspecified, length of silence is one to three seconds.]
6.   LS: About three years ago.
7. DA2: Tell me about why you came here.
8.   LS: I just came.
9.   ((Silence))
10.   LS: You know, I wanted to see the stars, Hollywood.
11.   ((Silence))
12. DA2: Uh huh
13.   LS: I didn't have no money.
14.   ((Silence))
15.   LS: I'd like to get a good place to live.
16.   ((Silence 5 seconds))

17. DA2: Go on. ((spoken simultaneously with onset of next utterance))
18. LS: There was some nice things I brought.
19.   ((Silence))
20. DA2: Uh huh
21. LS: Brought them from the rocketship.
22. DA2: Oh really?
23. LS: They was just some things I had.
24. DA2: From the rocketship?
25. LS: Right.
26. DA2: Were you on it?
27. LS: Yeah.
28. DA2: Tell me about this rocketship, Lisa. (1993, pp. 104–5)

Let us now examine the organization of this exchange, being especially sensitive to the issue of interactional competence. Throughout the exchange, the DA encourages Sellers to take extended and unfocused turns at talk by engaging in some very mundane interactional maneuvers. First, he alters the normal or expected sequence of question-answer adjacency pairs. In the 14 exchanges immediately prior to this extract, and continuing in lines 1 through 4, the DA asks a question, then follows Sellers's answers with additional questions, allowing no notable gaps between answers and next questions. A silence, however, follows line 4, where a question from the DA may have been expected. The gap in talk is eventually terminated (line 6) by Sellers's elaboration of her prior utterance. So far, so good. Participants appear conversationally competent, respecting principles of sequential organization and the flow of talk and interaction.

In line 7, the DA solicits further talk, but not in the form of a question. Instead, he makes a very general request for more information, but the adequacy of a response to this form of solicitation is more indeterminate than for a directly asked question. Sellers responds at line 8, but we now see that the DA's discretion is deeply implicated in the "adequacy" of her response. The completeness of the response depends, in part, on how the DA acknowledges it. In this instance, the DA does not respond at the first possible speaker transition point (after line 8). This prompts Sellers to elaborate her response. Again, the DA declines possible speakership. The pattern continues through line 20, with Sellers providing elaborations and the DA remaining silent or filling turn spaces with minimal acknowledgments or solicitation. Sellers's mention of a rocketship finally elicits an indication of apparent interest ("Oh really?") from the DA at line 22 and he asks a subsequent set of questions encouraging Sellers to talk about the rocketship.

This type of response marks a significant noticing that might accomplish several things. First, it can focus attention on the prior utterance so as to invite further talk on the subject. Such noticings may also call attention to the "faulted" quality of an utterance, suggesting the need for repair. For example, when the DA responded to Sellers's statement about the "rocketship," his use of "Oh really?" (line 22) could be heard as an expression of surprise or disbelief, an invitation for Sellers to dispel implied doubts by altering, repairing, retracting, or reframing the problematic utterance. Her indifference to the opportunity to retract or explain the claim may be interpreted as further evidence that she was incapable of recognizing and correcting conversational "gaffes" that any competent interactant would probably not make, and certainly would repair, if given the opportunity.

Clearly, this sequence of testimony, like other extended multi-unit turns at talk, is an interactional achievement (Schegloff 1982). The DA requested testimony from the patient, but repeatedly withheld acknowledgment of the testimony's adequacy, promoting more unfocused talk in the process. He encouraged Sellers to speak, using "Uh huh" to indicate an understanding that an extended unit of talk was in progress and was not yet complete (Schegloff 1982), and by declining possible turns at talk altogether. He resumed an active role in the dialog only after hearably "crazy talk" emerged, at which point he attempted to focus the discussion on the "crazy" topic and encourage Sellers to elaborate. For her part, Sellers sustained the ongoing conversation by filling silences that had begun to emerge at failed speaker transition points. She repeatedly elaborated responses, and eventually produced the "crazy talk" that was later cited as evidence of her incompetence. But, in a sense, it was her cooperation with the DA in extending the conversation, her conversational *competence*, that allowed for the emergence of that very talk.

At the completion of the hearing, the DA, in his summation, argued that Sellers was "gravely disabled" and should be hospitalized because she evidently could not manage the ordinary tasks of daily living due to her delusions. He claimed that "She lets her delusions come out even here in court, so I don't see how we can think she's capable of taking care of herself on an everyday basis."

The judge eventually ordered Seller's commitment to an inpatient psychiatric facility, explaining, in part, that Sellers's "performance on the witness stand" (referring to her "rocketship" references), combined with other problems identified by the testifying psychiatrist, indicated her inability to adequately care for herself if she was not hospitalized. Referring to her testimony about the rocketship, the judge noted that "she didn't have enough sense, or self control, or competence or whatever, to keep the conversation focused on things in this world. I just don't think she can handle other situations any better."

Up to this point, the analysis of the hearing has centered on the artful *hows* of interactional competence. But what happens if we bracket the *hows* of this sequence in order to look at *what* was said, and what resources were used to interpret it, just as the participants in the commitment hearing apparently did? Before, when we bracketed the substance and meaning of Seller's talk, the apparatus of conversation analysis revealed a quite competent interactant throughout the extract. Sellers responded in accountable fashion to all of the turn-taking contingencies of the conversation. She adroitly sustained the conversation, continuing her talk when her partner declined to speak at appropriate speaker transition points. The sequence was, by CA standards, perfectly intelligible and sequentially accountable.

But shifting the brackets, that is, changing our analytic orientation from *how* to *what*, leads to a virtual reversal of Sellers's competence. Turning the focus from *how* the conversation was accomplished to *what* was said keys us into different interpretive contingencies. Bracketing conversational mechanics allows us, like the judge and others, to focus more on the substance of Sellers's speech, on the meanings and wider implications of the content of her talk. In this regard, notice how differently Sellers's interactional competence was evaluated by the judge, who employed local interpretive resources and standards for his decision, standards oriented as much to what, as to how, the candidate patient engaged in the conversation. In the lived context of the commitment hearing, her conversational competencies could clearly be "seen but unnoticed," which is exactly what the judge did by focusing on "what everybody knew" about the possibility of civilian contact with rocketships and the like. "What everybody knows" and, most importantly, what need not be said, is that the cultural salience of speaking of contact with rocketships, under the circumstances, nondiscursively signaled "crazy talk" and incompetence in this court-room. Were the tone and dramatic presence of the hearing empirically available to us in the extract, it might not be far-fetched to add that the sheer scenic value of the exchange in lines 21 and 22 set the emotional basis for commitment. Indeed, for one sitting in the courtroom, there was an almost palpable sense that Sellers at that point had said things that virtually assured her commitment.

Let us briefly consider a second example from another commitment hearing. The following extract is a segment of cross-examination of a candidate patient that the judge claimed revealed the candidate patient's "mental incompetence." In his ac-count for involuntarily hospitalizing Henry Johnson (HJ) on the grounds of grave disability, the judge explained that Johnson's testimony was "confused and jum-bled." As the judge put it, "He didn't know what to say. He was stopping and start-ing, jumping from one thing to another. You can see that he can't focus on one thing at a time." A portion of Johnson's exchange with a district attorney is ex-tracted:

1. DA4: How you been feeling lately?
2. HJ: OK
3.   ((Silence))
4. HJ: I been feeling pretty good.
5.   ((Silence))
6. DA4: Uh huh
7.   ((Silence))
8. HJ: Pretty good, ummm all right
9.   ((Silence))
10. HJ: Got a job with (several words inaudible)
11.   ((Silence))
12. HJ: Pays OK, not bad.
13.   ((Silence 4 seconds))
14. HJ: My car got hit, an accident, really messed it up
15.   ((Silence))
16. HJ: Got to get it on the street
17.   ((Silence 5 seconds))
18. HJ: They gonna let us go to the truck out front?
19. DA: When you're all done here they might. (Holstein 1993, p. 108)

Here, the talk is discontinuous and multifocused, a speech environment charac-terized by failed speaker transition and recurrent silence. In court, the talk was heard as an individual's production, and was interpreted as symptomatic or probative of the patient's interactional incompetence. But, as in the previous extract, it is possi-ble to consider this halting, disjointed movement from one line of talk to another as a *collaborative* phenomenon that required Johnson's interactional competence for the sequence to emerge as it did.

For example, one might argue that many of the silences in the extract above resulted from the DA's refusal to assume a turn or, at minimum, acknowledge hearably complete utterances by Johnson. When Johnson offered topic-developmental utterances, the DA might have produced further questions, invitations, solicitations, or continuers to sustain the line of talk. Even minimal utterances and solicitations demonstrate recipient attention and invite further related talk (Maynard 1980). In the absence of these (as in lines 7–18), however, the line of talk can falter and silences may occur. Such silences may be heard as conversational difficulties, difficulties that implicate the prior speaker (in this case, Johnson), who may attempt remedial action.

One victim of a deteriorating line of talk is its topical continuity. Topic changes (that is, utterances that utilize new referents and implicate and occasion new lines of talk unrelated to talk in prior turns) and topic shifts (lesser changes in the ongoing line of talk) are common solutions to problems of producing continuous talk (Maynard 1980). For example, utterances that fail to generate either speaker transition or solicitations to continue may evoke silence. We can analyze the repeated silences above in these terms.

Maynard (1980) suggests that participants encountering silences often try to restore continuous talk, first by pursuing the ongoing line of talk, then, if this fails, by changing the line of talk. In the preceding extract, Johnson discussed how he was feeling in three utterances (lines 2, 4 and 8). The DA explicitly encouraged Johnson to continue only once (line 6). At line 10, Johnson shifted the line of talk, not abandoning the discussion of how he felt, but elaborating the reasons for his feelings. This received no acknowledgment, but Johnson continued to elaborate in a second utterance (line 12). The DA was again nonresponsive, so Johnson offered a new topic-developmental utterance, bringing up his recent automobile accident (line 14). This line and a subsequent elaboration (line 16) generated no response, and the testimony deteriorated into an extended silence. Johnson ended the silence with another topical offering in the form of a question, explicitly inviting speaker transition (line 18).

If we recognize an interactional basis for topical continuity, we cannot hold individual speakers solely responsible for maintaining a conversation's focus. As Maynard (1980) argues, topicality is constituted through joint conversational practices; it is more than a matter of content. Shifting the line of talk provides a procedural solution to problematic, nonresponsive speech environments. Changing the direction of the conversation, then, appears to be a pervasive and competent practice in environments characterized by repeated recipient silences. Analytically, we can appreciate this talk—talk that the court considers to be "incompetent"—as an interactional project that virtually depends upon the candidate patient's competence. In effect, under the circumstances, the candidate patient appeared to *competently* exhibit his *incompetence*.

Once again, the context of interpretation affects the substance of practical understandings. When we concentrate on explaining *how* the line of talk emerged, we get a different view than one gets from a more substantive stance. Ironically, in both of these examples, conversational actions that in a CA context would be considered

interactionally competent and uneventful were responsible for commonsense definitions of the practitioners' incompetence. We note this not to draw attention to any
deficiency of either evaluation, but to underscore the importance of various contexts to the interpretive process and to show how bracketing and unbracketing the
hows and *whats* of interaction gives us a more variegated view of social interaction.
In the world of everyday life, both *what* is done and *how* it is accomplished are
pointedly relevant to the outcomes of interpretive practice. As we argued earlier,
members' substantive resources and their artfulness must both be considered if we
are to understand the ways people define and engage lived experience. We need an
analytic vocabulary that is up to the task of capturing both sides of practice.

CONSTITUTIVE DESCRIPTION

Commonsensically, we refer to description as the process by which objects, ideas,
or events are more or less accurately represented. The definition relies upon the literal meaning of representation, that is, "re-presentation." This, of course, is an ide-
alization and suggests that the matters described meaningfully exist, separate from
any act of representation. Adequate description relies upon the describer's ability
to re-present, or accurately portray, the original.

Using a more constitutive idiom, we can frame description as an act of communication through which reality is substantively "talked into being."[3] From this standpoint, information, facts, and other reality depictions are formulated through descriptive activity (Gubrium and Buckholdt 1982; Gubrium and Holstein 1990,
1993b; Holstein and Gubrium 1994a). The accent here is on what is done with words,
less on how literal the process is. Interpretive practice provides a framework for this
activity.

Constitutively describing everyday life—its scenes and participants—is both artful and implicitly rhetorical (Burke 1989). Whereas the success of description, as it
is traditionally construed, might be couched in terms of accuracy, when description
is viewed as constitutive activity, the concern is more for *accountability*.
Descriptions must make sense; they must convince socially defined, culturally competent listeners that the objects, actions, or events in question warrant the attributions and categorizations that are bestowed upon them.

Descriptive discourse and actual interpretable occurrences are mutually constraining and elaborating (Bilmes 1986). Persons and situations, for example, take
on their known character as they are descriptively constituted, while, simultaneously, description and categorization orient to "what everyone knows" about the
types of people and circumstances in question if descriptions are to be compelling.
Artful description must therefore carefully craft images out of culturally shared vocabularies and understandings whose relevance to the descriptive task at hand can
be demonstrated. We will discuss some of the social mechanics of description in
this section, deferring our interest in circumstantial contingencies and resources to
the next chapter. Our intent is not to be comprehensive, but rather to highlight a
limited number of constitutive activities in order to illustrate the artfulness that suffuses descriptive practice. We continue to introduce terms of method talk along the
way.

Authorizing Description

In traditional discussions of social influence, variables associated with the authority of a claims-maker are often cited as determinants of whether or not the claim will be honored or accepted (see Cartwright 1959; Franzoi 1996). Whether the authority derives from social status, power, professional standing, special expertise, or charisma, it is argued that formulations offered by influential persons or persons occupying privileged positions are more likely to be accepted, or to outweigh or supplant formulations offered by the less influential.

In practice, however, the process is not as straightforward, not as predetermined as the more traditional view would have us believe. Such characteristics as power, status, and expertise have to be enacted—situationally invoked. They do not exist outside the matrix of interaction, but must be brought to bear interactionally on the matter at hand to take effect. Interpretive work has to be done in order for the characteristics to come into play.

This is not to say that these ostensible forms of authority are merely the artful creations of interpretive practitioners, who spontaneously generate the rhetorical resources they need to influence the task at hand. Rather, the artfulness is exhibited in how claims about status, power, and other sources of authority are accountably articulated with what is commonly known in a particular circumstance. This process and the resources it employs are reflexively related. As process is analytically foregrounded to promote its visibility, resources seem less salient, and vice versa. Neither one ever fully disappears, but instead merely awaits an analytic "unbracketing" to make its own importance evident. Let us explore some examples of how description is interactionally authorized, this time emphasizing the processual side over the substantive.

Consider how claims to professional standing, experience, or expertise might be used as forms of influence. In circumstances where such claims have currency, an experienced expert or professional is assumed to have more descriptive credibility than others (Miller 1991), but this rhetorical resource may also be mobilized locally to warrant the acceptance of allied descriptions. Take an exchange observed by Charles Suchar (1975) in a mental health clinic for emotionally disturbed children. The following are extracts from conversations between a child psychiatrist, Dr. J., and the counseling staff during psychiatric staffings, where the cases of several children are to be reviewed and evaluated by the psychiatrist. In the first extract, the psychiatrist and the child's counselor, Mrs. Star, are discussing the progress of a nine-year-old boy who has been described as having "childhood psychosis of a chronic nature." The child has been in the program for about one year and participants are evaluating his progress. The psychiatrist sounds hopeful, while the counselor seems to be pessimistic about the child's track record and future prospects:

> DR. J: I see something in him. I can smell it, something hopeful. Since he's rejected all avenues of pleasure, I don't think you should give him tasks to do. I think you're [Mrs. Star, the counselor] doing all right with him. . . . [To the program director:] I suggest we also begin seeing this mother and child together for a few visits for diagnosis.
>
> MRS. STAR: The father's a jerk—he's too rigid. I don't know if he'd like that.

Anyways, I don't know, he's [child] still twiddling [a major symptom]. It's so sad. . . . There's this kid in my neighborhood who's 20 and still does that. I don't know if [child] will ever change. It's so sad. . . .

DR. J: He [child] may do that at 20 also. He should have physical contact with someone. Mrs. Star, you're too pessimistic. . . . The hopeful thing with this type of kid is their opposition, I know. It takes experience with these kids to understand this. Once they give in and "yes" you all the time—they're cooked. Why don't you talk to him about his not talking. In time, he'll begin responding in a variety of ways, you'll see.

MRS. STAR: He *is* a great listener. I guess you're right. He knows what I'm saying. You can tell he knows. (Pp. 19–20, emphasis in the original)

Dr. J. and Mrs. Star seem initially to be at odds over both the description of the boy and what to do with him. Dr. J. "sees something [hopeful] in him," while Mrs. Star sees him as the type who is unlikely to change. Attempting to legitimate her claim, Mrs. Star invokes her knowledge of another case that she says is similar to the one under consideration. This might be seen as an appeal to specialized local knowledge. Dr. J. then speaks of the typical biography of "this type of kid," who "in time" will begin to respond if her suggestions are followed. Dr. J. suggests that her description may have greater merit than Mrs. Star's because, as Dr. J. claims, "I know" and "It takes experience" to understand these things, clearly implying Dr. J.'s superior, professionally grounded interpretive skill in such matters. Note that professionalism, experience, or local knowledge did not simply materialize, but were artfully and rhetorically brought to bear on the descriptive contest at hand. Just as Elijah Anderson's key informant, Herman, openly used Anderson—a Ph.D. candidate at the University of Chicago—to undergird his social status, Dr. J. applies a status claim to shape ongoing interaction in the staffing.

In another review, Dr. J. and a counselor-trainee, Mr. E., discuss a twelve-year-old boy who has been diagnosed as borderline schizophrenic. As in the preceding case, the boy has been in the program for about one year. Dr. J. portrays this boy in quite negative terms, calling him "pervasively anxious . . . absolutely driven by his anxiety," referring to him as a hyperactive child. Again, invoking the typical description of "such cases," Dr. J. claims expertise, this time in the latter part of her final utterance, where she once again invokes professional experience. Her rhetoric apparently brings the conversation, but not the disagreement, to an end:

DR. J: I'll tell you what he is, he's pervasively anxious, he's absolutely driven by his anxiety. [Addressing the boy's counselor, Mr. E:] If you really want to know what a hyperactive child looks like, you've got him. . . . Yeah, okay, he's begun to build controls for himself, but it was all built around his anxiety; all his activity is frenzy. . . . I think with him there is a vast split between what he says and what he feels. Most of what he says is garbage.

MR. E: [Visibly angered by the psychiatrist's last statement:] But sometimes he does mean what he says!

DR. J: But look, even from your material [progress notes written on a daily basis by counselors and submitted to the psychiatrist before the staffing] I get the feeling that what he verbalizes means nothing.

MR. E: But one time for example, he told me "I miss you" and he meant it.

DR. J: But that's different. Some things like that may touch him, but I'm still very dubious that words mean anything to him. I do not think words reach him at all. [The psychiatrist's tone of voice becomes more insistent and the counselor is still angered by the evaluation.] Look . . . Mr. E., I know what I'm talking about. I've seen cases like this before. It takes time to understand this. You must not kid yourself that what he says means anything. There's a lack of integration between his feelings and his words. (Pp. 20–21)

One might argue, as Suchar does, that the counselor-trainee ran up against the "cult of expertise" in this situation, but that would shortchange what those involved are doing with words. Experience and expertise were asserted in an accountable fashion, prompting the psychiatrist's descriptions, definitions, and proposals to prevail. In claiming that "I know what I'm talking about. I've seen cases like this before. It takes time to understand this," Dr. J. authorized her version of the case at hand in a way that resolved the discussion, at least for the moment. Her superior experience or expertise did not dictate this outcome from the outset, but was articulated from within the encounter itself, employing artful appeals to "outside" rhetorical resources. If she had not actually used these sources of influence, the authority of the case description might have developed along different lines.

Artfulness refers to the adroitness of practical reasoning. In the preceding extract, it would refer to the *use* of expertise (as opposed to some other resource such as professional standing) for authorizing description. A conversation analyst might trace how this is built up, utterance by utterance, in the interaction. But, an important feature of the exchange—its specific rhetorical quality—would be missing, something which is not noticeable in the turn-taking machinery of talk. In addition, by providing ethnographic evidence of "visible anger" and "tone of voice," Suchar informs us of the scenic, authorial presence of what is being conveyed, but not simply through words. In this case, the authority of, and challenges to, what is described, draw on unarticulated and unbracketed cultural resources that mediate the specific rhetorical force of usage in their own right.

While such unarticulated resources do not determine the developing shape of talk and interaction, they cannot be taken into account analytically by way of conversational material alone. But such culturally mediated emotional features of social interaction do condition what is otherwise being artfully developed. As we noted earlier, and as the emotionalists would remind us, ignoring them robs us of the animatedness and sheer scenic presence of what is being communicated, which, strictly speaking, is not revealed in speech exchanges. Simply analyzing conversational structure, in other words, does not make visible all forms of communication, which is a shortcoming of approaches like CA when they are exclusively concerned with the *hows* of conversational machinery.

If descriptive authority is achieved by enacting and mobilizing "outside" resources, description is also self-authorizing. By this, we mean that aspects of de-

scriptive discourse may work to insure that the description itself is taken as definitive. In a fascinating study of how laypersons come to define someone as "mentally ill," Dorothy Smith (1978) provides a language for unraveling several discursive techniques of this sort.

Smith's analysis centers on an extended interview conducted by one of her students in conjunction with a research project relating to definitions of deviance. The
key question asked of Angela, the interviewee, was: "Have you ever known anyone you thought might be mentally ill?" Angela responded to the question with a
narrative that described her friend, "K," as mentally ill, and offered several accounts
that she thought illustrated K's strange behavior. Working with the 138-line transcript of the interview, Smith carefully examined just how Angela, the "teller of the
tale," described K.

In her analysis, Smith explicitly focused on how the definition of K was achieved
within the act of conveying the description. Beginning from the presumption that
any object or event might be subject to more than one description, Smith analyzed
the text of the interview in order to explicate how the description itself was fashioned to encourage its credibility and acceptance, and how Angela established descriptive authority in the process. Smith explains that this began with Angela's very
first words in the interview: "My recognition that there might be something wrong
was very gradual, and I was actually the last of (K's) close friends who was openly
willing to admit that she was becoming mentally ill" (Smith 1978, p. 32).

This statement introduces a set of internal authorization practices that, according
to Smith, were "embedded instructions" within the description itself that subtly explained and guided how listeners were to understand what they were hearing. The
first thing to note is Angela's claim that she was a *friend* of K's who was stead-
fastly *reluctant* to accept the fact of K's mental illness. In claiming both friendship
and reluctance, Angela preempts any suggestion that her description is motivated
by anything other than the facts of the matter. The statement implies that Angela
would have no reason to mislead anyone about K; hence her descriptions can be
treated as credible. It instructs the listener to expect a truthful, even sympathetic,
description of K.

The opening statement also asserts that K was "becoming mentally ill," treating
this as a "fact" established prior to, and independent of, any accounts of it, or of attempts to overlook or excuse it. This has profound interpretive consequences because, as Smith points out, the fact "that we are told at the outset that K is mentally
ill authorizes the version of those who realized or came to admit the fact of her illness" (Smith 1978, p. 34). These first few words, Smith adds, serve as a template
for understanding all that follows in Angela's account.

Presented at the outset, the "fact" of K's mental illness serves as an interpretive
schema (Schutz 1970), a framework for making sense of subsequent claims.
Operating in a fashion similar to what Garfinkel (1967) describes as the "documentary method" of interpretation, any description or account now includes K's
mental illness as an incorrigible feature or pattern into which other observations
must fit. The asserted fact of K's mental illness thus makes any discrepancies between K's own accounts and those of others into further evidence of her illness.
After all, who could believe the explanations of a person known to be mentally ill?
K is thus disqualified from defining her own conduct, while Angela inherits defin-

itional privilege. Angela's accounts subsequently verify that the initial description is indeed valid, a process in which definition, in effect, documents itself.

The "fact" of K's mental illness authorizes other persons, but not K, to set the standards for what is to be interpreted as deviant and normal. If one is known, for all practical purposes, to be mentally ill, one cannot be the source of judgments about what is normal. Smith cites the following description of K's behavior that Angela mentioned in support of her definition of K. Recounting a series of incidents that illustrated K's strange behavior, Angela points out: "We would go to the beach or the pool on a hot day, and I would sort of dip in and just lie in the sun, while K insisted she had to swim 30 lengths" (p. 34). Notice how Angela's own behavior provides the standard for what is normal, the standard from which K's behavior deviates. The initial announcement of K's mental illness points the reader to Angela as the source of normative definition, because K is excluded from that process.

The way the swimming account is heard or read also depends upon the interpretive instructions embedded in the initial pronouncement. Description is commonsensically linked to fact so that one can claim descriptive privilege if one's descriptions are demonstrably "factual." The interpretive challenge, then, lies in *demonstrating* facticity. How is this done in the absence of the actual referent of the description in question?

Smith identifies another authorization practice that serves this purpose. Commonsensically, "facts" appear to be the same to independent observers, Smith argues. To claim something as a fact, one must show that proper procedures have been followed to establish it as "objectively" known. Smith suggests that the practical construction of a fact involves displaying that it is the same for everyone, and that witnesses' recognition of it as a fact (1) is based on direct observation, (2) is constrained by the nature of the object or event itself, and (3) is not determined by hearsay.

For example, Smith shows that Angela does not base her descriptive claims solely on her own observations. Instead, in a series of anecdotes, Angela refers to a number of persons who made similar related observations of K's bizarre behavior. By the end of the interview, five persons are introduced as witnesses to K's mental illness: Angela, Angela's mother, Trudi and Betty (friends of K's), and a woman friend of K's family. We might add that these are especially credible witnesses, since, again, each is likely to be seen as sympathetic to K and without motive to disparage her. Of course, these understandings rely upon cultural definitions of what it means to be a friend. Their analysis as such would require a shift in analytic focus to the interpretive resources employed to construct the descriptions. But given this background understanding, their presentation as a compilation of *independent* reports can be heard as factual, therefore authoritative, because they emanate from separate sources making empirical observations on different occasions, with nothing to motivate their common discovery other than K's behavior itself.

It is important to recognize that in telling her tale, Angela systematically added one account to the others, but implied no connection between witnesses or the events themselves. She did not merely tell of incidents revealing what she took to be K's troubles, but identified the separate accounts as independent sources of the "data" she was presenting. By artfully establishing their descriptions as independently "factual," Angela constructed them as collectively definitive. We should also point out that it is Smith's own method talk and bracketing operation that permits her to frame Angela's account as "facts-in-the-making" rather than merely a report of fact finding or factual reporting.

Mobilizing the Typical

It is not enough for description to emanate from an authorized source. It must also be cogent. Listeners must be compelled to think about and act towards what is described as if it were deeply and consequentially substantive. To achieve such mundane substantiality (Pollner 1987), interpretive practitioners must establish accounts as appropriate representations of their referent, all the while eliding the constitutive character of their project. To assemble convincing pictures of the world, the process of "worlding," as Pollner calls it, must proceed without notice.

Some of the invisibility of reality construction derives from its reliance on the typical and ordinary as means of interpreting experience. The use of the taken-for-granted proves to be both widespread and effective as a way of assigning sense to actions and experience. Let us examine some artful usages.

In day-to-day relations, people are confronted by experience out of which they must make sense and construct order. Upon encountering things and events, we often conclude that such-and-such occurrence is typical of this or that. Experience makes no sense until it has been categorized as evidently an instance of some known type, at least for the time being. Schutz (1970) calls this a process of *typification*. Experience, he suggests, is interpreted by casting various manifestations as elements of one or another ideal category or type that is part of a stock of knowledge at hand:

> All forms of recognition and identification, even of real objects of the outer world, are based on a *generalized* knowledge of the *type* of these objects or of the *typical* style in which they manifest themselves. . . . Each of these types has its typical style of being experienced, and the knowledge of this typical style is itself an element of our stock of knowledge at hand. This same holds good for the relations in which the objects stand to one another, for events and occurrences and their mutual relations, and so on. (Pp. 118–19, emphasis in the original)

Description tends to be formulated parsimoniously (Sacks and Schegloff 1979), through what Sacks (1972) calls "membership categorization devices." The use of a particular category or type implies a constellation of ancillary features that we take to be associated with the category (e.g., "elderly lady" might imply frailty or harmlessness). The application of a categorical description provides a basis for ascribing other characteristics, activities, and motives to objects and actions.

Typification is also a mundane form of explanation. Assigning an action to a typical category provides a set of typical motives for the action, as well as suggesting typically expected outcomes or possibilities. For instance, to say that an act of vandalism of school property is just an instance of adolescent boys acting out—"boys will be boys," so to speak—suggests that the motivation for the perpetrators' actions are not necessarily insidious, the damage done is not overly serious, and the perpetrators are likely to "outgrow" their misbehaviors. In other words, a typification offers a "vocabulary of motives" (Mills 1940) or an "account" (Scott and Lyman

1968) of what is said and done, elucidating and justifying what is simultaneously described.

There is much more at stake in the typification process than categorization and representation, however. Typification is consequential in that it guides and justifies courses of action. In representing a particular occurrence as typical of a category of occurrences, all features of the category reasonably accrue to the occurrence. For example, if an incident is typified as the act of a normally "childish" or "immature" adolescent, we might conclude that, for all practical purposes, the event was not especially damning or pathological. There would be no compelling reason to belabor the matter. As we noted earlier, we might conclude that the adolescent will eventually "grow up" and put such childishness behind him, thus interpretively normalizing the behavior.

In turn, the categorization of this adolescent as normal is corroborated as the incident in question is interpreted as one typical of a normal, if immature, child. The typification of the person and the definition of the act reciprocally document and confirm one another. The type of person involved makes the act understandable in a particular way, while the act—defined in this fashion—provides additional evidence that the person is behaving just like a member of the specified type.

Typifying the "same" act as deviant or pathological, of course, would suggest an entirely different response. It would be altogether reasonable to search for further evidence suggested by an attribution of deviance, which could mean attending closely to the individual involved for verbal or behavioral signs that would substantiate the categorization. Dismissing the act in question would be unreasonable. As before, the type (in this case, deviant), in turn, becomes more "apparent" as its concrete signs are identified, reciprocally documenting both the act and the category. As before, the assignment of experience to a particular category promotes distinctive constellations of understanding that carry evaluative implications with practical consequences.

The artfully practical side of typification has been documented in myriad everyday circumstances. Studies of human service settings such as welfare offices (see Miller 1991; Miller and Holstein 1995, 1996), homeless agencies (Spencer 1994), juvenile courts (Emerson 1969), schools (Cicourel and Kitsuse 1963), treatment centers for emotionally disturbed youth (Buckholdt and Gubrium 1979), and police departments (Cicourel 1968) are especially revealing since definitional eligibility must usually be established before services are rendered. Consider, for example, the practical implications that emerge for someone being typified as the "victim" of domestic violence or as a "battered woman" as opposed to the wife who had "a little disagreement with her husband." Donileen Loseke's (1989, 1992) analysis of staff members' definitional work at a battered women's shelter is exemplary. Loseke suggests that the typification process is central to nearly all consequential decision making at the shelter she studied. As a practical matter, any woman requesting services must descriptively fit the "battered woman" type or she will not be accepted as a client. The category, argues Loseke, comprises an open-ended constellation of characteristics and meanings, the application of which is by no means formulaic or automatic. Rather than simply matching the "objective" profile of the candidate client with a formal set of eligibility criteria, shelter workers adroitly articulate the salient characteristics of the presenting woman with the locally developed "battered woman type." The application of the type not only reflects collective understandings of what kind of women are "battered," but also draws upon local notions of what sort of women benefit from the shelter's services.

Take the following extracts from the "log book" in which shelter workers write entries briefly describing how they process each application for service. When a woman appears at the shelter, a worker interviews her, decides whether to accept her as a client, or refers her elsewhere, then writes a brief summary of the process and outcome in the log book. In the two extracts below, shelter workers formulate the prospective clients as exemplars of the "battered woman" type, using terms such as "very typical," and "classic battered case" as they construct the textual basis for admitting each woman to the shelter:

> Her doctor told her to get out (of her house) before it's too late. She sounded like a very typical battered woman. She cannot do anything, has lost all her friends, is always at home living this way. Her doctor told her that her physical problems were due to stress and will get better when she leaves him (her husband). She has been warned not to tell him she's leaving.

> She seems like a classic battered case. Had a long session with her, she was crying and very hurt. Absolutely no self-esteem, husband treated her like a child but she's still in love with him. . . . She feels very helpless and lonely. (Loseke 1989, p. 184)

Notice that the typification process relies upon the artful articulation of the case at hand with local understandings of just what constitutes the type, linking the *how* with the *what*. As Loseke explains, we see this in the first extract through the following features of the log entry: (1) the woman was depicted as a "battered woman" by citing a condition of current danger ("got out before it's too late"), (2) it was a situation of prolonged oppression ("always at home living this way"), (3) there were dire consequences of abuse ("her physical problems are due to stress"), (4) the woman lacked alternative resources ("she cannot do anything, has lost all her friends"), and (5) there was a prognosis justifying admission to the shelter (she "will get better when she leaves him"). Taken together, these characterizations provide an institutionally adequate definition of the "battered woman" for *this* shelter's purposes, at *this* particular time, under *these* circumstances.

While different, the second entry also contains a list of characteristics of the typical, said to be "classic, battered" case: (1) the woman was oppressed (her "husband treated her like a child") and (2) the woman subjectively felt demoralized and without alternatives ("very hurt, no self-esteem, helpless, lonely"). Again, the typical is crafted from local particulars.

Loseke points out that each of the entries simultaneously describes a "type of woman appropriate for shelter residence, a woman who needs the shelter, who could benefit from services, and who would likely become an acceptable member of the shelter commune" (Loseke 1989, p. 184)—the "battered woman." But the log entries depend on local knowledge about the shelter, its work, resources, and constraints for the internal logic of just what constitutes a "battered woman" to be fully understood. This logic must be apparent in its articulation of each case for the shelter workers' descriptions and admissions decisions to be fully accountable in practice.

Typifications cannot be understood separate from the conditions of their use. Indeed, the circumstances of usage can drastically differentiate what might on the surface seem to be similar types. On one occasion, for example, typifying an act as "immature" might mitigate the interpretation of misdeeds, as in the example of the "adolescent acting out." But for a seriously disgruntled wife, say, to typify her estranged husband as sexually "immature"—nothing more than an "immature little boy"—has much more derogatory connotations. Once again, we see the reflexive relation between articulation, circumstantial conditions, and meaning.

Using "Normal" Forms

As more or less global characterizations, typifications assert membership in a particular category. The act of casting a person as "a guy who seems to have his life together" or as "the kind of person who will go right off the deep end," classifies him as a "normal" member of the category to which he or she is assigned, irrespective of the way the category is evaluated. For example, describing a person as a "child molester" establishes him as a normal, typical member of the category, even as the category implies pathological abnormality.

Constitutive description relies extensively on ostensibly shared understandings of the normal ingredients of membership categories, in order to convey intended meanings in terms of familiar referents. The use of such normal forms capitalizes on "what everyone is presumed to know" about a particular category without having to specify a list of identifying characteristics. It depends at least partially upon the faith that an audience will fill in the details of what it means to be a particular type from a more-or-less culturally shared stock of knowledge—what Garfinkel (1967) calls institutionalized features of the collectivity.

Consider how normal forms are used in the course of involuntary commitment hearings, where descriptions of the candidate mental patient have immediate practical implications (Holstein 1993). While candidate patients are of course compared to specialized psychiatric types, such as "schizophrenic," more commonly, rather pedestrian categories are applied. In the following extract from a case involving Polly Brown, for example, Brown's hospitalization is sought based on a charge of grave disability: the DA alleges that Brown's bizarre, agitated behavior makes it impossible for her to get along with others, so she can't function socially. Part of the evidence for commitment involves an accusation that Brown threatened staff members on the psychiatric ward where she spent the past few days being observed and evaluated. At one point in the hearing, Brown's public defender attempts to argue that her outburst is understandable in light of its context, the behavior one might expect from anyone under the circumstances. The outburst, in other words, is an instance of what generally would be considered *normal in that circumstance*, not a normal instance of the clinically abnormal:

> As for her [Brown's] behavior in the hospital, we have heard that a nurse called her children bastards. I believe anyone would be agitated if they heard this sort of talk. She's protective like any mother would be. Any woman with children would be upset. (P. 153)

The PD's argument both explains the situational contingency that makes Brown's alleged outburst understandable and presents the reaction in relation to the normal, that is, in terms of what "anyone" might do, especially any mother. Providing a scenic description of Brown's behavior, the PD then establishes circumstantial "causes" by suggesting that what happened would have resulted for "anyone": the setting motivated the behavior. The normal form is constituted out of the circumstance at hand, then used as a standard of comparison, in effect doubly normalizing Brown's putatively abnormal behavior. Once again, we see the artfulness involved in producing both the normal, typical form, and in articulating the case at hand as an evidently clear instance of that typification.

Demographic categories such as gender, age, and occupation are frequently used to interpret the normal. Culturally assumed notions about the normal or conventional behaviors and traits of members of a particular class or group are applied to establish standards against which other cases can be compared. In Polly Brown's case, the membership categorization devices (Sacks 1972) "mother" and "family" were used to interpret the reasonableness of the patient's actions (she was being "protective," an expectable reaction from a "mother" when her "children" were disparaged).

Even the most casual acts of classification serve to typify in this way. Gender, for example, is invariably noted in simple forms of address (e.g., *Ms.* Smith, *Mr.* Jones) or in repeated use of personal pronouns (e.g., *He* did this and that; *She* has four children.). Such references are so routine and commonplace as to go virtually unnoticed, constituting "factual" representations that attract no special attention and appear on the surface to be unimportant. Yet they can serve as significant sources of perceptual and evaluative organization, providing implicit instructions for how to understand and relate to what is being described.

Returning again to the involuntary commitment process, we can see how simple references and depictions in terms of gender and age tacitly index particular traits, symptoms, and behaviors, providing a frame of reference for how these should be construed (Holstein 1987). As categorization devices, gender and age present commonsense models for depicting what culturally known types of people are like, and how members of such categories may be expected to behave. Arguments concerning psychiatric diagnosis or a patient's ability to live successfully in a community setting, say, often proceed within the framework of such depictions. For example, as a matter of practice, participants often contend that what may be considered mentally healthy *for a man* might be diagnosed as pathological *for a woman*, and vice versa.

Interpretation of this sort took place in a commitment hearing involving Kathleen Wells, a 32-year-old white female who was found living in a large cardboard box beneath a railroad overpass. While she was diagnosed as severely mentally ill and several problems were identified, Wells's hearing in Northern Court eventually turned to a discussion of the viability of her "living accommodations." Arguing for commitment, the DA pointed to the deficiencies of her existing situation, then used the patient's gender as a framework for claiming that the arrangement was especially untenable, as in the following extract:

Now I know Miss Wells claims that this [the cardboard box] is as good as the subsidized public housing programs the DSS [Department of Social Services] has suggested she look into, but we have to consider more than its construction aspects. . . . You can't allow a woman to be exposed to all the other things that go on out there under the [railroad] tracks. Many of those men have lived like that for years, but we're talking about a woman here. A sick and confused woman who doesn't realize the trouble she's asking for. She simply cannot live like that. That's no place for a woman, especially after dark. . . . She's not taking it [being a woman in the midst of men] into account. She doesn't realize how dangerous it is for her. It's up to the court to protect her. (Holstein 1993, p. 159)

The argument here is that the proposed living arrangement, while perhaps acceptable for a man, is inappropriate for a woman. Indeed, the transcript shows that the dangerous character of the setting, and its consequent untenability, was not fully apparent until the setting was described as the potential residence of a woman. The DA expressly references and uses the tacitly shared knowledge of the gendered nature of settings to make his case. Again, it is important to emphasize that this otherwise artful description relies upon available, culturally understandable images as resources for interpretation. Still, the DA has to invoke gender as a normal form to clearly establish the unsuitability of the situation, tying the *what* to the *how*. The tenability of the setting per se is not being evaluated, for it cannot be meaningfully removed from its links with its occupant's gender.

Age can be used similarly (Holstein 1990). In a case involving Jake Donner, for example, Dr. Haas, the psychiatrist who testified at Donner's commitment hearing, used normal expectations about persons of a particular age group to establish the inappropriateness of Donner's behavior. Consider how Haas employed age-related typifications in the following testimony:

Jake has the, shall we say, the enthusiasm of a much younger man. His landlord says he's out every night, and sometimes doesn't come back until the next morning. When I examined Mr. Donner he made no secret of his, let's say, passion for members of the opposite sex. He was extremely distraught about being hospitalized because he said he was dating several women and they would all be upset if he stopped coming round to visit them. He said some pretty outrageous things for a man his age. He claimed that he needed to have sex at least once a day or he would, as he put it, lose his manhood. And he said these women were anxious to oblige him. Now, here's a man in his fifties—what is he, fifty-five, sixty—saying the kind of things you'd expect from some teenager bragging to his buddies, but I'd have to say they were clearly inappropriate from him. (Holstein 1993, pp. 155–56)

Throughout his testimony, Haas elucidated much of Donner's symptomatology with reference to age. Diagnostic relevance was articulated by establishing a connection between Donner's age and interpretations of Donner's affect and behavior. Haas argued, for example, that Donner's tales of his sexual exploits were "outrageous" for a "man his age." What was tacitly taken to be normal for a man of this age underpinned the standards of appropriateness the doctor invoked. The sexual talk, for instance, was not intrinsically outrageous, but was portrayed as such only when it was linked to normative expectations for an older person who presumably would not be erotically inclined. Age provided an interpretive benchmark for understanding the conduct and claims in question.

As each of our examples illustrates, references to ostensibly normal forms appear to be constrained as much by speakers' pragmatic interests as by the objective characteristics of those to whom they refer. Altogether different meanings can be conveyed by the artful use of "normal" forms, depending upon the local objectives of description. The general point is that the meaning of any typification is artfully, yet circumstantially, organized. People actively formulate and use recognizable types, exercising creative discretion in how they assign and depict related attributes, but do so in relation to the interpretive contingencies of the case at hand. And once again, we should point out how we must continually shift our analytic brackets in order to understand the meanings that inform artfulness (as well as the artful practices that evince meaning).

Contrast Structures

Typifications are also used as points of descriptive contrast. Smith (1978) refers to these as "contrast structures" which are formulated so as to juxtapose characterizations of traits or behavior with statements that supply instructions for seeing the traits or behavior as anomalous or problematic. "Standard pattern rules" provide expectations about what events or behaviors follow from a characterization. Anomalies are accomplished by constructing relationships between such rules on the one hand, and descriptions of an object or instances of behavior, on the other, so that the former do not properly account for the latter. It then becomes "evident" that the object or behavior in question is anomalous.

Smith analyzes several contrast structures that develop in the interview with Angela concerning K's mental illness. The following portrayal by Angela provides an example. In the course of her description of "strange" things that K had done, Angela recounts the following:

(i) (K) would take baths religiously every night and pin up her hair
(ii) but she would leave the bath dirty. (P. 42)

In this example, part (i) presents a rule derived from routine features of K's behavior, then part (ii) shows that K also routinely violates that rule. The general expectation that is established is that given the facts of part (i), one would typically expect K to be "fastidious," oriented to and concerned about cleanliness. But instead of this, as part (ii) indicates, K leaves the bath dirty. Anomaly is produced because the expectation is that K should leave the bath clean after she is done. Following the rule, the hearer is left to infer that this is indeed "strange."

We saw the application of similar contrast structures in the preceding section, where gender- and age-related typifications were used to accentuate the problems of those to whom they were applied. While they were not all as concise as Smith's examples, each invoked discrepancies between what was normatively expected and what was observed. Recall, for instance, how Jake Donner's age and conduct were juxtaposed and compared with descriptions of behavior considered normal or appropriate for someone of a *different* age group. Where contrasts were expected, apparent similarities were pinpointed as signs of Donner's inappropriate behavior, and ultimately cited as symptoms of his illness. Donner's "enthusiasm" was portrayed as that of a "much younger man." In the ensuing discussion, Dr. Haas used this to document Donner's mental disturbance, framing it as age-inappropriate and symptomatic of psychiatric distress. Haas also compared Donner's claims about sexual needs and prowess to those of a boastful adolescent. The contrast drawn between what was considered normal for "a man in his fifties" and a "teenager" underscored the impropriety of Donner's claim. The doctor constructed anomalies by artfully crafting contrasts between Donner's reported behavior and that of the "normal" man of his type/age.

Let us add one final example from the commitment hearings to illustrate the production and use of contrast structures. A psychiatrist had examined candidate patient Gerald Simms, and, at the commitment hearing, testified that Simms should be hospitalized. Characterizing Simms as a "severely troubled man," the psychiatrist provided the following account for his diagnosis of schizophrenia:

> Mr. Simms suffers from drastic mood swings. His affect is extremely labile. One minute he'll be in tears, the next he's just fine. He fluctuates. His affect may be flattened, then elevated. One moment he'll be telling you about his cleaning business, then he'll flip out of character and cry like a brokenhearted schoolgirl over the most insignificant thing. Something that should never upset a grown man like Mr. Simms. During his periods of flattened affect, he seems to lose all interest. . . . His passivity—he's almost docile in a very sweet sort of way. He just smiles and lets everything pass. It's completely inappropriate for an adult male. (Holstein 1993, p. 155)

Here, the psychiatrist explicitly contrasts Simm's behavior with normal expectations for a person of his gender and age. Simms' emotions are portrayed as those of "a brokenhearted schoolgirl" crying over matters that should "never upset a grown man." His "passivity" is "inappropriate for an adult male." Simms's gender is made salient and consequential to the diagnosis, as it is displayed, juxtaposed, and contrasted with descriptions of behavior that is femalelike, or not properly masculine. Apparent incongruities are then cited as documents of mental illness. The production of contrast is central to making the description convincing, but the contrasts do not exist apart from the interpretive work done to establish them as relevant in the give and take of the hearing.

Metaphorical Usage

As with literary metaphors, everyday metaphors can be used as devices for understanding and experiencing one kind of thing in terms of another (Lakoff and Johnson 1980). We fashion descriptive metaphors to borrow or transfer meaning between interpretive domains, often importing the typically ordinary in order to interpret something new or unfamiliar, making sense of what might otherwise seem uninterpretable.

Consider the way a very ordinary metaphor is developed and used in the course of a discussion that took place during a meeting of an Alzheimer's disease caregivers' support group (Gubrium 1986a). One of the authors had been observing this group for several months and this was the first time the metaphor of the "hardy weed" was applied. The following extract starts when a caregiving spouse named Maude begins to talk about the energy it takes to be a responsible caregiver. Coincidentally, she notices a plant growing vigorously into the room from under a door to the outside. Other members of the group—Henry, Vera, Sam, and Anne, caregivers themselves—respond to what Maude indicates:

MAUDE: Would you look over there at that!
   SAM: What? What're you looking at? The door?
MAUDE: Sam, the weed. That little weed over there. See it. It's growing under the door from the outside.

HENRY: It's coming into the room for shelter. It's getting nippy out there and wants to come in.

MAUDE: That weed's got it rough out there by that busy street. [Elaborates] But it's makin' it. All that dust, grime, and traffic. It's hard on a weed. Kinda like us, I guess I was thinkin'. All the energy it takes. If we didn't have that kind of energy, we'd be dead by now.

VERA: All shriveled and dried up. No good to no one.

SAM: Ya got to give it to the weed. It's a survivor.

ANNE: Well, I ain't a weed. But if that's what it takes, ya keep right on agrowin' and gettin' to where you can survive and keep going. [Elaborates] Gosh, sometimes I think I won't be able to make it. He's [her demented spouse] gettin' awful heavy and he really can't help me any more. I'm going to need all the strength of that there old dandelion plant or I ain't goin' to make it.

MAUDE: If that weed can make it, so can we. That's what I'm thinking. You've gotta get up all your strength and just do it! [Getting up from her chair] I think I'll give that little old weed some water. We all need a boost and a bit of kindness, right? (Gubrium and Holstein 1995a, p. 564)

The exchange turns to other matters, but the weed is not forgotten. Repeatedly, group members refer back to this material reminder of their challenges as caregivers. Whenever the topic of persistence or endurance comes up, members use the weed to describe the kind of person it takes to deal with the trials and tribulations of dementia care on a daily basis. In subsequent meetings, as the weather changes and the weed withers, the group methodically alters its metaphorical usage, establishing new meanings that apply to different aspects of the caregiving experience. Members use the weed's withered condition to warn of possible things to come, of the effect of the rigors and stress of caregiving. They now see the weed in the context of the progressive burdens of care, poignantly conveying how the weed embodies the gradual but inevitable exhaustion of the caregiver.

Usage is a resourceful response to circumstance. In this case, caregivers make use of a meaningful feature of the immediate physical environment to interpret their situation.[4] They use the hardy weed to represent, even glorify, stamina and unappreciated persistence. They summon another ordinary image, of a withered weed, to convey something decidedly less sanguine in relation to the burdens of care that seem to mount in caregivers' lives. Contrasting communicative projects demand artfully variable usage, the result of which shows how the ordinary can be brought to bear in extraordinary ways. Images are summoned, elaborated and applied to meet the practical demands of everyday description. As we shall see in Chapter 8, artfully managed images can become local cultural resources for further interpretation of as yet unanticipated circumstances.

NARRATIVE PRACTICE

The recent growth of social research on narrative has contributed its own distinctive analytic terminology, bringing constitutive *how* questions to a crossroads with *what* concerns. While not neglecting the plots of narratives (the *whats*), qualitative researchers are increasingly attempting to understand the ways in which stories about experience are presented, structured, and made to cohere (the *hows*). As Catherine Riessman explains, analysis is moving beyond an interest in story content to questions such as "Why was the story told *that* way?" (1993, p. 2, emphasis in the original).

Part of the interest in narrative comes from the increasingly popular vision of lives as "storied" in one way or another (see, for example, Josselson and Lieblich 1995). Since stories have tellers, listeners, and circumstances for telling them (Bauman 1986), narrative analysis has begun to consider lives as acts of storytelling, attending to issues such as what life experiences get included and left out of narratives, how events are combined or emplotted, and how the overall course of life is framed in the process (Gubrium, Holstein, and Buckholdt 1994). There is a growing interest in how narratives structure perception, organize memory, and supply motives—in how storytelling is a part of human psychology (Gergen 1985; Sarbin 1986; Bruner 1987). Susan Chase (1995, p. 2) argues that sociological interests are also served by "taking narrative seriously" because narration, as a form of social interaction, "embodies the relation between narrator and culture," another way of bridging *hows* and *whats*. Donald Polkinghorne (1988) suggests that "narrative is the fundamental scheme for linking individual human actions and events into interrelated aspects of an understandable composite." Narrative schemes, he writes, "produce the particular form and meaning that is human existence" (p. 13).

We explore several aspects of narrative practice in the following sections. Once again, our aim is not to comprehensively review narrative studies, but rather to illustrate by exemplification the analytic idiom used to document the artful, interactional features of narration. We emphasize studies of narrative's ordinary contours, considering examples of storytelling and narrative description that may not have all the features of more formally crafted literary narratives or biographies, but which nonetheless put lives into narrative perspective.

While there is scholarly disagreement over just what a narrative is or how narration should be defined (see Polkinghorne 1988; Riessman 1993), for our purposes we will consider narratives to be accounts that offer some scheme, either implicitly or explicitly, for organizing and understanding the relation of objects and events described. Narratives need not be full-blown stories with requisite internal structures, but may be short accounts that emerge within or across turns at ordinary conversation, in interviews or interrogations, in public documents, or in organizational records (see Riessman 1993). As a meaning-making device, a narrative assembles individual objects, actions, and events into a comprehensible pattern; telling a story turns available parts into a meaningful whole. Contrasted, with, say, a mere list of objects or actions, a narrative can be seen to have a concerted order or structure, an orientation to the temporality of occurrences, and active, if flexible, linkages between elements.[5]

Narrative Linkage and Horizons

How are we to understand the meaning of what people tell us about their lives and experiences? One way is to turn to what they actively and artfully do with stories for the answer. As far as narrative practice is concerned, we need to consider how narrators link together aspects of experience and thereby meaningfully articulate the stories they tell. Understanding derives from the pattern of linkages, not from any single element. Meaning, in other words, *is* a linkage. Let us turn to narrative linkage as a meaning-making process, emphasizing the ways meaning is derived from how things are put together.

In practice, narration or storytelling comprises both matters told and the process of telling, both *whats* and *hows*. Narrative requires that various story elements be tied together in ways that produce coherent meaning. We can illustrate narrative production through the life stories of nursing home residents, which one of the authors gathered and analyzed as part of a study of the subjective meaning of the qualities of life and care in institutions (Gubrium 1993b). In these narratives, we see that stories are organized in complex ways to interpret and appreciate the diverse "qualities" of living in an institution. Given the opportunity to discuss in their own words the qualities of their lives and care in the nursing home, the residents offer accounts that are striking in the variety of concerns, pleasures, problems, and challenges conveyed, far more than the checklist of "qualities of life" that standard assessment instruments attempt to capture.

In the study, residents were asked to tell their life stories, following Bruner's (1986) procedure for eliciting subjectively relevant accounts of life. Interviewers encouraged residents to speak of the qualities of their care and lives in relation to lifelong experiences and to common public concerns such as the personal consequences of institutionalization. The researcher's leading question was, if residents were asked to be ethnographers of their own lives in the nursing home, how would they represent the quality of those lives?

The concept "narrative linkage" helps us to understand both what residents thought about their lives as a whole and how they articulated the various aspects in relation to their nursing home experience. Capable of being used either as a verb or a noun, narrative linkage can be viewed as both active and substantive. Viewed actively, linkage is the process through which elements of a life story are brought together and juxtaposed, combined into a complex ensemble of objects and/or events that together convey meaning. Viewed substantively, the linkages are the units of meaning that coalesce out of the narrative assembly process. As we look at these narrative linkages in the nursing home data, we can analyze both *what* is meant by the quality of life and *how* meaning is assembled.

We refer to patterns of narrative linkage as "horizons of meaning"; these are the contextual contours of the stories assembled by meaningfully linking together life experiences. Like Sacks's membership categorization devices, horizons are culturally mediated and suggest particular linkages and not others. That narration has horizons implies that, as listeners, we can discern a particular pattern in an unfolding story and can anticipate, even at the start, how a story will develop. Yet, at the same time, there are narrative nuances and elements of surprise, implicating the artfulness of storytelling and the elasticity of culture, suggesting further that horizons reflexively relate to storytelling. Horizons and linkages are thus mutually constitutive, reciprocally forming parts and connections into recognizable wholes. The same elements of experience can be linked together into differing configurations, taking on contrasting meanings as they coalesce in relation to distinct horizons.

Orienting to both linkage and horizon, let us look at how nursing home residents tie aspects of their institutional experience together, as well as how they make connections between the nursing home and life on the "outside," both past and present, in telling their stories. Consider the responses of two residents who made contrasting narrative linkages with, and between, life experiences. Bea Lindstrom's life story is told in terms of a personal ethic of distributive justice. According to Lindstrom, life for her has centered on the expectation that others should treat her fairly and that she, in turn, will never take undue advantage of them. She assiduously respects others' dignity and property and expects the same in return. Details of Lindstrom's childhood experiences, her marriage, her earlier adult life, and, now, her interpersonal relations in the nursing home are consistently told in these terms.

Like other residents who tie their stories together with this ethic, Lindstrom is enduringly vigilant. Her narrative is a tale of being constantly on guard, lest other residents or staff members invade her personal space or treat her badly. She claims she has been watchful her whole life. She repeatedly insists, however, that she is careful not to intrude into other residents' affairs nor to infringe on staff members' work. Above all, Lindstrom is militantly independent. Taken together, the narrative linkages in her story show a continuous preoccupation with such matters, the horizons of which serve to engross Lindstrom in the ongoing qualities of care and life in the nursing home.

An extract from an interview illustrates how Lindstrom links aspects of her life together with the threads of vigilance and independence (Carol is the interviewer):

CAROL: Let me ask you this, Bea. Describe for me a typical day in your life now.

BEA: I barely ever get out of this hole. I'd be so happy if I could. [Pause] I'll tell you how it is. They [staff members] wake ya up. You run to the john. That's how it is. And then you get dressed and you go, you go for breakfast. It's not too bad, but it's the same thing every morning. . . . So you're not interested in that. But anyway, there's coffee. And that's it. Ain't no home. Living here is a rough one. Ya got so many bosses here. I don't like bein' bossed . . . I don't take it. Always did. So that's my story. Like I said, this ain't home. It'd never make it. I don't know . . . too many bosses, I guess. . . . They come in the night and want you to go to bed and you're not sleepy. I won't do it. I'm not going to sleep because they want me to. It's my life too! [Pause] I'm a hellcat! . . . I certainly don't claim this here to be a part of my life. I don't claim it at all.

CAROL: Why do you say it's separate, that it's not part of your life?

BEA: Honey, I just don't like it. If I could do what I wanted to do and go and come when I wanted to. . . . Sure I would do what my husband would ask me to do. And he would do what I asked him to do, but we didn't tell one another they had to do it. I think that's the way it should be. And, honey, it sure ain't that way here. Every Tom, Dick, and Harry's always interferin' in your stuff. . . . I don't like this place. I want to get out and if I could get out, I'd go. I won't be happy here. I just like [pause] I feel like I'm in jail.

CAROL: I've heard other people say that.

BEA: Yeah, even the bed. [Strokes her bed] Run your hand over that.

CAROL: [Feeling the bedding] Plastic-feeling, not too comfortable.

BEA: [Sarcastically] I'm not gonna pee in the bed!

CAROL: I guess some of them [other residents] do.

BEA: Well, honey, I ain't some of them! They [the staff] don't remember that, honey. I asked them to take this thing [plastic sheet] out.

CAROL: They won't do it?

BEA: They won't do it! And it makes me mad as a hellcat. They got no respect for no one. Ya have to keep an eye on 'em all day and night. [Pause] Oh, hell, I'm just getting old and decapitated [sic]. . . . You have to keep an eye on them all the time. The treatment stinks. . . . I've got a mind of all the things I wanna do. That's what I wanna do and I don't like to be told how to do things and things. . . . A place like this, honey, ain't good for an old lady like me. We don't like no one mussin' with us. We keep to ourselves. (Gubrium 1993b, pp. 92–93)

Combined with Bea's other responses, the extract displays both of Lindstrom's abiding horizons: independence and vigilance. Note how she collects a variety of everyday occurrences together within these horizons, ultimately offering up a picture of the nursing home as a "jail" that strips her of her rights and freedom. The plastic sheet is not simply a discomfort but an assault on her dignity and independence. Her comments are woven around others' refusals to honor her requests and their inability to see her as she "really" is. This is linked to the staff's general lack of respect for residents. Bea narratively links those who offer no respect to her need to be constantly on the alert, to the need to "keep an eye on 'em" all the time. The horizons of independence and vigilance alternate, serving to cast the assembly of disparate incidents into the "jail" that is her nursing home experience. Linking nearly everything to these concerns, Lindstrom narratively appropriates her everyday vexations to the dominant horizons of her story. Given this pattern of linkages, we might guess that if we had heard more, or asked about other matters, we would likely be told more of the same story.

Compare this with resident Julia McCall's account, which constructs the qualities of life and care in her facility in terms that ultimately marginalize the quality of daily living. While the nursing home is salient to her, it is not nearly as important as "God's place." In Julia's words, she "loves the Lord" and thinks mainly of God's kingdom, not this world. Her story is suffused with references to religious beliefs and churchgoing. As she speaks of her life, Julia links each fact of her past and her present, from childhood to old age, with what she believes God intends for her in His grand design; she looks ahead to heavenly bliss. As the following extract illustrates, hers is a story narratively centered in the afterlife, mundane matters taking second place to otherworldly concerns (Jay is the interviewer):

JAY: Ms. McCall? Why don't you tell me a little about your life? . . .

JULIA: Well, you done asked, bless your heart. . . . I think I've had a pretty good life. I think the Lord's been good to me. I've been in church all my life. . . . I've been in this place for twelve years. That's a long time. . . . I've had a lot of pains and sickness, but I was pretty tough. I'm still livin', ain't I? The Lord provides, bless Him. I was raised to be a nice person. I was raised to go to church. . . . You know, I got a lot of friends. A lot of friends in here I don't know, but I think I have. . . . I got a lot of in here that, well, some's can be nasty, but they're still good people. I like my nurses. . . . They're better to me than anybody, even better to me than even my children. But really, they're all sweet, God bless 'em. God loves all his children, no matter. . . . I think I'm going to heaven from here. The Bible says that heaven's full, don't it? Well, I think He's got a place up there for me. . . .

JAY: If you could live your life over, what would you do differently?

JULIA: I don't know. I think I would just live it. . . . I wouldn't want to live it over. It might be worse. . . . I have never had anything that I really hated. I ain't really never hated nobody, have you? . . . I'm sorry for them some-times, aren't you? Like some's—some nurses and old ladies here—got bad attitudes. I'm sorry for them when they don't believe such a thing as God. . . . I've talked to some of them once and I don't think they've got good sense. I don't think they've ever read the Bible. But they all God's children. . . . Well, now, I don't have me anything much to look forward to here . . . but as I says, I'm looking to going to heaven and bein' up there. . . .

JAY: . . . But what about this place? Tell me about life in this place. How is the care here?

JULIA: Well, it's not too bad. There's some pretty nice people in here. I think some don't know much, but they can't help it. I think the nurses and the doctors is the smartest people there is, most of them anyhow. I got a sweet doctor. . . . I was real sick once, real sick. . . . I said, "Well why don't you just let me die?" He said, "I ain't gonna let you die 'cause you're too sweet to die." . . . I'm not afraid to die because I'm going to the right place. I think I'm going to meet my Savior. (Gubrium 1993b, pp. 71–75)

Additional responses show that against a horizon of otherworldly concerns, Julia's interest in the immediate quality of care and life in the nursing home is relatively minor. She is not oblivious to how the staff treat her, how clean the premises are, or how friendly other residents are. But as far as "lovin' the Lord" is concerned, the qualities of care and of life in the nursing home are, at best, worldly comforts, paling in comparison to salvation. At worst, the qualities are a source of minor daily irritations. Julia still finds it in her heart to accept those who vex her because, as she notes, "God loves all his children no matter." Throughout the interview, the in-terviewer attempts to steer the conversation to more mundane, worldly concerns, but Julia goes on to shrug off their importance, veering back to heaven, hell, God, and everlasting life. While other connections are evidently available, Julia contin-ues to use the "love of the Lord" to bring out the good in "all his children." As Julia tells her story, troubles and troublemakers of this life evaporate. They are hardly consequential in the greater scheme of God's ubiquitous and omnipotent love. Narratively linked to the future, Julia McCall's life on earth is merely a vehicle to a greater joy.

Such narratives show that the qualities of care and life are not simply assessments of daily living and caregiving, but are assembled into meaningful wholes composed of highly purposive linkages with lifelong experience. When residents are asked to tell their stories and speak of the qualities of care and of life in their own terms, they become narratively active subjects. The "quality" of care and life is diversely constructed, linked with, and given meaning in relation to, personal orientations, values, and conditions (see Holstein and Gubrium 1995a).[6]

Shifts in Narrative

While narrative linkages and their horizons guide and substantively structure accounts, they are neither singular nor immutable. Any one person may possess more than one narrative voice, which provides discursive grounds for recognizable shifts in horizons (Holstein and Gubrium 1995a). Speaking as a father, for example, a man might tell a completely different story of his own childhood exploits than he would speaking as a "drinking buddy" down at the bar. Given the possibility that narrators can assume various perspectives and speak with multiple voices, narrative shifts should be expected as various roles or perspectives are taken or provoked. Thus, a radical change in position or in a story line does not necessarily suggest narrative chaos or deception. To the contrary, it may simply signal that the narrator is reformulating a narrative line to voice different horizons and linkages.

Consider the following extract from data gathered as part of a study of institutionalized emotionally disturbed children (see Buckholdt and Gubrium 1979). The extract is drawn from a parent-effectiveness group meeting during a discussion of child-rearing practices. A mother of three was asked whether she modeled herself after her parents in disciplining her own children:

> It depends. When my kids are really bad, I mean really bad, that's when I think how my mother used to do with us. You know, don't spare the rod or something like that in those days? But, usually, I feel that Mother was too harsh with us and I think that that kind of punishment isn't good for kids today. Better to talk about it and iron things out that way. Still, like I say, it depends on how you want to think about it, doesn't it?

By the end of the extract, we learn that the "it depends" feature of this response marks the multivocal character of narrative production. To convey narrative meaning is to tell a story about the subject matter under consideration, embedding what is being talked about in further talk, which can be a story about storytelling (see Riessman 1993). In this regard, we can interpret this mother's statement as, initially, the beginning of a story about her parenting concerns "when [her] children are really bad." In this story, the mother comments that she thinks about discipline in terms of what her own mother did. She voices what her mother might have said. Her response is interpreted within an emergent chronicle of contingent intergenerational emulation. If she had continued with that story—developing its plot—she might have made narrative linkages with, say, the rampant breakdown of discipline in today's younger generation, something, she could have added, that was quite different in her parent's era. The mother paraphrased the maxim "spare the rod and spoil the child" to highlight such sentiments. In other words, the story she began to tell had a well motivated beginning, with linkages that could recognizably be developed into a predictable middle, and rationally conclusive end.

But mid-response, the mother shifts narrative gears, altering her story's horizon.

The initial, inchoate story highlighted the misbehavior of children in relation to generational differences. In that narrative context, her own mother served as a positive model for parenting. However, not far into that story, the phrase "but, usually" sets off a shift in linkages in which punishment rather than misbehavior is narratively foregrounded. While similar, linkages now orient more to consequences than causes. In that narrative context, this mother's story about her own mother's practices produces a negative model—of someone prone to exacting excess punishment. "Punishment" is tacitly divided into two categories, corporal and verbal, and the mother states that, currently, ironing things out is more effective. The kind of punishment her mother employed would not be "good for kids today."

At the end of the extract, the mother confirms the shift in horizon. Repeating "it depends," the mother elaborates on a story about storytelling that she only adumbrates at the start. She explains what it depends on, which amounts to "how you want to think about it." This not only signals the equally compelling narrative force of two quite different stories, with distinctive implications for plot development and contrasting consequences for domestic discipline, but it also evokes narrative reflexivity. The mother virtually tells her listeners that she is not just a narrator propelled by the stories to be told; she also is aware that she is *actively* involved in deciding which story to tell.

The last comment points to the agency of the storyteller, in particular the fact that storytellers need to decide what role or perspective to take when telling a story. Speakers convey this when they state that they have to think things over from various perspectives, that they recognize diverse contexts for interpretation, or that they need to take certain matters into account in deciding how they feel or what to say. This is an inchoate story in its own right, implicating important storytelling decisions, and knowledge about the *hows* of narration. In the preceding extract, it shows that the mother, as an active narrator, is not only telling stories, but is also constructing the relevance of possible versions of what she conveys at the same time. Viewing narration in this way allows us to take seriously what storytellers sometimes virtually tell their listeners: life is as much storied as it is lived (see Sarbin 1986).

Narrative Collaboration

Storytelling is not limited to single narrators. From one illustration to another, it has been evident that narratives are parts of conversations, artifacts of social interaction. To the extent that conversation is a collaborative venture, we may say the same for narrative. While stories have their tellers, storytelling unfolds in interactional context with audiences for whom narrative presentations must "mesh." Storytelling respects the normative expectations for turn-taking, speakership exchange, and the like. It takes conversational cooperation for stories and responses to emerge, for extended turns at talk to develop, turns long enough to accommodate narrative's descriptive needs (Jefferson 1978; M. Goodwin 1982; C. Goodwin 1984; Sacks 1986; Maynard 1996).

Stories are typically "invited," either explicitly or indirectly. For example, consider how interviewers collaborate with their respondents to produce extended narratives (Holstein and Gubrium 1995a). The process is far more active and complex than simply posing a question, then sitting back and waiting for the answer. Interview questions can be viewed as a form of *narrative incitement*. Using particular wording and questions, the interviewer can provide both motivation and precedence for answering in particular ways. Activities that have typically been seen as merely "rapport building" or "probing" (see Converse and Schuman 1974) serve to prompt, if not provoke, narrative roles and elaborations.

Narrative collaboration, however, is not confined to circumstances where stories are formally solicited. Nor is collaboration restricted to persons occupying formal roles as interviewers. In everyday interaction, we constantly construct stories in the course of conversation. Often their development receives more than mere "encouragement" from others who actively join the narrative process. Narration, for example, can involve multiple storytellers, full partners in jointly constructed narrative projects.

Consider the collaborative life story that was produced by nursing home resident Don Hughes. As part of the quality of life study discussed earlier (Gubrium 1993b, p. 141–48), interviews were conducted with widowed, single, and still-married residents living together. Don shared a room with his wife, Sue, at the Westside Care Center. Sue was 81 and Don was 88 years old. Don was formally designated the interview respondent, but the life story requested of him at the start quickly became something quite different, a narrative collaboration of everyone present. Sue was there while Don was being interviewed. As the interview unfolded, it soon became apparent that Sue did not much like Don's version of his life because it did not include her. From her standpoint, Don was telling his story as if Sue were missing from his life. Chiming in, she quickly urged Don to reconstruct the story's narrative horizons, which eventually reconstituted the story as one of the life they shared together. The interviewer (I) began by asking Don to describe his life:

> I: [To Don] I was hoping you'd tell me about your life.
> DON: I was a hobo!
> I: You were a hobo.
> SUE: [To Don] Why don't you tell her where you were born?
> DON: I was born in Minnesota and I left when I was 16 years old.
> SUE: Go on. So why did you leave?
> DON: Just to bum, see the country. So we went, another boy and myself. We went out west on the Northern Pacific Railroad. We was supposed to help put in signal posts. We worked there for a while and then went to Sheridan, Wyoming, and went from there up to the mountains. After that, we came home riding the rails. I stayed home for a couple of years and then a buddy of mine says, "Let's go to Florida." At that time, I says, "No." I knew a girl and her father was moving to California and he asked me if I'd drive his Ford there and I said, "Sure." So a buddy and me drove out to California, but when we got to the desert, the car broke down. We fixed it and drove to Sacramento. [Elaborates on his life in California and, later, his life "going East," and finally going to Florida.] We finally got down to Florida. He [Don's buddy] had been in the army and the government was allocating homestead exemptions in Florida at the time. He thought he might want one. We looked all over and there was nothing but swampland where we looked. So I came to this part of Florida here and we both were working. That's where I met my wife and that's the end of my life story.

SUE: [Sarcastically] Why don't you tell her that we got married in the meantime? I'm part of it, too, you know.

As Don continued, Sue teasingly insisted that the story include more of their life together. While the initial version dealt with Don's work experiences and "bummin' around," at Sue's insistence the story began to include marriage and family. We return to the interview as Don concluded a lengthy description of his many years working as a masonry contractor:

I: Was this after the depression?
DON: The depression was [pause]
SUE: It was just over.
DON: I walked ten miles to work for ten cents an hour. But you know I had a family and I wasn't lazy. But, anyway, after I worked for this fella, we had a big snow storm. [Elaborates] So we decided to come back to Florida. [Elaborates] We enjoyed life. She [Sue] had penicillin poisoning a couple of times. When I retired, I thought we had money to last.
SUE: You forgot to tell her one thing, that we built our own home stick-by-stick and every nail.
DON: Yeah. Anyway, our money didn't last. I got so's I couldn't work too much anymore and she got sick two or three more times.
SUE: [Chuckling] Just listen to him. In the meantime we had three more children. [Sarcastically] Remember that?
DON: Yeah, in the meantime we had three more children. That's all. That's it.
SUE: [Laughing] That's it? You're joking.

Following this, Don and Sue openly collaborated to embellish togetherness. The story was now *theirs*, not just a narrative of Don's individual experiences, as we see in the following extract:

DON: [Chuckling] This much I can tell ya. We've been married 63 years and enjoyed every bit of it. We worked together and never left. For instance, she had a bunch of girlfriends and she never went out at night. And I had boyfriends and I wouldn't go out at night. If we went to any place, we went together.
SUE: We traveled together. We went all over the country together. We didn't have such a bad life. We loved to camp. We loved to fish. We loved to do all kinds of outdoor sports. We like baseball, football. Name it. And we did all the things together. We never went to one place and let the other fella go another place.

The interview eventually turned to the nursing home. While the couple's earlier life had its disappointments, Don and Sue resented certain aspects of nursing home living even more. Still, one thing sustained the good life for them, something that Sue insisted upon including in their life story: togetherness. While Don and Sue teased each other with joking references to their respective foibles, they repeatedly affirmed their mutual affection.

As the interview progressed, the nursing home's shortcomings became marginal to the "sassiness" they called out in each other. The following extract shows that Sue and Don were more than mere nursing home residents with individual opinions about their current surroundings; they were, and would continue to be, the sassy couple they had delighted in being over the years. The long-standing linkages of togetherness, now established jointly, cast the nursing home's quality of life in a way that Don might never have conveyed if he had been interviewed alone. If the horizon of meaning that Don established at the very beginning of the interview had remained in place, the things Don mentions in the following extract as the nursing home's prisonlike quality of life would have contrasted mightily with his youthful free-spiritedness, casting the facility quite negatively. The narrative influence of Sue's "intrusions," however, diminishes the contrast, constructing the present quality of their lives in much more positive terms:

DON: [Chuckling] I was a no-good bum.

SUE: He's no bum. We're just as close as we were before and I love him. He's the only thing that makes this place tolerable. But he gets sassy sometimes and I have to knock him down a peg or two, but other than that, we still have fun together. He plays cribbage and cheats, but we still manage to get by. We gab and blab, about the old days, you know. That keeps us goin'.

Don: But this isn't the place for us. That's all I can say. It's too much like prison. If I didn't have her, I'd go crazy and so would she. [Elaborates] At least we have each other.

SUE: I know dear. We've had a good life, but now we're bitching like the devil. [Chuckling] I hope that isn't on the tape.

I: Well, it is.

DON: [To Sue, sarcastically] You mean to say you're not "itching" now?

SUE: [Chuckling] I didn't say "itching." I said "bitching." We still manage to giggle.

Conventional standards of evaluation for interview data would suggest that Sue's participation "contaminated" Don's interview. But if we abandon the individual respondent as our unit of analysis and focus instead on story and narration, there is no basis for invalidation. It may be neither Don's nor Sue's story, but the result is a narrative project that reveals both *how* a shared life can be assigned its rich "togetherness" and *what* that concurrently means to the couple who live it.

Biographical Work

Stressing the *hows* of storytelling that assemble personal experiences through time, we might consider the Hughes interview as an instance of *biographical work* (Gubrium, Holstein, and Buckholdt 1994). From this perspective, a life and the biography which is its story are interpretive accomplishments, created, sustained, and transformed through social interaction. If a life comes to have a distinct course of development, with phases, stages, peaks, or plateaus, this is as much a matter of getting the story into shape, as it is patterned progression through time. But, while biographical work has descriptive latitude, it also is oriented to practical considerations that prevent constructions from being capricious or arbitrary. Its artfulness orients to the consequential meanings of individual experiences, as well as to the circumstantial contingencies that influence storytelling.

Even though it may be tied to concrete events, biography is continually subject to reinterpretation. It is always to some extent the *biography-at-hand*, a story assembled for the purposes of the moment. In some place, at some time, an individual's past is contemplated for some reason. The specific context provides guidelines for what is relevant to incorporate into a biography. For example, when school staff members assign students to teachers and classrooms for the next school year, the pasts of individual students come into focus in terms of who should be assigned to which class and teacher (see Buckholdt and Gubrium 1979; Leiter 1974, 1980). For all practical purposes, the child's biography is now school-centered and its particulars assembled accordingly. Unrelated particulars are set aside, although they are always available for incorporation on other occasions, for different purposes.

An important condition of biographical work, which we develop in greater detail in the next chapter, is the availability of alternate models of the shape of a life or the pattern of progression through time. Life courses can take various and sundry forms, many of which have become popular and/or were originally part of scholarly writing or scientific research (see Kübler-Ross 1969). In particular circumstances, persons have at their disposal distinct models of personal progress through time that they apply to chronicle the course of their own or others' experience. For example, in certain support groups for the caregivers of Alzheimer's disease sufferers, caregivers learn to reckon the personal experience of caregiving in terms of distinct stages, while in other support groups, this is accomplished in relation to shifting interpersonal comparisons (Gubrium and Holstein 1993a). The groups' different resources for figuring the progress of the experience mediate participants' biographical work and views of individual pasts and futures.

But these models do not dictate biographical work. Because individuals are not "cultural dopes" (Garfinkel 1967), that is, mere puppets of conventional understandings and expectations, what biographical workers actually do with what is interpretively available is always artful. When several models of patterned progression are available, the course of experience that eventually emerges will be shaped by concern for what is circumstantially appropriate, understandable, or useful. Biographical work, then, is far from automatic; it is practical and capable of yielding elastic, even novel, formulations (see Gubrium and Holstein 1995b).

Much of the work of assembling a life story involves the management of consistency and continuity. This assures, as a practical commonsense matter, that in the biography that is produced, the past reasonably leads up to the present to form a plausible "life line." This is supported by the cultural imperative of biographical unity. As Goffman (1963) suggests, people assume that each individual has a single life course:

> Anything and everything an individual has done and can actually do is understood to be containable within his biography, as the Jekyll-Hyde theme illustrates, even if we have to hire a biography specialist, a private detective, to fill in the missing facts and connect the discovered ones for us. No matter how big a scoundrel a man is, no matter how false, secretive, or disjointed his existence, or how governed by fits, starts, and reversals, the true facts of his activity cannot be contradictory or unconnected with each other. (Pp. 62–63)

Even when the "facts" of a life suggest an unruly variability, the presumption of a single, coherent biography for each person guides how those facts are appraised and combined. Some may be deemed irrelevant to the biography at hand, and will thus be set aside or ignored. Or accounts may be formulated that cast some information as more factual than others. Gustav Ichheiser (1970) elaborates the theme of consistency in biographical work by suggesting that consistency-confirming information is actively searched for, even in its apparent absence:

> A man is under suspicion of murder. During the investigation certain definite abnormalities of his sexual behavior come to light, even though there is no evidence that they are related in any way to the committed murder. Again, the frequent reactions in many people, if verbalized, would read something like this: "This man whose sexual life deviates so strangely from the norm can also be expected to deviate from other social norms in any other respect." (Pp. 50–51)

Guided by interpretive schemas that virtually overpower some of the potential biography-building information at hand, singular, consistent biographies are constructed by reinterpreting emerging inconsistencies to fit expected patterns. In the process, old biographies are discredited, cast as flawed in order to sustain new images. For example, the *New York Times* (12/31/95) reports that accused Oklahoma City bomber Timothy McVeigh was remembered by childhood acquaintances as "utterly ordinary," but, as the article continues, this view is assimilated to the picture of McVeigh as a terrorist, a "loner who kept his violent thoughts to himself" in order to give the appearance of being ordinary.

Indeed, the appearance of normality itself may be interpreted as further evidence of underlying depravity. McVeigh was reported to be so nondescript in his youth that his former teachers didn't remember him at all. According to the *Times*, "Everybody who met him described him the same way: quiet, polite, neat." But as his connection to the destruction of a federal office building was publicized, readers were also informed that "criminologists say these traits are often the stuff of serial killers, terrorists, and other solitary murders." Like other such killers, he was said to have had deadly intentions all along, but managed to insidiously conceal them until they could be unleashed to achieve his violent objectives.

Such reconstructive biographical work is common in the news media. Even instances involving blatant inconsistencies can be molded into the prevailing pattern. In the case of mass murderer Charles Whitman, many "facts" were found to be utterly at odds with his identity as a killer, but the consistent biography still managed to prevail. By most accounts, Whitman had been the "all-American boy" before shooting fourteen people from atop a tower at the University of Texas. The search for further information revealed that Whitman had poached deer, tried to sell pornography, and gambled with known criminals. This information was assimilated into a biography that was positioned to question the all-American image. Nevertheless, the image proved substantial, so much so that a more popular explanation for the apparent discontinuity arose: Whitman suffered from a brain tumor. The seeming lack of a properly factual social or psychological account for Whitman's shootings led to the search for a reasonable biography linked to Whitman's body (Lofland 1969).

The extensive media coverage of Jeffrey Dahmer vividly displayed the diverse manifestations of biographical consistency at work, especially in relation to Dahmer's developmental life course (Gubrium, Holstein, and Buckholdt 1994). An admitted mass murderer whose long string of ghastly killings was discovered in 1991, Dahmer also had apparently cannibalized some of his victims. Over the course of his arrest and trial, accounts and explanations for Dahmer's behavior were offered by psychiatric experts, lawyers, law enforcement personnel, sociologists, people "on the street," and reporters, among others. Some commentators explained Dahmer's past in terms of his troubled relationship with his parents, claiming that this was a certain antecedent to, if not a cause of, Dahmer's killings. Instances of animal mutilation in Dahmer's childhood were assimilated to accounts of a "long-standing" disregard for life and a fascination with death and dismemberment. These facts of Dahmer's early years provided a basis for seeing a progressive pattern of development, with Dahmer "growing" from lesser to greater offenses. The course of his life and tragic behavior ostensibly made sense in light of this trajectory.

There were also noticeable absences from these media accounts. The public saw few references to warm or loving relationships, friendships, acts of kindness, indeed any accounts of behavior that might have made Dahmer appear to be anything other than the deranged murderer he was judged to be. Potentially "normal" activities of everyday life were ignored, or reinterpreted to better fit with what was "known." For example, a former resident of Dahmer's apartment complex, where several murders and dismemberments had occurred, provided the following description of his encounters with Dahmer:

> He was always real quiet. I'd see him and he'd just smile. He never said much, never did nothing you could notice. Never had nobody going in and out. It was real strange. You could just see he was a strange kinda guy. (WISN-TV: 2/29/92)

On the same news report, an African-American resident of the complex simply referred to Dahmer as "nothin' special, just your regular white guy" (WISN-TV: 2/29/92).

As the extract shows, what might otherwise be understood as "nondescript," ordinary behavior ("real quiet. . . . never said much, never did nothing you could notice") was interpretively transformed into evidence that Dahmer was "a strange kinda guy," with the implication that this was so all along. That he managed to appear innocuous, even benign, was cited as proof of what an insidious killer he "really" was underneath it all. The pattern of Dahmer's murderous character informed the meaning of his everyday behavior so that it was virtually impossible to see any normalcy in a man so thoroughly deviant. *In retrospect*, Dahmer's past was constructed to fit with the current descriptions and diagnoses of a deranged killer. His life virtually became a history of the present.[7]

*   *   *   *   *

While we certainly have not covered the entire range of interpretive practices, we have offered examples to illustrate a research idiom for documenting the deeply artful side of the process. This analytic language provides a way of seeing and describing just how adroit, industrious, and enterprising interpretive practitioners can be. This method talk is primarily motivated by, and itself motivates, questions concerning *how* reality is constituted. It invites us to examine artfulness, accordingly constituting the phenomena we describe.

In the next chapter, we shift our analytic brackets to the other side of interpretive practice, discussing the terminology developed to examine the substantive resources for, and conditions of, interpretation. The renewed language of qualitative method provides a means of analyzing such "external" factors without losing track of the agentic artfulness that is guided and informed, but not compelled, by them.

CHAPTER 8

Conditions of Interpretation

Attention to artfulness must be balanced by equal concern for the conditions of interpretation, for the substantive side of interpretive practice. This highlights the *whats* of experience, providing a basis for examining the circumstances of reality construction, the meaningful resources that are employed, and the realities that are produced and used in the process.

Concerns of this sort, in combination with *why* questions, dominate positivistic method talk. Most qualitative approaches tread carefully here. Naturalists are typically wary of explanatory vocabularies oriented to social forces that ostensibly constrain and motivate behavior. Ethnomethodologists eschew this language, preferring to treat it as an artifact of indigenous sense-making. They view it as a topic to be studied in its own right. Emotionalists carefully resist determinism, respecting the more spontaneous, passionate side of brute being.

Nevertheless, naturalists have traditionally used a language of rules, roles, norms, and the like to convey their interest in circumstantial influences on behavior. Ethnomethodolgists, despite their abiding emphasis on real-time, in-course constitutive practices, have always been attuned to the significance of discursive context. From Garfinkel's (1967) fundamental concerns for indexicality and reflexivity, to conversation analysts' attempts to describe the "context free" yet "context sensitive" character of ordinary talk-in-interaction (Sacks, Schegloff, and Jefferson 1974), ethnomethodologists have oriented to the *situated* accomplishment of social order in relation to talk and interaction. And emotionalists often focus on the experiential and emotional contexts of everyday life, especially in relation to the passions.

Still, none of these approaches strikes the balance needed to fully capture both the artful side and the substantive conditions of interpretation. When all is said and done, naturalism and emotionalism predominantly deal with the *whats* of experience, while ethnomethodology is captivated by concerns with constitutive *hows*. Perhaps it required the wide-ranging genius of Erving Goffman, whose analytic vocabulary does not clearly reflect any of these idioms, to sensitize us to the interaction between the artful and the substantive, even as he continued to emphasize the *whats* of everyday life.

GOFFMAN AS A POINT OF DEPARTURE

Just as we took ethnomethodology as an orienting vocabulary for examining the art-ful side of interpretive practice, we take Goffman as a point of departure for ad-dressing interpretive practice's substantive conditions. In some ways, Goffman is every bit as interested as are the ethnomethodologists in talk and interaction, but he does not assume such a fully constitutive position. In *The Presentation of Self in Everyday Life* (1959), for example, he portrays interaction in the highly active, cre-ative, agentic terms of the theater. Built across decades, the vocabulary is now clas-sic: performance, impression management, facework, self-presentation, expressions given and given off, definition of the situation, encounters, ritual, games, play, fram-ing, footing, fabrication, and many more terms make up Goffman's signature lan-guage.

Goffman focuses on certain conditions of interaction, most importantly those that bear on the management of moral order. While Garfinkel and the ethnomethodolo-gists set aside the substance of rules, norms, framings, and the like in order to make their interactive machinery visible, Goffman prefers to trace and discern how moral order itself offers a space for its embodiment and reenactment by individuals in re-lation to each other. In effect, he situationally unbrackets the ethnomethodological project, leaving actors socially monitoring and managing the talk and interaction they ongoingly construct. In this regard, Goffman's conceptual foundations are Durkheimian (see Cahill 1994; Collins 1980, 1985; Ditton 1980); he sees social re-ality as external to the individual, a constraint on personal action (Collins 1980; Manning 1980). Social order, for Goffman, depends upon moral demands and com-mitments, but these are of a particular nature:

> In their capacity as performers, individuals will be concerned with maintaining the im-pression that they are living up to the many standards by which they and their products are judged. Because these standards are so numerous and pervasive, the individuals who are per-formers dwell more than we might think in a moral world. But, *qua* performers, individuals are concerned not with the moral issue of realizing these standards, but with the amoral is-sue of engineering a convincing impression that these standards are being realized. Our ac-tivity, then, is largely concerned with moral matters, but as performers we do not have a moral concern with them. As performers, we are merchants of morality. . . . the very oblig-ation and profitability of appearing always in a steady moral light, of being a socialized char-acter, forces one to be the sort of person who is practiced in the ways of the stage. (Goffman 1959, p. 251)

It is an external moral order that is articulated "in the ways of the stage." Obligations for action are not regulated by internalized values, as they are for Parsons, say, but come by way of the operating drama of social life that accompa-nies specific situations. As Randall Collins (1980) summarizes, "In order to live up to this *external* morality, one is forced to have a non-moral, manipulative self" (p. 182, emphasis in the original).

According to Collins (p. 200), Goffman stresses the "hard external constraints of society upon what individuals can afford to do and believe," but he also allows for a certain flexibility. He situates actors in morally constraining social scenes, but the dramatic realization of moral imperatives is never fully scripted. Individual performance is dramaturgic; dramatic realization is extemporaneous. Goffman also stresses the ever-changing situational demands placed on moral actors, producing yet another source of interpretive variability. Still, as Collins also notes, Goffman thought there were limits to this variability: "The world is complex and shifting, but it is not infinitely so" (p. 200).

The concept of "framing" is central to Goffman's schema. Frames, Goffman argues, are constellations of meaning that inform the definition and understanding of situations and events. These organizing frameworks

are not merely a matter of mind but correspond in some sense to the way in which an aspect of the activity is organized. . . . Organizational premises are involved, and these are something cognition somehow arrives at, not something cognition creates or generates. Given their understanding of what it is that is going on, individuals fit their actions to this understanding and ordinarily find that the ongoing world supports this fitting. (1974, p. 247)

While the meaning of situations or actions may be transformed by active framing (and reframing, keying, and so forth, to use Goffman's vocabulary), meaning is never fully artfully constituted. The work of framing, keying, and the like is more reality manipulation and maintenance than it is the construction of reality *tout court*. Goffman pictures an actor who fashions definitions of the situation to suit practical moral needs, but this actor is a manager of the appearances of a deep moral order, not its creator. Moral order exists apart from the management activities. As Collins (1980) observes, "Goffman points to real sanctions in the material world as the ultimate grounding, and all transformations of it as secondary" (p. 204). Goffman is not so much interested in the moral reality of experience per se as he is in the everyday presentational work that orients to, and necessarily engages, it at the lived border of reality and representation (see Manning 1980).

Situational Analysis

Goffman's concern for the management of the moral order leads to his interest in the *situational* contours of social life: "My perspective is situational, meaning here a concern for what one individual can be alive to at a particular moment, this often involving a few other particular individuals and not necessarily restricted to the mutually monitored arena of face-to-face gatherings" (Goffman 1974, p. 8).[1] For Goffman (1964), "Social situations at least in our society constitute a reality *sui generis* as he [Durkheim] used to say, and therefore need and warrant analysis in their own right, much like that accorded other basic forms of social organization" (p. 134).

The domain of interaction is a characteristically ceremonial one, organized by elaborate rituals that are not simply the effects of a social liturgy (cf. Strong 1979). Rather, the "interaction order" consists of "systems of enabling conventions, in the sense of ground rules for a game, the provision of a traffic code, or the syntax of a language" (Goffman 1983, p. 5). Actors' orientations to this order are deeply moral, guided by principles outside themselves and residing in the situation itself. Agency is literally situated in the interaction order that serves to "insulate" agency from more distant forces, or at least mediate the influence of institutions.

"Social situatedness" thus assumes a commanding role in Goffman's method talk

(Maynard 1991a). The language of situated performance and framing addresses both action and its moral context, conveying the finesse of reality-defining action. His empirical and theoretical work clearly set a course that traverses the analytic terrain of interpretive practice. Yet, at the same time, Goffman posits an uninterpreted, obdurate reality underlying all situations and actions, a reality that resists interpretation.

While we agree that the moral order limits interpretation (not just anything goes, interpretively speaking), our view of interpretive practice suggests greater agency in the constitution of social meaning and reality than Goffman allows. His analytic vocabulary presumes moral order in principle and orients to its dramatic realization, but the artfulness of using and applying moral orders is restricted. Our sense of moral or normative order is equally in tune with ethnomethodology, which casts rules, not as determinants of social order, but as sense-making devices that are *used* to establish semblances of order (see Zimmerman and Wieder 1970). In this sense, rules serve as interpretive resources, not as determinate structures or directives. This perspective allows for agency in relation to *available* and *applicable* moral orders.

Goffman's situational emphasis also fails to capture the full range and complexity of moral orders that provide resources for, and, in turn, substantively condition interpretive practice. As important as situated interaction is, it increasingly unfolds in relation to a spectrum of institutional circumstances that warrant consideration. For example, organizational cultures, as they are reflexively enacted through local definitions, provide the grounds for interpretive work that Goffman all but ignores after the publication of *Asylums* in 1961 (Manning 1980). As Goffman's vision of the interaction order emerges, the institutional virtually gives way to the cognitive and the situational. While Goffman (1959) acknowledges the place of culture in situated interaction, he conceives of culture rather deterministically, describing it as "the moral values which influence activity in [social establishments or closed social systems]—values pertaining to fashions, customs, and matters of taste, to politeness and decorum, to ultimate ends and normative restrictions on means, etc." (p. 240).

Nevertheless, Goffman is an important forerunner of our attempt to substantively contextualize the artfulness of interpretive practice, especially in the way that he addresses the framing of talk and interaction. Following his lead, we now extend our analytic vocabulary to address broader contingencies of circumstance while still remaining faithful to a sense of constitutive agency by way of analytic bracketing. We use the term "circumstance" rather than "situation" to emphasize the local and institutional *conditions* of social interaction.

CONTINGENCIES OF CIRCUMSTANCE

As a matter of practice, interpretation takes place in real time, in concrete places, often in relation to highly particularized forms of knowledge (see Anspach 1987). These contingencies are both background for, and part of, the reality-construction process. A medical clinic, for example, provides a backdrop against which embedded interpretive activities can be understood. It furnishes both a language for, and of, action that distinguishes the setting as a "clinic" and the transactions conducted there as "medical." Foucault (1965, 1972, 1975) referred to these sited languages as *discursive structures* or *formations*—shared ways of communicating and putting into practice meanings that characterize particular sites at specific times. Simultaneously, a site such as a medical clinic is itself meaningfully constituted by virtue of the visible, hearable exchanges that take place there. This is the interactional scaffolding upon which clinical transactions are conducted, the very actions that comprise the clinic (see Maynard 1991b).

In practice, interpretation responds to proximate demands and concerns. As Goffman shows us, objects and actions can be variously "framed" or "keyed," changing their meaning in relation to circumstantial exigencies. Contextual demands may be formal, casual, or contrived. Interpretation may be taken for granted, its process and products virtually seen but unnoticed. Or it may be overtly political, invoking public "rhetoric" (Ibarra and Kitsuse 1993; Miller 1991), "publicity" (Gubrium 1993a), or "micropolitical" maneuvering (Emerson and Messinger 1977). Always tacitly persuasive, if only in terms of presumptively advocating one version of reality over another, interpretive activity may address particular audiences or "interpretive communities" (Fish 1980). Interpretation, then, is not so much situationally evanescent as it is conditioned by recollected experiences, anticipated futures, concrete objectives, localized functions, and available resources that can produce enduring, even anticipatable, effects.

Working Objectives

What is "seen" or "understood" in any particular circumstance is at least partially derived from what participants are attempting to accomplish. A teacher making placement recommendations, for example, describes students in terms of academic achievement, demonstrated competencies, and standardized, objective measures of potential and performance. He or she can describe the same students in entirely different terms when assessing their playground behavior. The very same student might be represented as "immature" when intellectual development is under consideration, but "quite grown up" when sociability is in question (see Cicourel and Kitsuse 1963; Gubrium, Buckholdt, and Lynott 1982).

The point is not that interpretation is inconsistent, but that it varies by virtue of its working objectives. These provide interpretive orientations that call up alternate sorts of framing. Objectives relate to schemes of understanding from which the observed "facts" of the matters at hand are articulated. Facts become pertinent in terms of an interpretive scheme, deriving their meaning from the understandings prompted by the task at hand (see Garfinkel 1967; Mehan and Wood 1975). For example, certain facts may have no apparent relevance to a juvenile court's assessment of a child's moral character, and thus be ignored in the court's proceedings. If the child is referred to a mental health facility, the clinical interpretation of the child may specify an entirely different set of facts as relevant, including those imposed in the court (see Emerson 1969; Gubrium, Holstein, and Buckholdt 1994). It is not simply that particular traits are emphasized in one setting and different characteristics are highlighted in the other. Rather, working objectives provide interpretive agendas—ways of looking at and seeing things—that formulate the meaningfulness of objects and actions, constituting the circumstantial facticity of the child's traits and record of conduct.

This produces definitional transformations based on the practical purposes at hand. The facts of family life, for example, relate to the working objectives of domestic interpretation. A teenager filling out a college admissions application may list her mother, father, and 10-year-old sister as family members, but rail that "I don't have a sister" when the 10-year-old spills grape juice on her white cashmere sweater. Later, the same teenager may express deep emotional attachment to her pet dog by firmly declaring him "a member of the family," thus constituting kinship in relation to emotional ties (see Levin 1993). Strictly speaking, as matters of practice, such facts must take "hyphenated" form: kinship-for-this-purpose, family-for-that-purpose, and so forth (see Gubrium and Holstein 1990).

Audiences and Accountability

As our previous example suggests, working objectives are not free-floating. They can have enduring circumstantial linkages that are closely tied to particular audiences. The linkages themselves can be distinctly embedded in particular institutions, providing a more socially articulated sense of interpretive accountability. That is, interpretations are accountable to the practical demands placed upon them, but those demands often materialize in the form of concrete (or imagined) persons or institutions for whom the interpretations will become matters of consequence. At the same time, the relation between working objectives, audiences, and institutions is not fixed. Who is obligated to address whom, and the aegis under which interpretation takes place, are real constraints, but in the give and take of social interaction, they are subject to constant definition and negotiation (Gubrium, Buckholdt, and Lynott 1982).

For example, staff members at a residential treatment center for emotionally disturbed children are required to set treatment objectives for children's problems and to interpret the problems to the children, parents, and funding agencies (see Buckholdt and Gubrium 1979). But the staff is not accountable to everyone in the same terms, nor are they similarly accountable to any one audience across situations. Assessments of treatment goals and a child's progress may thus vary by both audience and the circumstances of interaction. Staff members may offer one version of treatment and progress in a formal staffing session, for instance, and another when chatting with parents who have come to pick up their child for a weekend home visit.

The proximity as well as the identity of an audience conditions interpretation. One may see and say things one way in the immediate presence of an audience, where the audience directly witnesses how an interpretation is formed, but frame things quite differently when the audience is at a distance, where time and space allow for more interest-laden and contemplated formulations. The extent to which the audience directly participates in, or responds to, interpretation also conditions the process. The interpretive demands of informal grievance procedures, for example, are different from those of a court hearing, which are once again different from formal appeals procedures conducted through written application and document review (see Miller and Holstein 1995, 1996). The mere anticipation of a potential audience, whether or not the audience ever materializes, itself has an effect.

An example of the varied interpretations of patient "progress" in a physical rehabilitation hospital illustrates some of the circumstantial complications associated with audience (see Gubrium and Buckholdt 1982). Wilshire Hospital treated patients suffering from a variety of debilitating conditions such as stroke, brain trauma, spinal cord injuries, hip fractures, and amputations. Physical and occupational therapists provided exercise programs and professional counseling aimed at rehabilitating the patients to optimal functioning. Familial support was important to the overall effort, too, so family members were kept abreast of staff objectives including treatment goals, expected rates of progress, and discharge planning.

Staff at Wilshire interpreted treatment and progress in terms of several salient images, the most prominent being educational and medical images. When staff members worked with patients, they typically spoke of their clinical activity, assessments, and progress in an educational vocabulary. They represented current progress and future developments and prognoses in terms of motivation, teaching, and learning. Patients were reminded, for example, that staff could not "cure" their dysfunctions, only "teach" them how to overcome physical handicaps. Problems and barriers were not presented as medical or physiological hurdles; rather, they were conveyed as challenges to motivation and learning. When staff represented progress to third-party payers, however, they reported almost exclusively in medical terms. Progress was framed as the result of medical intervention. An audience of family members brought other complications. Either an educational or medical vocabulary might apply, depending on the apparent success of rehabilitation. Reports of good patient progress were offered in terms of effective clinical intervention, while disappointing news was cast in the language of educational deficit, lack of motivation, or poor learning habits.

This was especially complicated when audiences intersected, raising the question of which image of rehabilitation to key into, as much as how to communicate it. Consider what happened at a family conference attended by several staff members and an elderly stroke patient's sister and adult daughter. According to several staff reports, the patient was making good progress, even if it was not all that they had hoped for. The successful aspects of rehabilitation were conveyed in terms of clinical intervention and only in passing did one of the staff members note that they still needed to "get her [the patient] to push herself along" a bit more. Medical imagery clearly dominated the discussion.

Following these routine staff reports, the family members were asked if they had any questions. The patient's adult daughter prefaced her initial question with the statement, "Having been a physical therapist myself," whereupon the conversation immediately shifted into an educational framing of rehabilitation. Staff members and the daughter mutually elaborated on the day-to-day difficulties and "unknowns" of working with rehabilitation patients, focusing on the patient's interest in her own progress. At one point, the physical therapist remarked to the daughter:

Of course, you know the kinds of problems we have with getting them [patients] interested in their progress. You know how many of them come in here thinking that this is a hospital and it's going to cure them. You run up against that kind of thing all the time, and it's a real job just to get them to think in terms of pushing ahead on their own.

The adult daughter replied that she knew just what the physical therapist meant and, putting herself in the therapist's shoes, felt that her mother's progress ultimately was more a problem of motivation than it was a matter of medical intervention. In the course of this revamped discussion, the medical framing of the matter being discussed was displaced by an image of the educational and motivational realities of the case.

While audience, accountability, and objectives condition representation, it is important that we not conceive of these circumstantial contingencies too deterministically. Circumstance may prescribe interpretive relevances, but they do not dictate outcomes. For example, interpretation may speak to specific audiences, but it does not rigidly respond to them. Any circumstantial contingency, such as a sudden shift in audience, might in the course of interaction alter its status as a contingency and, as a result, change the working framework of interpretations.

At the level of social interaction, the meaning of things reflects both predictability and artfulness. Communication and related courses of action center on both the *whats* and the constitutive *hows* of interpretive practice. While, in the preceding example, the overall substance of what was going to be said by staff members to various audiences was predictable, this was subject to how those audiences presented themselves or how they were received. As we saw, as persons determined *how* they would interpret things, for all practical purposes, *what* was said virtually became self-evident, and predictable. Furthermore, staff members' formulations of who their audience was depended upon their knowledge of the accountable consequences of communicating to specific audiences in particular ways. Evidently, staff members "knew" that a family member who was admittedly one of their own, so to speak, could be counted upon for a predictably sympathetic response. Still, this could be undone in the course of interaction, as when "one of their own" reasserted his or her family status in the middle of a discussion of treatment effectiveness. In practice, the ongoing interpretive relation between these *what* and *how* concerns was enduringly discretionary; predictable, even ritual, outcomes depended on how the issues being addressed and discussed were interactively formulated.

INTERPRETIVE RESOURCES

As we mentioned earlier, practical objectives and audiences evoke distinctive interpretive orientations and frames of reference. Resources for interpretation are also vital ingredients for reality construction. Discursive conventions, structures, and meanings are significant circumstantial contingencies that comprise particular ways of seeing, talking, and understanding—the substantive ingredients of interpretation. To fully specify an idiom of interpretive practice, we need a vocabulary that conveys the building blocks as well as the activities and contingencies of meaning production. The key question here is, what substantive resources are available for assigning meaning to experience?

Occasioned Resources

It bears repeating that, while interpretive practice is constitutively artful, participants do not build reality from scratch, from the ground up, as it were, on each and every interpretive occasion. Rather, the interpretive work relies upon substantive resources for assigning meaning. Culture and social structure, of course, have long been regarded as sources of meaning and action (Durkheim 1961; Parsons 1937). Echoing Durkheim, Peter Berger (1963) tells us that

> society confronts us as an objective facticity. It is *there*, something that cannot be denied and that must be reckoned with. Society is external to ourselves. It surrounds us, encompasses our life on all sides. We are *in* society, located in specific sectors of the social system. This location predetermines and predefines almost everything we do, from language to etiquette, from the religious beliefs we hold to the probability that we will commit suicide. Our wishes are not taken into consideration in this matter of social location, and our intellectual resistance to what society prescribes or proscribes avails very little at best, frequently nothing. . . . [Society's] institutions pattern our actions and even shape our expectations. (P. 91, emphasis in the original)

Berger then tempers this harsh revelation by showing us how we continually rebuild the very "walls of our imprisonment":

> What happens in socialization is that the social world is internalized in the child. The same process . . . occurs every time the adult is initiated into a new social context or a new social group. Society, then, is not only something "out there," in the Durkheimian sense, but it is also "in here," part of our innermost being. . . . Society not only controls our movements, but shapes our identity, our thought and our emotions. The structures of society become the structures of our own consciousness. (P. 121)

Clearly, such a vision casts society and culture as powerful forces, making them the virtual architects of action. The view is striking for its imagery of societal predominance; external structures are both *totalized* and *determinant*, even while they are expressions of an internalized machinery. These are compelling resources indeed.

The lived border of reality and representation problematizes the very heart of this matter, however. While people, of course, dwell in society, its practical parameters are always subject to interpretation. In place of a "prison" of external and internalized rules and constraints, we suggest that culture and social structure offer what Foucault (1975) calls "conditions of possibility" for reality construction. Culture, for example, is not merely a set of rituals, rules, and fixed expectations; it doesn't furnish strict guidelines for behavior. Instead of the totalized museum of meanings that it is often taken to be, it is, in practice, a set of received, yet unfolding maps, recipes, and templates for how we might understand and respond to ourselves and others (see Geertz 1973). Cultural knowledge, as Geertz (1983) points out, is always local knowledge—mobilized in the here and now, for the practical purposes at hand.

From this, we can begin to consider how interpretive practice combines the circumstantial with the artful. As we will illustrate, interpretive resources exist as cultural conditions, awaiting the occasions of their applicability. They are used in diverse ways, typically quite astutely; resources are crafted to meet the demands of the occasion. Meaning is never completely predetermined; it must always be convincingly and accountably applied to concrete particulars. Practice engages institutional frameworks, formal and informal categories and vocabularies, long-standing cultural patterns, and other socially established structures of meaning (Geertz 1973, 1983), bringing them to bear in ongoing interpretive projects.

Still, as artful as they may be, interpretations typically appear quite familiar; they make sense (common sense) because they must resonate in some fashion with "what everyone knows to be so" or they run the risk of being socially irrelevant. Not only must descriptions be recognizable (Sacks 1974), but they must also be accountable in that they must convince socially defined, competent members that the circumstances in question warrant the attributions that are attached. Thus, while social reality is artfully constructed, this is accomplished in relation to substantive considerations.

But substantive resources themselves are not completely fixed; they are actively assembled from "cultural particulars," (Silverman 1985) which are enduringly available, yet contingently asserted. The stock of interpretive resources is thus occasioned in the sense that what is meaningfully brought to bear at any moment will be assembled, at that moment, from an available cultural inventory. Representation and reality, as we shall continue to see, move back and forth between the constitutive and substantive sides of practice.

Resources-in-Use

A renewed language of qualitative method emphasizes the analysis of the circumstantial contingencies of interpretation while avoiding the deterministic tenor of more positivistic vocabularies. The notion of *resources-in-use* supplies a shorthand for capturing important aspects of both sides of interpretive practice, simultaneously highlighting the substantive and the active. As Durkheim, Schutz, Foucault, and others remind us (using various terminologies), shared structures of meaning and discourse offer ways of orienting to objects and events that transcend individual formulations. They bring interpretive stability, reining in the social construction process so that it is not arbitrary. Signs cannot be inconsistently attached to their referents and still convey meaningful sense to other competent actors in an interpretive community. We cannot arbitrarily "make up" words, meanings, and their connection and hope to be understood.

On the other hand, words and their referents are not inherently or objectively meaningful (Saussure 1974). Nor is meaning a simple matter of convention. There is considerable variation and nuance in the merger of reality and representation. *Usage* is the modus operandi of this complex nexus. Wittgenstein put this in the simplest of terms: "One cannot guess how a word functions. One has to *look at* its use and learn from that" (1958, p. 109, emphasis in the original). Shared meaning occurs only through the accountable attachment of a description to an occurrence (the attachment of a medical category to a behavior, for example). What that occurrence is, which category is assigned, and audience recognition of the assignment are all deeply consequential to interpretive practice. One cannot simply designate meaning without orienting to the object of concern, available meanings, and contingencies of usage. Each provides concrete resistance to arbitrary interpretation.

As a matter of practice, interpretive resources are realized and become useful only in the *process* of their use. Mere availability does not insure that any particular resource will be brought to bear on any specific occasion. Myriad seemingly appropriate resources may tacitly "compete" for the opportunity to be applied in a particular instance. Previously uncontemplated resources may be conjured up to suit the needs of an occasion, and, if recognizably appropriate, become extemporaneously meaningful. This provides interpretive resources with the seemingly paradoxical, if not ironic, quality of being substantive and enduring, while also being emergent and circumstantial—balanced, in other words, at the lived border of reality and representation.

Take an instance of a very ordinary resource-in-use. The word "clock" commonly signifies a mechanical device for keeping track of the passage of time. Through metaphorical usage, however, the word and the object referenced can be made to represent all manner of things in circumstances where time is of the essence. In the data from a study of caregivers of Alzheimer's disease sufferers (Gubrium 1986a, 1986b), we noted, for example, how a ticking clock was appropriated to the description of the human self by a wife who had been providing home care for a demented and rapidly declining husband. He has been a longtime sufferer of Alzheimer's disease and now his wife is contemplating nursing home placement. When she is asked about how she will make the decision, she points to the clock on a nearby shelf and remarks, "That there clock's me. It'll keep ticking away until its time [to decide] and won't stop for a minute, until it winds down."

As she continues, we learn that "winding down" refers to the gradual decline and eventual ill health of the *caregiver*, not just to the disease sufferer. Caregivers, it is said, fail to look out for their own well-being; they don't keep an eye on the proverbial clock, needlessly wasting themselves away being martyrs for loved ones who have become mere shells of themselves. The clock is a descriptive resource for conveying a complex constellation of meanings associated with the passage of time: its inevitability, its personal irrecoverability, and its interpersonal resoluteness.

By way of further illustration, recall the example of the hardy weed that we presented in Chapter 7. The use of the weed demonstrated how meaning is artfully built up in talk and interaction. Of the many possible things that participants Maude and Henry might have noted about the weed (its noxious or intrusive qualities, for example), they selectively conveyed an image of hardship and endurance, explaining "That weed's got it rough out there. . . . But it's makin' it." Descriptively secured, the weed was brought to bear on the matters at hand. In Maude's words, the weed became a mirror image of their lives: "Kinda like us. I guess I was thinkin'. All the energy it takes. If we didn't have that kind of energy, we'd be dead by now." Meaning was appropriated, then artfully attached to the group by way of metaphor.

As artful as metaphorical usage is, the example also shows that the process relies upon well-known cultural images. The weed's durability and toughness in the face of adversity were locally crafted from understandings imported at least partially from outside of the give-and-take of the immediate situation. The descriptions relied upon what "everybody knows" about the character of weeds, but the shared imagery was tailored to current interpretive demands. Meaning was a product of *both* local application and preexisting interpretive possibilities, combined in usage. Even after the group established that the weed represented their collective hardiness and persistence, its meaning and use continued to be artfully and resourcefully formulated. Recall that at subsequent support group meetings, as the topic of discussion shifted to the progressive burdens of care, members adapted the weed imagery to show how the gradually withering weed embodied the ravages that accompany constant stress. The withering weed was used to show how the strains and hardships of caregiving can take their toll on even the hardiest of survivors. A preexisting and crafted resource was further shaped in terms of the culturally familiar to suit the interpretive demands of the occasion, once again demonstrating the reflexive relation between the *whats* and *hows* of interpretive practice.

LOCAL CULTURE

Recalling what Marx (1956) told us, people construct their lives, but not completely according to their own desires. The social construction process, he seems to be saying, is mediated by interpretive factors beyond individual control. Still, these factors come into play in concrete places, in real time, for immediately salient purposes in social interaction. This occasioned, practical usage is what Geertz (1983) had in mind when he argued that knowledge is "always ineluctably local" (p. 4).

As the corpus of local knowledge and practices coalesces, what we call *local culture* emerges as an interpretive resource. By this we mean the set of more or less regularized ways of assigning meaning and responding to things that is collectively derived and available for application within proximate circumstances (Gubrium 1989). Local culture is composed of recognizable categories, familiar vocabularies, organizational mandates, personal and professional orientations, group perspectives, and other similarly delimited frameworks for organizing meaning. Its domains are relatively bounded and distinct; small groups; formal organizations; social collectivities organized around characteristics like race, gender, or age; and other relatively circumscribed provinces develop their own modes and materials for reality construction. But local culture is not a fixed set of injunctions or absolute directives. It conveys relatively stable and distinct ways of conceptualizing experience that are subject to reformulation and application. While local culture may inform particular interpretations and supply the vocabulary for their articulation, it does not dictate what is interpretively constructed.

Our use of the term "local" is intended as an *experiential* designation rather than a purely geographic label. For example, multiple local cultures may simultaneously inhabit the same geographic site. Or the relative prominence of local cultures may vary from time to time within the same setting. In a residential treatment center for emotionally disturbed children (see Buckholdt and Gubrium 1979), for example, interpretations of the children's problems emphasized psychological and behavioristic formulations of disturbance and treatment. But at the end of the working day, as staffing changed and concerns shifted to the mundane details of getting the children fed and off to bed, the phenomenon of disturbance "escaped," as David Silverman (1989) puts it, as staff oriented to the children as good or fussy eaters and light or sound sleepers. On weekends especially, the language of disturbance was supplanted by less therapeutic terms of reference. For instance, the received rhetorical force of the phrase "It's the weekend!" was used by the children as justification for temporarily suspending the consequences of not adhering to the center's token economy. This aspect of local culture was virtually anchored in time—here one day, gone the next—its borders as much temporal as geographic.

Local culture may also have specific organizational moorings. That is, interpretive resources and orientations can be *organizationally embedded* (Gubrium 1987; Gubrium and Holstein 1993b), reflecting the distinct perspectives, meanings, and priorities of formally organized settings, disciplines, or collectivities. For example, interpretation may echo professional orientations, such as a psychiatrist's, as opposed to a social worker's, point of view in a community mental health clinic. As we will argue, everyday life is more and more conducted within formally organized settings, so the articulation of meaning increasingly accords with organizationally promoted ways of making sense of experience.

Taking these terms together, our method talk detotalizes the more deterministic use of related concepts, offering instead analytic tools for capturing how interpretive practitioners think and talk about experience within the relatively circumscribed domains of their everyday lives. The idea of a general culture, as some anthropologists conceive of it for example, is too broad to represent diversely meaningful and applicable wholes. Culture writ large may indeed provide grounds for interpretation, but not in the imperious, dogmatic fashion that traditional formulations often imply.

We must also emphasize that local culture implies culture-in-use. As such, it potentially involves multiple layers of interpretive resources and constraints. Contingencies intersect to confront interpretive practitioners with a vast array of complex options and constraints. Race, gender, professional affiliation, physical location, biographical particulars, and myriad other factors come together at the nexus of interpretive domains and demands, to be sorted and used. Given these complexities, it is virtually impossible for interpretation to be dictated by any single source, in any totalized fashion. Indeed, layered contingencies are the source of vast interpretive variation.

Local Cultural Diversity

Consider how diversely formulated experience can be. Part of the field study of caregiving for Alzheimer's disease sufferers involved observation of a variety of caregiver support groups (see Gubrium 1986a). The groups provided an opportunity to document the emergence and operation of distinct interpretive resources as they were brought to bear on various aspects of the caregiving experience. Some groups were composed of spouses, mainly the elderly wives of demented husbands, who cared for their husbands at home. A few groups were limited to the adult children of demented parents, usually caregiving daughters. Many groups had a mixture of caregivers, including siblings and friends.

The support groups had a variety of goals and leadership styles. Some groups were didactic; others were more socioemotional. But these emphases could vary with the topic of discussion. Related to this, a leadership style might be formally specified for a group, such as the professional facilitation of a nurse or social worker, but the character of facilitation also varied again depending upon the particular issues under consideration. Groups might embrace a professional–medical leadership and orientation on some occasions, only to turn decidedly antiprofessional when certain caregiving issues, such as the incurability of the disease, became topical (Gubrium 1987).

Regardless of goals or leadership style, the groups developed distinct ways of sharing the caregiving experience. For example, in one of the groups, images of ideal caregivers provided interpretive templates for formulating the personal meaning of caregiving. One caregiver, Jessica, who was no longer an active participant in the group, nonetheless was taken to be an exemplar of "total devotion." As group members considered the various activities and sentiments that accompanied caregiving in the home, or that surrounded the question of institutional placement, they used Jessica's legendary experiences to assess how they were doing in comparison. In the local context of caring for a loved one, Jessica was the unflagging caregiver who bore up under the unrelenting burden of the "36-hour day." That phrase, borrowed from the disease's broader public culture (evidenced in promotional literature, self-help books, and widely distributed videotapes), pointed to caregivers' common sense of burden, which, in turn, was locally exemplified by Jessica's efforts.

Jessica, however, did not always serve as a positive standard of comparison. When discussion turned to the personal and familial consequences of not being able to "let go" of hopelessly failing loved ones and place them in nursing homes, Jessica could be cited as an example of "overdevotion." In this context, group members often referred to her to describe how caregivers can refuse to acknowledge the "reality" of the disease, "denying" that loved ones could deteriorate beyond recognition. Here, again, terms of reference such as "denial" took broader cultural understandings on board for local usage. On such occasions, Jessica was still a local exemplar, though she was not to be emulated. Her case was used to evaluate whether others were also "denying," that is, failing to be realistic about the decreasing benefits of continued home care. Jessica served as the basis for assessing whether one was "going too far" in one's devotion and becoming the "second victim" of the disease, caught in a spiral of overdevotion and self-neglect. Jessica's exemplary status thus shifted from being a positive to a negative standard of comparison. In this regard, local culture exhibited topical slippage; Jessica's exemplary status in the group was artfully applied according to communicative need.

Not all of the groups studied called on such singularly prominent exemplars. Support groups that failed to develop icons of caregiving and their accompanying folklore provided a wider spectrum of options for the interpretation of experience, challenging group members to continually design evaluative footing for interpersonal comparison. The related local culture of such groups flowed with the descriptive details and contrasts of individual participants' reports of daily caregiving experiences. This, too, was mediated by broader cultural understandings, but they were applied more directly to individual differences, not indirectly by way of legendary exemplars.

Each group developed distinct resources for interpreting the caregiving experience, even though they stood in similar relation to the disease's public culture. Potential resources that were commonly employed in one group might be virtually ignored in others. Interpretive practice thus reflected local variability in what might be meaningfully useful.

Making Culture Local

Local cultural resources do not simply present themselves for use, either as descriptive background or as a set of antecedents. They evolve from both external sources and interpretive activities in their own right. By way of illustration, let us turn to another set of examples from the Alzheimer's disease caregivers' support groups.

In the course of sharing caregiving experiences, group participants often find themselves immersed in discussions of family matters. Despite the well-intentioned interest in problems of caregiving that is voiced from many quarters—medical, psychological, legal, and custodial—it is generally believed to be the sufferer's family who can best offer the kind of love and attention needed to cope with the disease. When family care and the attendant hardships are at issue, especially in connection with family responsibility, participants often ask each other what it actually means to "be family" or act as a family member (see Gubrium and Holstein 1990).

This leads to other emotionally charged questions. What does it mean to be family in light of the mental demise of a loved one? What should a family do for the disease sufferer? How much is enough? What is too much? What should be expected from any member? Each question raises the possibility that one's concern will be judged unfamilial, not adequate for close kin. As participants address the questions, they reveal underlying presumptions about how to interpret the parameters and contours of family life, presumptions grounded in related local cultures of domesticity (see Gubrium and Holstein 1990, 1993b; Holstein and Gubrium 1994a, 1995b).

Perhaps the most poignant concern is the decision to institutionalize a loved one. In the Alzheimer's caregiving experience, institutionalization is always a looming eventuality, one faced with trepidation. Typically, the family is considered to be, as Christopher Lasch (1977) puts it, the disease sufferer's final "haven in a heartless world." In light of this sentiment, caregivers wonder whether it is realistic or selfish to consider both the sufferer's increasing care requirements and the growing burden on the lives of other family members. Does the decision to institutionalize mean that relatives have abandoned a loved one, are mainly thinking of themselves, and are thus no "real" family at all to the member in need?

The broadcast media, documentary films, Alzheimer's Association newsletters, and popular caregiver handbooks regularly present caregivers with ways of thinking about such questions. Family members are also introduced to exemplars of individual caregiving and disease experience. Local chapters of the Alzheimer's Association provide links between the disease's public culture, support groups, and individual households. Support group participants draw upon all of these sources of meaning as they search for answers to questions about the caregiving experience.

The proceedings of a support group show just how prominently aspects of the disease's public culture can figure locally. In one session, two caregiving wives, Sheila and Sandra, described their worries over how they would manage their husbands' increasing confusion and physical needs. They spoke of their love and devotion, of how, as one of them put it, "I'm going at it alone and, so far, I'm holding up." They also expressed fear that it might be just a matter of time before each would collapse from the overwhelming burden of it all. Gilda, the group's facilitator, responded sympathetically but firmly to their laments. In the process, she referred to a well-known source of information about the caregiving experience:

Look, I know what you're going through. I've been through it myself. I really feel for you, as we all do I'm sure. But you have to start thinking a different way about it. All I've been hearing just now is "I this," "I that," "I'm taking care of him," "I'm holding up until now." Well, my dears, are you ever going to stop and think that it's not all you? Sure, it's all very hunky-dory that Sheila's daughter is supportive and has been very complimentary. "A perfect daughter," you said? Well, my dears, there's a family here. Let's turn this around a bit, please. You've all seen *Someone I Once Knew* [a widely distributed documentary film portraying five families' experiences with the disease]. Well, then, what's the family really doing? After all, it's not just your husband; it's their father. It seems to me there's a bigger problem here. What should the family be doing? (Gubrium and Holstein 1990, p. 63)

Both Sheila and Sandra were reluctant, as Sandra stated, "to bring them [family members] into it." They felt their duties as wives obligated them to assume the full burden of care. What was more, Sheila added, "My son and daughter have families of their own to think about." Still, Gilda insisted on drawing their attention to what Gilda repeatedly called the "wider picture." Her comments made it evident that the wider picture meant the family entity as a whole, separate from each and every one of its members. As Gilda spoke, she again drew upon the public culture of the disease:

Ask yourself this, will you? You've both been around for a while, right? You read the newsletters from National [Alzheimer's Association headquarters] and the *36-Hour Day* [a popular caregiver handbook] and you saw those films we show at chapter [meetings]. Did you ever stop to think that you all might be one of those families? Forget that sister for a minute, or that daughter of yours, Sheila; what kind of family are you? Just ask yourself that. I remember how I was. It wasn't that long ago either, I might add. I'd read the stuff and poured over it. Over and over. But I kept saying to myself, "No, that's not us." Well, my dears, it took Judy here [another facilitator] to nearly pound my head against the wall to wake me up to the fact that one of those pathetic devoted wives I had read about was really me! I remember Judy telling me, "That's your family all right." It struck me like lightning because I hadn't really thought of us [family members] as any kind of family at all. (Gubrium and Holstein 1990, p. 63)

Public culture is literally invoked here; films and literature are cited by name. Still, such interpretive resources do not simply assert themselves, determining the meaning of the experiences to which they are applied. While these resources were available to participants, they had little impact on Sheila and Sandra until Gilda invoked their relevance and utility. Moreover, the resources were not imported wholesale. Rather, as the extracts show, select knowledge about the Alzheimer's caregiving experience was concretely articulated with particular details of the matters under consideration.

If the disease's public culture offers a stock of options for interpretation and is used to frame biographical particulars, in the end, the public culture's realization awaits local staging. On one hand, various forms of publicity remind caregivers and others that it is the family that ultimately matters most as a source of care. Only the family can make "real" sense of the burdens of care and the "actual" interests of the sufferer. Indeed, the public culture has a distinctly antiprofessional theme that undergirds the emphasis on self-help, further implicating the family as a source and network of unlimited devotion.

On the other hand, caregivers also encounter images of "realistic" families. These are families who are said to have realized that institutionalization is a most humane course of action and, in any case, is inevitable. While the true family puts it off as long as possible, loving and judicious kindred realize what is in the best interest of all concerned. They must act realistically. At the risk of caregivers themselves becoming totally incapacitated and the family falling apart, it is believed that being responsible eventually means relieving the burden of care and placing the hopelessly deteriorated loved one in the care of those better suited to the task. Ironically, it is sometimes suggested that, if the dementia sufferer were aware of it, he or she would argue that the disease eventually prevails on the family to act in the most familial way possible, that is, in the way that is best for all members. In this regard, "being family" suggests being realistic and, ultimately, ending the torturous, possibly destructive, burden of care.

These options confront support-group members with alternate senses of what it means to "be family." They are presented, sorted, and selected according to local specification. This was illustrated at a support group meeting where discussion centered on a particularly distraught and overburdened wife, Kitty. It was Kitty's second marriage, and while she and her now demented husband John had no children, he had two daughters from a previous marriage that Kitty loved as her own. She had been a mother to them for over three decades. Presenting this background, Kitty added that she and John had been totally devoted to each other through the years, "like a marriage made in heaven." Tearfully, Kitty then reported that John was at the point where she had to tend to virtually all his needs—eating, toileting, dressing, grooming, and moving about—reminding her listeners of what all had heard time and again. It was the familiar story of a spouse's and family's resolute devotion to one of its members.

The group sympathized with Kitty, noting that her devotion exemplified true loving concern and care. Other participants presented similar stories, underscoring the matter of what a good family should be. But at one point, group facilitator Rhoda, an experienced caregiver who had already placed her husband in a nursing home, asked Kitty if she had considered the possibility that she was overburdening herself. Rhoda explained that, while she recognized and understood Kitty's devotion, perhaps Kitty was ignoring herself and the rest of the family. Wasn't it possible, Rhoda continued, that Kitty's family was in the process of breaking down while John was "really in never-never land," completely oblivious to the situation?

Kitty listened intently, said that she had asked herself the same questions, but tensely concluded that she could not admit that John was "gone." Calling on the group to recognize what the evidence did not show, she explained that perhaps, deep down inside, John was still there, "maybe cold and lonely and really trying to reach out." She pointedly asked the group whether any of them could actually admit that their spouses were totally gone, even though they were obviously demented. The poignancy of the remark was evident, even if it was unspoken. The momentary silence was only broken by audible sighs and whimpers, clear signs of the emotional salience of the scene. Rhoda heightened the tension by emphatically replying that she thought Kitty was "denying," not willing to admit that she was destroying herself and the rest of her family by refusing to admit that John was gone. Rhoda then referred to the kind of family who never fully realizes what it means to be family in these circumstances because they cannot face the fact that it "is time," referring to the need to consider nursing home placement. Recalling a participant whom the group members knew very well, she argued that caring enough meant giving up on what now was really "just the shell of a former self," as the former participant had ultimately done with her loved one.

Animatedly, Kitty, Rhoda, and others made culture local by articulating received themes with interpersonal particulars. While the disease's public culture was familiar, its resources were mediated by group members' individual contributions, points of view, and personal sentiments, as well as by the collective experience of the group as a whole. Individual experiences and their crosscutting understandings informed the diverse family characterizations that were produced, all of which fed into the constellation of local meanings of domesticity and responsible caregiving.

Local Constructs

Local culture need not merely be an adaptation of "outside" resources. Participants can inventively assemble their own relatively stable and useful frameworks for processing experience. Such was the case when nursing home resident Maida Wood, her circle of friends, and others defined family in terms unexpected, even resented, by Maida's relatives. While the concept of family is, of course, used in diverse ways throughout society, the ways that the term was applied by Maida and her friends became, in the context of nursing home living, a creative element of resistance in Maida's relations with her children. Kinship took on meaning in connection with local usage.

Gossip had it that Maida first came to the nursing facility after she was abruptly ushered from her home into a medical courier van under the pretext of being taken to see her doctor. Instead, she was delivered to a nursing home and admitted to a personal care unit. Her daughter and son explained to the staff, and later to Maida, that it was the only way they could get Maida admitted, because, as the daughter put it, "Mother just wouldn't hear of it."

Maida was confused at first, and "co-operated" in the admission process. She later reported that she did not know where she was, even though she had been repeatedly reminded that Lakeview was her new residence. Bewildered by the deception and abrupt change of scene, she said she had no idea why she had been placed in the facility after the "medical people" had finished with her. Through great effort, she tried to compose herself, locate her whereabouts, and find a reasonable explanation for what had happened. Lakeview staff considered her to be disoriented, which was not out of the ordinary for someone newly admitted to a nursing facility.

As time passed, Maida grew resentful. When she learned that her children had planned the placement well in advance, she felt betrayed and resigned herself to the loss of family loyalty. Who could she now trust when her own family had double-crossed her? Her children's visits were decidedly uncomfortable, even though both the son and daughter apologized repeatedly and explained that they felt they had no alternative. They were considerate and never relaxed their concern for Maida's welfare, visiting her often and regularly taking her on outings.

Meanwhile, Maida began to adjust to her new surroundings. She was increasingly drawn to a small circle of residents in the home, two women and a man, with whom she became fast friends. They were so visibly close that they became known through-out the facility as "Maida's group." When a member of the group was ill, the oth-ers would be highly solicitous and wary of staff intervention. When any of them was temporarily absent from the home, the others became anxious about how things were going for the missing member.

As time passed, the group members came to express their mutual affection by re-ferring to each other in familial terms. Freda, the eldest, was often called the "mother" or simply "grandma Freda." Group members referred to Sara, who was sixty-eight years old and at least ten years the others' junior, as "the baby." Sarah relished the appellation and used it herself to describe her role in the group. Both group members and the staff, especially the nurses aides on the floor, began to speak of the group as a "family," elaborating the vocabulary in the same way the group did as they described members' roles and relationships.

But this was not "one big happy family" from all points of view. Maida's son and daughter bristled at Maida's use of kinship terms to refer to her friends. They grew irritated by the group's constant presence when they visited and by reports of member's veritable familial concern for each other. Maida repeatedly asserted that no real children would have done what the son and daughter had done in placing her in "a final resting place" against her wishes. She never hesitated to remind her children that she had a "genuine" family now: Sara, Freda, and Harold.

Needless to say, the children were upset by this, and interpreted Maida's "familylike" conduct as a further sign of confusion and disorientation. Accord-ing to them, she had lost all sense of reality where domestic relations were con-cerned. The children complained to the Lakeview social worker and sought the support of sympathetic nurses, at one point even trying to have members of Maida's group transferred to other floors. When Maida's group disrupted the customary older of the unit, staff members, too, grew resentful. Indeed, at one point, when the children's and staff's irritations seemed to boil over, staff members openly considered disbanding the clique because, they argued, all its members were patients and had caring families of their own to think about. When the irritations subsided, however, staff members indulged the familylike alliance, even en-couraged it.

It was clear that who Maida's family was, in practice, was not simply a matter of biological ties. As far as Maida and her group were concerned, Maida's son and daughter were no family at all. Interpreted against the group's emergent standard of sensitive, mutual caring and concern, which members occasionally vociferously used to assign meaningful kinship, the son and daughter were derelict, hardly wor-thy of being called "children." As Maida claimed, Sara, Freda, and Harold proved to be just what she expected of family.

Maida's group was intent on viewing its social relations in terms of the familial framework they had in part developed to address Maida's placement and relations with her children. Interpretations of family membership—who was family—could not be disentangled from the local culture of domesticity built up around the group's, and especially Maida's, circumstance in the nursing home. Familial understandings and representations issued from the distinctive organization of the circumstance, its unique hardships and opportunities, and the developing interpersonal definitions, commitments, and resentments.

For Maida's group and select staff members, family discourse became the mechanism for conveying the local meaning of social ties. The discourse and its meanings were reflexively artful and rhetorical. Indeed, the operating familial structure of the group rose and fell discursively with various interpretive challenges to its assignment. When Maida's relations with her son and daughter were especially bitter, family rhetoric was loud and brash. In her children's and friends' presence, Maida gleefully discounted the son and daughter's status as children and touted the familial roles group members had taken on. The son and the daughter responded in kind, challenging the groups' familial claims, which often brought the daughter to tears. When Maida's relations with the children were less strained, however, family discourse and the rhetoric of domestic irresponsibility were muted.

It is important to add that what Maida, her group, and others constructed locally was not a simple, straightforward link between the *whats* of family discourse and the *hows* of usage. When relations between Maida and her children were especially bitter, what was actually said about kinship and familial commitment was dramatically emphatic. The social relevance of what was said and how it was formulated was underscored by emotional forcefulness. As Goffman and the emotionalists would remind us, the sheer scenic presence and animatedness of what was said and done appropriated meaning in its own right. We know the local relevance of what Maida and her group construct because talk and interaction drew upon the moral significance of affective expressiveness to enhance the link between *how* and *what*. What was said and how it was used were thereby more interpersonally consequential for those concerned than they otherwise might have been.

INSTITUTIONAL SITES/SIGHTS OF LOCAL CULTURE

Writing about medical "perception," but suggesting interpretive implications far beyond the clinic, Foucault (1975) argues that the possibilities of apprehending and understanding—even seeing—things are embedded in, and depend upon, historically situated, disciplinary "gazes." Foucault suggests that the fundamental ways of viewing the world that characterize a community of practices (such as the medical community) virtually establish what might be perceived and what remains invisible. Disciplinary "codes of knowledge," he argues, meaningfully organize our views. They are more broadly implicative than situational framings (such as Goffman emphasizes) in that institutions, professions, disciplines, and the like provide enduring representational strategies and resources. Interpretive practice becomes especially complex when it is mediated by diverse professional or disciplinary perspectives that might occupy the same organization. In effect, the *sites* of local culture can be venues for a variety of *sights*.

Organizational Perspectives

Consider, for example, the vision of family that conditions interpretive work at Wilshire Rehabilitation Hospital, and compare it to the situated culture of family developed by Maida's group in the preceding section. While Wilshire successfully guides recovery, patients are seldom fully rehabilitated when they are discharged. The possibilities and problems that might arise in home care situations are therefore deeply influential in discharge planning. Typically, this extends to the need to define who the family is for the purposes of continuing care. Biological or legal ties are only candidate qualifications for family membership. Above all, what is sought is a "family-for-discharge-purposes," one that will "be family" throughout the ongoing rehabilitation process As a result, family membership assignment is strongly grounded in the local rehabilitation culture.

Those engaged in discharge planning undertake their deliberations in relation to shared understandings of what it means to be familial, but, as we noted earlier, their views are also organizationally embedded. Jobs provide alternative perspectives for deciphering who could "really" be a family member and who may only appear to be, further articulating the familial. Following one Wilshire family conference, for example, two members of an elderly stroke patient's rehabilitation team, a physical therapist and a social worker, met to discuss the patient's discharge destination. They agreed that the patient should not return to her own home because she could no longer get around the house on her own, nor navigate the neighborhood's changing social terrain. In fact, they noted, the patient's son had already put the house up for sale. The patient would either go to live with her younger, widowed sister in the sister's apartment, or move into her son's much larger house. Both had offered to provide her a home.

As team members discussed the case, it was clear that they were engaged in more than simply choosing between placement options. They were commonly seeking *familial* care, but doing so according to disciplinary perspectives. In anticipation of these deliberations, the physical therapist had completed an environmental assessment of both candidate households, and, while she found the son's house more wheelchair accessible, she hesitated to recommend placing the mother with the son, claiming that the son "certainly didn't act like one." The therapist explained that everything she had seen and heard led her to believe that the "so-called son" considered his mother to be "just so much human baggage," soon to be tucked away in a bleak back bedroom where she would not interfere with *his* family life. The therapist took umbrage at how the son kept referring to what *his* family needed, as opposed to what his mother required. She interpreted this to mean that the son did not include the mother in his family and therefore would not seriously attend to her rehabilitation. From the therapist's point of view, being family in this case meant that the son should include his mother in domestic life, which, according to the therapist, would optimize her functioning. The therapist remarked that the son's eagerness to sell his mother's house confirmed the therapist's feeling that the son was not at all sensitive to his mother's needs; he was no son at all. She concluded that it would be in everyone's best interest to discharge the patient into the care of her evidently more conscientious sister.

The social worker, however, focused on two other considerations. She believed that she knew more about the "dynamics" of the case because she had frequently dealt with the son and the sister by telephone and in office visits while the patient was hospitalized. According to the social worker, both the son and the sister appeared very supportive, keeping track of the mother's progress and offering to do what they could to facilitate optimal functioning. The social worker also pointed out that both sister and son had actively participated in the hospital's support group for families of stroke victims, which she facilitated, and they seemed eager to learn whatever they could about stroke rehabilitation and long-term prospects for recovery. She concluded that, in her professional judgment, in as much as both the son and the sister were knowledgeable about stroke hospitalization, either's home could provide an adequate discharge destination. The social worker did admit to "subtle bias" against the son, stemming from the son's alleged cold manner, but she argued that team members should take care not to let personal prejudices affect their objectivity.

While there was disagreement in the appraisal of family status in the case, each interpretation was nonetheless accountably oriented to parameters informed by the culture of rehabilitation. Family status was assessed in terms of how the son and sister might contribute to the ultimate goal of optimal functioning. Perceptions of "family" in this context produced views of family-for-rehabilitation-purposes. The hyphenation is important because, while textually awkward, it signals the exact empirical entity under consideration—not the family per se, but family as viewed in, or seen from, this particular site. A lack of hyphenation, by the same token, would suggest that family (or any other social object) could be written about, designated, or defined as if its meaning were evident separate from the conditions of interpretation.

The local culture brought to bear in family perceptions at Wiltshire was decidedly different from the one observed in Maida's nursing home group. The group's culture of concerned care focused on trust and affectional bonds, whereas the Wilshire Hospital team opened the family to view in more professional terms, in specific relation to formal rehabilitation goals. While trust and affection were of interest to the rehabilitation team, they were taken to be only two among many other "clinical" ingredients of the case. While the physical therapist's and the social worker's perspectives were somewhat at odds, these represented differences in interpretation that were likely to be repeated, time and again, within the local scheme of things.

Disciplinary "gazes" can become even more evident when formal sites are compared. We see this in the contrast between family appraisals fashioned under the perceptual aegis of rehabilitation or nursing home residence and similar assessments made in a court conducting involuntary commitment hearings. While commitment decisions orient to a variety of practical considerations, one prominent concern is the availability of tenable living arrangements for the candidate patient (see Holstein 1984, 1993). If a tenable situation in the community is not available, involuntary commitment is likely. In court proceedings, however, tenability is judged in terms of effective custody, not rehabilitation or affectional ties. By and large, judges orient to community placement destinations in terms of the availability of someone to contain the sorts of disturbances that mentally ill persons are expected to cause. They are looking for the presence of a competent caretaker to supervise the released patient.

Consider how this custodial orientation conditions the assessment of a candidate patient's family and proposed living situation (see Holstein 1993). Mental patient Charles Fonville sought his release from involuntary commitment after a series of incidents of bizarre public behavior, claiming that he would resume his program of medications and move in with his brother, his brother's common-law wife, and a third person who Fonville claimed to be a cousin. The judge gave the following account for his decision to continue the commitment:

> I see no choice in this matter. Mr. Fonville here wants to live at home, but there's no one there who can be trusted to keep an eye on him. There's no one to keep him from going off the deep end and causing the kind of trouble that brought him here in the first place. No family, no one to look after him at all. . . . There's no one to keep him out of trouble.

Note in this instance how the judge withheld family assignment, based on his opinion that the group in question would not "look after" Fonville, explaining that there was "no one to keep him out of trouble." There was no mention of therapy, recovery, or rehabilitation. Nor were candidate family members' affectional commitments questioned. Rather, the custodial orientation directed family assessments to qualities that bore significantly on how the candidate patient would be controlled if he should act up in the future (something which, in most cases, is assumed to be a virtual certainty). For the practical purpose at hand, the judge saw the family in terms related to the capacity to contain disorderliness, not in connection with rehabilitation or emotional bonds, a view embedded in the court's, especially the judge's, disciplinary understanding.

Disciplinary Intersections and Practical Usage

Still, as we noted earlier, local culture—disciplinary, formal, or informal—is neither automatic nor preordained in its application. Returning to our original contention that interpretive practice is both artful and substantive, let us illustrate how multiple disciplinary "gazes" can inform the local culture of police work. An incident involving the apprehension of a person alleged to be mentally ill is instructive in this regard (Gubrium and Holstein 1990).

Officer Roberta Jones of the South City police department's Community Service Division was called to respond to a civilian complaint that a young African-American, Rodney Keats, was disrupting a residential neighborhood. Keats was reportedly terrorizing a stretch of sidewalk, ranting incoherently and brandishing a broomstick at concerned onlookers and passersby. Jones approached the youth cautiously, talked him into sitting down in the shade of a tree to discuss the situation, and convinced Keats to surrender the broomstick. As she tried to decipher the events that led to the bizarre and unsettling incident, Jones searched for both a working interpretation and a practical solution to the problem at hand: what was going on and what was she going to do about it?

Technically, Jones did have grounds for citing Keats for disturbing the peace, assault, and trespassing. But Keats appeared to be psychiatrically troubled; he seemed disoriented, agitated, and delusional. Local police wisdom informed Jones that jail was no place for a "crazy" person. "Any cop knows" that persons with mental problems will be exploited, perhaps to the point of physical harm, if they are jailed for what might ostensibly have been criminal violations.

Overlaying this was Jones's orientation to the "social work" side of her Community Service Division appointment, as it was sometimes called by her colleagues on the police force. Jones had received special training in dealing with psychiatric problems and was an experienced navigator of the local mental health service system. Local statutes made it possible to transport a dangerous mentally ill person to the county hospital, where the person could be admitted, involuntarily if necessary, for observation and treatment. Such hospitalization, however, was contingent upon the availability of a bed on the emergency psychiatric ward. Only six such beds existed, and Jones knew they almost certainly would be occupied. In all likelihood, Keats would be turned away. If Jones insisted that this was a "special" case, she might get Keats admitted, but she also knew from experience that her pleas of special circumstance were likely to be a major issue when Keats was evaluated for involuntary commitment. To insist on his temporary admission was tantamount to insuring his subsequent long-term hospitalization. As necessary as this sometimes was, Jones knew that few prospective mental patients look forward to commitment.

Finding herself at the virtual intersection of two professional "gazes," police work and community mental health care, Jones came to interpret Rodney Keats's problems in relational and custodial, as much as in psychiatric, terms. Far from being a puppet of circumstantial contingencies, she took local understandings and events into account in articulating the current and prospective meaning of things. Having a variety of interpretive resources at her disposal, it was her task to make sense of the situation in a way that addressed the practical relevancies at hand, in light of her immediate responsibilities and interpretive dispositions.

Drawing initially upon her "peacekeeping" mission as a police officer, Jones set out to bring the disturbance under control. Keats had been complaining that the "gang" of neighbors he was assaulting were "after his mind," so Jones tried to convince him that his best chance for keeping them at bay was to keep his mind "private" and stay out of any conversation that might expose his mental workings. At the same time, Jones began to negotiate some sort of community custody for Keats, hoping to keep him out of harm's way until she could arrange outpatient help.

To that end, Officer Jones asked Keats where he lived. He said he lived down the street, and directed Jones to a small duplex in a row of modest, slightly deteriorating houses. Jones asked Keats whom he lived with, and Keats responded "my momma." A middle-aged African-American woman answered the door and, after she inquired into the circumstances of Keats's "arrest," asked what she could do to "keep Rodney out of trouble." The following exchange then took place:

OFFICER: Are you the boy's mother?
WOMAN: As much as he's got.
OFFICER: Well, where is his mother? Where does she live? Does the boy have a
         family?"
WOMAN: She lives across town, but she don't have nothing to do with him.
OFFICER: Well who are you?
WOMAN: Esther Franks, I'm his momma.
OFFICER: Just a minute. Who's the mother? What are you saying here?
WOMAN: I'm Rodney's momma. I raised him since he was a baby. He's mine to
        look after, so I got to claim him. (Gubrium and Holstein 1990, p. 119)

Jones sought more than mere clarification of familial status. Her interpretive task was to discern family in terms of who was "really" responsible for Keats's care and supervision. From that viewpoint, it was of little concern to Jones that the woman had only tenuous kinship ties to Keats. Actually, further inquiry revealed that the woman was the former common-law wife of Keats's now-deceased uncle. Jones's immediate objective and her present professional "gaze" led her to look for someone who would care for Keats in a familial manner; formal ties were clearly a secondary consideration.

Other interpretive layerings also played into Jones's assessment of the situation. For example, she brought her own experience as a black woman to bear on the matter. Jones knew that kinship could be organized in complex ways in the African-American community (see Stack 1974), and took that into account in figuring the familial claims Ms. Franks was making. As a black woman, Jones had an "insider's" understanding of what Franks was conveying about family relations in her comments.

Eventually, Jones concluded that, as far as she could tell, Esther Franks met the demands of family status better than did Keats's "mother," who had long since abandoned him. Jones decided to leave Keats in Franks's care. After a lengthy discussion with Franks regarding Keats' problems, and detailed instructions on how to enroll him in a community mental health program, Jones returned to the police station. She called the mental health center and made arrangements for Keats to be seen the next day, telling a therapist that Keats's "mother" would accompany him to the intake visit. Jones then filed a police report on the incident, indicating that after restoring order to the situation she left Keats at home with his "family" and arranged for his "mother" to call her, Jones, if any further trouble arose.

Esther Frank's family status in relation to Rodney Keats was debatable on both legal and biological grounds, yet within the circumstances confronting Officer Jones, "motherhood" was unequivocally assigned. Franks and Keats talked of each other as mother and son. It was clear to Jones, given her interpretive orientations and practical agendas, who Rodney's family needed to be at the moment. What is more, Jones brought a particular stock of knowledge to the situation that contained a model of family that could be articulated with the relationship that she encountered. Ultimately, Rodney Keats's "family" emerged out of Jones's contextually sensitive, culturally informed definition of the situation, from Jones's judicious sifting of representational resources.

To make analytic sense out of Officer Jones' decisions, we need to examine both the real-time interactional circumstances of Jones's assessment and the cultural background against which she interpreted the situation. It is important to remember that, while local culture and organizational orientation are commanding conditions of interpretation, setting and circumstance do not determine interpretive practice. They provide resources, orientations, and objectives, but not injunctions or directives. Interpretive practitioners are never mere extensions of organizational "thinking" (M. Douglas 1986); nor are they "cultural dopes" (Garfinkel 1967). Therefore, we need an analytic strategy and vocabulary that apprehends and conveys the multiple layerings and interpretive artfulness of culture-in-use. Research requires both close observation of the interactional circumstances within which decisions are made and a broader ethnographic awareness of the diverse interpretive resources that bear upon them.

In the preceding case, our method talk clearly addressed both the *whats* and the *hows* under consideration. The researcher had spoken with Officer Jones at length at the police station, had interviewed other officers in her division, had spoken with and observed staff in local community mental health agencies (partially focusing these discussions on the agencies' working relations with the police), and had accompanied Jones for a short time on the job before actually observing the events reported. Whenever possible, the researcher made detailed notes of talk and social interaction. Naturalistic methods, combined with more ethnomethodological data-recording techniques, facilitated an analysis that focused both on how Jones interactionally interpreted the matters at hand and on the way local culture conditioned interpretation. Alternatively bracketing *whats* and *hows* at the lived border of reality and representation, the researcher was able to document the interpretation and use of "family" at the site of its construction.

THE COMPARATIVE ETHNOGRAPHY OF INTERPRETIVE PRACTICE

From these illustrations, it's apparent that the meaningful *whats* and the constitutive *hows* of interpretation are especially visible when different sites are compared. This allows us to highlight the activities, perspectives, and resources characterizing a particular site by noticing how they differ from those operating in other sites. A renewed language of qualitative method thus encourages the comparative ethnography of interpretive practice, alternately focusing on both the artful processes and the substantive conditions of meaning-making and social order. Such a strategy draws upon the strengths of naturalism and emotionalism by maintaining a concern for *what* is going on while describing socially constituting *hows*, ethnomethodology's mission.

A growing number of qualitative researchers are interested in developing this focus. Maynard (1989), for example, notes that (naturalistic) ethnographers have traditionally asked "How do participants see things?" implying the naturalistic assumption that reality lies outside the interpretive practices through which it is apprehended. Discourse studies, according to Maynard, ask "How do participants do things?" suggesting that reality is interactionally accomplished. While his own work typically gives priority to the later question (see, for example, Maynard 1984), Maynard doesn't want to ignore the former. He notes that, in the interest of studying how members *do* things, ethnomethodologically inspired discourse studies have tended to de-emphasize factors that condition constitutive interaction. Recognizing that "external social structure is used as a resource for social interaction at the same time as it is constituted within it," Maynard suggests that ethnographic and discourse studies can be mutually informative, allowing researchers to better document the ways in which the "structure of interaction, while being a local production, simultaneously enacts matters whose origins are externally initiated" (p. 139). "*In addition* to knowing how people 'see' their workday worlds," writes Maynard, researchers should try to understand how people "discover and exhibit features of these worlds so that they can be 'seen'." (p. 144, our emphasis).

Expressing similar interests and concerns, Mehan has developed a discourse-oriented program of "constitutive ethnography" that puts "structure and structuring activities on an equal footing by showing *how* the social facts of the world emerge from structuring work to become external and constraining" (1979, p. 18, emphasis in the original). Mehan examines "contrastive" instances of interpretation in order to describe both the "distal" and the "proximate" features of the reality constituting work people do "within institutional, cultural, and historical contexts" (1991, pp. 73, 81).

Beginning from ethnomethodological and discourse analytic footings, Silverman (1993a) likewise attends to the institutional venues of talk and social construction (also see Miller and Silverman 1995). Praising ethnography that exhibits constitutive sensibilities, he suggests that discourse studies that consider the varied institutional contexts of talk bring a new perspective to qualitative inquiry.[2] Smith (1987) expresses a similar interest in "institutional ethnography" in relation to her feminist program for describing lived realities from the standpoint of women. And recently, Gale Miller (1994) proposed "ethnographies of institutional discourse." Such an approach, he argues, would serve to document "the ways in which setting members use discursive resources in organizing their practical actions, and how members' actions are constrained by the resources available in the settings" (p. 280). Thus, we hear more and more qualitative researchers calling for an approach that addresses both constitutive *how* and substantive *what* questions.

Let us illustrate how comparative study facilitates such an approach by describing in detail an ethnography of two family therapy agencies (Gubrium 1992; cf. Rosenblatt 1993). The study deals with how the local therapeutic cultures embodied in the two settings enter into the production of domestic order and disorder. One of the agencies, Westside House, offers a program of outpatient family therapy, following the "brief" model (Haley 1976; de Shazer 1982, 1985; de Shazer and Berg 1988). The other agency, Fairview Hospital, is a private psychiatric facility with inpatient services. It provides individual and family therapy, combining a variety of therapeutic techniques and orientations, from twelve-step programs to "toughlove." While there is no age limit for treatment in these agencies, the study focuses on family-oriented interventions aimed at the domestic troubles of children, adolescents, and young adults said to be "out of control."

We begin with glimpses of how the comparative ethnography of practice reveals the social construction of domestic order at Westside House. One day, as the researcher is waiting to begin his observations, he notices Donna Reddick, a counselor, greet and chat with a family arriving for its second session at the agency. The case is a court-ordered referral for drug counseling for the teenage son who had been arrested for cocaine possession. Reddick doesn't see the father and asks the mother if she expects her husband to show up. The mother says that their car has a flat tire and that her husband is out in the parking lot fixing it and will be a bit late. Reddick peeks out the window, sees no one, and remarks for all to hear that it is important to start on time since she has another appointment immediately after this one.

Five minutes later, the father enters, sits down at the far end of the reception area with his family, and quietly speaks with his son. Reddick eventually notices the father's arrival and asks the family to go into her office and make themselves comfortable. Before she joins them, the receptionist, Paula, catches her eye and comments: "The old man [father] doesn't seem to be too interested. I didn't think he was going to show. Do you believe that flat tire story? [Pause] The last time, he was a half hour late. Did you get much on him? I'd bet he's not around much."

Reddick answers that she doesn't know much about the father, but that "Mom seems to run the show," as she puts it, speculating that this is the reason the son is out of control. This is the researcher's first hint of the way that staff at Westside attend to family authority.

Reddick and Paula continue to chat, exchanging views on how the father fits into the family picture. At one point Paula remarks: "You know, he could have sat down next to his wife. But he's always kinda in the background. To me, that says something. I mean, why should he always be in the background?" Reddick initially discounts the relevance of the father's choice of seats:

Well, I wouldn't read too much into it this time, Paula. After all, he did come in late because of the flat and all. [Chuckles sarcastically about the father's attempted deception] It's only natural to sit down over there when ya come in [next to the door]. Just because he sat over there [nodding to the left] doesn't mean anything, I don't think. [Pause] Then again, you never know. Didn't he just stand there the last time they were in here and let the kids sit? Right? Maybe he just likes to stand. [Both laugh.] (P. 47)

Mundane exchanges such as these offer initial clues to Westside House's therapeutic culture, and further observations unveil links between abstractions such as domestic order and family hierarchy, and behavior displays such as choice of seating position. Much as Wieder's ethnography of the halfway house presented the researcher with a way of understanding what was being *done* through the telling of the convict code, observations in the therapy agency provide insights into the orientations and meanings that guide the counseling staff's interpretations of domestic order. As we saw in Wieder's study, local culture operates like a set of interpretive instructions. At Westside House, talk that relates seating position in the room and social position in the family reveals how staff members actually "see" (construct) domestic order and disorder. In time, the researcher will learn that seating position is taken to be a concrete sign of how members relate to one another in the home, even if on this occasion Reddick provisionally discounts it.

With this in mind, now consider the researcher's next observations during the counseling staff's video review of a therapy session at the same agency. Counselors routinely meet with an outside consultant to discuss videotapes of family counseling sessions. The purpose is to learn to be more effective by observing and sharing ideas about how colleagues manage the give-and-take of the therapy process. Before starting the videotape, Keith Borelli, a counseling intern, introduces the case. He describes a session involving a twenty-five-year-old man named Chuck, who is in court-ordered counseling because he "beat up" his thirty-eight-year-old wife, Rosie. As Borelli details the case, others join in. One of the counselors points out the thirteen-year age difference between Chuck and Rosie. Another says Chuck is "just a baby," and others elaborate on the mother–child metaphor. Chuck, they eventually surmise, is the "helpless young boy" whose every move is dominated by his overbearing wife, who's nearly "old enough to be his mother." One counselor claims that Rosie is a strong, even hard, woman. Others note that this "dysfunctional arrangement"—a man with a wife thirteen years his senior—must be at the root of the couple's problems. In the counselors' eyes, age differences are evidently also hierarchical and signal domestic order.

Borelli continues, reporting that Rosie claims drugs are involved in the situation, a fact Chuck has denied. Borelli explains, "From what I can figure, they both beat each other up." According to Borelli, small incidents escalate into big battles, but Chuck is the only one who has been charged with battery. Borelli then discusses another family member, Rosie's twenty-one-year-old daughter. Borelli reports that Chuck has said he will walk out of the session if the subject of the daughter comes up.

The counselors then begin a lengthy discussion of the small age difference between Chuck and his stepdaughter and the "power thing" that apparently exists between the two of them. The counselors eventually agree that the wife's and daughter's ages, relative to Chuck's, make for a highly volatile situation that is difficult for Chuck to handle. As one counselor remarks, "You can see why he explodes and escapes [by using drugs]; none of them listens to him."

Borelli finally starts the videotape. As the counselors watch, family members in the tape come into the room and take their seats. The consulting therapist, Dick Billings, asks everyone to pay close attention to where family members sit:

Now, let's see where they decide to sit themselves down. Maybe we can pick up some of the relations there. [Asks Borelli to restate the spouses' age difference.] Let's see if Mom takes the power seat. [Asks Borelli to stop the tape momentarily.] Where do you think she'll sit? (P. 53)

A lengthy discussion ensues concerning the relation between domestic authority and the position of the chairs in the counseling room. Some see the "power seat" as the chair in the middle. Others guess that Mom's authority will lead her to the seat closest to the counselor because that seat, located next to a seat of formal power in the counseling room, is also a power seat. Even while there is disagreement, a tacit rule seems to be operating, urging everyone to read signs of domestic authority from seating arrangement. The counselors form working hypotheses about family functioning accordingly.

Borelli restarts the tape. The counselors then see Chuck take the seat closest to the counselor. Rosie takes the middle seat, and the oldest daughter seats herself between Chuck and Rosie. In a telling exchange, Billings leans forward and asks if anyone has noticed where the oldest daughter sits. "Yeah, she's sitting right between Chuck and Rosie!" blurts Borelli. Billings responds didactically:

That's right. Good. That's just what we'd expect if the daughter is joining Mom against Chuck. It's a classic arrangement. Mom's at the center. The henpecked husband is at the end and the daughter who is old enough to be his wife, but isn't even his daughter, makes sure that she takes her place in the power structure. (P. 57)

The counselors temporarily set aside the hypothesis that Mom would take the presumptive "power seat" next to the counselor and continue to watch the tape. They now focus on the daughter's location and what it says about Chuck's relationship with his wife. As the discussion develops, Gary Nelson, one of the counselors, recalls the alternative power seat hypothesis, suggesting that maybe both Chuck and Rosie occupy power seats and are themselves vying for authority, with the daughter being more or less irrelevant to their power struggle. Counselor Nancy Cantor vigorously objects, pointing to family members' physical comportment—*how* they appear to be seated, not just where.

> Oh, come on, Gary. Look at them. Just look. [Pointing to the monitor] We all know what's going on. You can see what's happening. The guy [Chuck] is caught in a vice. It's written all over the daughter's face. Look how she's sitting there. She's just right in there next to Mom and doesn't want Chuck to get any closer. She's protecting Mom and Mom knows that she can get the daughter to keep him at bay, right? You can see that, too, how the age thing is coming into play. Mom's the oldest and she's got the floor. (Pp. 57–58)

From the observations in this session, and from what was seen and heard in the reception area, the contours of Westside's image of domestic order begin to take shape for the researcher. As the counselors point to the physical signs of family order and disorder on the video monitor, they virtually talk order into being. We learn that the functional family is locally viewed as a hierarchy of authority, with appropriately distributed rights and obligations. A functional family has parents or other responsible adults in control, making the consequential decisions of the home. The therapeutic aim is to reestablish this authority when it has eroded, putting the parents in control, preferably with the father at the top of the hierarchy, his wife at his side, nearby. Counselors are constantly alert for signs of disrupted hierarchy and treat the minutest details of seat selection and comportment as therapeutically telling.

It is important to point out that what the researcher collaterally observes in the fieldwork at Fairview Hospital is indirectly affecting what he notices at Westside. The contrasts in local culture, especially the agencies' dramatically different models of domestic order, inform the researcher's interpretation of Westsiders' actions as much as what he gleans on site at Westside from talk and interaction alone. In time, the researcher will learn that quite similar signs are used to represent domestic order in the two agencies, even though the signs are taken as evidence of distinctly different family structures. Comparing the two sites shows the researcher that the virtually identical *hows* of the individual agencies lead to contrasting conclusions regarding *what* might and might not be going on in the home. For example, as we will see shortly, at Fairview Hospital, comportment is read for signs of emotional bonds, not authority. Comparing the agencies brings this into bold relief as the constitutive process is temporarily bracketed in order to concentrate on substantive meaning.

Sensitized by such comparisons, the researcher is increasingly attuned to the separate cultures of domestic order. Consider what emerges from his observations of another videotaped therapy session at Westside in which counselors articulate additional nuances of seating arrangement and comportment. In this case, counselors are reviewing a tape of a mother and her twin sons' therapy session. Leila Korson, a counseling intern, and former schoolteacher, introduces the tape, telling the counselors that the mother is divorced and depressed, while the twins are constantly disruptive at school. The following extract shows how, in the counselors' talk, the twins' status as troubled youth is embodied in seated posture and discussed in the vocabulary of power and domination.

Korson starts the tape, and the counselors (including Gary Nelson, Nancy Cantor, Tammy Horton, and Donna Reddick) turn to the monitor, where they expect to "see" what Korson has just described. They listen as Korson, on tape, asks the boys how it feels to grow up as twins. Nelson then tells Korson to put the tape on pause and to identify each person on the monitor. As Korson does, she comments on family members' seating arrangement, pointing to comportment as indicative of what another counselor will soon call "not a very healthy home":

KORSON: This one [twin Johnny] was kinda quiet at first. I couldn't get him to say anything. Later in the session, he moved over here [points to his current seating position] and then he started to talk more, like he was the boss around home. I think he's the dominant one [twin]. Look at the way he's sitting. [Johnny sits upright and forward in his chair.] He's like that all the time, even when he was sitting over here [points to the seat at the right, out of camera range].

CANTOR: Now he's in the power seat and he feels more comfortable [pause] more like himself.

HORTON: Yeah, like he feels at home.

REDDICK: The mother, to me, is giving mixed messages to the boys about living at home and going to the father [who lives nearby]. She tells them if they don't behave, they can just get out of the house and go to their father. Then she tells them that they better behave or they'll turn out just like him.

HORTON: [Pointing to the monitor as she restarts the tape] Yeah [pause] and just look at that kid [Johnny]. Look at how he sits at the edge of the chair [pause] like he's going to jump all over Mom if she dares to cross him. Just look at him! It's written all over him. That look he's giving her. My God, it's just telling her [mother] that he's in charge. And he knows it. If she crosses him, he'll just march over to Dad and live there.

CANTOR: And would you look at the other one [twin]. He's watching his brother real close-like, waiting to see what to do. And would ya look at Mom! [All watch the monitor for a few seconds] Look at how she looks down at the floor all the time, like she's being stepped on as Johnny gets going. You can see what a bad scene it is. That's not a very healthy home. No wonder those boys are delinquent. (Pp. 62–63)

The counselors point to the monitor as if they were actually witnessing domestic disorder before their very eyes. With comments such as "Look at Mom," "Just look at him," and "That's not a very healthy home," the speakers sound as if they are directly observing the household's social order and, at the same time, how the twins figure into it. They use body signs to concretely and locally reference and constitute what is otherwise abstract, namely, domestic disorder and delinquency. We actually see and hear local culture being brought to bear in interpretive practice.

Now, compare this with what the researcher observed at Fairview Hospital. While ostensibly offering similar services, but calling it family *therapy* not family *counseling*, Fairview staff orients differently to domestic order. This is apparent during a multifamily group therapy session. Speaking of what it means to be a home and family, therapist Dave Shindell explains to the group of parents:

Family operates on a real emotional level called "love." That's the bottom line. You've got it other places of course but the family's unique because that's the source. That's what family is all about and that, unfortunately, is also where all the trouble comes from. Then expectations work on in over that, like "you do this and if you want me to do that, then you'll have to do so-and-so." So expectations fall in there. There are all kinds of conditions put in the way, like power trips. [Elaborates] That, my friends, is when you fail to love, to recognize the other person for themselves, deep inside. You've got feelings and you've got love. What happens when unconditional love is there, the child starts to grow . . . and others grow and trust, too. It's real, real important to be consistent with your adolescent in this way. [Elaborates] That's what makes a home a home. There's no place quite like it. You know it. I know it. If you're inconsistent, you risk questioning that basic love that's the family and that holds things together. (P. 134)

Later, another therapist, Tim Benson, offers the following comments in a therapy group:

If you ask me, I'd say, off hand, that 95% of the homes these days are dysfunctional. You name a family and I'll bet you I can show you a home where feelings are all screwed up. I'd say there are probably fewer than 2% of the homes that you could really call loving homes, you know where everyone has respect for the other guy's feelings and shares feelings and knows how to give when someone is hurting, you know, recognize feelings. [Elaborates] And, ladies and gentleman, that's what we're up against and what we're here for: to help you share those feelings, get them out on the table and try to rebuild your families. Love's where it's at. When love breaks down, that's when the trouble starts. (P. 135)

Such comments articulate the contrasting culture of domesticity that permeates Fairview. Whereas Westsiders view parental authority as the foundation of domestic order, Fairview staff members observe order in the expression of feeling. With this as background, the researcher can begin to hear and, especially, to understand how domestic order is constructed in actual group discussions at Fairview. Consider an example from another group therapy session. Shindell is responding to an angry teenager by explaining the need to sit down and talk in order to effectively convey feelings. Ricky Watson, the teenager, has just stood in the middle of the room and angrily told his mother that he is not going to "take it anymore," that neither his mother, who is present, nor his father realizes what it is like to be "grounded" because of the "littlest" things." Before Ricky finishes, Shindell interrupts, and several parents and another adolescent patient, Bill, join in:

SHINDELL: Okay, Watson, I think we've heard enough. We've . . .
   RICKY: [Continuing] It's not fair. I get grounded just because . . .
SHINDELL: [Interrupting] We heard you, Ricky. You can sit down now. You've told your side of it. [Ricky slowly takes his seat. There's a long pause. All eyes are on Ricky and his mother. Shindell continues.]
SHINDELL: [To Ricky] You've come across loud and clear. [To the group] I think we should ask ourselves, "Has Ricky really communicated what he feels?" [To Ricky] You say they ground you for the littlest thing? But do you bother to ask them how they feel about what you did to deserve that? I don't think so. Maybe the more important question is,

"Did you really *tell* Mom how you feel?" I think all of us would agree that we heard you loud and clear. The question is, "What did we hear?" [Pause] Think about it. [Looks around the room] Anyone. What would you hear if someone was standing there, just three feet away from you, yelling at the top of his voice at you about something?

DAD A: I'd say I'd be hearing a lot of screaming and yelling.

MOM B: I'd say, "There's a pretty disturbed teenager."

RICKY'S MOM: That what Ricky's like lately, shouting, racing around the room, mouthing off, standing right in front of me and his dad and swearing like a sailor. It's a wonder his dad doesn't haul off and brain him when he's like that. Ricky never sits down and tells you what's on his mind. No sir. He's got to be on a soapbox with a loudspeaker.

SHINDELL: I think what we're hearing here is the first thing about how not to communicate. No one is going to say anything to anyone when he's standing there yelling. I'm sure that's not what anyone of us believes is effective. I think the first thing is that we have to learn to just sit down and . . .

BILL: [Interrupting] You have to sit tight for five minutes, Ricky-boy, and think about what you're doing instead of yelling and starting into it, right off the bat like that.

SHINDELL: That's the first thing. If you don't sit down and deal with this rationally . . . get down to business . . . no one's going to hear anything you're saying, no matter how much you say or how loud you say it.

BILL: [Chuckling] That's right, Ricky-boy. [Singsong] You got to sit a little; smile a little; put your feet on the ground a little. [All laugh] Seriously, Watson, you got to put your feelings on the table, man, or you're gonna get nowhere fast. (Pp. 192–93)

With the knowledge that Fairview therapists consider love, emotion, and respect for one another's feelings to be ingredients of the functional family, we can appreciate this extract for the way it conveys the need to share fairly. From the responses to Ricky, we hear tacit reference to the local image of a "democracy" of emotions in which everyone gets his or her say. In the functional home, a person honestly conveys what he or she feels and permits others to do the same. Note, for example, how Shindell stresses Ricky's inability to relay what he really feels and, equally important, how Ricky ignores others feelings. To Shindell, this represents poor communication.

The idea of a democracy of emotions is very abstract, not something readily observed. The same can be said of a hierarchy of authority. Comparative ethnography helps the researcher discern just what signs are used locally, and how they are interpreted, to detect and construct family order. As we mentioned earlier, signs of domestic order are seen in similar kinds of behaviors and gestures at both Fairview and Westside. But *how* culture is embodied tells us little about *what* local culture is at the two agencies. Seating, comportment, and the like are significant in both agencies, but they do not convey the same meanings at both places. Exclusively attending to the *hows* of the process in either setting would fail to reveal the local constitutive significance of *what* is under consideration. However, with the *whats* of local culture in mind (and with the *hows* temporarily bracketed), the researcher begins to understand why, say, seating at Fairview refers more to being seated than to the particular seat selections of family members. "Sitting down" is thought to be more conducive to communication and the reception of feelings than standing up. The father who sits down while describing his unruly son's behavior is considered more likely to convey authentic feelings and actually be heard than the father who stands up and intimidates listeners. Comportment, especially "sitting back," reflects communicative receptivity. The mother who not only sits down to communicate, but sits back in her chair, is seen as better equipped to empathetically listen to her daughter's anxious complaints about a boyfriend's drinking than the mother who sits at the edge of her chair and appears ready to cut her daughter off at any moment. Family members who speak in an inviting and calm tone of voice and who, in turn, show evidence of being prepared to "actively listen," facilitate the expression of feelings.

As the researcher continues to compare interpretive practice at the two agencies, we get a more vivid picture of just how differently they constitute the family. While similar signs are taken to embody domestic order, they are viewed as representing quite different entities in the local scheme of things. At Westside, staff interpret a parent who, during a therapy session, seats himself or herself prominently in the room, presents confidently, and speaks forcefully, as being in a proper position of authority at home. This is the way parents should act, as Westsiders would see it. Typically, parents, especially fathers, counseled at Westside do not behave in this way. Westsiders take this as a marker, if not a cause, of families' domestic troubles.

Conversely, the rare father who at Westside House selects a "power seat" and presents in a clear and commanding manner, tolerating no interruptions from other family members, is said to be showing that he is in charge at home, that the family is functioning well. Staff at Fairview, however, would view a similarly presenting father as using power to spoil what should be a proper democracy of emotions, where every member has the opportunity to share his or her own feelings. In this case, the father's comportment would be viewed as a sign of family disorder.

Taken together, these comparisons provide ways of highlighting aspects of local culture and its articulation. The artful practice of reading physical signs of domesticity from seating and comportment is common to both settings. A comparison of the settings allows us to hold artfulness constant in this regard in order to see the interpretive effects of local culture. Comparative analysis and analytic bracketing enable the researcher to concentrate for the time being on interpretive resources, while not forgetting the constitutive process. Following that, the researcher may shift attention back to artfulness, but always with a background awareness of substantive conditions.[3]

CHAPTER 9

Explanation and Deprivatization

To this point, we have skirted the question that seems to motivate much social research: the question of *why*? As noted earlier, qualitative researchers typically approach this question cautiously, sometimes with great trepidation. Explanation is tricky business, one that qualitative inquiry embraces discreetly in light of its appreciation for the complexity and indeterminacy of social life. It's one thing to describe what's going on, or how things or events take shape. Qualitative researchers have faith in their ability to address these as empirical matters. But the question of *why* things happen can lead to inferential leaps and empirical speculations that can propel qualitative analysts far away from their stock in trade. Still, explanation often goes hand in hand with description. The challenge is to respond to the *why* question in ways that are empirically and conceptually consonant with qualitative inquiry's traditional concerns.

In order to ask *why*, we need a domain of explanation for whatever is to be explained. The familiar distinction in sociology between macrosociological and microsociological domains, for example, specifies two kinds of explanatory footing. Most commonly, macrosociological variables are used to explain microsociological phenomena (e.g., using the rural/urban or the traditional/modern distinction to explain qualities of face-to-face relationships). Parsons's (1951) social system framework was once a leading model of this type of explanation, using macrolevel systemic variables to explain functioning and variation in individual lives and actions.

When qualitative researchers raise *why* questions, they typically entertain them within the empirical purview of the here-and-now or the there-and-then, in the vicinities of lives in progress. Their explanatory position is close to the lived border of reality and representation. Their method talk warily broaches the macrosociological because macrolevel explanation commonly diverts attention from that border. Because qualitative researchers' instincts tell them to respect the common threads that distinguish their craft, they look for explanatory space and footings that accommodate these epistemological orientations and empirical priorities.

EMERGING EXPLANATORY FOOTINGS

One way for qualitative inquiry to approach *why* questions without hazarding its leading empirical interests is to build from its traditional focus on the *whats* and *hows* of social life. Explanatory footings can be found at the intersection of concerns for what is going on in relation to how it is structured, in the space we ourselves have created to analyze interpretive practice. Following naturalistic impulses, for instance, we can first address the issue of what the social world is like; then, by temporarily suspending belief in the realities of that world, we can shift our attention to answering questions of how the representations of those realities come to be taken as real in practice. We may even begin to ask about the functions of recurrent constitutive processes (Silverman 1993a). But as we attend to social construction, we must remember that the *whats* of the social world always inform our understanding of the *hows*. And, as the emotionalists remind us, we must not lose track of the poignantly scenic matters that seem to disappear in constitutive analysis. Taken together, these reciprocal *what* and *how* concerns offer a basis for answering a variety of *why* questions.

Explaining the Natural

Naturalists such as Whyte, Liebow, and Anderson are primarily disposed to carefully document unknown or poorly understood domains of everyday life, making use of certain circumstantial *whats* to explain others. Typically, they do not invoke broader external variables (broad *whats*) to explain the particular local *whats* in question. Recently, some sociological ethnographers, including Michael Burawoy and his associates (1991), have argued against this localizing tendency, asserting that ethnography needs to be "unbound" from this. The issue is, to some extent, a matter of emphasis, but more importantly, it is one of empirical risk. Locating themselves at the lived border of reality and representation, naturalists tend to emphasize the fine-grained details of everyday life, while being less concerned with the ostensibly distant conditions that affect it. They search closer to home for answers to *why* questions. "Unbinding" ethnography to identify distant conditions can risk giving short shrift to the fine points of, and ways in which, everyday realities are lived and represented. It also opens qualitative inquiry to the possibility that everyday life might be portrayed as a mere reproduction of the so-called broader realities. This is not to suggest that naturalistic studies should reject macrolevel explanations, only that the risk of eclipsing the common threads of qualitative inquiry for totalized explanation lurks threateningly in the background.

Analytic bracketing offers naturalists a more indigenous kind of empirical footing for asking a different kind of *why* question, one that Anderson adumbrates in *A Place on the Corner*. This kind of *why* question relates reality to the representational side of the lived border. Never doubting the realities of everyday life, the naturalist typically observes and documents the social organization of those realities. But, switching analytic gears and bracketing belief in the realities, the naturalist can raise the question of why they take the shape and form they do. Reality-constructing mechanisms provide one sort of answer. The *how* of constitutive process offers empirical footing for answering *why* reality appears as it does.

Anderson points us in this direction when he states that, as pervasive and powerful as the external social world is in organizing his informants' desires, hopes, and courses of action, it is a world those men contribute to, and construct, as much as it is one that shapes their lives. By introducing the question of how the culture of respect is constructed, Anderson sets the grounds for documenting the ways in which his informants' talk and interaction produce culture in the immediate circumstances of their lives. This helps explain the culture's shape and persistence.

Explaining the Emotional

Analytic bracketing provides a similar kind of empirical footing for asking *why* questions in relation to emotionality. Like the naturalists, the emotionalists concern themselves with *what* questions, but the emotionalists' *what* questions are about matters ostensibly more poignant and the answers often considered to be hidden from view. Theirs is an orientation to the deeper *whats* of everyday life as a source of answers to the questions of why lived experience takes the shape it does The circumstantial contours of emotional expression, of course, do add an explanatory element of their own.

The rub is that while feelings, sentiments, and passions are considered to be prime sources of talk and interaction, talk and interaction *express* that emotional experience. The question is, how do qualitative researchers know what others feel if those feelings are not adequately conveyed in words? In addition, researchers must conscientiously attend to what they themselves communicatively convey about feelings in order to insure that what they offer adequately reflects what ubiquitously permeates the experiential world. As Wittgenstein (1958) argued, something categorical and public must be applied in order to turn privacy into meaningful awareness. Researchers must convey the ineffable in some way that does representational justice to what cannot be expressed. This is a conundrum indeed. Expressing something inexpressible is a practical challenge to everyday actors and an analytic and representational challenge to emotionalist researchers.

Recall, Douglas's (1985) instructions for creative interviewing. The technique was presented as a means both to plumb the inner depths of experience and to incite respondents to disclose what they feel but usually hide from view. In search of answers to questions about what lies within, Douglas raises myriad procedural questions that are aimed at the creative interviewer more than at the respondent. Later emotionalists investigate subjectivity less by probing it than by reenacting it. Again, the concern is with procedures for communicating emotional experience. Methodology becomes less a means of obtaining these data than it is data itself. As we illustrated earlier, Ellis and Bochner (1992) wrote a play about an abortion decision in order to convey through sights, sounds, and performance the depths of experience, which would be lost in mere words.

Procedure here is tantamount to subject matter. Reversing the positions of what ethnomethodologists call topic and analytic resource, latter day emotionalists turn to their own "ethnomethods," from poetry to plays, as a way of conveying subjectivity. They don't analyze the methods, but, rather, attempt to reenact them. Methods are to be applied and appreciated, not researched in their own right. Following postmodern sentiments, there is little to distinguish between subject and researcher. Rather, it is people's emotions as such that are center stage, especially the researchers'.

At the same time, the relation between the deep and mysterious *whats* of emotional experience on the one hand, and the *hows* of emotional expression and communication on the other, offers empirical footing for two different kinds of explanation. Characteristically, emotionalists remain concerned with questions of why feelings are uncommunicated and why, if they are expressed, they often do not convey what is actually felt. As we illustrated in Chapter 4, we can attempt one kind of explanation by bracketing the reality of emotional experience in its own right to examine the talk and interaction that emotionalists employ to realize subjectivity. Our ethnomethodologically informed analysis of Ellis and Bochner's play showed that the judicious use of quotation marks and the actors' positioning on stage served to distinguish the public from the private, and ostensibly invisible, side of emotionality. The authors used very public and recognizable meaning-making devices to communicate private experience. Asking why feelings were now being revealed, we turned to how emotionality was methodically being constituted for an answer.

Reversing this, we can offer another explanation by bracketing our attention to constitutive *how* matters in order to ask what cultural resources were used to convey emotionality. While we identified two communicative techniques Ellis and Bochner used within the play to distinguish the private from the public, it is important to note that employing a dramatic form of representation, that is, a play, is a kind of rhetorical move in and of itself. Culturally, drama and other more "literary" forms of expression are held to be somehow more in tune with the deeper realms of lived experience than is cool, dispassionate academic text. Capitalizing on romanticist sensibilities, the emotionalists draw upon communicative resources that are culturally and historically associated with emotional expression. Dramatic or poetic modes of representation *do* feelings in a culturally recognized way; they do not merely convey what feelings are like. Knowing *what* culture provides offers explanatory footing; asking why feelings are being revealed, we can turn to the cultural configurations of emotionality as much as to methods of communication for an answer.

Explaining the Constitutive

Given their concern for *how* reality is constituted, ethnomethodologists care less about why participants construct what they do, why specific meanings enter into these activities, or why particular outcomes are produced. Jack Katz (1994, p. 254) notes that conversation analysis tends to neglect many questions about the factors that condition the production of talk and interaction:

> The conversation analysts show us such phenomena as the intricate [internal] monitoring of turn taking and the subtle achievement of repairs to potential misunderstandings in face-to-face, or ear-to-ear (e.g., phone) discourse, but they happily build an instructive corpus of empirical findings on universal aspects of conversational practice without a concern to establish the contingencies governing the motivation to enter and sustain conversations (Sacks 1992; Schegloff 1979).[1]

Katz's concern with the "contingencies governing" the presence or absence of talk and interaction directs us to possible *why* questions relating to the constitutive *hows* of conversation (see Moerman 1992). Again, analytic bracketing permits us to begin with the typical ethnomethodological interest in constitutive practice, then turn to the conditions bearing on the production of talk and interaction. As a result, we might explain why talk and interaction are occasioned as they are and, relatedly, why certain topics and not others come into play in conversational practice. Like other explanations, these require distinct analytic footing in the empirical world, in this instance, footing located in the context and conditions of interaction. *Why* questions are thus placed separate from, but along side of, the *hows* of reality construction that typically captivate ethnomethodology.

This provides ethnomethodology with fertile grounds for explanation. As Silverman (1993a) notes in discussing the practical relevance of qualitative research generally, and his own research on HIV counseling in particular, there can be no basis for dealing with *why* questions unless we also consider the broader contexts of communication. Looking at his own research situation, he explains:

> Our research has much to say about how counselors can organize their talk in order to maximize patient uptake (Silverman, Bor, Miller, and Goldman 1992). However, without organizational change, the impact of such communication techniques alone might be minimal or even harmful. For instance, encouraging patient uptake will usually involve longer counseling sessions. Experienced counselors will tell you that, if they take so long with one client that the waiting period for others increases, some clients will simply walk out—and hence may continue their risky behavior without learning their HIV status. (P. 193)

What Silverman is saying here is that one must be familiar with the *whats* of organizational conditions in sites where HIV counseling takes place in order to understand why particular kinds of talk take place at all. What is going on substantively also comes to bear on what functions are performed by particular conversational mechanisms.

Ethnomethodological explanation thus requires a deeper consideration of the substantive contexts of interpretive practice than conversationally oriented ethnomethodology typically allows. Recent studies of institutional talk have begun to take institutional contingencies into account, however. This research is looking into the ways in which the locally organized *whats* of communicative practice—for example, particular types of turn taking, conversational monitoring, and repair that occurs under the aegis of medical encounters, legal hearings, or television interviews—can be used to answer *why* particular conversational matters are routinely developed, interrupted, or repaired.

Another ethnomethodologically grounded strategy for considering the contextual *whats* in relation to the *hows* of interpretive practice is to undertake collateral studies of varied sites of talk and interaction. We considered this strategy in Chapter 8 by comparing the communicative organization of family therapy in two different agencies. The advantage of this strategy for addressing *why* questions is that the organizational and local cultural characteristics of the sites can provide a basis for formulating constructively oriented typologies of such sites, which, in turn, can serve as broader-based sources for explanation. For example, in the family therapy study, the agencies were distinguished from one another according to their local cultures of domestic order. Knowledge of these cultures helps us to explain why therapeutic talk is meaningfully organized in the ways that it is in the respective sites. As far as the social construction of domestic disorder is concerned, how participants "do" family can be partially explained by the *type* of interpretive orientation that serves as an institutional resource for meaning-making.

What a typology adds is an analytic basis for understanding the range of meanings that might be locally produced. It helps us anticipate changes in interpretations of domestic order and family functioning when the institutional therapeutic philosophy or model of therapy changes. Typologies are more general sources of explanation for local talk and interaction than analyses informed by the understandings gained from single institutional sites. Should a typology have systematic theoretical linkages with other sources of explanation, the possible answers to locally oriented *why* questions would become even more elaborate. For instance, a typology of possible discourses of sickness available in a particular professional domain would help to explain the forms of talk and possible discursive grounds for resistance or reformulation that develop in ongoing social interaction within that domain.

Addressing *Why* by Way of *What*

It should go without saying that these overtures to explanation are not meant to be leaps into causal analysis or the theoretical elaboration of macrostructures. Instead, they suggest that we can address *why* questions by considering the contingent relations between the *whats* and *hows* of social life. Conditions of interpretation, for example, provide the contingent *whats* of talk and constitutive interaction. While looking at an in-depth interview or observational data, for instance, we might be interested in how people narratively assemble their lives or in how the everyday realities of work life in a particular setting are constructed so as to give them a semblance of authenticity. But our appreciation for both sides of interpretive practice leads us to ask questions about what those actual lives are about and what models of authenticity are available to those in the concrete setting under consideration, allowing us to answer *why* questions about the *hows* by way of *what*.

Invoking these *whats* involves method talk that takes us beyond, but does not eclipse, issues of how the matters under consideration are constituted. For example, in *A Place on the Corner*, Anderson begins to write about the culture of respect as a social construction, and it soon becomes evident that the particular culture and connotations of respect constituted in the vicinity of Jelly's bar and liquor store are not necessarily the same as they are in other urban locations. Returning to Anderson's text, on the very first page of his opening chapter, he repeatedly sensitizes the reader to the "thereness" of local life and the difference it makes in how respect is experienced. One sentence reads, "The urban poor and working-class people are likely to experience their local taverns as much more than commercial businesses" (p. 1). A few sentences later in the same paragraph, Anderson writes about these people, "This is their place." And, finally, at the end of the paragraph comes a sentence that distinguishes the "thereness" of this place from the "thereness" of other places. It is a way of informing the reader that what is forthcoming matters as much for what is known about everyday life as how the life under consideration is put together: "Other settings, especially those identified with the wider society, with its strange, impersonal standards and evaluations, are not nearly as important for gaining a sense of personal self-worth as are the settings attended by friends and other neighborhood people." Anderson is urging us to recognize that denizens of urban locations like the place on the corner are more enduringly involved in the construction of respect than those in most other places. That is why the social construction of respect there is so important.

Similarly, Wieder, the ethnomethodologist, is centrally concerned with how a code of conduct is used to constitute the moral affairs of the staff and residents of the halfway house, but it is evident throughout *Language and Social Reality* that usage applies locally consequential meanings. The specific vocabulary of this particular code—when it is used, in what circumstances, with what implications—matters just as much as the fact that the code is used at all as a reflexive sense-making device. It is not usage and reflexive constitution alone that make the code important or interesting. Reflexive usage produces, organizes, and manages a *convict* code, with its attendant configuration of cultural meanings. This code is not about kids snitching on one another for breaking classroom rules. Rather, the halfway house code deals with snitching as it relates to criminal life, covert drug use, maintaining life-and-death loyalties, offering dangerously risky resistance, and showing highly enterprising solidarity. Sacks (1992) makes abundantly clear that the content of culture (in this case, the particular code) does matter in how reality is constituted. As Sacks might have explained using the idea of a membership categorization device, the categorizational consequences of snitching in relation to the convict code are distinctly different for the organization of talk and interaction than the consequences of openly snitching in grade school. The former could lead to "serious," if not life-threatening talk and interaction; the latter might result in mere teasing or mild rebukes.

Still, when Anderson, Wieder, Sacks, and others attend to the *whats* of everyday life, they do not analytically capitulate to broader social structures. While they formulate explanations in terms of what are taken to be important cultural configurations, each one seems to remember that lived experience can easily be eclipsed and its inventiveness shortchanged in method talk that speaks only of "social conditions," "explanatory variables," or "historical forces." This is precisely what Whyte suggests when he writes on the first page of the Introduction to *Street Corner Society*: "Cornerville people appear as social work clients, as defendants in criminal cases, or as undifferentiated members of 'the masses.' There is one thing wrong with such a picture: no human beings are in it" (1943, p. xv).

This is anything but a romance with the natives. At stake here is the hard-nosed, scientific sentiment that, if we are to understand the organization of experience—whether it is the ordinary details of people's lives, the constitutive practices of talk and interaction, or the full scenic presence of their thoughts and feelings—we need to place ourselves close to the lived border of reality and representation. Causal variables or distal forces should not displace the lived experience of those who are the subjects of inquiry.

Addressing *Why* by Way of *How*

The explanatory space of interpretive practice also extends in the other direction, to its artful side, allowing us to answer *why* questions about the *whats* by way of *how*. One of the issues we raised earlier in discussing *Street Corner Society* was Whyte's neglect of interpretive perspective. While Whyte's story, of course, is renowned for its sociological originality, it is largely a story put together by Whyte from Doc's

point of view. Even though Whyte informs us that Doc's story is virtually everyone's in Cornerville, we wondered if this would include, say, Cornerville women's
points of view. Would the bravado be there? Would the same themes of loyalty,
kinship, and racketeering be foregrounded? How would women depict Cornerville
social organization? While we might guess that many of the *whats* that Doc, Chick,
and the other men describe would be included, would the *hows* of the storytelling
be the same? As Lila Abu-Lughod (1991, 1993, p. 4) might remind us, Cornerville
women could very well write their world differently (also see Moore 1988).

Of course, we can only guess at how Cornerville women would put "their story"
together. Chase (1995), however, examines differential storytelling in her recent
study of the work narratives of women school superintendents. Her aim is to explain the diverse representational *whats* of a professional career by analyzing in-
depth interviews with women from various racial and ethnic backgrounds who work
as school superintendents in both rural and urban environments. The women all tell
of professional power and success, on the one hand, and discrimination encountered
in a white and male-dominated occupation, on the other hand. Still, their stories end
up being quite different, and Chase asks why is it that a common experience results
in such diverse narratives? Why do the superintendents produce such disparate versions of reality? Her explanation implicates the *hows* of storytelling in relation to
two distinct, but experientially shared whats: the cultural discourses of individual
achievement and of inequality:

> My interest lies in understanding relations among culture, narrative, and experience—in
> understanding how women make sense of their experiences by narrating them within a par-
> ticular cultural context. . . . My [own] narrative shows that as women recount their experi-
> ences, they simultaneously draw on and struggle with various cultural discourses—networks
> of meaning—about individual achievement and inequality. Through that narrative process,
> women construct self-understandings that both shape and are shaped by those cultural dis-
> courses. (P. x)

Chase's method talk is revealing. While she refers to the rather familiar *whats* of
these superintendents' careers, she is reluctant to conclude that these themes of
achievement and inequality are simply reproduced by them. What Chase calls "cultural discourses" are not narrative templates that determine how the women articulate the histories and sentiments of superintendency. Rather, as Chase's material illustrates, the women are *active* storytellers. They not only convey, but construct
their work narratives. While both the interviewers and the women superintendents
call upon the cultural discourses of achievement and inequality to frame their questions and answers, the resulting portraits of careers are adroitly crafted in relation
to biographical particulars. How these women produce and relate their distinct narratives is as important as what is being said in common.

Chase presents four case studies from her sample of 27 interviews. Let us briefly
compare two of them. Ana Martinez, a Hispanic woman, highlights competence and
excludes talk of discrimination in her career narrative. While Ana is asked about
both the successes and the elements of inequality that shaped her career, topics which
she acknowledges as relevant to the lives of women superintendents, she avoids talk
of discrimination. Like the other women, she has trouble combining the contradic-

tory themes of success, inequality, and discrimination into the same narrative. Chase asks herself, "How can she [Ana] connect this story about subjection [to discriminatory practices] to her broader story about professional competence and commitment?" For Ana, the solution is to construct a story whose success is built on a clear narrative separation of applicable discourses. According to Chase, Ana's way of resolving the narrative tension is to exclude themes of discrimination from her narrative. Tellingly, Ana offers a "metastatement," or comment about what she is communicating in response to a follow-up question about whether ethnicity figured in her career: "Uh because [pause] although I recognize the inequities that exist I don't dwell on them. [Chase: hm hmm] I don't talk a lot about them" (p. 82).

Margaret Parker, an African American, narrates the two discourses differently, putting her own artful gloss on the woman superintendent's story. Rather than suppressing themes of inequality and discrimination, Margaret weaves them into a narrative of resilience. Her story uncovers layers of vulnerability and strength. As a woman and an African American seeking success in what is largely a white man's world, Margaret is admittedly vulnerable to discrimination throughout her career. She tells the story of job discrimination many times. But she also reveals sources of inner strength. While Margaret was discriminated against, her ability to work through the consequences adds to a tale of personal strength in the face of adversity, narratively enhancing her success and career achievements. At one point, Margaret tells how she was able to deal with an especially painful discriminatory situation, in which she uses the discourse of inequality in support of, not against, the discourse of achievement. The following comments refer to her way of handling her relations with the man who was hired for a job that should have been hers:

And my people who were working with me were saying [whispering], "Boy how is she doing it? How is she taking it?" [Return to normal voice] Especially when the guy came on board [pause] and he was introduced to the cabinet as the assistant superintendent and everybody's eyes sort of propped on me and I'm sitting here holding back all of my feelings 'cause I'm very pained, no question about that. [Chase: hm hmm] Um [pause], but I went right ahead doing my job and people'd see him and me standing talking together. They'd see us eating lunch together you know [Chase: hm hmm] and uh that's just who I am. [Chase: hm hmm] That's just who I am. (Pp. 136–37)

Chase's analytic move in the direction of the *hows* of narrative allows her to explain what the women portray. Through the women's narratives, Chase describes the cultural contours of job success in the face of inequality, but her elaboration of the biographical particulars of each story tells us *why* culture is more complex than a configuration of exportable meanings or even a multilevel layering of categories and understandings. Culture or, in this case, the meaning of achievement in the face of inequality is not simply a shared story of encountering and overcoming discrimination, complex as that might be. Rather, meaning is artfully woven together using what culture provides to produce multiple versions of career success in the circumstances under consideration. The result is a notion of culture that is "thick" with separately activated nuances of meaning, reflexively constructed, adjusted, and adapted in relation to biographical contingencies.

While Chase uses the *hows* of narration to explain the meaning of career stories, she never loses sight of the *whats* under consideration. She zeros in on the adversities of inequality and discrimination, which are culturally recognizable "background expectancies," using what is culturally available to formulate her interview questions. Her research project is conceptualized in terms of what is collectively understood to be real and significant. Chase then explains her respondents' stories in relation to *how* they actively construct and present their careers in narrative format.

DEPRIVATIZATION AND INTERPRETATION

Contemporary social life, it seems, is conducted in a virtual plethora of public sites and locations, interpreted from diverse perspectives, more and more of them formally organized. Indeed, people-defining organizations (see Holstein 1992) may be the hallmarks of contemporary Western society, where life is increasingly carried out in relation to professional and disciplinary practices (Foucault 1978; Presthus 1978; Ahrne 1990; Giddens 1992; Drucker 1993). If explanatory footings can be found at the intersection of social circumstance and constitutive action, we have more reason than ever for examining the ways in which organizational circumstances and resources incite and condition reality construction.

Large-scale and small-scale organizations and their distinct moral orders touch nearly all aspects of daily living, from domestic relations, to personal troubles, to public policies. One way of characterizing this is to say that matters of everyday life are interpretively formulated in *public* circumstances. Organizations and their agents make it their business to evaluate our lives and experiences so that they can address, assess, and ameliorate the practical challenges of day-to-day living. In doing so, they become the virtual sources of experiential definition—purveyors of social reality, so to speak. Borrowing Norbert Wiley's (1985) apt term, we can say that the descriptive contours of everyday life and the interpretation of experience have become "deprivatized" (see Gubrium and Holstein 1995a, 1995b, 1995c; Holstein and Gubrium 1995b).[2]

If we extend method talk to the proposition that experience in the modern world increasingly comes to us in the guise of formally incited stories, we can then begin to consider explanation in terms of the growing narrative deprivatization of interpretive practice. This offers us ways of accounting for both the broad diversity and the familiarity of interpretations. Particular sites condition interpretation in a relatively stable fashion, which accounts for similarities in the interpretations that are produced. Variations in meaning derive from the multisitedness, and of course, the related artfulness, of interpretive practice. Deprivatization thus serves as a source of explanation for both interpretive variability and stability.

Recall, once more, the comparative analysis of the family therapy agencies in Chapter 8. Our analysis suggested that distinct local cultures of interpretation provided different interpretive resources and orientations for assessing troubled lives and families. Westside House, with its vision of family as a hierarchy of authority, supplied resources and standards for evaluating family troubles that contrasted with Fairview Hospital, with its emphasis on affective linkages. If asked why signs of trouble might be read differently in the two agencies, we could turn to the local cultures of the two sites for at least a partial answer.

As we illustrated earlier, physical comportment during therapy sessions is read in both settings for signs of domestic disorder. But local culture provides quite different interpretive schemes to inform the readings. For example, in observing a group family therapy session, therapists at Westside might take the central seating position of the father as an empirical indication that the father is responsibly assuming a rightfully authoritative status at the top of a decision-making hierarchy that must be properly aligned for the family to function. The very same choice of seating position, read against the interpretive background of Fairview's model of the family as a democracy of emotions, is likely to engender an entirely different interpretation, especially if the father uses his position to dominate talk and interaction. It might be said, for example, that the father was drawing the family circle out of balance, possibly asserting himself in ways that prevented free and equal communication and the open display of feelings. Physical comportment in this case embodies dysfunctionality.

The point here is not that one agency provides a more plausible interpretive framework than the other. Nor are we saying that the signs of domestic order and disorder can be read in a predictable fashion. Rather, we are suggesting that local culture provides relatively stable orientations and resources—or "conditions of possibility (Foucault 1975, p. xix)—for interpretation. These establish loose parameters and expectations for the kinds of interpretations that readily "make sense" in the institutional context of the settings under consideration. By understanding how, and with what tools, interpretive practitioners "make sense" under specified circumstances, we are also able to explain variation in interpretive outcomes. Broadly speaking, we can explain that family functioning and dysfunctionality are differentially constructed in talk and interaction in the two therapy agencies as a result of their respective deprivatizations of domestic order (Holstein and Gubrium 1995b).

Let us consider another illustration of how the deprivatization of interpretation, in particular, its organizational embeddedness, helps to explain interpretive variability. In this case, we focus both on diverse ways of assessing the social form "family" under different, organizationally grounded interpretive conditions, and on how personal troubles come to be defined in organizationally preferred terms. The case involves the client of a community mental health system, and staff members of two organizations affiliated with it (Holstein 1988b). The client, Harriet Baker, was the 47-year-old mother of three grown children. Harriet lived with her husband in an isolated rural area in the upper Midwest. She had a history of psychiatric problems and was enrolled in the local Community Support Program (CSP) to receive help.

The Northwoods County CSP was mandated to provide practical assistance to chronically mentally ill persons who were attempting to live with minimal supervision in de-institutionalized, community circumstances. While CSP personnel oriented to the emotional and psychiatric well-being of their clients, their primary day-to-day work entailed assisting clients to accomplish the routine tasks of community living: managing a household, shopping for groceries, keeping various appointments, and the like. In this respect, Harriet did not demand much from the CSP, and she and her husband had managed to get by on their own since their three children had come of age and left home.

However, there were looming problems. Harriet's husband had reported several times that Harriet had become extremely agitated, claiming to hear voices in her head. He also reported that she had become forgetful and negligent, and had lost the patience required to complete even the simplest household tasks.[3] Twice she had wandered away from the house into the surrounding woods, and her absence was not noticed until her husband returned from work to find her missing. Both times, the sheriff's department had to search the woods to find her. Although she was unharmed, and did no harm, Harriet could not say where she was going, what she was doing, or when she intended to return from her excursions. She would only say that she needed to get out of the house because it was "closing in on me."

The CSP social worker managing the case was concerned because Harriet had been her client for several months and had not seemed to improve in her ability to run the household. Indeed, Harriet's competence in managing her daily affairs now seemed to be declining. The CSP social worker began to doubt the feasibility of allowing Harriet to remain at home and sought the advice of a colleague, a county Department of Social Services (DSS) social worker, who was familiar with Harriet's problems. In their discussion, the CSP social worker tentatively proposed the possibility of seeking psychiatric hospitalization for Harriet, even if it had to be done against her will:

> We just don't have any other way of looking out for her. Harriet's really isolated out there and we just can't keep track of her. I visit as often as I can and her support worker goes at least once a week, but we can't replace her family. All she has is Jack [Harriet's husband] and he's not there during the day and sometimes not even at night. Her family should look out for her, but since Janie [Harriet's youngest daughter] moved, nobody's there. Harriet really needs more help if she's ever going to learn to live with her problem and now she seems to need someone watching her day and night. It's either her family or the hospital, and right now the hospital may be more of a family than she's got at home. (P. 269)

The CSP social worker's suggestion to hospitalize Harriet oriented to several aspects of the organizationally embedded interpretive framework that characterizes the CSP. Most notably, the organization's custodial and management concerns shaped the way that the social worker discerned and articulated Harriet's present situation. The problem, from this perspective, lay in Harriet's penchant for disappearing and her inability to maintain a household. Articulated in these terms, Harriet's problems implicated her family life, which was all but nonexistent. The CSP image of family was a supportive network of ever-present caregivers. The domestic arrangement of the Baker household failed to provide much of anything in that regard. The interpretive problem in this case was formulated in terms of who was "looking out" for Harriet, which was cast, at least in part, as a familial responsibility. As the social worker described Harriet's domestic relations, she said Harriet's family was virtually absent and called the mental hospital "more of a family than she's got at home."

The DSS social worker, however, was not convinced that hospitalization was warranted. We can trace this disagreement, again at least in part, to the different organizational priorities, mandates, and interpretive proclivities that he brought to the case. The DSS social worker was also the county's mental health specialist, and although Harriet was not technically his client, he had provided Harriet's family with informal "family counseling" for several years. Because the DSS worker was a practicing therapist, his professional and organizational commitment was to ameliorating *psychiatric* troubles, especially the affective distress that was thought to upset daily functioning. While concerned with problems of everyday living, the DSS worker focused much more on Harriet's emotional well-being than did the CSP worker, whose own organizationally mandated attention emphasized the custodially practical. Note how the DSS worker described Harriet's situation. The orientation to intervention is distinctly different from what we heard from the CSP worker in the preceding extract:

She [Harriet] really does need to have someone look after her, but I'm not so sure that she wouldn't get worse if she was sent to Milford [the psychiatric hospital]. If she was put away, she'd have nothing left. No house, no family. She'd think nobody cared and she wouldn't have anybody to care about. I'm afraid that having no family at all would make her mighty unhappy. She doesn't have much of a family now, but it's more than Milford would be. . . . That's no family. She could really get messed up. (P. 270)

As the DSS worker articulates the problem and evaluates the proposed solution, he is primarily concerned with how Harriet might respond *emotionally* to being hospitalized fifty miles from home. His emphasis on the affective components of Harriet's mental health moved custodial concerns to the background as he focused on how hospitalization would disrupt Harriet's already unstable life, which "could really get messed up." Hospitalization was framed as an unappealing response to Harriet's troubles. When viewed in terms of affective criteria and the family's purported natural caring and caregiving function, the hospital, which the CSP social worker portrayed as "more of a family than she's got at home," was cast as "no family at all."

If we ask *why* these depiction's of family and personal troubles are so different, the organizational conditioning of interpretation clearly supplies one sort of answer. In this case, the social workers offered understandings of what Harriet's problem was and how it should be handled in terms that were informed, if not dictated, by their respective professional senses of what constitutes healthy lives and living environments. The two social workers' professional orientations and affiliations, in effect, led them to construe family quite differently. Their interpretations articulated institutionalized priorities and perspectives as much as they spoke of differential person perception.

The variability we see here is not merely about whether or not Harriet has a family. Rather, it represents a clash of formally incited talk and interaction that results broadly from the deprivatization of interpretation. The two social workers thought about and understood "family" in different, yet institutionalized, ways. It was two distinct modes of understanding, not discrepant information or correctable oversight, that cast the mental hospital as "family" in one scenario and the all-but-vacant household as "family" in another. Conversely, such modes of understanding transcend individuals but, in practice, leave CSP personnel likely to agree with the CSP social worker, while other "therapists" will tend to sympathize with the DSS worker regarding the familial assessment. This stability represents more than professional or organizational loyalty. Organizational embeddedness produces persons who confront the world in terms of distinct interpretive possibilities. While organizations and institutions may not simply produce persons of like mind, they do "think" for their participants, in a manner of speaking, by providing vocabularies and encouraging their interpretive practitioners to talk and act in relation to particular resources, goals, and outlooks (Douglas 1986). At the same time, we must remember that organizational views must be articulated with actual experience, reminding us that organizational perspective does not merely speak for itself, but also must be artfully and accountably asserted.

DIVERSITY AND DEPRIVATIZATION

With life more and more intertwined with the discourses of organizations and institutions, people are likely to call upon (or be called upon by) professionals and agencies to interpret, define, and respond to their personal questions, dilemmas, and troubles. Human service agencies abound, offering help and advice at every turn. Schools, day care centers, and churches socialize the young, while "12-step" programs and support groups see us through midlife and the later years. And these are but a small fraction of the settings that typify contemporary life. On any given Sunday, for example, one can scan the local newspaper—say, in Gainesville, Florida—and find literally dozens of self-help and support groups listed for recovering alcoholics, families of alcoholics, codependents of substance abusers, cancer sufferers, survivors of cancer, Gulf War veterans, victims of sexual assault, perpetrators of domestic violence, AIDS victims, the friends and significant others of AIDS sufferers, right-to-lifers, and transvestites and their spouses, among many others. Robert Wuthnow (1994) has estimated that 40 percent of the U.S. population participates in such groups, seeking personal meaning and community.

As more and more organizations and their agents are charged with assessing or facilitating talk about personal experience, meaning becomes ubiquitously deprivatized. Reality is increasingly constructed from distinctive circumstances, so that personal and social objects take hyphenated form: "the-family-according-to-this-agency," "dysfunctional behavior-from-that-professional standpoint," "personality-as-viewed-by-this-expert," and so on. The diversity of interpretations, it seems, is limited only by their representational forms. The multisitedness of the deprivatized world evokes definitions of experience as distinct as the occasions and conditions that incite related talk and interaction.

Consider the variety of interpretations encountered by a twelve-year-old boy and his family as they traversed the organizational terrain of human service agencies in search of help for some "problems of youth" (see Gubrium, Holstein, and Buckholdt 1994). Charles Grady was originally referred to a child guidance clinic, the result of a run-in with the police. At the time, Charles had a history of disruptive behavior in school and a growing list of informal encounters with the law. He was continually "acting out" and fighting with other boys his age and older, seemingly always "looking for trouble." When the police picked him up for "loitering" with a group of "rowdy" boys at a fast-food restaurant, the police department's juvenile officer told Charles and his parents that Charles would either have to enroll in the clinic's Delinquency Prevention Program or face charges in juvenile court. The family opted for the clinic.

This particular clinic had several departments and programs that provided outpatient therapies and services for children presenting emotional and related troubles. A central principle guiding the Delinquency Prevention Program was that juveniles often engaged in deviant and disruptive activities because of "peer-group pressure." One of the clinic's goals was to provide positive alternatives to gang influences. Charles was initially assigned to a peer group led by a counselor, Mr. Burke. Under Burke's professional guidance, Charles was integrated into adult-supervised, peer-oriented activities that took him away from his normal after-school routines and involved him with new "friends."

Providing a rationale for this treatment plan, Burke explained that the problem with "boys like Charles" was that they were at a developmental stage where they were extremely susceptible to the influence of peer group members whom they looked up to or admired. Evidently, Charles showed signs of gravitating toward gang membership. According to Burke, "Preadolescence is a time when kids are looking for acceptance, approval, anything to prove that they belong," and Charles was right at that stage. Charles's misbehavior in school, his brushes with the law, and his tendency to get into fights and skirmishes were all proof that he was trying to impress others, to become a part of a crowd of "undesirables." Burke's particular perspective located Charles at a stage in life characterized by extreme social vulnerability.

Three weeks into the program, Charles was again in trouble, this time for vandalizing school property. The police took him to the clinic, where his troubles were the source of much consternation. At a subsequent meeting, his case was reevaluated by the Youth Programs supervisor and a staff therapist, Mr. Miller. In the course of the discussion, Miller noted the results of the cognitive and emotional development tests Charles had taken when he first arrived at the clinic. He then recommended further psychological evaluation, and, following a two-hour interview with Charles, offered an alternate perspective on Charles's problem. Writing in Charles's case file, Miller suggested that Charles's "antisocial outbursts" resulted from "misdirected frustration and energy." Shifting the interpretive criteria for evaluating Charles's conduct from the social to the psychosexual, Miller explained that Charles was "going through a difficult adolescence. He has difficulty adjusting to newly developed sexuality and physical maturity. . . . He vents his feeling and frustrations in aggressive outbursts and senseless acts of hostility and destruction." Miller recommended that Charles begin weekly therapy sessions, informing the supervisor that "Charles's psychosocial development and social skills haven't caught up with his hormones" (Gubrium, Holstein, and Buckholdt 1994, p. 153).

Alternative professional perspectives and related organizational mandates gave rise to contrasting interpretations of the boy and his behavior. Charles's developmental stage was transformed from that of a socially vulnerable "preadolescent" when subject to the "gaze" of Mr. Burke's Delinquency Prevention Program, to a "psychosexually maladjusted adolescent" when viewed from Mr. Miller's psychotherapeutic perspective. As the interpretive circumstances surrounding Charles's evaluation changed, so did the meaning, cause, and patterning of his troubles.

Charles continued to participate in clinic activities. He attended his therapy sessions without major incident for another month, but there were occasional reports from school and clinic personnel that he was still prone to disruptions and fighting. Entirely coincidentally, Charles's parents decided to send him to a summer camp and took him to a physician for a required physical examination. At the physician's office, Charles's mother apparently mentioned Charles's recent troubles. She later told the supervisor at the clinic that the physician, Dr. Cook, had mentioned the possibility that her son was "hyperactive." Cook apparently had done some tests and written a prescription for Ritalin, the pharmacological treatment of choice for hyperactivity. Mrs. Grady quoted the doctor as saying, "Charles acts so immature because he probably has some sort of medical disorder." Only partly in jest, Mrs. Grady added, "It's either Ritalin for him, or Valium for me."

Once again, as interpretive jurisdiction shifted, so did the nature of Charles's troubles. The transformation from typically vulnerable preadolescent, to maladjusted teenager, to an organically "immature" boy highlights the variety of interpretations that can flow from the diverse circumstances through which a single life might pass. Not only does deprivatization provide possibilities for such diversity, it also simultaneously supplies elasticity in the realities under consideration (Gubrium and Holstein 1995b, 1995c). Charles's clinical record, that is, his institutionally constructed identity, was a product of professionally and organizationally grounded interpretive work that shaped and reshaped his life and experience. Each version was locally accountable to the distinctive representational concerns, demands, and predispositions of the circumstances in which it was embedded.

This interpretive diversity is reminiscent of some postmodernist descriptions of experience in an electronically mediated world of evanescent images. Epstein (1996) refers to it as a "wilderness of mirrors." From a postmodernist standpoint, meaning is cast adrift in a decentered, polysemic, and reflexive space of floating signs and symbols. Yet, even if we appreciate the postmodern sensitivity to reality's fluid character, its rampant abstractions do not always accord with empirical observation. While "the field" may not be as well-defined, definite, and singular as, say, the naturalists conceive of it, fields nonetheless do pose concrete conditions for interpretive practice that remain more or less obdurate, no matter how "field" is defined. Reality is *some place*, even if that place hardly resembles a geographic area. The reality of a political economy of signs, or the swirling experience of an electronically mediated, fast-paced, sign-consuming world, also has its moorings, as tenuous or variable as they might appear to be.

Lyotard (1984) himself suggests that something like a condition of deprivatization may be at work in producing postmodern fluidity. His view gives us purchase on a means of grounding meaning and explanation when he likens the current dizzying array of experience to variable, yet socially organized, language games, as we noted in Chapter 5. Drawing from Wittgenstein (1958), he poses the possibility of locating reality at the "crossroads of pragmatic relationships." In doing so, Lyotard helps to retrieve the concrete sites of everyday practical activity, including the myriad and diverse sites for representing reality we have used for purposes of illustration.

Adapting Foucault (see Dreyfus and Rabinow 1982), we conceive of these language games as sited or institutionalized discursive formations. Some sites might be constituted as an intersection of multiple language games, thus providing grounding and organization for familiar interpretation on the one hand, and for considerable variation on the other. Other sites might be more homogeneous. However organizationally varied, the representational gambits of these institutionalized language games are far from predetermined since they are enduringly subject to interpretive practice. As Lyotard (1984, p. 17) suggests, "the limits the institution imposes on potential language 'moves' are never established once and for all (even if they have been formally defined)." Perhaps Lyotard had something similar to interpretive practice in mind when he described his "pragmatics of knowledge" in terms of institutionalized, yet indeterminate, practice. Surely, empirical work like Chases's (1995) study moves along similar lines.

The notion of deprivatization provides a basis for depicting the fluidity of contemporary reality in less epistemologically radical terms than skeptical postmodernism would have it. By giving Lyotard's and others' postmodernist arguments a slightly modern twist—incorporating the sorts of grounding provided by deprivatization—we can reappropriate contemporary experiential reality for general sociological explanation. We can then proceed to seek answers to questions of *why* by tracing the diversity and differentiation of contemporary life to the proliferation of institutional sites that increasingly serve as representational resources for constituting the real (see Gubrium and Holstein 1994c, 1995b, 1995c; Holstein and Gubrium 1995b).

REFLEXIVELY REASSERTING THE COMMON THREADS

As we have shown, analyzing interpretive practice requires a commitment to working back and forth between its artful and its conditional sides. It encourages the researcher to alternate between questions concerning *what* is going on, under *what* conditions, and *how* that is being accomplished. Analytic bracketing is the method for achieving this. Neither side of practice is emphasized more than the other. The interplay and tension between the two sides animates analysis. Combined, they provide a multidimensional space for raising *why* questions, while remaining situated at the lived border of reality and representation.

The interplay, however, locates us in somewhat unfamiliar territory as far as the common threads of qualitative inquiry are concerned. For the most part, qualitative researchers adopt strategies that orient to the social world from the bottom up. Most naturalists strive to see social reality from actors' points of view, and emotionalists want to delve below the surface, seeking deep disclosure. Conversation analysts and some ethnomethodologists contend that analysis must begin with the communicative machinery of interaction in order to properly understand how more fully elaborated social forms are accomplished or structured. Others come at it differently. Burawoy (1991), for example, leans toward a "macro" approach, suggesting that we relate to social structural forces and document how they are played out in the scenes of everyday life (cf. Smith 1987). Giddens's (1984) concept of structuration also links macro- and microlevel phenomena in a more top-down fashion.

Viewing the two sides of interpretive practice as in dialectical relationship deprivileges the distinction between the two strategies; neither takes precedence over the other. Like two sides of the same coin, interpretive artfulness and substantive conditions mutually inform one another, so that they can never be fully separated. The most the researcher can do is to temporarily bracket one or the other in order to address its counterpart. The bracketing is decidedly heuristic, because knowledge of what is confined within the brackets insists on informing the analysis. One cannot understand artfulness without reference to its circumstances; conversely, the realities of everyday life are embodied in and through meaning-making processes. It is specious and unproductive to insist that qualitative inquiry separate, or assign different priority to, phenomena that are reflexively related.

The dialectical approach ultimately provides a more morally self-conscious basis for reasserting the common threads of qualitative inquiry. It permits a kind of indigenous analytic reflexivity without hazarding postmodern empirical nihilism. Following Rosenau's (1992) distinction, the reflexivity is empirically affirmative, not skeptical. Analytic bracketing offers a way of deconstructing realities without losing analytic footing precisely because of its dualistic formulation. Alternating back and forth, interactionally constitutive groundings are available for deconstructing meaning, then substantive foundations provide the platform for making constitutive interaction meaningful. Bracketing the natural and emotional allows us to deconstruct nature and its passions, while retaining empirical footing in artful methods of reality construction. Bracketing artfulness allows us to deconstruct the social constitution of the real while retaining empirical footing in culture and meaning.

Equally important, shifting between *what* and *how* questions keeps the analysis of interpretive practice self-consciously attentive to both the world researched and the researcher. Concern for reflexivity promotes analysis that alternately interrogates the substantive "authority" of the "realities" behind researchers' descriptions, then, in turn, questions the constitutive omnipotence of researchers' representational practice. It is analytic bracketing's own "built-in" brand of postmodernism.

This self-conscious dialectic complicates, but does not obliterate, the common threads of qualitative inquiry. The interrelated analysis of both sides of interpretive practice sacrifices a degree of parsimony in exchange for a more nuanced understanding of the *reflexive complexity* of social life. Because the dual approach emphasizes the emergent and contingent nature of social reality, it underscores the traditional "antitotalizing" spirit of qualitative inquiry, retaining a role for both individual agency and circumstantial influence. This, in turn, encourages a theoretical minimalism that guards against both a priori assumptions and deterministic modeling.

The traditional *working skepticism* of qualitative inquiry is broadened by orienting to interpretive practice. Analytic bracketing allows us to expand skepticism in empirically productive ways as we alternately suspend belief in reality and in representation as a way of better understanding reciprocal influences in the diverse *heres* and *theres* of contemporary life. This, of course, requires an even deeper *commitment to close scrutiny*, since both the constitution and reproduction of social life are now more fully open to examination than ever. The research challenge is to develop techniques for exploiting the new analytic terrain. In the process, more *qualities of social life* and *senses of the subjective* are brought to light, making the field of inquiry richer and more challenging.

A renewed language of qualitative method widens the *focus on social process*, sharpening the view of practice. Perhaps we are merely recalling Marx, but interpretive practice as we construe it involves more than the strategic or constitutive work of "doing" social life. It also necessarily includes the local and more distantly related elements of circumstance that are incorporated into and condition that work. The method talk through which we realize this emphasis on practice stands between, and draws from, the other qualitative research idioms, allowing us to cross-fertilize matters of meaning, culture, emotion, and the play of signs. Its vocabulary offers qualitative inquiry a means of describing the simultaneously constructed yet conditionally durable world.

By focusing on intersecting levels of meaning that are constituted, articulated, and manipulated in the myriad settings of everyday life, qualitative inquiry self-critically accepts the challenge to make sense of a reflexively dynamic, yet substantive reality. Those engaging a renewed language of qualitative method are never permanently situated at a particular vantage point on empirical reality. Instead, they exchange analytic footings, moving step by bracketed step, from one representational site to another, tuning into the talk and interaction of interpretive practitioners who collectively enact their worlds in relation to what is meaningfully available and accountable.

Notes

Chapter 1

1. The fantasy conversations in the following paragraphs are loosely based on, or inspired by, actual conversations we have heard "in the halls," as well as by passages in a variety of texts that give eloquent voice to diverse research approaches. Those from whom we most concretely borrow include the following: Babbie (1995), Baudrillard (1983b, 1988a, 1988b), Bulmer (1984), Douglas (1977, 1985), Ellis (1991a, 1991b), Ellis and Flaherty (1992), Emerson (1988), Lyotard (1984), Pollner (1987), Schneider (1991, 1993), Zimmerman and Pollner (1970). We will revisit several of these idioms in subsequent chapters.

2. There are myriad ways in which we might classify and contrast qualitative research approaches. Norman Denzin and Yvonna Lincoln (1994), for example, attempt a detailed classification in their *Handbook of Qualitative Research*. Our choice has been to focus on some rather broad criteria for grouping that derive from the fundamental assumptions and research questions underpinning the respective approaches.

Obviously, as with any organizing scheme, ours takes the risk of underemphasizing, transforming, or ignoring some very important contributions. For example, by deciding not to highlight "theoretical" paradigms, we downplay what are often viewed as the major contributions of symbolic interactionism. Our justification relates to the diversity of applications and orientations within symbolic interactionism that can easily be expressed in naturalistic (see Lofland and Lofland 1995), constitutive (see Blumer 1969), emotionalist (see Denzin 1989a), and even postmodernist (see Denzin 1991, 1992) terms. In a related way, there are major qualitative researchers who do not easily fit any theoretical classificatory schema. Erving Goffman comes immediately to mind. Our choice has been to show how such researchers bridge different approaches, or extend the major idioms in ways that modify, innovate upon, and renew more established frameworks.

Another obvious omission from our idioms is "feminism." Again, this does not reflect a failure to appreciate the myriad substantive and methodological contributions of feminist scholars (see Harding 1987; Reinharz 1992) as much as it represents our unwillingness to confine feminist scholarship to a single qualitative idiom. Qualitative feminist research is conducted in many voices, and there are massive feminist contributions within each of the idioms we have singled out for discussion. To indicate just a few, naturalistic feminist studies include Daniels (1988), Hochschild (1983, 1989), Rubin (1976), Stack (1974), and Thorne (1993). Feminist contributions to ethnomethodology and related constructionist approaches include Baber and Allen (1992), Kessler and McKenna (1978), Kitzinger (1987), and West and Zimmerman (1987). Emotionalist work with feminist sensibilities includes Ellis and Bochner (1992), Ellis and Flaherty (1992), Warren (1988), Richardson (1992), and Krieger (1979, 1983). Postmodernist work in a feminist mode includes Clough (1992), Gordon (1990), Richardson (1990, 1991), and Trinh (1989). Some feminists move between or outside our major idioms; Dorothy Smith brings the vocabulary of Marxism and ethnomethodololgy to her feminist studies (1987, 1990); Marjorie Devault combines naturalist and constructionist impulses in her study *Feeding the Family* (1991); and Carol Brooks Gardner presents a Goffmanesque hybrid of naturalistic interactionism in her book on public harassment, *Passing By* (1995), to single out a few.

Just as feminism speaks in many idioms, so do qualitative research programs orienting to race (see Collins 1989), ethnicity (see Nagel 1994, 1996), and sexuality (see Gamson 1995; Seidman 1992). Our failure to discuss them separately and in depth is not meant to diminish their presence in the qualitative research enterprise. Rather, we hope to appreciate and emphasize their diverse contributions throughout.

3. Another, more naturalistic, kind of *how* question differs from this constitutive *how*. The naturalistic *how* refers to natural processes of social interaction by which social roles and relationships are staged and strategically managed, how they function. Symbolic interactionists, especially those working with a dramaturgical or strategic interaction vocabulary, highlight these performative hows, bringing into view the myriad techniques for managing roles and relationships. See Ditton (1980), Goffman (1959, 1961, 1963), and Stone and Farberman (1970) for a dramaturgic emphasis. For a strategic interaction emphasis, see Dietz, Prus, and Shafir (1994); J. Lofland (1976); and Lofland and Lofland (1995). And, for empirical examples, see Charmaz (1975, 1991); Dietz, Prus, and Shafir (1994); L. Lofland (1972, 1973); Karp (1973); and (Unruh 1983). Indeed, the *Journal of Contemporary Ethnography*, which was founded under the name *Urban Life* by the Loflands, has an ongoing tradition of publishing articles with performative naturalistic (performative *how*) emphases.

The constitutive *how* question, in contrast, is more the bailiwick of ethnomethodologists and related constructionists. They emphasize the ways in which both naturalistic *whats* and *hows* are constituted, sustained, and managed in everyday life. A major interest is in how these constitutive practices go "seen but unnoticed" (Garfinkel 1967), allowing the features of everyday life to present themselves to participants as natural, not constructed.

Note that both symbolic interactionists and ethnomethodologists use the term "manage" as part of their vocabulary of *how* concerns. For symbolic interactionists, the term refers to the management of ongoing social life, especially roles and relationships, within a more or less taken-for-granted social reality. For ethnomethodologists, however, the term signals the ongoing construction of social reality, with its attendant reality-maintenance and reality-management work.

Chapter 2

1. Anthropology is equally deeply embedded in a naturalistic tradition but it typically has turned its gaze to distant cultures and settings. Recently, however, anthropologists have been at the forefront of new, more self-conscious approaches to qualitative research; see Clifford (1983), Clifford and Marcus (1986), Geertz (1973, 1983, 1988), Hodder (1994), Marcus (1994), and Moerman (1974, 1992).

2. This tradition of naturalism continues to animate countless empirical studies and methods texts (Vidich and Lyman 1994), but it is important to distinguish it from the equally active, but analytically more self-conscious, naturalism of ethnomethodology (see Chapter 3). In ethnomethodology, the natural itself becomes topical, focusing on *how* that which is taken to be natural in the world of everyday life comes to be accepted as such by its members. There is an explicit interest in "the natural" as a members' project. The related *whats* of the social world are set aside and subjected to the question of how they mundanely become what they are naturally taken to be (Pollner 1987).

We should also distinguish the traditional form of naturalism from what Lincoln and Guba (1985) once called "naturalistic inquiry" (also see Erlandson et al. 1993). Guba and Lincoln (1994) now suggest that their project is better described as "constructivism."

3. As we will see in Chapter 5, part of the recent crisis of representation stems from the realization that ethnographic omnipresence and insight, which naturalists traditionally assign to themselves and to key informants, is equally bound to ethnographic authority.

4. Recent critics argue that ethnography is essentially an *ethnographic story*. The language of "being there," "their worlds," and "their stories" becomes a kind of storytelling, which erodes the naturalist's project. This narrative critique follows from a different analytic language, whose method talk has been critically developed by Geertz (1988) and others (Atkinson 1990; Clifford and Marcus 1986; Clough 1992; Van Maanen 1988, 1995a, 1995b). We will discuss this at greater length in Chapter 5. Simply put, Geertz, Clifford, Marcus, and others argue that, insofar as ethnographies are presented as "their stories," they are as much an artifact of the ethnographic authority in, and descriptive conventions of, writing such stories, as they are actual representations of "their worlds."

Chapter 3

1. *Member* is a key concept in ethnomethodology. As Garfinkel and Sacks (1970) emphasize, the term is not used merely to reference a person; it also refers to one who has a mastery of the natural language of a setting or community. Natural language competence is indicated by one's ability to be "heard to be engaged in the objective production and objective display of commonsense knowledge of everyday activities as observable, reportable phenomena" (p. 342). To be a member is to display the commonsense or mundane reasoning that defines a linguistic community.

2. Schwartz and Jacobs (1979) call this kind of researcher a "reality reconstructor" and discuss the pros and cons of drawing upon culture that is common to both researchers and informants to describe life within that culture.

3. See Bloor (1988), Emerson and Pollner (1992), and Rochford (1992), for discussions of the various aspects of attempts at member validation.

4. Consider, for example, the unavoidable irony inherent in an ethnomethodological account of astronomers' work that frames the "optic pulsar" as a "cultural object" (Garfinkel, Lynch, and Livingston 1981). Ethnomethodological and other constructionist studies have frequently documented the social constitution of the commonplace, for example, gender (Garfinkel 1967), intelligence (Pollner and McDonald-Wikler 1985), mental abilities and disabilities (Marlaire 1990), mind (Gubrium 1986b), family (Gubrium and Holstein 1990), ethnicity (Moerman 1974), profession (Dingwall 1976), suicide (Atkinson 1978), students (Holstein 1983), victims (Holstein and Miller 1990), and children's' worlds (Corsaro 1986) and this tends to give the studies an unavoidable "debunking" undertone.

5. While ethnomethodology was once accused of being a divisive, solipsistic, self-indulgent "sect" by the president of the American Sociological Association (Coser 1975), its practice is now widespread in the United States, the United Kingdom, and Europe (see Fehr and Stetson 1990; Maynard and Clayman 1991). Along with other versions of social constructionism, it is also developing a presence in Japan (see Ayukawa 1995; Nakagawa 1995), and there is a considerable body of English language literature currently in translation.

6. Others are not so quick to concede the prominence of CA, nor its direct connection to ethnomethodology (see Atkinson 1988; Lynch 1993; Lynch and Bogen 1994; Watson and Seiler 1992).

Chapter 4

1. Similar criticism has come from within ethnomethodology (Moerman 1992; Lynch and Bogen 1994). For example, Dusan Bjelic and Michael Lynch p. (1992, p. 76) have commented on the "absurd" accounts of situated competencies of everyday work that result when conversation analysts limit their examination of the talk and interaction entailed to the discursive machinery of speech exchanges. As Bjelic and Lynch note, "Although we agree that tape-recorded and transcribed records may offer a convenient *indexical surface* for addressing the situated organization of practical actions, we do not think the analysis of 'talk *qua* talk' can adequately come to terms with the disciplinary activities out of which 'talk' arises" (p. 44, emphasis in the original). As we shall elaborate in chapters that follow, we share this reluctance to confine analysis to talk *qua* talk. But we also resist the radical situationalism with which Lynch and others flirt (see Bogen and Lynch 1993, Lynch 1993), preferring to allow space for explanation in relation to variable interpretive conditions.

2. Douglas and his associates' existential sociology was, in many ways, a direct response to what they considered the rationalist excesses of ethnomethodology. But they, too, were influenced by symbolic interactionist tradition. The resurgence of emotional sociology in the 1980s and into the 1990s also responds to the postmodern debate and postmodernism's anti-enlightenment sentiments.

3. This extends, both directly and indirectly, to the larger historically and culturally based literature on the body that is, in certain respects, highly philosophical. See, for example, Foucault (1972, 1973, 1975, 1978, 1979, 1980); Falk (1994); Frank (1990); Featherstone, Hepworth, and Turner (1991); Glassner (1988); Schilling (1993); and Turner (1984).

4. In conversation analysis in particular there is a rhetorical, yet theoretically necessary, penchant for method talk that sounds scrupulously analytic and objective. For example, rather than writing that a "troubles recipient" seriously responds to something or relates to the previous speaker, Gail Jefferson (1984) writes that the recipient respectively "produces a recognizably serious response" (p. 346) and "a recipient displays affiliation with a prior speaker" (p. 348). This illustrates an important feature of CA's analytic vocabulary: its descriptions of action tend to rely upon textual forms that distance subjectivity. The CA idiom is composed of terms especially coined to maximize the sense that only that which is locally visible (hearable) shall be incorporated into analysis. This heightens the impression of (cool) objectivity and painstaking empiricism.

The vocabulary also tends to suppress individual agency, designed as it is to minimize reference to nonvisible, internal, motivational, and psychological states. As Pertti Alasuutari (personal communication) has noted, conversation analysts appear to prefer to write "P produces a narrative" than to write "P tells a story," because the latter reads too much of the subject, and subjectivity, into what is conveyed.

Similarly, CA often prefers the term "overlapping utterances" to "interruptions" because the latter signals a possible intentionality that cannot be discerned from the overlapping talk itself.

These, and other, rhetorical devices applied in CA succeed because they incorporate the cultural signaling of empirical objects, as opposed to subjects. This is precisely CA's intent: to convey conversation in terms of observable sequential exchanges, not internal or dispositional motivations. Regarding Jefferson's and similar CA method talk, the rhetorical effect is further enhanced because the choice of guiding metaphors ("production") as well as much of the vocabulary ("apparatus," "mechanism," "scaffolding," "repair," and so forth) is highly mechanistic, taken from the world of mechanical action.

To recognize the rhetorical aspects of description, however, is not to invalidate it (see Chapter 5 and Atkinson 1990). Indeed, our own research, like all others', whether conversation analytic or otherwise, is unavoidably rhetorical in one way or another.

5. As we will illustrate later in the chapter, this provides the basis for ethnomethodological analysis of the communicative machinery of the passions.

Chapter 5

1. This sharp turn follows decades of more empirical critique that represented the self's trials as stemming from moral uncertainty, inequality and domination, organizations and the technological rationalization of everyday life, and their related "anonymizing" tendencies, all of which have roots in classical social theory. See, for example, C. Wright Mills's (1951) discussion of the manipulation and selling of self; David Riesman's (1950) depiction of the inner- and other-directed self; Goffman's (1959) presented self; Peter Berger, Brigitte Berger, and Hansfried Kellner's (1973) homeless mind; and Robert Bellah and his associates' (1985) self that is lived for itself and through others, all of which lead us, classically, to Kenneth Gergen's (1991) view of the saturated self. Equally important are commentaries deriving from feminist, gay/lesbian, cultural, interactionist, critical, psychiatric, and political economic perspectives.

For discussion of postmodernism more generally and its relation to social theory, see Alexander (1991), Antonio (1991), Bauman (1988), Best and Kellner (1991), Bogard (1990), Katovich and Reese (1993), Kellner (1988), Lash (1990), Lemert (1991), Norris (1990), Richardson (1991), Rogers (1992), Seidman (1991), and Seidman and Wagner (1992).

2. Rosenau's (1992) characterization of postmodernism as either affirmative or skeptical suggests that it is the skepticals who are smitten by this crisis, who give up on empirical reality altogether. According to Rosenau, affirmative postmodernism retains an empirically grounded, yet antipositivistic, view of the relationship between reality and representation. See Gubrium and Holstein (1994) for the application of a version of affirmative postmodernism (or late modernism) to the production of selves in contemporary life.

3. There are, of course, other versions of the idiom (see Best and Kellner 1991) and we offer this version only as one possible exemplar that is relevant to qualitative inquiry.

4. The related "wordiness" of conversation analytic fields has been represented by some as the ultimate naturally occurring social reality (see Boden and Zimmerman 1991; Schegloff 1987, 1991). For a critique of this view, see Silverman and Gubrium (1994).

5. The televised Super Bowl recently has been interspersed with animated beer advertisements that depict a football game in progress, complete with touchdown scoring beer cans and beer bottle referees. The ads themselves have been advertised in advance, with all the attendant excitement and commentary usually associated with the "real" game, and they unfold, play by play, in step with the on-field game. The on-field event and the animated "simulation" blur in a swirl of "de-differentiation" (Lash 1990) that makes it hard to distinguish the entertainment from its sponsorship, the "signified" from its "simulacrum."

6. Sociological and postmodernist sensibilities are also mixed in a variety of projects that are sometimes called "social studies of science" (see Latour 1987; Latour and Woolgar 1979; Woolgar 1989b).

7. Denzin (1991, p. viii) distinguishes between the postmodern era or condition and postmodern theory. The postmodern era is the period of late capitalism, especially the decades following World War II and postmodernism is the emotional experience of living in this era. For Denzin, postmodern theory, especially as formulated by Baudrillard, is bereft of both historical and concrete empirical footing. While

Denzin's is a study of postmodern (cinematic) society, he proceeds without a totalized postmodern theoretical skepticism.

8. The kinds of texts referenced include texts by postmodern and modern social theorists, on the one hand, and the six award-winning films, on the other. Arguably, from a radically postmodernist perspective, there is a third kind of text that does not receive Denzin's critical attention: lived experience. A fully skeptical postmodern reading, in Rosenau's (1992) sense of the term, would set all three texts side by side for rhetorical examination, playing each off the others for comparative claims to the real. For example, the representational structure of "being there," which Geertz (1988) describes in his examination of the ethnographic writings of Claude Levi-Strauss, Edward Evans-Pritchard, Bronislaw Malinowski, and Ruth Benedict, might be compared to Hollywood representations of the "primitive" (cf. Torgovnick 1990). In limiting his textual analysis to the "two kinds of texts listed earlier," Denzin understandably chooses to straddle the modern and postmodern in order to engage a critical reading, thus appropriating the crisis of representation for his distinctly modernist, cinematically empirical project.

9. The work of naturalistic researchers has been disproportionately subjected to rhetorical analysis. Clough (1992), Van Maanen (1988), and Atkinson (1990) each concentrates on them. The rhetoric of the emotionalists has received less attention, although Silverman (1985, 1993b), Gubrium (1992), and Holstein and Gubrium (1995a) have commented on the rhetoric of feelings in everyday life. The "reality" of ethnomethodology and conversation analysis still awaits the kind of systematic rhetorical treatment Atkinson applies to urban ethnographies (see also Pollner 1991, 1993; Schneider 1993). Besides the objectifying linguistic strategies of conversation analysis (see Chapter 4, note 4), another point of departure might be the ethnomethodological penchant for referring to certain forms of talk as "naturally occurring," implying that other forms, such as those arising in survey interviews, are not naturally occurring. See Holstein and Gubrium (1995a) for an argument about the social conditions under which interviews could be conceived as naturally occurring forms of talk.

Chapter 6

1. This touches on the distinction Atkinson (1992) makes between the faithfulness and the readability of accounts in qualitative research. According to Atkinson, the distinction is a tense one. Any attempt to make the report of multifaceted, multilayered, and multivocal features of social life readable is likely to be unfaithful to these complexities and enduring nuances because they are difficult, if not impossible, to put into writing. Conversely, being faithful to the complexities is likely to result in an unreadable account. This representational tension is an indigenous feature of qualitative research, for which researchers have developed an abiding tolerance.

2. This is David Silverman's (1993b) strategy when he suggests that we have become an "interview society," not just a society studied by means of interviewing. By this, he means that more and more of our lives are presented and structured through interviews of one kind or another (e.g., media interviews, employment interviews, eligibility interviews). He has also argued that we inhabit a "counseling society," which emphasizes interviewing's often therapeutic function (Miller and Silverman 1995). Under the circumstances, we might begin to think of all formally incited talk and interaction, including the survey interview, as "naturally occurring." This would warrant bringing interview data into the purview of qualitative inquiry as authentic talk and interaction, not simply as a secondary gloss on what is otherwise "really" experienced (see Holstein and Gubrium 1995a).

This, of course, has immediate methodological implications for the issue of validity. Validity is a concern in survey research (as well as other forms of social research) precisely because the survey instrument is conceived of as a categorically distinct phenomenon, set apart from its subject matter. Taken conventionally, the interview schedule is the instrument and the respondent's experience is the subject matter from which the instrument collects information. When the interview becomes part of the reality of experience because our contemporary lives are being interpreted, both to ourselves and to each other, in interview-like terms, then the interview becomes subject matter itself. This, of course, means that the problem of validity disappears, since the interview is explicitly part of the phenomenon of interest, not simply a possible source of distortion.

3. Being distant from this border risks the opposite, namely, the incorporation of the representational into the real, forming a positivism unconcerned with the complex and constructive subjective elements of lived experience.

4. The postmodern road in anthropology, for example, from *Writing Culture* (Clifford and Marcus 1986) to *Recapturing Anthropology* (Fox 1991), has clear signposts of choice and hopefulness.

5. Silverman (1985, 1993a) suggests that this goal is difficult to achieve because of sociology's tendency to approach its phenomena in terms of polarities. Traditional theoretical formulations are commonly built on oppositions such as reality versus representation, macro versus micro structures, public versus private, and thought versus feeling. Indeed, the polarities serve to divide and categorize kinds of sociological theory and method, and would even divide the preceding vocabularies, were we not planning to join them in dialectical relationship.

Rather than conceiving the polarities as inherent divisions of experience and incorporating them wholesale into our analytic vocabularies, Silverman urges us to think of them as indigenous categories, forms of collective representation writ both small and large (cf. Durkheim 1961). This would permit us to study, for example, how members of a social setting attribute blame for their troubles, whether, say, to social conditions or to personal failures, or even to uncontrolled passions. This casts members as macro/micro theorists in their own right. In this approach, qualitative method's special sensitivity becomes a sensitivity to *members'* own method talk and use of polarities.

6. "If men define situations as real, they are real in their consequences" (Thomas 1931, p 50).

7. Recall Wieder's halfway house study, in this regard. While his ethnomethodological analysis was clearly oriented to how the convict code was used to convey a local sense of social order, he did not ignore what was being said and the objects and actions to which words referred in the setting, the bailiwick of the naturalist. Wieder's goal was to describe how the code was used to constitute the halfway house as a social setting, and how the code itself was reproduced through its articulation with ongoing activity in the setting. Wieder noted that the code itself was not recognizable except through its linkage to the setting. Its workings could be understood only if one was familiar with the halfway house, its participants, and the activities to which the code referred. In other words, understanding required a familiarity with this world and its stories. Wieder did not attempt to analyze disembodied, decontextualized passages of talk to demonstrate how the code was used. To the contrary, he continually provided the organizational context for who was speaking, to whom, in what circumstances, and about what topics, in order to make the mechanics of "telling the code" intelligible. Issues of what was going on and how it was happening could not be separated, either methodologically or conceptually.

8. Giddens's concept of structuration attempts a related synthesis from a different point of departure. According to Giddens (1984), structuration is a practical, discursive process whereby the ordinary "doing" of social structures such as class, community, family, and the self is constitutive of their broader presence in our lives. But practice is approached top-down rather than bottom-up. From the top down, a priori structures, while they are claimed to be constituted in practice, are nonetheless characteristically overrationalized and neatly packaged according to theoretical specification. Wanting to answer the questions, say, of why social structures do what they do, structuration gets the job of social structure done, but quite idealistically.

9. Ethnomethodologists tend to emphasize the here and now of interaction. While they carefully document the discursive organization of usage in talk and interaction, a focus on speech alone would not readily reveal, say, what is meaningful or influential, but unsaid. We might know from long-term observation, for example, that an institutional setting promoted a macro, as opposed to a micro, understanding of the causes of personal troubles. But this local understanding would not necessarily appear within indigenous conversational exchanges, or even a series of exchanges. The difference between such institutionalized macros and micros would only become empirically evident when institutional settings were viewed ethnographically and compared over time. Strictly speaking, if we limited our analysis to situated spates of real-time talk and interaction, it would not even occur to us to wonder *why* such differences existed, to ask how discursive differences derive from distinct institutional commitments.

Recently, this *why* question has been taken up in studies of "talk-at-work" or institutional talk (see Silverman and Gubrium 1994). Attempts are being made to document the *how* of talk and interaction as they relate to the *what* of diverse institutional settings (see Boden and Zimmerman 1991; Drew and Heritage 1992). This also allows researchers who document linkages between *hows* and *whats* to explain why talk is locally organized the way it is. The problem is that strict adherence to the exclusive reality of talk and interaction provides no integral theoretical grounds for considering *what* and *why* questions. For strict adherents, *what* and *why* enter into studies as matters of scene setting. After studies of talk and interaction "at work" are located in particular institutional settings, then questions of the relation between ethnomethods (representation) and institutional meanings (realities) are considered.

10. If we confine ourselves to describing resources and interactional strategies whose use is apparent to members, then we all but deny the possible importance of "silent" conditions and socially conditioned silence. While we appreciate the conversation analytic insistence on confining analysis to the hearable/observable, this stance rules out the possibility that unspoken factors could condition real-time interaction. Ethnographic observation has repeatedly shown this to be a viable, if not prevalent, possibility. See Miller (1993).

Chapter 7

1. The number of conversational mechanisms documented by CA is impressive, including the following: opening conversations; asking questions; offering answers; giving directions; ending conversations; misunderstanding; conversational repair work; puns and joke telling; the conversational formulation of context; storytelling; timing in conversation; side sequences in talk; booing; troubles tellings; overlaps and interruptions; conversational acknowledgments; topic selection; development; and change; narrative practices; explanations; conversational formulations; collaboration and dispute; mutual monitoring of participants' talk in conversation; perspective display sequences; blaming; agreement and disagreement with assessments; legitimizing and authorizing conversational claims; forgetfulness, and accusations. See Fehr and Stetson (1990) for an extensive bibliography.

2. Involuntary commitment hearings vary somewhat from one jurisdiction to another, but they generally include a set of common components and orientations. Typically, a psychiatrist, a psychologist, or an MD testifies as to the psychiatric troubles of the person whose involuntary hospitalization is being sought. These witnesses invariably recommend commitment, based on danger to self or to others, or due to grave disability. Next, the candidate patient testifies on his or her own behalf. These are usually the only witnesses called. Direct examination and cross-examination are conducted by a member of the district attorney's office (representing the state) and the candidate patient's representative, almost always a lawyer from the public defender's office. After hearing testimony, a judge will often continue the questioning, then make a decision to hospitalize or release the candidate patient. While this description may make hearings sound perfunctory, that is generally not the case, and a wide range of consequential issues are typically discussed. See Holstein (1993) or Warren (1981) for further descriptions of these proceedings.

3. Other discursive forms besides talk are equally constitutive, so, while we may emphasize talk and interaction as descriptive activities, we do not intend to exclude more textually mediated kinds of description (see, for example, Smith 1987, 1990).

4. We must remember that the metaphor of the weed is at least partially imported to the group as a preexisting set of meanings and associations that are culturally shared. After all, the group did not invent the notion of weeds as hardy survivors. We discuss this as a feature of resources-in-use and the multilayeredness of meaning in Chapter 8.

5. Much research with sociolinguistic underpinnings has addressed the issue of narrative structure in the wake of the work of writers like Ferdinand de Saussure (1974), explicating systems of meaning within language, the structures of narrative that provide its internal scaffolding, and the functions that constitute a narrative (Propp 1968; Labov 1972; Polkinghorne 1988; Riessman 1993; Silverman 1993b). Some have approached narrative structure dramaturgically (Burke 1989). Conversation analysts and others have attended closely to how a story is conveyed, looking at the utterance-by-utterance structuring and sequencing of narrative tellings (C. Goodwin 1984; M. Goodwin 1982; Jefferson 1978; Sacks 1992).

6. Of course storytellers are free, in principle, to link together their experiences in whatever way they wish and make meaning accordingly. But they are nonetheless accountable for what is said and, in that regard, listeners respond to what is recognizably sensible and acceptable, given emerging patterns of linkages or horizons of meaning. The sudden emergence or gradual development of a new narrative horizon would cause a listener to wonder why and provide grounds for a shift in responses. As we noted earlier, narrative linkages and their horizons are reflexively related in practice; narrative is as much a matter of active telling as of the things told.

7. The awesome power of biographical consistency should, by now, be apparent. Proceeding retrospectively, practical biographers can work back from the present to create the past that is needed to motivate the present and the currently anticipated future. This, in effect, means that a life course is always and only provisional; it is constantly subject to reinterpretation in light of each new development. The implication, of course, is that there is no assurance for parents of currently well-behaved children that they are raising good citizens, not homicidal maniacs.

The constitutive power of biographical work, however, is mainly retrospective. Accused "Unabomber" Theodore Kaczinski, for example, is said to match almost perfectly the developmental history and psychological profile assembled by a former FBI agent who was working on the case (NBC-TV News, 4/14/95; ABC-TV News, 4/14/95). In retrospect, Kaczinski—extremely intelligent, reclusive, possessed of a flair for explosives since childhood—presents us with a "Unabomber" incarnate. For better or worse, however, such profiles have little predictive utility. Consider what might occur if the FBI's psychological workup had been used to screen candidate Unabombers. Specifying an intelligent but socially awkward introvert, "hypereducated," disenchanted with aspects of the social and political climate of his times, an intense person with festering resentments toward what might to others seem trivial matters, the Unabomber profile would likely fit most of the readers of this text, and would surely single out the authors.

Chapter 8

1. This characterization of "situation" differs slightly from one offered in Goffman's (1964) article "The Neglected Situation," where the situation is defined as an occasion of "mutually monitoring possibilities." On such occasions, participants find themselves accessible to the "naked senses" of others who are present and are themselves so available.

2. Moerman (1988) makes a similar argument in the anthropological literature.

3. Conversation analysts are increasingly researching "talk at work" as a way of dealing with the cultural contours of social interaction. The term refers to talk that occurs in institutional settings (see Drew and Heritage 1992; Boden and Zimmerman 1991). The argument is that ostensibly distinct patterns of talk and interaction are constitutive of particular settings. This is tricky though, because researchers designate and describe particular cultural contexts *before* the analysis of the conversations that those conversations are said to reveal. CA would have us believe that setting, as a distinct context for talk and interaction, can be visibly (hearably) constituted *in the machinery of talk* itself (see Schegloff 1991). This would mean that no scene-setting would be necessary (or even have to be provided) for the production of the discursive context to be apparent. One wonders if what is demonstrated in these studies could have been produced in the unlikely event that no prior knowledge of the setting had been available, or if prior knowledge were rigorously bracketed.

The issue here is very much a problem of method talk. Studies of talk at work typically introduce empirical (conversational) material with informational statements about the settings in which the material was gathered. Institutional studies always admit to being about conversation in *some* context, but even the myriad CA studies of telephone interaction make that discursive context available to readers before the analysis begins. Indeed, titles of research reports literally announce cultural context at the start. For example, one of Heritage's (1984a) articles is entitled "Analyzing News Interviews: Aspects of the Production of Talk for an Overhearing Audience." Immediately, the reader knows and, in a manner of speaking, is prepared to get the gist of, what conversation is doing in what follows. In a word, the *productivity* of talk relies as much on this analytically underrecognized, naturalistic start as on what the analysis proper aims to show. In such studies, culture inevitably sneaks in the front door, in titles and "incidental" stage setting. Apparently, analysts fail to recognize that some measure of discursive context is being imported to inadvertently assist in the explanation of how context is indigenously constructed.

Strictly speaking, the researcher cannot hope to attribute culture completely to the organization of talk and interaction per se when everything but conversational machinery is disattended. Analytically, one must at some point reappropriate culture and meaning to talk and interaction in order to know what is artfully and methodically going on in that talk and interaction. Centered as analytic bracketing is on both sides of interpretive practice, there is theoretical warrant for the continual reappropriation of meaning.

Chapter 9

1. Katz goes on to argue that the typical engrossment of other qualitative researchers in the local *whats* of social reality needn't lead them to ignore *why* questions either. He points out that naturalistic studies with historical and political bases of interest have been especially successful at considering *why* questions. Their researchers' examination addresses decidedly local *whats* in relation to contexts of broader *whats*, but, significantly, always in relation to the local. Katz explains, for example, that Kai Erikson's (1966) study of the persecution of "wayward Puritans" in seventeenth-century Massachusetts informs us not only that documented talk and interaction served to produce deviance among those suspected of witchcraft and consorting with the devil, but also that the Puritan ethos and related social and political context of the setting in which this occurred offered reasons for why talk and interaction took the direction they did at the time.

2. Suggesting that interpretation has become deprivatized invites a reconsideration of the traditional distinction between the experientially public and the experientially private. In offering the concept of deprivatization, we are not simply suggesting that what had previously been private is now organizationally public. Rather, our point is also that, as a "genealogy" of knowledge, the private (and the public), in practice, is *constructed* at the same time that social discourse turns to issues of privacy (see Dreyfus and Rabinow 1982). Deprivatization is a condition of social discourse that, of course, has organizational underpinnings in related institutional developments.

Other social theorists present similar views. For example, in *The History of Sexuality, vol. 1*, Foucault (1978) argues that, contrary to both popular and scholarly opinion, the Victorian age was not the zenith of privacy, but, rather, was a time of massive transformation of private issues into public discourse. Tracing this to earlier times, he writes, "since the end of the sixteenth century, the 'putting into discourse of sex,' far from undergoing a process of restriction, on the contrary, has been subjected to a mechanism of increasing incitement" (p. 12). Foucault uses the term "sex" to refer to all manner of intimacies. What some figured to be distinctly and properly private was becoming "private" by "going public" through the proliferation of a *discourse of privacy*. It is important to emphasize that "going public" and "transformation" do not indicate a process of historical emergence as much as they signal the cultural construction of privacy through the proliferation of privacy-constituting vocabularies.

Giddens (1992) describes a related "transformation of intimacy," arguing that sexuality, love, and eroticism—intimate relations in general—have become "plastic," freed from an intrinsic connection with reproduction and, more important for our argument, freed from an ostensibly private realm. Focusing on popular notions of privacy gone afoul, such as interpersonal "codependency," Giddens describes how myriad domains of public life constitute and diversify the private as never before. This undermines the dichotomy between private and public spheres. It is not that the private sphere is being destroyed by forces of public life, but that privacy looms ever larger as a concern as it is increasingly rendered problematic as a distinct domain of experience.

We can infer from Foucault and Giddens that there might be something to gain by abandoning the traditional distinction between the public and the private as empirical or analytic polarities. Indeed, we ourselves feature the public–private divide as a discursive product of interpretive practice (Gubrium and Holstein 1990, 1995c; Holstein and Gubrium 1995b. Also see Silverman 1993a).

3. In her book *Madwives*, Carol Warren (1987) presents case material with similar readings of wives' "dysfunctionality" in the cultural context of the United States in the 1950s. She argues that signs of "madness" (schizophrenia) in the family circle were read as much against publicly recognized domestic roles as they were viewed as mental aberration. Indeed, up to a point, bizarre thoughts and talk were considered normal for the so-called "second sex." This suggests that, as long as women's domestic routines were functioning as expected, their mental aberrations were unlikely to acquire clinical designations of pathology.

References

Abu-Lughod, Lila. 1991. "Writing against Culture." Pp. 137–62 in *Recapturing Anthropology*, edited by Richard Fox. Santa Fe, NM: School of American Research Press.

Abu-Lughod, Lila. 1993. *Writing Women's Worlds: Bedouin Stories*. Berkeley: University of California Press.

Adler, Patricia A. and Peter Adler. 1991. *Backboards and Blackboards*. New York: Columbia University Press.

Adler, Patricia A. and Peter Adler. 1994. "Observational Techniques." Pp. 377–92 in *Handbook of Qualitative Research*, edited by N. Denzin and Y. Lincoln. Thousand Oaks, CA: Sage.

Ahrne, Goran. 1990. *Agency and Organization*. London: Sage.

Alexander, Jeffrey. 1991. "Sociological Theory and the Claim to Reason: Why the End Is Not in Sight." *Sociological Theory* 9:147–53.

Anderson, Elijah. 1976. *A Place on the Corner*. Chicago: University of Chicago Press.

Anspach, Renée. 1987. "Prognostic Conflict in Life-and-Death Decisions: The Organization as an Ecology of Knowledge." *Journal of Health and Social Behavior* 28:215–31.

Antonio, Robert J. 1991. "Postmodern Storytelling versus Pragmatic Truth-seeking: The Discursive Basis of Social Theory." *Sociological Theory* 9:154–63.

Atkinson, J. Maxwell. 1978. *Discovering Suicide*. London: Macmillan.

Atkinson, Paul. 1988. "Ethnomethodology: A Critical Review." *Annual Review of Sociology* 14:441–65.

Atkinson, Paul. 1990. *The Ethnographic Imagination*. London: Routledge.

Atkinson, Paul. 1992. *Understanding Ethnographic Texts*. Thousand Oaks, CA: Sage.

Ayukawa, Jun. 1995. "The Construction of Juvenile Delinquency as a Social Problem in Post World War II Japan." Pp. 311–29 in *Perspectives on Social Problems, vol. 7*, edited by J. Holstein and G. Miller. Greenwich, CT: JAI Press.

Babbie, Earl. 1995. *The Practice of Social Research*. Belmont, CA: Wadsworth.

Baber, Katherine M. and Kathleen M. Allen. 1992. *Women and Families: Feminist Reconstructions*. New York: Guilford.

Baudrillard, Jean. 1981. *For a Critique of the Political Economy of the Sign*. St. Louis: Telos.

Baudrillard, Jean. 1983a. *Les Strategies Fatales*. Paris: Grasset.

Baudrillard, Jean. 1983b. *Simulations*. New York: Semiotext.

Baudrillard, Jean. 1988a. *America*. London: Verso.

Baudrillard, Jean. 1988b. *Cool Memories*. New York: Verso.

Baudrillard, Jean. 1991a. "La guerre du Golfe n'a pas eu lieu." *Liberation*, March 29.

Baudrillard, Jean. 1991b. "The Reality Gulf." *The Guardian*, January 11.

Bauman, Richard. 1986. *Story, Performance, and Event: Contextual Studies of Oral Narrative*. New York: Cambridge University Press.

Bauman, Zygmunt. 1988. "Is There a Postmodern Sociology?" *Theory, Culture, and Society* 5:217–37.

Becker, Howard S. 1958. "Problems of Inference and Proof in Participant Observaton." *American Sociological Review* 23:652–60.

Becker, Howard, Blanch Geer, Everett Hughes, and Anselm Strauss. 1961. *Boys in White*. Chicago: University of Chicago Press.

Bellah, Robert N., Richard Madsen, William M. Sullivan, Ann Swidler, and Steven M. Tipton. 1985. *Habits of the Heart*. Berkeley: University of California Press.

Benveniste, Emile. 1970. *Problems in General Linguistics*. Miami, FL: University of Miami Press.

Berger, Peter L. 1963. *Invitation to Sociology*. Garden City, NY: Anchor Books.

Berger, Peter L., Brigette Berger, and Hansfried Kellner. 1973. *The Homeless Mind*. New York: Vintage.

Berger, Peter L. and Thomas Luckmann. 1966. *The Social Construction of Reality*. Garden City, NY: Doubleday.

Best, Joel. 1995. "Lost in the Ozone Again: The Postmodernist Fad and Interactionist Foibles."*Studies in Symbolic Interaction*. 17:125–30.

Best, Steven and Douglas Kellner. 1991. *Postmodern Theory*. New York: Guilford.

Bhabha, Homi K. 1992. "Postcolonial Authority and Postmodern Guilt." Pp. 56–66 in *Cultural Studies*, edited by L. Grossberg, C. Nelson, and P. A. Treichler. New York: Routledge.

Bilmes, Jack. 1986. *Discourse and Behavior*. New York: Plenum.

Bjelic, Dusan and Michael Lynch. 1992. "The Work of a (Scientific) Demonstration." Pp. 52–78 in *Text in Context*, edited by G. Watson and R. Seiler. Beverly Hills, CA: Sage.

Bloor, Michael J. 1988. "Notes on Member Validation." Pp. 156–72 in *Contemporary Field Research*, edited by R. Emerson. Prospect Heights, IL: Waveland.

Blumer, Herbert. 1969. *Symbolic Interactionism*. Englewood Cliffs, NJ: Prentice-Hall.

Bochner, Arthur P. and Carolyn Ellis. 1996. "Taking Ethnography into the Twenty-First Century." *Journal of Contemporary Ethnography* 25:3–5.

Boden, Deirdre and Don Zimmerman (eds.). 1991. *Talk and Social Structure*. Cambridge: Polity.

Bogard, William. 1990. "Closing Down the Social: Baudrillard Challenges Contemporary Sociology," *Sociological Theory* 8:1–15.

Bogdan, Robert and Steven J. Taylor. 1975. *Introduction to Qualitative Research Methods*. New York: Wiley.

Bogen, David and Michael Lynch. 1993. "Do We Need a General Theory of Social Problems?" Pp. 213–37 in *Reconsidering Social Constructionism*, edited by J. Holstein and G. Miller. Hawthorne, NY: Aldine de Gruyter.

Bosk, Charles. 1979. *Forgive and Remember*. Chicago: University of Chicago Press.

Bottomore, T. B. 1956. *Karl Marx*. London: Watts and Co.

Brissett, Dennis and Charles Edgley (eds.). 1990. *Life as Theater: A Dramaturgical Sourcebook*. 2d. ed. Hawthorne, NY: Aldine de Gruyter.

Brown, Richard Harvey. 1987. *Society as Text*. Chicago: University of Chicago Press.

Bruner, Jerome. 1986. *Actual Minds, Possible Worlds*. Cambridge, MA: Harvard University Press.

Bruner, Jerome. 1987. "Life as Narrative." *Social Research* 54:11–32.

Buckholdt, David R. and Jaber F. Gubrium. 1979. *Caretakers*. Newbury Park, CA: Sage.

Bulmer, Martin. 1984. *The Chicago School*. Chicago: University of Chicago Press.

Burawoy, Michael. 1991. *Ethnography Unbound*. Berkeley: University of California Press.

Burke, Kenneth. 1989. *On Symbols and Society*. Chicago: University of Chicago Press.

Cahill, Spencer E. 1994. "Following Goffman, Following Durkheim into the Public Realm." Pp. 3–17 in *The Community of the Streets*, edited by S. Cahill and L. Lofland. Greenwich, CT: JAI Press.

Cartwright, Dorwin (ed.). 1959. *Studies in Social Power*. Ann Arbor: University of Michigan Press.

Charmaz, Kathy. 1975. "The Coroner's Strategy for Announcing Death." *Urban Life* 4:296–316.

Charmaz, Kathy. 1991. *Good Days, Bad Days: The Self in Chronic Illness and Time*. New Brunswick, NJ: Rutgers University Press.

Chase, Susan E. 1995. *Ambiguous Empowerment: The Work Narratives of Women School Superintendents*. Amherst, MA: University of Massachusetts Press.

Cicourel, Aaron V. 1964. *Method and Measurement in Sociology*. New York: Free Press.

Cicourel, Aaron V. 1968. *The Social Organization of Juvenile Justice*. New York: Wiley.

Cicourel, Aaron V. 1974. *Cognitive Sociology*. New York: Free Press.

Cicourel, Aaron V. and John I. Kitsuse. 1963. *The Educational Decision-Makers*. Indianapolis: Bobbs-Merrill.

Clemmer, Donald. 1940. *The Prison Community*. Boston: Christopher Publishing House.

Clifford, James. 1983. "On Ethnographic Authority." *Representations*. 1:118–46.

Clifford, James. 1988. *The Predicament of Culture*. Cambridge, MA: Harvard University Press.

Clifford, James and George E. Marcus (eds.). 1986. *Writing Culture*. Berkeley, CA: University of California Press.

Clough, Patricia Ticineto. 1992. *The End(s) of Ethnography*. Thousand Oaks, CA: Sage.

Collins, Patricia Hill. 1989. *Black Feminist Thought*. Boston: Unwin Hyman.

Collins, Randall. 1980. "Erving Goffman and the Development of Modern Social Theory." Pp. 170–209 in *The View from Goffman*, edited by J. Ditton. London: Macmillan.

Collins, Randall. 1985. *Three Sociological Traditions*. New York: Oxford University Press.

Connor, Steve. 1989. *Postmodern Culture*. Oxford: Blackwell.

Converse, Jean and Howard Schuman. 1974. *Conversations at Random*. New York: Wiley.

Corsaro, William. 1986. *Children's Worlds and Children's Language*. Hawthorne, NY: de Gruyter.

Coser, Lewis A. 1975. "Two Methods in Search of a Substance." *American Sociological Review* 40:691–700.

Danforth, Loring. 1982. *Death Rituals of Rural Greece*. Princeton, NJ: Princeton University Press.

Daniels, Arlene Kaplan. 1988. *Invisible Careers*. Chicago: University of Chicago Press.

de Man, Paul. 1986. *The Resistance to Theory*. Minneapolis: University of Minnesota Press.

Denzin, Norman K. 1971. "The Logic of Naturalistic Inquiry." *Social Forces* 50:166–82.

Denzin, Norman K. 1984. *On Understanding Emotion*. San Francisco: Jossey-Bass.

Denzin, Norman K. 1985. "Emotion as Lived Experience." *Symbolic Interaction* 8:223–40.

Denzin, Norman K. 1988. "Blue Velvet: Postmodern Contradictons." *Theory, Culture, and Society* 5:461–73.

Denzin, Norman K. 1989a. *Interpretive Interactionism*. Newbury Park, CA: Sage.

Denzin, Norman K. 1989b. *The Research Act. 3d ed.* Englewood Cliffs, NJ: Prentice Hall.

Denzin, Norman K. 1991. *Images of Postmodern Society*. London: Sage.

Denzin, Norman K. 1992. *Symbol Interactionism and Cultural Studies*. Oxford: Blackwell.

Denzin, Norman K. 1993. "Rain Man in Las Vegas: Where Is the Action for the Postmodern Self?" *Symbolic Interaction* 16:65–77.

Denzin, Norman K. and Yvonna S. Lincoln (eds.). 1994. *Handbook of Qualitative Research*. Thousand Oaks, CA: Sage.

Derrida, Jacques. 1974. *Of Grammatology*. Baltimore: The Johns Hopkins University Press.

deShazer, Steve. 1982. *Patterns of Brief Family Therapy*. New York: Guilford.

deShazer, Steve. 1985. *Keys to Solutions in Brief Therapy*. New York: Norton.

deShazer, Steve and Insoo Berg. 1988. "Constructing Solutions." *Family Therapy Newsletter* 6:42–43.

Devault, Marjorie. 1991. *Feeding the Family*. Chicago: University of Chicago Press.

Diamond, Timothy. 1992. *Making Gray Gold*. Chicago: University of Chicago Press.

Dietz, Mary L., Robert Prus, and William Shaffir (eds.). 1994. *Doing Everyday* Life. Toronto: Copp Clark Longman.

Dingwall, Robert. 1976. "Accomplishing Profession." *Sociological Review* 24:331–49.

Ditton, Jason (ed.). 1980. *The View from Goffman*. London: Macmillan.

Douglas, Jack D. 1977. "Existential Sociology." Pp. 3–73 in *Existential Sociology*, edited by J. D. Douglas and J. M. Johnson. New York: Cambridge University Press.

Douglas, Jack D. 1985. *Creative Interviewing*. Beverly Hills, CA: Sage.

Douglas, Jack D. and John M. Johnson (eds.). 1977. *Existential Sociology*. New York: Cambridge University Press.

Douglas, Mary. 1986. *How Institutions Think*. Syracuse: Syracuse University Press.

Drew, Paul and John Heritage (eds.). 1992. *Talk at Work*. Cambridge: Cambridge University Press.

Dreyfus, Hubert L. and Paul Rabinow. 1982. *Michel Foucault: Beyond Structuralism and Hermeneutics*. Chicago: University of Chicago Press.

Drucker, Peter. 1993. *Post-Capitalist Society*. New York: Harper.

Durkheim, Emile. 1961. *The Elementary Forms of the Religious Life*. New York: Collier Macmillan.

Durkheim, Emile. 1964. *The Rules of Sociological Method*. New York: Free Press.

Eagleton, Terry. 1983. *Literary Theory*. Minneapolis: University of Minnesota Press.

Eco, Umberto. 1994. *The Island of the Day Before*. New York: Harcourt Brace and Co.

Edgerton, Robert B. 1967. *The Cloak of Competence*. Berkeley: University of California Press.

Edmondson, Ricca. 1984. *Rhetoric in Sociology*. London: Macmillan.

Ellis, Carolyn. 1991a. "Emotional Sociology." *Studies in Symbolic Interaction* 12:123–45.

Ellis, Carolyn. 1991b. "Sociological Introspection and Emotional Experience." *Symbolic Interaction* 14:23–50.

Ellis, Carolyn and Arthur P. Bochner. 1992. "Telling and Performing Personal Stories." Pp. 79–101 in *Investigating Subjectivity*, edited by C. Ellis and M. G. Flaherty. Newbury Park, CA: Sage.

Ellis, Carolyn and Michael G. Flaherty (eds.). 1992. *Investigating Subjectivity*. Newbury Park, CA: Sage.

Emerson, Robert M. 1969. *Judging Deliquents*. Chicago: Aldine.

Emerson, Robert M. (ed.). 1988. *Contemporary Field Research*. Prospect Heights, IL: Waveland.

Emerson, Robert M., Rachel I. Fretz, and Linda L. Shaw. 1995. *Writing Ethnographic Fieldnotes*. Chicago: University of Chicago Press.

Emerson, Robert M. and Sheldon Messinger. 1977. "The Micro-politics of Trouble." *Social Problems* 25:121–34.

Emerson, Robert M. and Melvin Pollner. 1992. "Difference and Dialogue: Members' Readings of Ethnographic Texts." Pp. 79–98 in *Perspectives on Social Problems, Vol. 3*, edited by J. Holstein and G. Miller. Greenwich, CT: JAI Press.

Epstein, Jonathan (ed.). 1996. *Wilderness of Mirrors: Symbolic Interactionism and Postmodernism*. New York: Garland.

Erikson, Kai. 1966. *Wayward Puritans*. New York: Wiley.

Erlandson, David A., Edward L. Harris, Barbara L. Skipper, and Steve D. Allen. 1993. *Doing Naturalistic Research*. Newbury Park, CA: Sage.

Estroff, Sue E. 1981. *Making it Crazy*. Berkeley: University of California Press.

Fahim, Hussein (ed.). 1982. *Indigenous Anthropology in Nonwestern Countries*. Durham, NC: Carolina Academic Press.

Falk, Pasi. 1994. *The Consuming Body*. London: Sage.

Featherstone, Mike. 1988. *Postmodernism*. Special issue of *Theory, Culture, and Society*, vol. 5.

Featherstone, Mike, M. Hepworth, and Bryan Turner (eds.). 1991. *The Body: Social Process and Cultural Theory*. London: Sage.

Fehr, B. J. and Jeff Stetson. 1990. "A Bibliography for Ethnomethodology." Pp. 471–559 in *Ethnomethodological Sociology*, edited by Jeff Coulter. Aldershot, UK: Edward Elgar.

Fields, Belden A. 1988. *Trotskyism and Maoism: Theory and Practice in France and the United States*. New York: Praeger.

Filmer, Paul, Michael Phillipson, David Silverman, and David Walsh. 1973. *New Directions in Sociological Theory*. Cambridge, MA: MIT Press.

Fine, Gary Alan. 1983. *Shared Fantasy*. Chicago: University of Chicago Press.

Firth, Raymond. 1936. *We, the Tikopia*. London: Allen & Unwin.

Fish, Stanley. 1980. *Is There a Text in This Class? The Authority of Interpretive Communities*. Cambridge, MA: Harvard University Press.

Foucault, Michel. 1965. *Madness and Civilization*. New York: Random House.

Foucault, Michel. 1972. *The Archaeology of Knowledge*. New York: Pantheon.

Foucault, Michel. 1973. *The Order of Things*. New York: Vintage.

Foucault, Michel. 1975. *The Birth of the Clinic*. New York: Vintage.

Foucault, Michel. 1978. *The History of Sexuality, vol. 1*. New York: Random House.

Foucault, Michel. 1979. *Discipline and Punish*. New York: Vintage.

Foucault, Michel. 1980. "Body/Power." Pp. 55–62 in *Michel Foucault: Power/Knowledge*, edited by C. Gordon. Brighton, UK: Harvester.

Foucault, Michel. 1988. "The Ethic of Care for the Self as a Practice of Freedom." Pp. 1–20 in *The Final Foucault*, edited by J. Bernauer and D. Rasmussen. Cambridge, MA: MIT Press.

Fox, Richard G. 1991. *Recapturing Anthropology*. Sante Fe, NM: School of American Research Press.

Frank, A. 1990. "Bringing Bodies Back In." *Theory, Culture, and Society* 7:131–62.

Franzoi, Steven L. 1996. *Social Psychology*. Dubuque, IA: Brown and Benchmark.

Gamson, Joshua A. 1995. "Must Identity Movements Self-Destruct? A Queer Dilemma." *Social Problems* 42:390–407.

Gans, Herbert. 1962. *The Urban Villagers*. New York: Free Press.

Gardner, Carol Brooks. 1995. *Passing By: Gender and Public Harrassment*. Berkeley: University of California Press.

Garfinkel, Harold. 1967. *Studies in Ethnomethodology*. Englewood Cliffs, NY: Prentice-Hall.

Garfinkel, Harold (ed.). 1986. *Ethnomethodological Studies of Work*. London: Routledge and Kegan Paul.

Garfinkel, Harold. 1995. "Shop Floor Achievements and Shop Floor Theorizing in the Work of Designed Enterprises: Constituents of the Shop Floor Problem." Presented at the Annual Meeting of the American Sociological Association, August, Washington, D.C.

Garfinkel, Harold, Michael Lynch, and Eric Livingston. 1981. "The Work of a Discovering Science Construed with Materials from the Optically Discovered Pulsar." *Philosophy of the Social Sciences* 11:131–58.

Garfinkel, Harold and Harvey Sacks. 1970. "On the Formal Structures of Practical Actions." Pp. 337–66 in *Theoretical Sociology: Perspectives and Developments*, edited by J. C. McKinney and E. A. Tiryakian. New York: Appleton-Century-Crofts.

Geertz. Clifford. 1973. *The Interpretation of Cultures*. New York: Basic.

Geertz, Clifford. 1983. *Local Knowledge: Further Essays in Interpretive Anthropology*. New York: Basic.

Geertz, Clifford. 1988. *Works and Lives: The Anthropologist as Author*. Stanford, CA: Stanford University Press.

Gergen, Kenneth J. 1985. "The Social Constructionist Movement in Modern Psychology." *American Psychologist* 40:266–75.

Gergen, Kenneth J. 1986. "Correspondence versus Autonomy in the Language of Understanding Human Actions." Pp. 136–62 in *Metatheory in Social Science*, edited by D. Fiske and R. Schweder. Chicago: University of Chicago Press.

Gergen, Kenneth J. 1991. *The Saturated Self*. New York: Basic.

Giallombardo, Rose. 1966. *Society of Women*. New York: Wiley.

Giddens, Anthony. 1984. *The Constitution of Society*. Berkeley: University of California Press.

Giddens, Anthony. 1992. *The Transformation of Intimacy*. Stanford, CA: Stanford University Press.

Glaser, Barney G. and Anselm L. Strauss. 1965. *Awareness of Dying*. Chicago: Aldine.

Glaser, Barney G. and Anselm L. Strauss. 1968. *Time for Dying*. Chicago: Aldine.

Glaser, Barney G. and Anselm L. Strauss. 1967. *The Discovery of Grounded Theory*. Chicago: Aldine.

Glassner, Barry. 1988. *Bodies*. New York: Putnam.

Goffman, Erving. 1959. *The Presentation of Self in Everyday Life*. New York: Doubleday.

Goffman, Erving. 1961. *Asylums*. Garden City, NY: Doubleday.

Goffman, Erving. 1963. *Stigma*. Englewood Cliffs, NJ: Prentice-Hall.

Goffman, Erving. 1964. "The Neglected Situation." *American Anthropologist* 66:133–36.

Goffman, Erving. 1974. *Frame Analysis*. New York: Harper & Row.

Goffman, Erving. 1983. "The Interaction Order." *American Sociological Review* 48:1–17.

Goodwin, Charles. 1984. "Notes on Story Structure and the Organization of Participation." Pp. 225–46 in *Structures of Social Action*, edited by J. M. Atkinson and J. Heritage. Cambridge: Cambridge University Press.

Goodwin, Margaret H. 1982. "'Instigating': Storytelling as Social Process." *American Ethnologist* 9:799–819.

Gordon, Avery. 1990. "Feminism, Writing, and Ghosts." *Social Problems* 37:501–16.

Gordon, David F. 1987. "Getting Close by Staying Distant: Fieldwork with Proselytizing Groups." *Qualitative Sociology* 10:267–87.

Guba, Egon G. and Yvonna S. Lincoln. 1994. "Competing Paradigms in Qualitative Research." Pp. 105–117 in *Handbook of Qualitative Research*, edited by N. Denzin and Y. Lincoln. Thousand Oaks, CA: Sage.

Gubrium, Jaber F. 1975. *Living and Dying at Murray Manor*. New York: St. Martin's.

Gubrium, Jaber F. 1986a. *Oldtimers and Alzheimer's: The Descriptive Organization of Senility*. Greenwich, CT: JAI Press.

Gubrium, Jaber F. 1986b. "The Social Preservation of Mind: The Alzheimer's Disease Experience." *Symbolic Interaction* 6:37–51.

Gubrium, Jaber F. 1987. "Organizational Embeddedness and Family Life." Pp. 23–41 in *Aging, Health, and Family: Long-Term Care*, edited by Timothy Brubaker. Newbury Park, CA: Sage.

Gubrium, Jaber F. 1988a. *Analyzing Field Reality*. Newbury Park, CA: Sage.

Gubrium, Jaber F. 1988b. "Incommunicables and Poetic Documentation in the Alzheimer's Disease Experience." *Semiotica* 72:235–53.

Gubrium, Jaber F. 1989. "Local Cultures and Service Policy." Pp. 94–112 in *The Politics of Field Research*, edited by J. Gubrium and D. Silverman. London: Sage.

Gubrium, Jaber F. 1992. *Out of Control: Family Therapy and Domestic Order*. Newbury Park, CA: Sage.

Gubrium, Jaber F. 1993a. "For a Cautious Naturalism." Pp. 89–102 in *Reconsidering Social Constructionism: Debates in Social Problems Theory*, edited by J. Holstein and G. Miller. Hawthorne, NY: Aldine de Gruyter.

Gubrium, Jaber F. 1993b. *Speaking of Life: Horizons of Meaning for Nursing Home Residents*. Hawthorne, NY: Aldine de Gruyter.

Gubrium, Jaber F. and David R. Buckholdt. 1982. *Describing Care: Image and Practice in Rehabilitation*. Boston: Oelgeschlager, Gunn & Hain.

Gubrium, Jaber F., David R. Buckholdt, and Robert J. Lynott. 1982. "Considerations on a Theory of Descriptive Activity." *Mid-American Review of Sociology* 7:17–35.

Gubrium, Jaber F. and James A. Holstein. 1987. "The Private Image: Experiential Location and Method in Family Studies." *Journal of Marriage and the Family* 49:773–86.

Gubrium, Jaber F. and James A. Holstein. 1990. *What Is Family?* Mountain View, CA: Mayfield.

Gubrium, Jaber F. and James A. Holstein. 1993a. "Family Discourse, Organizational Embeddedness, and Local Enactment." *Journal of Family Issues* 14:66–81.

Gubrium, Jaber F. and James A. Holstein. 1993b. "Phenomenology, Ethnomethodology, and Family Discourse. Pp. 649–70 in *Sourcebook of Family Theories and Methods*, edited by P. Boss, W. Doherty, R. LaRossa, W. Schum, and St. Steinmetz. New York: Plenum.

Gubrium, Jaber F. and James A. Holstein. 1994. "Grounding the Postmodern Self." *Sociological Quarterly* 35:685–703.

Gubrium, Jaber F. and James A. Holstein. 1995a. "Individual Agency, the Ordinary, and Postmodern Life." *Sociological Quarterly* 36:555–70.

Gubrium, Jaber F. and James A. Holstein. 1995b. "Life Course Malleability: Biographical Work and Deprivatization." *Sociological Inquiry* 65:207–223.

Gubrium, Jaber F. and James A. Holstein. 1995c. "Qualitative Inquiry and the Deprivatization of Experience." *Qualitative Inquiry* 1:204–222.

Gubrium, Jaber F., James A. Holstein, and David R. Buckholdt. 1994. *Constructing the Life Course*. Dix Hills, NY: General Hall Press.

Haas, Jack and William Shaffir. 1987. *Becoming Doctors*. Greenwich, CT: JAI Press.

Habermas, Jürgen. 1971. *Knowledge and Human Interests*. Boston: Beacon Press.

Haley, Jay. 1976. *Problem-Solving Therapy*. New York: Harper & Row.

Hammersley, Martyn. 1990. *Reading Ethnographic Research: A Critical Guide*. London: Longman.

Harding, Sandra (ed.). 1987. *Feminism and Methodology*. Bloomington: Indiana University Press.

Hebdige, Dick. 1988. *Hiding in the Light: On Images and Things*. London: Routledge.

Heritage, John. 1984a. "Analyzing News Interviews: Aspects of the Production of Talk for an Overhearing Audience." In *Handbook of Discourse Analysis, vol. 3: Genres of Discourse*, edited by T. van Dijk. New York: Academic.

Heritage, John. 1984b. *Garfinkel and Ethnomethodology*. Cambridge: Polity.

Higgins, Paul C. and John M. Johnson (eds.). 1988. *Personal Sociology*. New York: Praeger.

Hilbert, Richard A. 1990. "The Efficacy of Performance Science: Comment on McCall and Becker." *Social Problems* 37:133-135.

Hilbert, Richard A. 1992. *The Classical Roots of Ethnomethodology*. Chapel Hill: University of North Carolina Press.

Hochschild, Arlie R. 1973. *The Unexpected Community*. Berkeley: University of California Press.

Hochschild, Arlie R. 1979. "Emotion Work, Feeling Rules, and Social Structure." *American Journal of Sociology* 85:551–75.

Hochschild, Arlie R. 1983. *The Managed Heart*. Berkeley: University of California Press.

Hochschild, Arlie R. 1989. *The Second Shift*. New York: Viking.

Hodder, Ian. 1994. "The Interpretation of Documents and Material Culture." Pp. 393–402 in *Handbook of Qualitative Research*, edited by N. Denzin and Y. Lincoln. Thousand Oaks, CA: Sage.

Holstein, James A. 1983. "Grading Practices: The Construction and Use of Background Knowledge in Evaluative Decision-Making." *Human Studies*. 6:377–92.

Holstein, James A. 1984. "The Placement of Insanity: Assessments of Grave Disability and Involuntary Commitment Decisions." *Urban Life* 13:35–62.

Holstein, James A. 1987. "Producing Gender Effects on Involuntary Mental Hospitalization." *Social Problems* 34:141–55.

Holstein, James A. 1988a. "Court Ordered Incompetence: Conversational Organization in Involuntary Commitment Hearings." *Social Problems* 35: 458–73.

Holstein, James A. 1988b. "Studying 'Family Usage': Family Image and Discourse in Mental Hospitalization Decisions." *Journal of Contemporary Ethnography* 17:261–84.

Holstein, James A. 1990. "The Discourse of Age in Involuntary Commitment Proceedings." *Journal of Aging Studies* 4:111–30.

Holstein, James A. 1992. "Producing People: Descriptive Practice in Human Service Work." *Current Research on Occcupations and Professions* 6:23–39.

Holstein, James A. 1993. *Court-Ordered Insanity: Interpretive Practice and Involuntary Commitment*. Hawthorne, NY: Aldine de Gruyter.

Holstein, James A, and Jaber F. Gubrium. 1994a. "Constructing Family: Descriptive Practice and Domestic Order." Pp. 232–50 in *Constructing the Social*, edited by T. Sarbin and J. Kitsuse. London: Sage.

Holstein, James A. and Jaber F. Gubrium. 1994b. "Phenomenology, Ethnomethodology, and Interpretive Practice." Pp. 262–71 in *Handbook of Qualitative Research*, edited by N. Denzin and Y. Lincoln. Thousand Oaks, CA: Sage.

Holstein, James A. and Jaber F. Gubrium. 1995a. *The Active Interview*. Thousand Oaks, CA: Sage.

Holstein, James A. and Jaber F. Gubrium. 1995b. "Deprivatization and Domestic Life: Interpretive Practice in Family Context." *Journal of Marriage and the Family* 57:607–22.

Holstein, James A. and Richard S. Jones. 1992. "Short Time, Hard Time: Accounts of Short-Term Imprisonment." Pp. 289–309 in *Perspectives on Social Problems*, edited by J. Holstein and G. Miller. Greenwich, CT: JAI Press.

Holstein James A. and Gale Miller. 1990. "Rethinking Victimization: An Interactional Approach to Victimology." *Symbolic Interaction* 13:103–122.

Holstein James A. and Gale Miller (eds.). 1993. *Reconsidering Social Constructionism: Debates in Social Problems Theory*. Hawthorne, NY: Aldine de Gruyter.

Hughes, Everett C. 1971. *The Sociological Eye: Selected Papers*. Chicago: Aldine.

Ibarra, Peter R. and John I. Kitsuse. 1993. "Vernacular Constituents of Moral Discourse: An Interactionist Proposal for the Study of Social Problems." Pp. 25–58 in *Reconsidering Social Constructionism: Debates in Social Problems Theory*, edited by J. Holstein and G. Miller. Hawthorne, NY: Aldine de Gruyter.

Ichheiser, Gustav. 1970. *Appearances and Realities*. San Francisco: Jossey-Bass.

Irwin, John. 1970. *The Felon*. Englewood Cliffs, NJ: Prentice-Hall.

Jackson, M. 1989. *Paths toward a Clearing: Radical Empiricism and Ethnographic Inquiry*. Bloomington: Indiana University Press.

Jacobus, M., E. F. Keller, and S. Shuttleworth. 1990. *Body/Politics: Women and the Discourses of Science*. New York: Routledge.

James, William. 1950 [1890]. *The Principles of Psychology*. Vol. 1. New York: Dover.

Jefferson, Gail. 1978. "Sequential Aspects of Storytelling in Conversation." Pp. 219–48 in *Studies in the Organization of Conversational Interaction*, edited by J. Schenkein. New York: Academic Press.

Jefferson, Gail. 1984. "On the Organization of Laughter in Talk about Troubles." Pp. 346–69 in *Structures of Social Action*, edited by J. M. Atkinson and J. Heritage. Cambridge: Cambridge University Press.

Johnson, John M. 1975. *Doing Field Research*. New York: Free Press.

Johnson, John M. 1977. "Ethnomethodology and Existential Sociology." Pp. 153–73 in *Existential Sociology*, edited by J. Douglas and J. Johnson. New York: Cambridge University Press.

Jones, Richard S. and Thomas Schmid. 1997. *Doing Time: Prison Experience and Identity*. Greenwich, CT: JAI Press.

Josselson, Ruthellen and Amia Lieblich (eds.). 1995. *The Narrative Study of Lives: Interpreting Experience*. Thousand Oaks, CA: Sage.

Karp, David A. 1973. "Hiding in Pornographic Bookstores: Reconsiderations of the Nature of Urban Anonymity." *Urban Life* 1:427–51.

Karp, David A. 1996. *Speaking of Sadness: Depression, Disconnection, and the Meanings of Illness*. New York: Oxford University Press.

Karp, Ivan and Martha B. Kendall. 1982. "Reflexivity in Fieldwork." In *Explaining Human Behavior*, edited by P. Secord. Beverly Hills, CA: Sage.

Katovich, Michael A. and William A. Reese. 1993. "Postmodern Thought in Symbolic Interaction: Reconstructing Social Inquiry in Light of Late-Modern Concerns." *Sociological Quarterly* 34:391–411.

Katz, Jack. 1988. *Seductions of Crime*. New York: Basic Books.

Katz, Jack. 1994. "Jazz in Social Interaction: Personal Creativity, Collective Constraint, and Motivational Explanation in the Social Thought of Howard S. Becker." *Symbolic Interaction* 17:253–80.

Keats, John. 1958. *The Letters of John Keats 1814–1821*, edited by H. E. Rollins. Cambridge: Cambridge University Press.

Kellner, Douglas. 1988. "Postmodernism as Social Theory: Some Problems and Challenges." *Theory, Culture, and Society* 5:239–70.

Kellner, Douglas. 1992. "Popular Culture and the Construction of Postmodern Identities." Pp. 141–77 in *Modernity and Identity*, edited by S. Lash and J. Friedman. Oxford: Blackwell.

Kemper, Theodore. 1990. *Social Structure and Testerone*. New Brunswick, NJ: Rutgers University Press.

Kessler, Suzanne J. and Wendy McKenna. 1978. *Gender: An Ethnomethodological Approach*. Chicago: University of Chicago Press.

Kitsuse, John I. 1962. "Societal Reactions to Deviant Behavior: Problems of Theory and Method." *Social Problems* 9:247–56.

Kitzinger, Celia. 1987. *The Social Construction of Lesbianism*. Beverly Hills, CA: Sage.

Kleinman, Sherryl. 1984. *Equals before God*. Chicago: University of Chicago Press.

Kleinman, Sherryl and Martha A. Copp. 1993. *Emotions and Fieldwork*. Newbury Park, CA: Sage.

Kotarba, Joseph A. 1977. "The Chronic Pain Experience." Pp. 257–72 in *Existential Sociology*, edited by J. Douglas and J. Johnson. Cambridge: Cambridge University Press.

Krieger, Susan. 1979. *Hip Capitalism*. Beverly Hills, CA: Sage.

Krieger, Susan. 1983. *The Mirror Dance*. Philadelphia: Temple University Press.

Kübler-Ross, Elisabeth. 1969. *On Death and Dying*. New York: Macmillan.

Kuhn, Thomas S. 1962. *The Structure of Scientific Revolution*. Chicago: University of Chicago Press.

Kundera, Milan. 1984. *The Unbearable Lightness of Being*. New York: Harper & Row.

Labov, William (ed.). 1972. *Language in the Inner City*. Philadelphia: University of Pennsylvania Press.

Laçan, Jacques. 1977. *Ecrits*. New York: W.W. Norton.

Lakoff, George and Mark Johnson. 1980. *Metaphors We Live By*. Chicago: University of Chicago Press.

Lasch, Christopher. 1977. *Haven in a Heartless World*. New York: Basic.

Lash, Scott. 1990. *Sociology of Postmodernism*. London: Routledge.

Lash, Scott and Jonathan Friedman (eds.). 1992. *Modernity and Identity*. Oxford: Blackwell.

Latour, Bruno. 1987. *Science in Action*. Cambridge, MA: Harvard University Press.

Latour, Bruno and Steve Woolgar. 1979. *Laboratory Life: The Social Construction of Scientific Facts*. London: Sage.

Leiter, Kenneth. 1974. "Adhocing in the Schools: A Study of Placement Practices in the Kindergardens of Two Schools." Pp. 17–75 in *Language Use and School Performance*, edited by Cicourel et al. New York: Academic Press.

Leiter, Kenneth. 1980. *A Primer on Ethnomethodology*. New York: Oxford University Press.

Lemert, Charles. 1991. "The End of Ideology, Really." *Sociological Theory* 9:164–72.

Lepenies, Wolf. 1988. *Between Literature and Science: The Rise of Sociology*. New York: Cambridge University Press.

Levin, Irene. 1993. "Family as Mapped Realities." *Journal of Family Issues* 14:82–91.

Liebow, Elliot. 1967. *Tally's Corner*. Boston: Little, Brown.

Lincoln, Yvonna S. and Egon G. Guba. 1985. *Naturalistic Inquiry*. Beverly Hills, CA: Sage.

Lindesmith, Alfred R., Anselm L. Strauss, and Norman K. Denzin. 1988. *Social Psychology*. Englewood Cliffs, NJ: Prentice-Hall.

Lofland, John. 1969. *Deviance and Identity*. Englewood Cliffs, NJ: Prentice-Hall.

Lofland, John. 1976. *Doing Social Life*. New York: Wiley.

Lofland, John and Lyn H. Lofland. 1995. *Analyzing Social Settings*. Belmont, CA: Wadsworth.

Lofland, Lyn H. 1972. "Self-Management in Public Settings." *Urban Life* 1:93–108.

Lofland, Lyn H. 1973. *A World of Strangers*. New York: Basic Books.

Loseke, Donileen R. 1989. "Creating Clients: Social Problems Work in a Shelter for Battered Women." Pp. 173–94 in *Perspectives on Social Problems, Vol. 1*, edited by J. Holstein and G. Miller. Greenwich, CT: JAI Press.

Loseke, Donileen R. 1992. *The Battered Woman and Shelters*. Albany, NY: SUNY Press.

Lyman, Stanford. 1990. "Anhedonia: Gender and the Decline of Emotions in American Film, 1930–88." *Sociological Inquiry* 60:1–19.

Lynch, Michael. 1993. *Scientific Practice and Ordinary Action*. New York: Cambridge University Press.

Lynch, Michael and David Bogen. 1994. "Harvey Sacks's Primitive Natural Science." *Theory, Culture, and Society* 11:65–104.

Lynch, Michael and Steven Woolgar. 1988. "Sociological Orientations to Representational Practice in Science." *Human Studies* 11:99–116.

Lyotard, Jean-François. 1984. *The Postmodern Condition*. Minneapolis: University of Minnesota Press.

Manning, Peter K. 1980. "Goffman's Framing Order: Style as Structure." Pp. 252–84 in *The View from Goffman*, edited by J. Ditton. London: Macmillan.

Marcus, George E. 1994. "What Comes (Just) after 'Post'? The Case of Ethnography." Pp. 563–74 in *Handbook of Qualitative Research*, edited by N. Denzin and Y. Lincoln. Thousand Oaks, CA: Sage.

Marcus, George E. and M. J. M. Fischer. 1986. *Anthropolgy as Cultural Critique*. Chicago: University of Chicago Press.

Marlaire, Courtney L. 1990. "On Questions, Communication, and Bias: Educational Testing as 'Invisible'

Collaboration." Pp. 233–60 in *Perspectives on Social Problems, Vol. 2*, edited by G. Miller and J. Holstein. Greenwich, CT: JAI Press.

Marx, Karl. 1956. *Selected Writings in Sociology and Social Philosophy*, edited by T. B. Bottomore. New York: McGraw-Hill.

Matza, David. 1969. *Becoming Deviant*. Englewood Cliffs, NJ: Prentice-Hall.

Maynard, Douglas W. 1980. "Placement of Topic Change in Conversation." *Semiotica* 30:263–90.

Maynard, Douglas W. 1984. *Inside Plea Bargaining*. New York: Plenum.

Maynard, Douglas W. 1988. "Language, Interaction, and Social Problems." *Social Problems* 35: 311–34.

Maynard, Douglas W. 1989. "On the Ethnography and Analysis of Discourse in Institutional Settings." Pp. 127–46 in *Perspectives on Social Problems, Vol. 1*, edited by J. Holstein and G. Miller. Greenwich, CT: JAI Press.

Maynard, Douglas W. 1991a. "Goffman, Garfinkel, and Games." *Sociological Theory* 9:277–79.

Maynard, Douglas W. 1991b. "Interaction and Asymmetry in Clinical Discourse." *American Journal of Sociology* 97:448–95.

Maynard, Douglas W. 1996. "On 'Realization' in Everyday Life: The Forecasting of Bad News as a Social Relation." *American Sociological Review* 61:109–131.

Maynard, Douglas W. and Steven E. Clayman. 1991. "The Diversity of Ethnomethodology." *Annual Review of Sociology* 17:385–418.

McCall, Michal M. and Howard S. Becker. 1990. "Performance Science." *Social Problems* 37:117–33.

McKinney, John C. 1966. *Constructive Typology and Social Theory*. New York: Appleton-Century-Crofts.

Mehan, Hugh. 1979. *Learning Lessons: Social Organization in the Classroom*. Cambridge, MA: Harvard University Press.

Mehan, Hugh. 1991. "The School's Work of Sorting Students." Pp. 71–90 in *Talk and Social Structure*, edited by D. Zimmerman and D. Boden. Cambridge: Polity.

Mehan, Hugh and Houston Wood. 1975. *The Reality of Ethnomethodology*. New York: Wiley.

Miller, Gale. 1978. *Odd Jobs*. Englewood Cliffs, NJ: Prentice-Hall.

Miller. Gale. 1981. *It's a Living*. New York: St. Martin's.

Miller, Gale. 1991. *Enforcing the Work Ethic: Rhetoric and Everyday Life in a Work Incentive Program*. Albany, NY: SUNY Press.

Miller, Gale. 1994. "Toward Ethnographies of Institutional Discourse." *Journal of Contemporary Ethnography* 23:280–306.

Miller, Gale and James A. Holstein. 1993. *Constructionist Controversies: Issues in Social Problems Theory*. Hawthorne, NY: Aldine de Gruyter.

Miller, Gale and James A. Holstein. 1995. "Dispute Domains: Organizational Contexts and Dispute Processing." *Sociological Quarterly* 36:37–60

Miller, Gale and James A. Holstein. 1996. *Dispute Domains and Welfare Claims*. Greenwich, CT: JAI Press.

Miller, Gale and David Silverman. 1995. "Troubles Talk and Counseling Discourse." *Sociological Quarterly* 36: 725–47.

Miller, Leslie J. 1993. "Claims-Making from the Underside: Marginalization and Social Problems Analysis." Pp. 349–76 in *Reconsidering Social Constructionism: Debates in Social Problems Theory*, edited by J. Holstein and G. Miller. Hawthorne, NY: Aldine de Gruyter.

Miller, Steven M. 1952. "The Participant Observer and Over-Rapport." *American Sociological Review* 17:97–99.

Mills, C. Wright. 1940. "Situated Actions and Vocabularies of Motive." *American Sociological Review* 5:904–13.

Mills, C. Wright. 1951. *White Collar*. New York: Oxford University Press.

Mills, C. Wright. 1959. *The Sociological Imagination*. New York: Oxford University Press.

Moerman, Michael. 1974. "Accomplishing Ethnicity." Pp. 54–68 in *Ethnomethodology*, edited by R. Turner. Harmondsworth, UK: Penguin.

Moerman, Michael. 1988. *Talking Culture*. Philadelphia: University of Pennsylvania Press.

Moerman, Michael. 1992. "Life after C.A." Pp. 20–34 in *Text in Context*, edited by G. Watson and R. Seiler. Newbury Park, CA: Sage.

Moore, Henrietta. 1988. *Feminism and Anthropology*. Minneapolis: University of Minnesota Press.

Nagel, Joane. 1994. "Constructing Ethnicity: Creating and Recreating Ethnic Identity and Culture." *Social Problems* 41:152–76.

Nagel, Joane. 1996. *American Indian Ethnic Renewal: Red Power and the Resurgence of Identity and Culture*. New York: Oxford University Press.

Nakagawa, Nobutoshi. 1995. "Social Constructionism in Japan: Toward an Indigenous Empirical Inquiry." Pp. 295–310 in *Perspectives on Social Problems, Vol. 7*, edited by J. Holstein and G. Miller. Greenwich, CT: JAI Press.

Norris, Christopher. 1982. *Deconstruction: Theory and Practice*. London: Routledge.

Norris, Christopher. 1990. *What's Wrong with Postmodernism*. Baltimore: Johns Hopkins University Press.

Paget, Marianne A. 1995. "Performing the Text." Pp. 222–44 in *Representation in Ethnography*, edited by J. Van Mannen. Thousand Oaks, CA: Sage.

Park, Robert E. 1950. "An Autobiographical Note." Pp. vi–ix in *Race and Culture*. Glencoe IL: Free Press.

Parsons, Talcott. 1937. *The Structure of Social Action*. New York: McGraw Hill.

Parsons, Talcott. 1951. *The Social System*. New York: Free Press.

Paules, Greta. 1991. *Dishing It Out*. Philadephia: Temple University Press.

Perrucci, Robert. 1974. *Circle of Madness*. Englewood Cliffs, NJ: Prentice-Hall.

Pfohl, Stephen. 1992. *Death at the Parasite Cafe*. New York: St. Martin's.

Polkinghorne, Donald E. 1988. *Narrative Knowing and the Human Sciences*. Albany, NY: SUNY Press.

Pollner, Melvin. 1974. "Sociological and Commonsense Models of the Labeling Process." Pp. 27–40 in *Ethnomethodology*, edited by R. Turner. Harmondsworth, UK: Penguin.

Pollner, Melvin. 1987. *Mundane Reason*. New York: Cambridge University Press.

Pollner, Melvin. 1991. "Left of Ethnomethodology: The Rise and Decline of Radical Reflexivity." *American Sociological Review* 56:370–80.

Pollner, Melvin. 1993. "The Reflexivity of Constructionism and the Construction of Reflexivity." Pp. 199–212 in *Reconsidering Social Constructionism*, edited by J. Holstein and G. Miller. Hawthorne, NY: Aldine de Gruyter.

Pollner, Melvin and Robert M. Emerson. 1988. "The Dynamics of Inclusion and Distance in Fieldwork Relations." Pp. 235–52 in *Contemporary Field Research*, edited by R. M. Emerson. Prospect Heights, IL: Waveland.

Pollner, Melvin and Lynn McDonald-Wikler. 1985. "The Social Construction of Unreality: A Case Study of a Family's Attribution of Competence to a Severely Retarded Child." *Family Process* 24:241–54.

Poster, Mark. 1988. "Introduction." Pp. 1–9 in *Jean Baudrillard: Selected Writings*. Stanford, CA: Stanford University Press.

Presthus, Robert. 1978. *The Organizational Society*. New York: St. Martin's.

Propp, Vladimir I. 1968. *The Morphology of the Folktale*. Austin: University of Texas Press.

Psathas, George. 1995. *Conversation Analysis*. Thousand Oaks, CA: Sage.

Reinharz, Shulamit. 1992. *Feminist Methods in Social Research*. New York: Oxford University Press.

Richardson, Laurel. 1990. *Writing Strategies*. Newbury Park, CA: Sage.

Richardson, Laurel. 1991. "Postmodern Social Theory: Representational Practices." *Sociological Theory* 9:173–79.

Richardson, Laurel. 1992. "The Consequences of Poetic Representation." Pp. 125–37 in *Investigating Subjectivity*, edited by C. Ellis and M. Flaherty. Thousand Oaks, CA: Sage.

Richardson, Laurel and Ernest Lockridge. 1991. "The Sea Monster: An Ethnographic Drama and Comment on Ethnographic Fiction." *Symbolic Interaction* 14:335–40.

Riesman, David. 1950. *The Lonely Crowd*. New Haven: Yale University Press.

Riessman, Catherine. 1993. *Narrative Analysis*. Thousand Oaks, CA: Sage.

Robbins, Thomas, Dick Anthony, and Thomas E. Curtis. 1973. "The Limits of Symbolic Realism: Problems of Emphatic Field Observation in a Sectarian Context." *Journal for the Scientific Study of Religion* 12:259–72.

Rochford, E. Burke, Jr. 1992. "On the Politics of Member Validation: Taking Findings Back to Hare Krishna." Pp. 99–116 in *Perspecitves on Social Problems, Vol. 3*, edited by J. Holstein and G. Miller. Greenwich, CT: JAI Press.

Rogers, Mary F. 1992. "Teaching, Theorizing, Storytelling: Postmodern Rhetoric and Modern Dreams." *Sociological Theory* 10:231–40.

Ronai, Carol R. 1992. "The Reflexive Self through Narrative." Pp. 102–24 in *Investigating Subjectivity*, edited by C. Ellis and M. Flaherty. Newbury Park, CA: Sage.

Rorty, Richard. 1979. *Philosophy and the Mirror of Nature*. Princeton, NJ: Princeton University Press.

Rosenau, Pauline Marie. 1992. *Post-modernism and the Social Sciences*. Princeton, NJ: Princeton University Press.

Rosenblatt, Paul C. 1994. *Metaphors of Family Systems Theory*. New York: Guilford.

Rubin, Lillian B. 1976. *Worlds of Pain: Life in the Working Class Family*. New York: Basic Books.

Ryan, Michael. 1988. "Postmodern Politics." *Theory, Culture, and Society* 5:559–76.

Sacks, Harvey. 1963. "Sociological Description." *Berkeley Journal of Sociology* 8:1–16.

Sacks, Harvey. 1972. "An Initial Investigation of the Usability of Conversational Data for Doing Sociology." Pp. 31–75 in *Studies in Social Interaction*, edited by D. Sudnow. New York: Free Press.

Sacks, Harvey. 1974. "On the Analyzability of Stories by Children." Pp. 216–32 in *Ethnomethodology*, edited by R. Turner. Harmondsworth, UK: Penguin.

Sacks, Harvey. 1986. "Some Considerations of a Story Told in Ordinary Conversation." *Poetics* 15:127–38.

Sacks, Harvey. 1992. *Lectures on Conversation, vols. 1 and 2*. Cambridge, MA: Blackwell.

Sacks, Harvey and Emanuel A. Schegloff. 1979. "Two Preferences in the Organization of Reference to Persons in Conversation and Their Interaction." Pp. 15–21 in *Everyday Language Studies*, edited by G. Psathas. New York: Irvington.

Sacks, Harvey, Emanuel A. Schegloff, and Gail Jefferson. 1974. "A Simplest Systematics for the Organization of Turn-taking in Conversation." *Language* 50:696–735.

Said, Edward W. 1978. *Orientalism*. New York: Vintage.

Sanders, Clint R. 1989. *Customizing the Body*. Philadelphia: Temple University Press.

Sarbin, Theodore R. (ed.). 1986. *Narrative Psychology: The Storied Nature of Human Conduct*. New York: Praeger.

Saussure, Ferdinand de. 1974. *Course in General Linguistics*. London: Fontana.

Scheff, Thomas J. 1990. *Microsociology: Discourse, Emotion, and Social Structure*. Chicago: University of Chicago Press.

Scheff, Thomas J. and Suzanne M. Retzinger. 1991. *Emotions and Violence*. Lexington, MA: Free Press.

Schegloff, Emanuel A. 1979. "The Relevance of Repair to Syntax-for-Conversation." Pp. 266–96 in *Syntax and Semantics 12: Discourse and Syntax*, edited by T. Givon. New York: Academic Press.

Schegloff, Emanuel A. 1982. "Discourse as an Interactional Achievement." Pp. 73–91 in *Georgetown University Roundtable on Languages and Linguistics*, edited by D. Tannen. Washington, DC: Georgetown University Press.

Schegloff, Emanuel A. 1987. "Between Macro and Micro: Contexts and Other Connections." Pp. 207–34 in *The Macro-Micro Link*, edited by J. Alexander, B. Giesen, R. Münch, and N. Smelser. Berkeley: University of California Press.

Schegloff, Emanuel A. 1991. "Reflections on Talk and Social Structure." Pp. 44–70 in *Talk and Social Structure*, edited by D. Boden and D. Zimmerman. Cambridge: Polity.

Schegloff, Emanuel A. 1992. "Introduction." Pp. i–lxii in *Harvey Sacks: Lectures on Conversation, Vol. 1*, edited by G. Jefferson. Oxford: Blackwell.

Schegloff, Emanuel A. and Harvey Sacks. 1973. "Opening up Closings." *Semiotica* 7:289–327.

Schilling, Chris. 1993. *The Body and Social Theory*. London: Sage.

Schneider, Joseph. 1991. "Troubles with Textual Authority in Sociology." *Symbolic Interaction* 14 296–319.

Schneider, Joseph. 1993. "'Members Only': Reading the Constructionist Text." Pp. 103–116 in *Reconsidering Social Constructionism: Debates in Social Problems Theory*, edited by J. Holstein and G. Miller. Hawthorne, NY: Aldine de Gruyter.

Schutz, Alfred. 1967. *The Phenomenology of the Social World*. Evanston, IL: Northwestern University Press.

Schutz, Alfred. 1970. *On Phenomenology and Social Relations*. Chicago: University of Chicago Press.

Schwartz, Howard and Jerry Jacobs. 1979. *Qualitative Sociology*. New York: Free Press.

Scott, Marvin and Stanford Lyman. 1968. "Accounts." *American Sociological Review* 33:46–62.

Seidman, Steven. 1991. "The End of Sociological Theory: The Hope." *Sociological Theory* 9:131–46.

Seidman, Steven. 1992. *Embattled Eros*. New York: Routledge.

Seidman, Steven and David G. Wagner (eds.). 1992. *Postmodernism and Social Theory*. Oxford: Blackwell.

Shaffir, William B. and Robert A. Stebbins. 1991. *Experiencing Fieldwork*. Thousand Oaks, CA: Sage.

Shalin, Dmitri N. 1993. "Modernity, Postmodernism, and Pragmatist Inquiry: An Introduction." *Symbolic Interaction* 16:303–32.

Silverman, David. 1985. *Qualitative Methodology and Sociology*. Aldershot, UK: Gower.

Silverman, David. 1989. "Six Rules of Qualitative Research: A Post Romantic Argument." *Symbolic Interaction* 12:25–40.

Silverman, David. 1993a. *Interpreting Qualitative Data*. London: Sage.

Silverman, David. 1993b. "Kundera's *Immortality* and Field Research: Uncovering the Romantic Impulse." Unpublished manuscript, Department of Sociology, Goldsmiths' College, University of London.

Silverman, David, R. Bor, R. Miller, and E. Goldman. 1992. "Advice-giving and Advice-reception in AIDS Counseling." Pp. 137–59 in *AIDS: Rights, Risk, and Reason,* edited by P. Aggelton, P. Davies, and G. Hart. London: Falmer Press.

Silverman, David and Jaber F. Gubrium. 1994. "Competing Strategies for Analyzing the Contexts of Social Interaction." *Sociological Inquiry* 64:179–98.

Smith, Dorothy E. 1978. "'*K*' is Mentally Ill: The Anatomy of a Factual Account." *Sociology* 12:23–53.

Smith, Dorothy E. 1987. *The Everyday World as Problematic*. Boston: Northeastern University Press.

Smith, Dorothy E. 1990. *The Conceptual Practices of Power: A Feminist Sociology of Knowledge*. Boston: Northeastern University Press.

Smith, Paul. 1989. "Writing, General Knowledge, and Postmodern Anthropology." Discourse 11:159–70.

Snow, David A. and Leon Anderson. 1993. *Down on Their Luck: A Study of Homeless Street People*. Berkeley: University of California Press.

Spector, Malcolm and John I. Kitsuse. 1987. *Constructing Social Problems*. Hawthorne, NY: Aldine de Gruyter.

Spencer, J. William. 1994. "Homeless in River City: Client Work in Human Service Encounters." Pp. 29–46 in *Perspectives on Social Problems, vol. 6,* edited by J. Holstein and G. Miller. Greenwich, CT: JAI Press.

Spradley, James P. and Brenda J. Mann. 1975. *Cocktail Waitress*. New York: Wiley.

Stacey, Judith. 1990. *Brave New Families*. New York: Basic.

Stack, Carol. 1974. *All Our Kin*. New York: Harper & Rowe.

Stone, Gregory P. and Harvey A. Farberman (eds.). 1970. *Social Psychology through Symbolic Interactionism*. Waltham, MA: Xerox College Publishing.

Strong, Phil. 1979. *The Ceremonial Order of the Clinic*. London: Routledge.

Suchar, Charles S. 1975. "Doing Therapy: Notes on the Training of Psychiatric Personnel." Presented at the Annual Meeting of the Midwest Sociological Society, April, Chicago.

Suttles, Gerald. 1968. *The Social Order of the Slum*. Chicago: University of Chicago Press.

Sykes, Gresham. 1958. *Society of Captives*. Princeton, NJ: Princeton University Press.

Thomas, W. I. 1931. *The Unadjusted Girl*. New York: Harper.

Thorne, Barrie. 1979. "Political Activist as Participant Observer: Conflicts of Commitment in a Study of the Draft Resistance Movement of the 1960s." *Symbolic Interaction* 2:73–88.

Thorne, Barrie. 1993. *Gender Play: Girls and Boys in School*. New Brunswick, NJ: Rutgers University Press.

Torgovnick, Marianna. 1990. *Gone Primitive*. Chicago: University of Chicago Press.

Trinh, Minh-ha. 1989. *Woman, Native, Other*. Bloomington, IN: Indiana University Press.

Turner, Bryan S. 1984. *The Body and Society*. Oxford: Blackwell.

Turner, Roy. 1989. "Deconstructing the Field." Pp. 13–29 in *The Politics of Field Research*, edited by J. Gubrium and D. Silverman. London: Sage.

Ulmer, Greg. 1983. "The Object of Post-Criticism." Pp. 111–25 in *The Anti-Aesthetic: Essays on Postmodern Culture*, edited by H. Foster. Port Townsend, WA: Bay Press.

Ulmer, Greg. 1989. *Teletheory: Grammatology in the Age of Video*. New York: Routledge.

Unruh, David R. 1983. *Invisible Lives*. Beverly Hills, CA: Sage.

Van Maanen, John. 1988. *Tales of the Field*. Chicago: University of Chicago Press.

Van Maanen, John. 1995a. "An End to Innocence: The Ethnography of Ethnography." Pp. 1–35 in *Representation in Ethnography*, edited by J. Van Maanen. Thousand Oaks, CA: Sage.

Van Maanen, John (ed.). 1995b. *Representation in Ethnography*. Thousand Oaks, CA: Sage.

Vidich, Arthur J. and Stanford M. Lyman. 1994. "Qualitative Methods: Their History in Sociology and

Anthropology." Pp. 23–59 in *Handbook of Qualitative Research*, edited by N. Denzin and Y. Lincoln. Thousand Oaks, CA: Sage.

Warren, Carol A. B. 1987. *Madwives: Schizophrenic Women in the 1950s*. New Brunswick, NJ: Rutgers University Press.

Warren, Carol A. B. 1988. *Gender Issues in Field Research*. Beverly Hills, CA: Sage.

Warren, Carol A.B. 1981. *The Court of Last Resort*. Chicago: University of Chicago Press.

Watson, Graham and Robert M. Seiler (eds.). 1992. *Text in Context: Contributions to Ethnomethodology*. Newbury Park, CA: Sage.

West, Candace and Don H. Zimmerman. 1987. "Doing Gender." *Gender and Society* 1:125–51.

Whalen, Jack. 1992. "Conversation Analysis." Pp. 303–10 in *Encyclopedia of Sociology, vol. 1* edited by E. Borgatta. New York: Macmillan.

Wieder, D. Lawrence. 1988[1974]. *Language and Social Reality*. Landham, MD: University Press of America.

Wiley, Norbert. 1985. "Marriage and the Construction of Reality: Now and Then." Pp. 21–32 in *The Psychosocial Interior of the Family*, edited by G. Handel. Hawthorne, NY: Aldine de Gruyter.

Wittgenstein, Ludwig. 1958. *Philosophical Investigations*. New York: Macmillan.

Whyte, William Foote. 1943. *Street Corner Society*. Chicago: University of Chicago Press.

Wolff, Kurt H. 1964. "Surrender and Community Study." Pp. 233–64 in *Reflections on Community Studies*, edited by A. Vidich, J. Bensman, and M. Stein. New York: Wiley.

Woolgar, Steve. 1988. "Reflexivity Is the Ethnographer of the Text." Pp. 14–34 in *Knowledge and Reflexivity*, edited by Steve Woolgar. London: Sage.

Woolgar, Steve. 1989a. "The Ideology of Representation and the Role of the Agent." Pp. 131–44 in *Dismantling Truth*, edited by H. Lawson and L. Appignanesi. New York: St. Martin's.

Woolgar, Steve. 1989b. *Knowledge and Reflexivity*. London: Sage.

Woolgar, Steve and Dorothy Pawluch. 1985. "Ontological Gerrymandering. The Anatomy of Social Problems Explanations." *Social Problems* 32:214–227.

Wuthnow, Robert. 1994. *Sharing the Journey: Support Groups and America's New Quest for Community*. New York: Free Press.

Wuthnow, Robert, James D. Hunter, Albert Bergesen, and Edith Kurzweil. 1984. *Cultural Analysis*. London: Routledge and Kegan Paul.

Zimmerman, Don H. 1970. "The Practicalities of Rule Use." Pp. 221–38 in *Understanding Everyday Life*, edited by J. Douglas. Chicago: Aldine.

Zimmerman, Don H. 1988. Preface to *Language and Social Reality*, by D. Lawrence Wieder. Lanham, MD: University Press of America.

Zimmerman, Don H. and Melvin Pollner. 1970. "The Everyday World as a Phenomenon." Pp. 80–104 in *Understanding Everyday Life*, edited by J. Douglas. Chicago: Aldine.

Zimmerman, Don H. and D. Lawrence Wieder. 1970. "Ethnomethodology and the Problem of Order." Pp. 287–302 in *Understanding Everyday Life*, edited by J. Douglas. Chicago: Aldine.

Name Index

Subject Index